SISTER ELISABETH FEDDE
"To Do the Lord's Will"

Elisabeth Fedde
and the Deaconess Movement
Among the Norwegians in America

Gracia Grindal

Lutheran University Press
Minneapolis, Minnesota

Sister Elisabeth Fedde: "To Do the Lord's Will"
Elisabeth Fedde and the Deaconess Movement
Among the Norwegians in America
By Gracia Grindal

Cover painting by Dale Redpath, 2014. Commissioned by the author for this project. Those wishing giclee copies should contact the author.

Library of Congress Cataloging-in-Publication-Data applied for.

ISBN-13: 978-1-932688-98-6
ISBN-10: 1-932688-98-6

Lutheran University Press, PO Box 390759, Minneapolis, MN 55439
www.lutheranupress.org
Printed in the United States of America

Dedicated to Paul and Dorothea Ofstedal,
good friends in the Lord,
who know these stories in their hearts

Sister Elisabeth Fedde

CONTENTS

KAISERSWERTH
DIACONESS HYMN

By Theodore Fliedner

Blessed fount of heavenly gladness,
 Jesus, whose are all our powers,
Thee in sickness, want and sadness,
 To behold and serve is ours.

If we bear the sick man's burden,
 Lord, in thankful love to Thee,
Thou wilt say to us in guerdon:*
 Come ye blessed, come to me.

Where the child with love is tended:
 Where the tears of want are dried;
Where the prisoner is befriended,
 Thou art Shield, Reward and Guide.

Give more love, that fire from heaven;
 Send that Love that longs to bless,
That it may increase like leaven
 Till it grows pure happiness.

Tr. Catherine Winkworth

*guerdon = reward

INTRODUCTION

What follows is the story of Sister Elisabeth Fedde (1850-1921), the deaconess whose vision, sturdy character, and accomplishments helped create what became several modern institutions of mercy still flourishing in America. It is a legacy of surprising substance for a single woman of her time. In telling her story, which she clearly wanted told, I have had a plethora of sources, all of which have needed careful examination and study in order to determine which accounts were the most accurate. She left a diary, a copy of which was given to me by the Evangelical Lutheran Church in America (ELCA) archives, and two slightly different versions of her memoirs (*Optegnelser*). Where and when the diary was found is not known, but it gives us a daily record of Sister Elisabeth's life from her arrival in New York City on April 10, 1883, until May 1888. It is often difficult to decipher, and the paper is in bad condition, but it gives us her experiences in a kind of raw and unmediated style that is very helpful to the biographer. In addition, we also have her manuscript, *From My Deaconess Time* (*Fra min diakonissetid*), a scrawled and very difficult to decipher memoir written between 1897 and 1920, which Kristin Kavli Adriansen transcribed to typescript. Fedde clearly had her diary at hand as she wrote these two versions of the memoirs, each very similar to the other. "Søster Elisabeths Optengnelser" was published in twelve issues of the *Nordisk Tidende* on the fiftieth anniversary of the founding of her work in 1883 and then later printed in *Lutheraneren*, the Norwegian-language church paper of the Norwegian Evangelical Lutheran Church (NELC). Sister Elisabeth had asked that her memoirs not be published until after her death.

Her nephew, Waldemar Reiersen, brought the *Memoirs* to America some time before 1933, the year that *Nordisk Tidende* printed them, partly because they were about the beginnings of the hospital, but also because they gave a rare picture of the founding of the Norwegian colony and the history of Brooklyn in the last half of the nineteenth century.[1] Since she based her memoirs on her diary, some stories from the diary are expanded, some left out. We cannot be sure exactly when they were written, but we do know it was after she left Brooklyn for good in 1896. Like all memoirs, hers are burnished by time as Fedde recalls her experiences in the light of her own more mature contemplation and reflection. While very well written, they are not immediate. She does not recall dates correctly in these later works, and the biographer has to check carefully to see whether or not the date is right. Her recollections show her to have grown into a more gracious and even funny person as she gives us accounts of events which may not necessarily have amused her when they happened. Fedde, a gifted person—nurse, administrator, spiritual guide—also shows herself to be a gifted writer. One colleague compared her favorably with George Eliot, the novelist who skillfully used vivid details to put us in the scene.

In addition to Fedde's accounts, several others attempted to tell her story based on these sources. They are also helpful, but a bit messy and have to be read carefully. Beulah Folkedahl's translation of the diary, which appeared in the *Norwegian American Historical Review,* vol. XX, left out half of the diary, so readers of the English sources are at a disadvantage compared to those who can read Norwegian. Folkedahl's translation left out details I consider to be crucial in drawing a picture of Sister Elisabeth. They leave us with an abbreviated insight into Fedde's feelings and thoughts. In addition to the translation, Folkedahl was working on a history of Fedde and the Brooklyn hospital as well, now in the Norwegian American Historical Association archive. Although somewhat inchoate, it is filled with details I trust but cannot always verify outside of giving her credit. There is also *The Borrowed Sister* by Rolf Johnsrud (Augsburg Publishing House, Minneapolis, 1951), based on the Norwegian sources, especially her *Optegnelser* from the *Nordisk Tidende.* It served the good purpose of telling her story in English. It treated Fedde as something of a saint, a portrait which neither she nor her contemporaries would have thought appropriate, although she was admired by many, especially those with whom she worked at the end of her career. By then, she had made peace with herself and her calling—and maybe even the debilitating chronic disease she suffered in the last years of her life, a condition about which she never specifically complained.

Fedde, like many saints, was a driven visionary, the kind that is often difficult to get along with in daily life. Both Johnsrud and others who have attempted to tell her story by putting her in the best light possible have passed over the disagreements she had with her boards and colleagues. For me, those disagreements are at the heart of finding out who she was. They give us a glimpse into the time in which she lived and the difficulties she experienced as a woman working to exercise her calling in a culture unfamiliar with the deaconess vocation and the public role she had as a woman. She lived at the beginning of the time when the roles of women were expanding. The minutes of the board meetings and other contemporaneous records have been crucial in drawing a faithful portrait of her, as have newspaper articles and reports, along with some few letters from archives, especially the Augsburg College Archives in Minneapolis. These have all been invaluable and give us a better insight into most of the troubles Fedde experienced both in Minneapolis and the Brooklyn Motherhouse.

When one looks at what Fedde accomplished in a very short time, founding what later became huge modern medical complexes in mere weeks, and then thinks of how today such projects would involve years of planning, feasibility studies, and proposed financial campaigns, one has to marvel at her grit and vision, despite all the trouble she had to endure to realize her dreams for the deaconess movement in America.

One learns some about the life and times of the Lutheran Deaconess movement through her life story, but to tell the story well it is also necessary to present some of the important parts of Lutheran deaconess history as well as the history of the Norwegian American Lutheran churches in which she worked during her years in the United States. While for many readers those histories of theological and cultural debates may seem dry and dusty detours along the way, they help us understand how these controversies, about which church historians have spent lifetimes reading and writing, affected actual persons, especially women. Putting Fedde into these histories greatly improves my own understanding of their impact on the lives of both men and women at the time and of her work and her time. I have tried to relate them as vividly as I could, sometimes using the techniques of fiction (although never straying from the original sources except insofar as I produce some dialogue that is not in the records, but would almost have to be there) so as not to lose the reader in the alphabetical soup of Lutheranism in the United States. It can be daunting to figure out these traditions. Because Lutheran church history has been written to tell the stories of church merger negotiations and deals slenderly with the work of congregations, and the laity—especially the women—we know little about the work of women in these traditions. Their stories have not been told because women were not at the table during the delicate theological deliberations that ultimately brought most Norwegian Lutherans in America together into one church body, the Norwegian Evangelical Lutheran Church, in 1917. Telling the story of a woman from this time gives a richer texture to our collective memories.

I am increasingly convinced, as I have sorted through the many primary sources she left us, that one of the main goals of her later life was to tell this story so that it would not die. Reading her accounts in her own handwriting gives one a better sense for her story. Fedde wanted to be remembered because she knew her experience was unique and part of an important history. She wanted people to know how hard she had worked to establish these institutions and do the will of the Lord. For that reason I have tried not to leave any stone unturned—and there are lots of them out there—to get her story told with fuller detail and nuance.

To do this I have had to trouble librarians, archivists, and friends around the world. I am deeply grateful to Luther Seminary which gave me the sabbatical time to begin the work, and to the librarians there, especially Karen Alexander and Bruce Eldevik who were always available to help me find arcane resources in libraries around the world. The summer of 2011 I visited Kaiserswerth where the deaconess movement among Lutherans began. Dr. Norbert Friedrich, director, welcomed me graciously and showed me the grounds. I attended Sunday services in the Motherhouse church and was shown the museum and archives. Since then the Kaiserswerth archivist Annett Buettner has been most generous in sharing images and other information that improve the quality of this work. Later that fall I visited the Lovisenberg Diaconal Hospital in Oslo where Beret Hovland opened up the deaconess archives and gave me invaluable advice along with copies of important documents that have been crucial to my understanding of Fedde. Also thanks to Yngve Nedrebø at the Bergen Statsarkiv who helped uncover some last pieces in the mystery, as well as the librarian Pam Berven in Egersund, Norway, where Elisabeth lived out her last days. My cousin Tårån Kivle Petterson and her husband Steiner have also offered me help with old Dano-Norwegian expressions and nursing lore.

I have tried to be appropriately scrupulous in my attributions of sources. Much of the material from Elisabeth's Diary is my translation and paraphrasing of it, but when I quote the translations of others, I credit them. This is also true of the *Memoirs* (*Optegnelser*), all of which are my translations, since these were not translated. Translations and paraphrases into English of an original source can be tricky. I have tended to indent long direct translations, but not paraphrases. In most cases Sister Elisabeth is the basic source I am using for the story. Sometimes when the material seems to run on for a while without attribution, the footnote at the end of the material will note the source.

Kristin Anderson, archivist at Augsburg College, has been most kind in helping me track down leads in the archives there, as have librarians at the Minnesota Historical Society. Kari Bostrom of the Luther Seminary archives has always been ready with sources, as has Joel Thoreson at the ELCA archives in Chicago. Don Stiger at the Lutheran Medical Center in Brooklyn, which counts Fedde as its founder, spent the good part of a morning driving me around to the various Fedde sites along with supplying access to pictures of the old hospital and buildings where Fedde lived and worked.

Karen Fedde May, who was married to one of Elisabeth's grand-nephews, has become a good friend and supporter of this book, giving me family information and pictures, some of which appear here. Other family members in Norway such as John Dancke have also been quick to share materials with me. Pastor Kirsti Mosvold, head pastor at Lovisenberg Diakonale Sykehus, helped me make some crucial connections in Norway. More connections came to me through the generosity of Kristin Kavli Adriansen, nurse in Stavanger whose master's thesis on Fedde helped give me entrée to the family and its archives. Without her contacts and support my work would have been much the poorer. In addition, Dr. Kristin Norseth at Menighetsfakultet in Oslo has also been a good conversation partner in this work. Inez Olson Schwarzkopf, an old friend and friend of the Minneapolis deaconess community, has also been helpful in reading the manuscript and giving me good feedback. To them all I am most grateful.

Paul and Dorothea Ofstedal, dear friends, have been godsends to me as they have read and proofread my manuscripts. To them I dedicate the book. Paul's grandfather, Andreas A. Øfstedal, was rector at the Chicago Deaconess Motherhouse. Dorothea's father, Pastor J. C. Jerdee, was pastor at the Beloit Children's Home in Iowa. He served alongside his wife Dora, an R.N. who used her public health training in Minnesota and the former Yugoslavia after World War I to lead the health services at the Beloit Children's Home between 1935 and 1939. Both Paula and Dorothea bring special connections to the subject of this book.

My nephew's wife, Melinda Knatterud, accompanied me on my trip to Lutheran Medical Center in Brooklyn and took pictures of the Elisabeth Fedde display there. Finally, the new digitalization of practically everything has helped immeasurably. I was able to find references to Elisabeth Fedde in the Library of Congress digitalized papers and the Norwegian newspapers now available on line from the National Library of Norway, to say nothing of the digital archives of the Norwegian church and its records. These have become extremely valuable to genealogists and researchers and very helpful to me.

Thanks also to Karen Walhof and Lutheran University Press for her support of this project. Her encouragement and interest have been vital. All have contributed to making the book more accurate. The mistakes, of course, are all mine, but many fewer because of their help. For that I am most grateful. We do not work alone in this business, and this list of colleagues and friends is ample evidence for that.

Soli deo Gloria!

CHAPTER ONE

THE CALL

Sister Elisabeth adjusted her deaconess cap and tied it under her chin more securely. She was expecting a guest. The late summer afternoon was oddly cool for early September, but the dank air from the Mississippi and the pollen floating invisibly on the air around them made her sneeze. She was in West Salem, Wisconsin, visiting Mrs. Helen Johnson, an old friend from Mandal. They had talked into the night as they caught up on gossip from the old country. During their noon meal, Elisabeth had told Helen about her journey through Missouri to visit an uncle, John Hanson, and her cousin, Marie, daughter of her late aunt, her mother's sister, Oline Sofie. What she had seen there of American Reconstruction shocked her: former slaves working their small plots, living in their newly-built little homes, evidence of the slave holders fathering children to increase the number of slaves, the lively worship services she had observed among them, and the way the pastor had passed the collection plate around until he got what he needed. It was a completely different world to her from either Norway or Brooklyn where she now headed The Norwegian Lutheran Deaconess Home and Hospital. She had come to know Mrs. Johnson back in Norway while visiting her sister and brother-in-law in Mandal, a small village on the Skagerrak, the arm of the North Sea that rolls between Mandal and Skagen, Denmark, with its gleaming white sand beaches that had become the playground of Scandinavia's artists.

They were preparing to meet a friend from Christiania, Pastor Olaf Guldseth, who knew the deaconess community there. Also a newcomer, he had heard from Mrs. Johnson that Elisabeth was coming to town on the train from Mason City the day before. He was eager to see her. He had something to tell her.

The coffee cups clinked as Helen set the table and brought out the waffles with the newly preserved strawberry jam and freshly churned butter. The pastor and her company deserved some of the best Norwegian goodies.

They heard him knocking at the door. Pastor Guldseth was a thin man with a dark beard, closely shaven and neatly trimmed. Helen, greeting him politely, invited him in. He took off his hat, shook hands with Elisabeth, and sat down at the table. He and his wife, Lise, had arrived four months before, on May 5, 1888, on the *Geiser* ship of the Thingvalla Line in New York, and had visited Sister Elisabeth in Brooklyn. A newly ordained pastor, he was ready to take up his call in Eleva, Wisconsin, some miles south of Eau Claire.

Olaf Guldseth

After their coffee and a few pleasantries, especially about Guldseth's new call, the pastor got to the point. He had come to tell Sister Elisabeth that she should go to Minneapolis on her trip to the Upper Midwest. The General Council of Lutheran Churches was meeting there; Dr. Spaeth, the president of the council, was speaking on the deaconess movement. Dr. Passavant, known as the father of the deaconess movement in America would be there too. "You would enjoy hearing them both," he urged, setting down his coffee cup quietly.

Sister Elisabeth knew and admired Passavant. He had even asked her to be the Sister Superior at the Pittsburgh Motherhouse a few years before. She would enjoy seeing him again. The idea intrigued her. Where would she stay? Mrs. Johnson had a good friend in Minneapolis who ran a boarding house there. She was sure Elisabeth could find a room with her.

Tickets to Minneapolis were half price at the time because of the national conferences scheduled there during September. In addition, Guldseth said, his friend Georg Sverdrup, the president of Augsburg Seminary, was interested in the deaconess movement. Sverdrup's sister-in-law, Elise Heiberg, at that time was working in the deaconess hospital in Christiania, and both Guldseth and Fedde knew her.

After their meal, Sister Elisabeth considered the idea. She promised Guldseth she would pray about whether to go or not. She had been exhausted when she took the train from Brooklyn to Chicago then to Dalton, Missouri, to visit her family. Her health had suffered from stress and overwork. She had left the Brooklyn work just as they had started building a new hospital. She had worked hard getting the plans done and the community to support it. She was confident it would progress well without her. Now she was rested. As she prepared for bed and began her evening devotions, she prayed for guidance. To do God's will was her prayer. She rose from her knees and went to bed, confident that she would have an answer in the morning. When she awoke the next morning, she decided that it would be worth it to see Minneapolis, the destination of many Norwegians passing through Brooklyn. Several days later, when Mrs. Johnson heard from her friend that she did have rooms for them, she decided to go. Sister Elisabeth had never been so far west or north. She knew that many of her countrymen had come to the Upper Midwest to find new lives. Now she would see for herself the rolling expanses of country attracting them. She was eager to see it. She would leave the next day.

As the train swayed and clattered on its way beside the Mississippi River she could see both the youngest and older part of what she once called this "praiseworthy nation." The river towns where they stopped to let off passengers and refuel were older by some fifty years than the towns and cities above the river. This new land seemed bustling with energy and power. One wonders what she was thinking as the train chugged along the Mississippi River into St. Paul and the Union Depot where that year 150 trains departed every day carrying over eight million people a year in and out of the city. Did she have any idea of what was about to happen? We do not know.

The train lurched to a stop in the station. Sister Elisabeth, with the others, stepped off the train through the throngs of German, Swedish, and Norwegian Lutherans rushing to find rooms in the Cities. She found a horse and buggy taxi to take her to the home of Helen's friend in Minneapolis, some miles to the west. The house was filled with visitors. Elisabeth's room was small, but she made herself at home. Before she retired for the evening, she received a letter from Pastor M. Falk Gjertsen, of Trinity Congregation in Minneapolis. He had heard from Guldseth that she was in town. Could she meet with him tomorrow? He had some questions to ask her. With her usual curiosity, she looked forward to the next day when she would tour the city, one of the fastest growing in the country, and then speak with the pastor. Once again, as she went to bed, she prayed that in all things she would be obedient to God's will.

Pastor Gjertsen could scarcely contain his excitement when he heard Fedde was in town. Long-time pastor of Trinity Congregation in Minneapolis, and city leader, he saw his chance. It had been a dream of his and his congregation to call a deaconess from Norway and ask her to begin a Motherhouse in the city. Just two years before, Marie Heiberg, the president of the Tabitha Society at Trinity, had written the Deaconess Motherhouse in Christiania to ask if it could send a sister to Minneapolis to work among poor Norwegians there. If she came, she could establish a Motherhouse to train deaconesses that would serve in Minneapolis but also go from there to other cities in the region to work with the poor and sick.[2] With Fedde there, that dream seemed closer than ever. Gjertsen had already spoken with some of the other American Lutheran church leaders in town for the week. Several had experience in building Motherhouses, none more than William Passavant. Gjertsen invited them all to his home for a meeting. They could advise him on how to build a Motherhouse in Minneapolis. For him the stars seemed to have aligned. It was time to begin. As a visionary, he knew this was the time. No wonder he was excited. Those gathered in his living room that September day in 1888 represented a confluence of various histories, which make this account both complicated and rich. To understand it, several stories need to be told, all of which give a picture of Lutheranism in America at the end of the nineteenth century. It was quite a day—that chilly, rainy day in Minneapolis so many years ago.

M. Falk Gjertsen

The Personae

The third week of September 1888, the convention of the General Council of Lutherans in America was meeting in the newly refurbished St. John's English Lutheran Church on Fifth Street and Eighth Avenue in Minneapolis. Delegates included many luminaries from what is still known as the Muhlenberg tradition of Lutheranism in America, centered in Philadelphia, Pennsylvania.[3] Swedes were also filling the city to celebrate the 250th anniversary of their immigration to America. At the same time, the leadership among the Norwegian-American Lutherans was meeting in Minneapolis, making plans for a merger that would create the largest Norwegian American Lutheran church, with some 152,000 souls. It must have been a heady time for these men in the young, bustling city. Never before had all these Lutherans been together in one place and in such numbers.

When Sister Elisabeth was ushered into the Gjertsen parsonage, the men all stood up. The aging William Passavant stepped over to greet her warmly. As she shook his hand, she automatically curtsied, as younger Norwegian women had been taught to do on meeting their elders. She knew him fairly well. She had met him early in her time in Brooklyn, when she had gone to the Wartburg Orphanage he ran in Mount Vernon, New York. Three years before, in 1885, he had written her to ask her to work for him at

William Alfred Passavant

the deaconess house in Pittsburgh, a job she had declined. She knew as well that no one in America could speak on Deaconess Motherhouses with as much authority as Passavant. Forty years before he had traveled to Kaiserswerth, Germany, to visit the Deaconess Motherhouse there in order to persuade Theodor Fliedner (1800-1864) to send four deaconesses to America to help found a Motherhouse in Pittsburgh, and later in Milwaukee, Wisconsin. Passavant's presence must have seemed like a benediction for these younger Norwegians. As Sister Elisabeth had come in, he was telling the younger men of his trip to Minneapolis some thirty years before, in 1856, when it was still Indian hunting grounds, as he was looking to establish an English-speaking Lutheran congregation in St. Paul. In 1881 he would return twice in order to make arrangements to buy the Swedish Augustana church in downtown Minneapolis, to house such a congregation. His presence at the General Council convention in 1888 must have seemed to him, now an old but spry man, a kind of valedictory trip. His dream had come true. The church had been refurbished and remodeled with a new parsonage on the same lot, just east of where much later the Humphrey Dome stood. St. John's was to be dedicated in its new location during the meeting of the General Council. M. Falk

St. Johns in Minneapolis where the convention of the General Council was held

Gjertsen and the Norwegian contingent had not come to the Cities until after 1873, when Augsburg Seminary had moved there. They must have found Passavant's knowledge of the city fascinating, as he had been there sixteen years before they had. Just as significant for all Lutherans in America would be the introduction of the *Common Service* prepared by members of the General Council. It would soon be adopted for use by every Lutheran body in America. An exciting time indeed!

Beside him stood the courtly Dr. Adolf Spaeth (1839-1910) who had just given a speech on the deaconess movement to the convention which no doubt the men, and probably Sister Elisabeth, had all heard.[4] Sister Elisabeth had met him and his wife at other deaconess meetings in the East. Spaeth, of Philadelphia Seminary, had completed eight years as president of the General Council. He worked comfortably in both elegant English and fine German, but Fedde could hear the German accent in his greeting. A member of the Phila-delphia board of the deaconess home, he was an

Adolf Spaeth

intellectual defender of the movement. His formidable wife, Harriet Reynolds Spaeth (1845-1925), daughter of Philadelphia Professor Charles Porterfield Krauth (1823-1883), the leading American Lutheran theologian of the day, would later translate from German a book on the history of the movement. It was published the year after her husband's death. She and her husband were devoted to the idea of a diaconate for women, and they had been influential in its flourishing in America, just as it reached its peak in numbers and enthusiasm.

Across the room was the president of the Norwegian-Danish Conference, Pastor Gjermund Høyme (1847-1902), who in 1890 would become the president of the new United Norwegian Lutheran Church. She could speak his language, she noted, as she greeted the younger man with the long dark beard and penetrating eyes. A rising star with a poetic flair, he liked the idea of a Deaconess Motherhouse. Melchior Falk Gjertsen (1847-1913), her host, now taking her elbow and guiding her across the room, was one of the best preachers in the Twin Cities. He served on the Minneapolis School board, the library board, a political club known as the Viking Club. He was a hymn writer, novelist, and publisher of popular songbooks: *Songs of the Homeland* (*Hjemlandssanger,* 1877) and later *The Song Book* (*Sangbogen,* 1899). A mover and shaker, he had helped to establish a board of charities and corrections in Minneapolis and a Norwegian version of the YMCA, and belonged to the Prohibition Society in the city. Anyone wanting to start a project of any kind among Norwegians in the city at the time would want him to be on the committee, if not the leader of it.[5] He well deserved his reputation as an eloquent preacher, she thought, as he moved around the room introducing her to his guests.

She followed, as Gjertsen directed her toward their other countrymen. She shook hands with President Georg Sverdrup (1848-1907), whose sophisticated Bergen dialect and cool steady gaze and quiet demeanor impressed her. Next to him was Sven Oftedal (1844-1911), brother of Lars Oftedal, her pastor in Stavanger, who had persuaded her to send the application letter to the deaconess institution in Christiania. She watched Oftedal's eyes move quickly about the room,

Sven Oftedal

his frank appreciation of the attractions of the serving girl bringing them coffee, and his rich eloquent voice as he sat down casually in the rocking chair and swung back to take the measure of the group. He was, with Sverdrup, the leading professor at Augsburg Seminary. He belonged to Gjertsen's congregation and occasionally served with him as pastoral associate or member of the Trinity board. In 1869, The Norwegian-Danish

Conference (1870-1890) had founded Augsburg Seminary in Marshall, Wisconsin, under the leadership of Professor August Weenaas (1835-1921). Oftedal, professor of New Testament, had a long history of supporting women's causes, ever since he had founded *The People's Paper (Folkebladet)* in 1880, the newspaper of the Conference. Sverdrup, president of Augsburg Seminary and professor of Old Testament, had been editor of several journals, including *The Quarterly (Kvartalskrift)* and *The Lutherans (Lutheraneren)*. Sverdrup had quite enough to do as president of the seminary without taking on another task as daunting as this. Elisabeth's practiced medical eye noted the weariness in Sverdrup's aspect, and she wondered about his health. Recently widowed, he needed help raising his young family. The need for such an institution, however, interested him, and he most of all had the organizational heft to get such an institution going. Now that they were planning the new United Church with its many more resources, they were able to think big.

The need for a Norwegian hospital and other institution of mercy in Minneapolis, one that would train young women to be deaconesses to help in these matters, was clear to all sitting in the Gjertsen living room. When Gjertsen had found her and persuaded her to come to the meeting, he had said, "You are the first deaconess we have seen here, and we must learn how to build such an institution in Minneapolis from you."[6] Sister Elisabeth wrote in her memoirs that "because we were there he called a meeting of the most influential men in the Lutheran church who, at the time, were in town." At the meeting, she wrote, the "eloquent Gjertsen" began speaking about their hope to have a Deaconess Motherhouse in Minneapolis, as did Professor Sven Oftedal, also well-spoken by her account. In his recollection of the event, Sverdrup indicates they found her after the meeting, but Sister Elisabeth writes she was there, remembering how she told those gathered in Gjertsen's parsonage about her work in Brooklyn.[7]

The men eyed each other as she spoke. Oftedal leaned forward in his chair. They all looked expectantly at her. The only sound for the moment was the creaking of Oftedal's chair. Passavant cleared his throat and pointed at her, "In order to establish a motherhouse, you need a deaconess." According to Sister Elisabeth everyone turned to her and said, "Now you have to stay here."

She looked around the room at them as they waited. She thought of the hospital being built in Brooklyn as they spoke. She could not, she told them. She had obligations to her work as Sister Superior in the Deaconess Home and Hospital. Her vacation was over, and she was expected to return to Brooklyn soon. To a man, however, they urged her to stay. The door was now open, she realized, and, as one accustomed to following the Lord's will, she thought she had better not close it. If you leave, they told her, the work would never be established in Minneapolis. A wealthy gentleman, the banker Reinert Sunde (1842-1923), owner of the Scandia bank on Fourth and Cedar in Minneapolis, stood up and said, "I have a home at 2731 Hennepin Avenue that could be used for such a house if we can begin such an organization. You can have it free for the first two years." She was somewhat unsure what to do but wanted to do God's will. What was God's will? God's will had to be hers. What would she do?

Augsburg and Minneapolis

At the time of the meeting in the Gjertsen parsonage, Minneapolis was booming. In the decade from 1880 to 1890, its population had more than tripled from 47,000 to 156,000. Known as the Mill City, it milled

Minneapolis flour mill

the grain from the surrounding Minnesota and Dakota prairie farms. From there the flour was transported south on the Mississippi by flatboat or via rail to commercial centers both east and west. That year—1888— was an especially exciting year because James J. Hill had just opened his Great Northern railroad from St. Paul to Butte, Montana. In seven years (1895) it would be possible to travel from Minneapolis to Seattle on his Great Northern railway. These expansions made Minneapolis a more convenient destination than ever before, and the ebullience with which the Lutherans agreed to meet in Minneapolis, gateway to the Pacific Northwest, matched the ebullient optimism of the builders of the Northwest, as it was called at the time.

For many reasons, Gjertsen, Oftedal, and Sverdrup were eager to found a Deaconess Motherhouse in Minneapolis, a center for Scandinavian Lutherans. At the time there was no hospital for Norwegians in the Upper Midwest where Norwegians were quickly populating the new land, homesteading the verdant prairies, building new towns and cities. The idea of a Motherhouse for the training of deaconesses who would follow their countrymen into the new territories settled by Norwegians was to be applauded. Although the education of young women was not Sverdrup's purpose in the training of deaconesses, he did note that it was one way to provide an education for women who wanted to serve in some kind of public ministry in the church.[8] Augsburg Seminary, like Luther College, exclusively educated young men for the ministry. But Sverdrup knew the question of higher education for women was beginning to loom over all educational institutions in the country as was the question of women's rights.

Sverdrup's interest was consistent with his vigorous pietism and, very likely, his own personal experience. Sverdrup's first wife, Catharine Elisabeth Heiberg (1854-1887), had died the year before. A relative

Georg Sverdrup

from Norway had come to take care of the children temporarily, but Sverdrup needed help again. Catherine's sister, Elise Susanna Heiberg (1864-1942), would come a year later in 1890. She had enrolled at the Motherhouse in Christiania (Oslo) on September 14, 1884, and at that time was working in the pharmacy at the state hospital (*Rikshospitalet*) where she would work until 1889, when, on August 22, she left Christiania for Minneapolis to care for Sverdrup's children, her nieces and nephews. He had been in Christiania as a student when the deaconess house there was built by people he admired, and he very likely had heard a good bit about the Motherhouse from Elise's letters. It is not surprising that he would write several speeches and articles on the diaconate published in *Folkebladet* and later in his collected works. Like the others he traced the idea back to Scripture and Lutheran theology, as well as the work of Theodore Fliedner (1800-1864) in Germany, whom he had closely studied. By the time of the meeting at the Gjertsen home, there were sixty Motherhouses and over 6,500 deaconesses worldwide. Minneapolis as the growing center of Norwegian Lutherans would easily support such an institution.

This was also a hopeful time for the Norwegians in Minneapolis. The city was quickly becoming a center of the Norwegian-American population and a natural place for Norwegian institutions. With the coming merger of the United Norwegian Lutheran Church in America in 1890, these leaders believed Augsburg Seminary would become the major Norwegian-American institution of learning in the region. A Deaconess Motherhouse would add to Augsburg's influence. The signs were good for them and their optimism well-founded as they looked forward to becoming the largest and most vigorous of the Norwegian Lutheran bodies in America. As they sat in Gjertsen's living room, a gleaming future rose before them. They looked at Sister Elisabeth. What would she say?

Sister Elisabeth Fedde

When the young Tonette Elisabeth Fedde (1850-1921) left her home by the Feda fjord in 1874[9] near Flekkefjord, in southwestern Norway to pursue her training at the new Deaconess Motherhouse in Christiania, she knew she was entering a new calling for a woman, one about which she knew very little. She had been brought up on the Fedde farm, in the county now known as West Agder, but in her time Lister and Mandal. Her parents, Andreas Villumsen (1814-1873) and Anne Marie Olsdatter

Feda valley with church, Elisabeth's home marked by arrow

FEDDE FAMILY

Feda Church, 2013

(1818-1864), were landed farmers (after her father left his life at sea to care for her mother) and faithful Christians who cared for the poor and needy if they presented themselves at their door.[10] Her family, part of the peasant (*bønder*) class, had family connections with the leadership class in Norway, known as the people of condition. Her grandmother was the daughter of Maren Dancke Eiberg, married to a ship captain who served the Danish king.

Elisabeth had been born on Christmas Day, December 25, 1850, and baptized at the Feda church the next day. Her family of eight siblings lived in a home very near the church, so the young Elisabeth and her brothers and sisters could play in the church yard beside Feda fjord.[11] Elisabeth had received a typical elementary education and read the materials available to every pious Norwegian Lutheran at the time: the Bible, the hymnal,

Inside Feda Church, 2013

Adolph Tiedemand's painting of catechization in the Norwegian church

and Martin Luther's Small Catechism as elaborated on extensively in Erick Pontoppidan's *Truth Unto Godliness,* which added over 700 questions to be answered by the catechumens. This book had shaped Norwegian spiritual life for nearly 200 years, since entry into the civil life of the realm required confirmation, meaning the young had to memorize at least some of this material.[12]

Not long after her mother died, in 1863, when Elisabeth was only thirteen, she began to "read for the minister" on her way to being confirmed. On October 8, 1865, she was confirmed.[13] The church book which recorded her confirmation also included her grade: Very good. (*Meget godt*). In her autobiographical letter and application to study at the Deaconess Motherhouse in Christiania, written June 26, 1874, she said that at her confirmation service she had promised Pastor Bang (1840-1913)[14] and the Lord with "her whole heart to renounce sin and trust in God, but then I fell away into the world with all its joys." This statement is typical of pietists when describing life before their conversion. As a young woman without a mother, and a father not quite wealthy enough to send his daughter to school away from home, Elisabeth was sent to learn housekeeping or the domestic arts from a neighboring housewife when she was about eighteen. After two years there, she moved to Stavanger to take a job in the home of a shoemaker. At the time, even if she did not feel herself to be a good Christian, she knew the shoemaker's home was not right for her. She thanked the Lord for protecting her from falling into gross sin during that time, and had prayed that she could find a Christian home where she could serve in a better environment. Her prayer would soon be answered.

Hans Nielsen Hauge

To understand the motivations of the Norwegian Americans in Gjertsen's living room one has to understand a bit of the religious situation in Norway at the time. Hans Nielsen Hauge (1771-1824) from Fredrikstad, south of Christiania on the eastern side of the Oslofjord, was the layman whose spiritual experience while plowing his fields on April 5, 1796, changed him and ultimately Norway. Hauge had been singing a hymn as he was working and suddenly felt as though he had been struck by a light that left him senseless for some time. He awakened a different man, wanting to love, obey, and serve God and his neighbor. After some days considering what he should do to respond to what he believed to be God's calling, he began to travel around the

Hans Nielsen Hauge

country with his books, holding meetings, writing letters, preaching the Gospel, singing hymns, knitting while he walked, attracting young people who would walk with him on his way, seeking his spiritual counsel and practical advice. His work helped spark a revival in Norway.

The state church at the time opposed Hauge's fervor because as a layman he was a threat to its authority. It arrested him several times for having religious meetings without being a properly ordained pastor in the Norwegian state church. They tried to stop his movement by using a law against him called the Conventicle law which banned such meetings. It had been passed in 1741 to hinder independent religious groups such as the Moravians from encroaching on the state church. When Hauge seemed a threat, he was thrown into jail on several charges, frequently that of being a vagrant without the proper papers. His chief offense, however, in the eyes of the law was breaking the Conventicle Law. Finally, the church and state put him in jail where he languished nearly ten years, ca. 1804-1814, a time that broke his health but not his movement. He believed that the laity could preach, both men and women, if they had the gift. He chose women for his leadership circle as well as men.[15] When he died in 1824, his revival had changed the religious lives of many Norwegians and the entire country. His most recent biographer, Dag Kullerud, called him the first modern Norwegian because he had awakened Norway from its sleep. His movement broke both the power of the state church and the mercantilist economic system that had been in power when he began his ministry.[16]

Without him, scholars have wondered if Norwegians would have had the courage and spiritual fortitude to have come to America and to have built prosperous commuties on the prairies. Fedde could be counted as being a part of that revival in its second generation.

Stavanger

When Elisabeth went to work in Stavanger, she was going to the right place for her at the time. Stavanger, on the southwest coast of Norway, was part of what was called the Bible Belt of Norway. Hans Nielsen Hauge's revival had a big impact on the area. His friend, Jon Haugvaldstad (1770-1850), a leader of the mission movement of Norway, continued Hauge's work in the region and helped to found the Stavanger Mission High School in 1843. Many Norwegian missionaries went from there to serve in various places around the world. The school and mission societies in Stavanger made it a center of revival and

Jon Haugvaldstad

mission concerns. The Iver Siqveland (b. 1815) family asked Elisabeth to work for them in their home where she would also continue to learn skills that helped in the managing of a household. From his wife, Johanne Helene Siqveland (b, 1815), she learned many important things. Elisabeth wrote:

> The Mrs. was a very kind and understanding housewife. With her I experienced a good preparatory school for the vocation I would later enter. She was very precise, and I, who had very much missed my mother, received a good foundation from her.[17]

Siqveland, a broker by trade and a wealthy man, supported many causes dear to the hearts of the pietists: foreign and home missions, deaconess hospitals and motherhouses, orphanages, and senior's homes. The Siqveland home contained edifying classics beloved by Lutheran pietists: John Bunyan's *Pilgrim's Progress*, Christian Scriver's *The Soul's Treasury* (*Seelenschatz*,) but especially Philip Jakob Spener's *The Practice of Christianity* (*Kristendoms Øvelse*) which the young Elisabeth eagerly read. She remembered all her life how Siqveland had walked back and forth in the house singing the good old hymns dear to the hearts of Norwegian pietists. He and his wife were kind to the young Elisabeth, she reported. They let her go home to be with her father during his final illness. For this she was grateful. When her father died, on October 24, 1872, the sorrow of losing him caused Elisabeth to pray that God would help her, now alone in the world without a home. After a struggle, which she reported in language very typical of pietists, to "rid herself of the world," she asked God to change her heart. On November 12, 1872, it happened. Suddenly she felt completely new and cleansed of her sin. "I was so glad I hardly felt myself walking on earth!"[18]

The young Elisabeth soaked up the earnest Christianity of the Siqvelands and prayed she would be led into some kind of Christian service, but as a young woman she admitted she did not know what might be possible. "What might God's will be? Fields of service for women are limited, and even of those few I am not informed."[19] About the time of her struggle to find a place in the world, difficult because she was now alone without father or mother, deaconesses from the Christiania Motherhouse had appeared in Stavanger and had begun to serve the sick and indigent. A seamstress who frequented the Siqveland home had noticed Elisabeth's conscientious work and told her, "Elisabeth, you ought to be a deaconess." This was a new idea for the young woman. She had seen a few deaconesses dressed in the garb and wondered if they were Roman Catholic nuns. "How could I do that?" she asked. "There is a house in Christiania where Christian women who desire to serve the Lord among the sick and the needy can be admitted and trained for that purpose," the seamstress replied.

At first she rejected the idea of becoming a deaconess, with their "white scarves with hats on top and black shawls," but after the religious crisis brought on by the death of her father, she began to think she was being called into such service.[20] As Elisabeth prayed, she struggled to discern God's will for her, wanting to offer her whole life to God. In the mean-

Iver Siqveland's letter for Elisabeth

time, she went to meet with two deaconesses in Stavanger to ask them about their life and work at the Motherhouse in Christiania. They encouraged her and gave her information about the strict rules by which they lived. She approved of the rules and thought they made her more certain of her call.

Sometime later Elisabeth went to Mrs. Siqveland and said, "I want to be a deaconess!" Mrs. Siqveland agreed that Elisabeth should pursue the vocation and offered to help the young woman with her application. She knew many involved with the Deaconess Motherhouse in Christiania, especially Cathinka Guldberg, the mother superior. Siqveland's son, Johannes, who had studied theology in Christiania, knew the deaconess community well and helped her apply.

Many founders of the Deaconess Motherhouse in Christiania were part of a group of friends well known to the Siqvelands, so things moved quickly once Fedde made known her wish to enter the diaconate. The young Siqveland sent her a letter telling her how to apply for admittance to the Motherhouse: 1) write a spiritual autobiography, 2) give her reasons for applying, and 3) get recommendations from a pastor and employer (see Appendix 3). She quickly completed the application. While she was praying and wondering whether or not she should actually send

Lars Oftedal

in her letter of application, she went to consult the influential Pastor Lars Oftedal (1838-1900), the leader of Bethania prayer house, where she went every Wednesday evening to hear him teach Luther's *Small Catechism* as explained by Pontoppidan. Prayer houses (*bedehuser*) were built after the end of the Conventicle Act in 1842 by pietists who wanted a place to meet outside the church for prayer and small group meetings.

Lars was a brother of Sven Oftedal, professor at Augsburg Seminary. Lars Oftedal was at the peak of his enormous spiritual influence in Norway, so it is not surprising she sought him out as a trusted spiritual advisor. In her letter of application Elisabeth noted that after hearing of the Motherhouse, she felt more and more called to become a deaconess. Her application closed with the confidence that God would do what was right for her.[21] Her visit with Oftedal ended with his saying, "Outside my door is a post box. Put your letter in it." She did. Very soon thereafter, she was accepted by the Motherhouse in Christiania.[22]

Along with his commendation of Fedde to the Deaconess Motherhouse, Siqveland, according to the requirement of employers who recommended a student, also promised to take her back into his employ if for some reason things did not work out for her at the school.[23] This assured that the young women, many of whom were poor, would not be abandoned to the streets (see Appendix 3).

The Deaconess Motherhouse in Christiania

On December 1, 1874, Fedde left her home in Feda for Christiania to begin a new life in a new profession that few knew about. On Saturday, December 5, 1874, when she stepped across the threshold of the Motherhouse, she could hardly imagine what was about to happen to her. Immediately a new life began.[24]

When Elisabeth applied to be admitted to the Motherhouse in Christiania, the deaconess movement had already become well established in Norway. Not long after its first year in 1868, fourteen young women had been admitted as future sisters. When Elisabeth arrived in 1874, six years after its founding, it

Mother Cathinka Guldberg

was a growing concern. Not surprisingly the house was closely connected to the two original deaconess houses in Germany: Kaiserswerth, where Theodore Fliedner had established the first Motherhouse, and Neuendettelsau, Bavaria, where Wilhelm Loehe had founded a similar order. Cathinka Guldberg (1840-1919), the first

Sister Superior in Norway, had trained at Kaiserswerth; her close associate, Ulrikke "Rikke" Nissen (1834-1892), had been at Neuendettelsau and spent a short time at Kaiserswerth. Nissen became the teaching sister, responsible for the education of the deaconesses. This meant that the Christiania Motherhouse where Sister Elisabeth had gone to live and study was led by two women who had studied at each of the founding Motherhouses in Germany.

Theodore Fliedner

To understand the growth of the Deaconess movement in the nineteenth century, especially the Motherhouse in Christiania, it is necessary to consider its origins in the life and work of Theodore Fliedner, a pastor in Germany, who as a boy had lived through the ravages of the Napoleonic Wars. In 1820, Fliedner passed his exams for ordination and began

a ministry as a teacher in the home of a wealthy merchant in Cologne. Soon he was appointed rector of a church in Kaiserswerth, a small town on the Rhine, where centuries before Frederick Barbarossa had built a castle. Kaiserswerth, now a suburb of Düsseldorf, was mostly Catholic at the time. Because of the extreme poverty in his congregation and the needs of the local prison, Fliedner traveled throughout the region collecting money for the work of both the

Theodore Fliedner

congregation and the prison. In doing so he gained experience in raising money for the poor, as well as a better sense for the appalling conditions in the prisons, especially for women. He had been moved by the pressing concern to help the neighbor and felt a desperate need for some kind of revival in the Lutheran church of the day, especially one that would bring Christian love and kindness to people suffering from extreme poverty, consequences of the brutal Napoleonic wars which had swept across Germany with particular fury, and dislocations caused by the Industrial Revolution. Fliedner was trying to meet the challenges obvious to everybody. He and his wife began to study the ancient office of the diaconate to see if it might be answer to the need around them During this same time, Karl Marx (1818-1883) printed his *Communist Manifesto* (1848) and began working on *Das Kapital,* both of which attempted to revolution-ize the entire society in order to deal with the same economic distress the

Johann Hinrich Wichern

Fliedners were also trying to alleviate. The Fliedners wanted to help the suffering by build-ing orphanages, children's homes, refuges for pregnant girls, and hospitals for the sick and dying. Heirs of the pietist movement which had gone cold during the Enlightenment, Fliedner and another German contemporary, Johann Hinrich Wichern (1808-1881), began estab-lishing such institutions. Fliedner, who had grown up in extreme poverty, was eager to help the poor, or "the least of these," as Jesus had urged in his parable of the last judgment in Mat-thew 25. Fliedner took a trip to visit the orphanage at Halle, near Leipzig, established over a century earlier by one of the fathers of pietism, August Hermann Francke (1663-1727). There he found rich resources for many of his ideas about helping the "widow and orphan" since Francke had founded one of the first orphanages in Germany. The theological educa-tion Fliedner received at the university did little to quench his thirsty spirit. The habits of the Enlightenment prevailed in the lives of many pastors and professors he met: they preferred worldly amusements to life in service and study of God's Word. Fliedner was moved by the need around him and wanted to act out of his Christian faith.

The Fliedners were not alone in their concerns. To further his under-standing of what could be done for people suffering such dire situations, Fliedner traveled to England and Scotland where he met many who would become helpful advisors and colleagues, especially in regard to the conditions of women's prisons. In an effort to help female ex-convicts who gave evidence of wanting to reform their lives, in 1840 he established a halfway house in Kaiserswerth where twenty-eight former prisoners could live in comparative comfort and safety.

While this was a commendable work, it was not enough for the restless Fliedner, who wanted to establish a more effective way for Chris-tians to provide such acts of mercy. Soon he began thinking of reviving the ancient order of deaconess in the same spirit as the early apostles.

The first hospitals had been established by Greek Christians in the early centuries of the church, when orders of sisters cared for the sick. After the Reformation, in areas where Lutherans dominated, with the closing of the convents such institutions had disappeared. They did not reappear until the likes of Fliedner came along. Since people knew nothing of germs and the importance of cleanliness, hospitals became places of pestilence themselves. Most nursing at the time was done at home by women who often had three generations to nurse: parents, children, and husbands, brothers and other relatives. In existing hospitals nurses were poorly regard-

Kaiserswerth deaconess

ed and untrained, often known as "drunken menials." Hospitals, such as they were, had no sense for cleanliness. At the time of Florence Nightingale's reforms, nursing was a disreputable profession. Lytton Strachey, in his biographical essay on Nightingale wrote:

> A "nurse" meant then a coarse old woman, always ignorant, usually dirty, often, brutal, a Mrs. Gamp in bunched-up sordid garments, tippling at the brandy bottle or indulging in worse irregularities. The nurses in the hospitals were especially notorious for immoral conduct; sobriety was almost unknown among them; and they could hardly be trusted to carry out the simplest medical duties.[25]

Human waste, vermin, unwashed bedclothes in closed unventilated quarters were the rule rather than the exception. After the turn of the century, a population explosion began when many more children survived to adulthood. A significant number of women who did not find husbands financially able to marry needed to have places to live and work where they could be safe and prosper. At the time, single women could inherit their father's property in most Western countries, but if they had no resources or promise of an inheritance, it was nearly impossible to make a living in a career other than being a maid or governess—as Elisabeth knew very well after her father died. For women in Elisabeth's day it was vital to have a source of support. Women without such support often had no alternative but the brothel. It is difficult for us today to understand how very limited the choices for women were then. Elisabeth well understood this as she looked for a way to serve her Lord—and support herself. The diaconate looked like a healthy alternative to several unattractive possibilities if marriage was not possible.

Women's Choices

It was a different dilemma for women of affluence. As single women they could inherit their father's wealth, but when they married that wealth became their husbands. Wealthy single women like Florence Nightingale avoided marriage for several reasons, including her ferocious devotion to the nursing profession and the fact that the marriage contract treated them and their inheritance as the property of their husbands. In this scenario, the husband then became the woman's legal guardian as her father had been. The early feminists focused on this situation when they first began agitating for their rights. The women's movement in America had its official beginning at the 1848 convention in Seneca Falls with

Three different deaconess garbs—Berlin, Leipzig, Stockholm—in a painting still hanging in Fliedner's office

COURTESY OF FLIEDNER CULTURAL FOUNDATION KAISERSWERTH

Elizabeth Cady Stanton (1815-1902) and Susan Brownell Anthony (1820-1906) which resulted in the *Declaration of Sentiments and Rights*. In *The Declaration* one of the sentiments (really complaints) was that marriage made a woman "civilly dead" because all her wealth and resources after her marriage belonged to her husband. It is not surprising that the first women's struggle for rights centered around this question, moving only later to the quest for suffrage. American states began granting married women the right to inherit property in 1849, long before suffrage was granted. In 1893, at the Chicago World's Fair, Lucy Stone, an abolitionist and suffragette, now grown old in the struggle, noted that "Wives, widows, and mothers seemed to have been hunted out by the law on purpose to see in how many ways they could be wronged and made helpless. A wife by her marriage lost all right to any personal property she might have."[26] Now things had been much improved, for which Stone said women should be grateful.

Because, at the time, the vote was associated with property women with property were the first to vote in municipal elections for school board or other such public offices before universal suffrage. This began happening in the late nineteenth century in America and Norway. Although there are instances of brave and unattached women striking out on their own before the mid-nineteenth century, it was after the American Civil War, with the open American frontier and the continuing passage of laws giving women more rights, that women in significant numbers trained to become teachers, secretaries, or doctors and later nurses, many of whom remained single. Schools such as St. Olaf College in Northfield, Minnesota, admitted women because there was a market for such women in the labor force. A woman alone, with no prospect for or interest in marriage, might look upon the vocation of a deaconess as a safe and good vocation.

Women As Deaconesses

Fliedner, among others, had heard how much women had done for soldiers during the Napoleonic Wars, and he began to wonder if it would be good for such women to live together and receive an education that would prepare them for a religious vocation that included nursing skills. Using the words of Jesus in Matthew 25, "I was sick and you visited me," he began considering how to create a place where women could train to be nurses and at the same time be educated as spiritual counselors. While the Fliedners were praying about the challenges before them, the largest house in Kaiserswerth came up for sale. In an act of faith, the Fliedners bought it and miraculously received the necessary funding from their community to pay for it and move in. In May 1836, Fliedner signed the statutes for a Deaconess Society for Rhenish Westphalia, and the house was soon readied for the young women. What they needed now were young women who were ready and willing to live such a life. As the Fliedners prayed and collected money, Gertrude Reichardt (1788-1869), a

Gertrude Reichardt

woman of forty-eight, came to them seeking a position. The daughter of a doctor, she had helped her father treat his patients, so she was well-trained for such a ministry and profession. Other women applied, and soon the Fliedners had a Motherhouse established.

All this time Fliedner was ably assisted by his wife, Friederike Wilhelmine Münster (1800-1842). He had met her while looking for help with women prisoners. In 1828 they married, and they had ten children, not all of whom survived infancy. Fliedner considered her the first deaconess. She had encouraged him to buy the first building and to open the first Motherhouse even before they had any sisters. She had the gift, according to Harriet Spaeth, wife of Adolph, of "sanctified insight" which kept her husband from making many a mistake.

Friederike Fliedner

> The order, simplicity, and frugality which she taught and practiced were, especially in the beginning, of incalculable value. With large-hearted charity toward all who were in need of help, she understood how to combine a manly energy in the case of those inclined to abuse it [sic]. She was one of those rare souls who understand not only how to bear courageously their own heavy burden, but at the same time to give strength and assistance to others.[27]

Fliedner treated the sisters in the Motherhouse, as it came to be called, like his daughters, teaching them Scripture, training them in the role of the office of deaconess, and leading them in family devotions every evening. During the day they were instructed in the arts of nursing by a doctor and Sister Gertrude. A mere six years after the first sister had been admitted, more than forty sisters lived with them, and the hospital had over 200 beds. Through the 1840s the movement spread quickly through Germany and Europe. When the revolutions of 1848 broke out, partly because the needs of people were so dire, much of the work of Fliedner and others who had turned their attentions to the needy (such as Wichern at his Rough House [*Rauhes Haus*] for boys in 1833) began to be seen as necessary and important for the stability of the entire society. After the death of his first wife, Friederike, in 1842, Fliedner married Caroline Beartheu (1811-1892) of Hamburg in 1843. Caroline, like Friederike, became a close associate of her husband and worked hard organizing and running the establishment during Fliedner's long trips away raising money and establishing new houses in Germany, the Middle East, and even America. After his death in 1864, she continued the work

The first Mrs. Fliedner and Pastor Fliedner in their office in Kaiserswerth

of the Motherhouse as Mother Fliedner until her own death in 1892. In 1846, Pastor Passavant had come to Kaiserswerth to learn about establishing a Deaconess Motherhouse in Pittsburgh. Three years later, in 1849, after the civil turmoil in Europe had settled somewhat, Fliedner began his extensive travels to spread the idea of the Deaconess movement abroad. The summer of 1849, about forty years before the meeting in Minneapolis, he had gone to North America by way of Bremen and London at the request of Passavant. Four sisters traveled with him, and they helped establish the Motherhouse in Pittsburgh. Fliedner's work and ideas began spreading around the world, partly because Fliedner began editing a magazine, *Friends of the Sick and Poor: A Journal for the Diaconate of the Protestant Church,* in which he told of his travels and urged the adoption of Motherhouses where they could be supported by the local population.

Caroline Beartheau, Fliedner's second wife

Kaiserswerth when Florence Nightingale visited. The arrow indicates her room.

Florence Nightingale in Kaiserswerth

On July 31, 1850, Florence Nightingale visited the Motherhouse in Kaiserswerth. She had hoped to go there since hearing of it in 1846, but she was restrained by her mother who continued to hope she would marry and give up her passionate concern for the reform of nursing. After a time in Egypt and Athens, Nightingale found her way to Kaiserswerth and came to be good friends with the Fliedners with whom she corresponded for many years. As she left the Motherhouse she signed the guestbook, "Florence Nightingale, who, with an overflowing heart, will always think of the kindness of all her friends at dear Kaiserswerth. I was a stranger and ye took me in. Kaiserswerth, August 13, 1850."[28] She returned as a student in 1854 and counted this time as crucial to her understanding of her own vocation. Upon leaving she wrote in her di-

Florence Nightingate

ary, "Left Kaiserswerth feeling so brave, as if nothing could ever vex me again."[29] As she set up a home for old women who had lost their fortunes, she wrote to Caroline Fliedner to say that she was thinking of Kaiserswerth as she was building the institution:

> I sometimes envy my dear sisters at Kaiserswerth a little, they have a father and a mother, so much guidance and spiritual help. The paid attendants who work with the three probationers cause me endless trouble, they have neither love nor conscience. How fortunate I should be if we had none but Sisters. I do not think that this institute is suitable for the Deaconess organization. My intention is to stay for a few years—my difficulties here are certainly an excellent training for me; and then I shall attempt the real task—on a better basis, I mean in a public hospital.[30]

These comments indicate she understood the problems with employees as opposed to the dedication of the sisters. She would go on to adopt many practices from Kaiserswerth in her lifetime, indirectly spreading the fame and practices of the Lutheran Deaconess Motherhouse around the world.

Nightingale and the Profession of Nursing

Florence Nightingale was the most famous trailblazer in the effort to reform and improve the profession of nursing around the world. Her experience as nurse to the British soldiers in the Crimea showed her to be not only a pioneer in nursing but also an incredible administrator. In fact, that turned out to be her greatest gift. She was able to see how to keep the wards for the soldiers clean, how to give them nutritious food and good ventilation, as well as clear the sewers of Scutari where the troops were stationed. As important as her personal attention to patients was her force of personality, which persuaded the military and the British bureaucracy to change old routines and protocols. At this distance her achievements seem nothing short of phenomenal. When she started her work in Crimea, four out of ten soldiers were dying of disease, not of their wounds. By the time she has completed her reformation of battle nursing procedures, only twenty-two out of a thousand perished.[31]

After gathering facts for the Royal Commission on the Health of the Army, she began to advocate sanitary conditions as most important in medical treatment. "Fear of dirt is the beginning of good nursing" was her mantra, no doubt a play on the biblical dictum, "The fear of the Lord is the beginning of wisdom."[32]

These new practices, when adopted, slashed the instances of cholera, typhus, typhoid, and dysentery caused by unsanitary conditions. Her book, *Notes on Nursing: What It Is And What It Is Not* (1859), was a short primer on nursing, brimming with common sense about matters of health. She defined nursing as "the proper use of fresh air, light, warmth, cleanliness, quiet, and the proper selection and administration of diet—all at the least expense of vital power to the patient."[33] She recommended 1) keeping the patients properly ventilated, neither too hot or cold; 2) learning how to delegate treatments to others when you are not there; 3) keeping noise down; 4) providing the patient some variety of stimulus; 5) good nutrition; 6) clean beds and bedding; 7) light; 8) clean rooms and walls; 9) personal cleanliness on the part of the nurse; 10) keeping ones advice and commentary about the patient confidential and useful; 11) close observation of the patient.[34] While these may seem self-evident to us, in her time they were medical breakthroughs. In addition to working with the sick, she also thought that nurses could improve the health of the poor by teaching them better sanitary habits. About this she was also right. Her work resulted in a reform of the nursing profession in England, America, and soon around the world.

Nightingale's forceful personality and fierce religious persuasions made her into something of a saint during her lifetime: people trusted her and wanted to follow her example and advice. Her life and work, urging the importance of these new kinds of practices in the health system, brought her into contact with feminists around the world. John Stuart Mill famously asked her to be on his Women's Suffrage Society which was formed in 1867. Her response to him was telling:

> "That women should have the suffrage, I think no one can be more deeply convinced than I," Florence replied, "But it will probably be years before you obtain it. In the meantime, are there not evils which press more hardly on women than not having a vote? For instance, until a married woman can be in possession of her own property, there can be no love or justice."[35]

While she had her criticisms of the feminist movement, she agreed that the ideology that made women into nearly helpless beings was

The Motherhouse in Kaisersworth today

bad.[36] In the meantime, however, her reputation and her thinking about the profession of nursing spread around the world.

Fliedner's work was part of that reform, and as far reaching, but today virtually unremarked. Before the close of the decade, there were Motherhouses in Constantinople, Smyrna, Alexandria, Sidon, and Beirut. When Fliedner died October 4, 1864, he left behind a legacy of prison reform, halfway houses for women convicts, asylums for the "insane" (as they were called), as well as schools that prepared young women to teach, be nurses, and build orphanages and old people's homes—however Christians wanted to do something to serve their neighbors. Most important, however, was his remarkable legacy in the deaconess houses around the world.

Wilhelm Loehe's Deaconess House In Neuendettelsau

A few years after Fliedner began his work at Kaiserswerth, Pastor Johan Konrad Wilhelm Loehe (1808-1872) in Neuendettelsau, Bavaria, began a similar work. In 1853, Loehe published a tract, "Reflections on the Female Diaconate within the Protestant Church of Bavaria" (*Bedenken über die weibliche Diakonie innerhalb der Protestantischen Kirche Bayerns, insonderheit über zu errichtende Diakonissen Anstalten*). In it he set forth several propositions about the need for and possibilities of such an office in the church. His major assertions were somewhat similar to

Fliedner's: 1) Clergymen visiting the sick noticed that the women who were caring for them seemed to have a special gift with the sick. 2) These women, if given an education, could be a blessing to the sick and needy in their district because their training would be beneficial to all. 3) These institutions would be attended by girls from any Christian tradition, but they would not take the place of other schools for girls in the upper classes. This training would be beneficial to the entire community since women had a natural aptitude for being merciful and this education would be a general education. 4) Deaconesses, whether married or single, could apply their gifts to ministering to suffering humanity. 5) These institutions for deaconesses would become like seminaries to

Johan Konrad Wilhelm Loehe

train nurses for spiritual service in asylums, kindergartens, governesses, as missionaries. 6) Such institutions would be formed around hospitals so the sisters could get a practical education as well. 7) These institutions could be in either city or country where the leaders as persons would be more important than the institution.

To that end he organized a Motherhouse which opened on May 9, 1854 above a tavern in Neuendettelsau. His poem, "What Do I Wish?"

The Deaconess Motherhouse at Neuendettelsau

became one of the most commonly repeated and memorized slogans for the deaconess community around the world:

> What do I wish?
> I wish to serve.
> Whom do I wish to serve?
> The Lord, in His poor and needy ones.
> And what is my reward?
> I do not serve either for regard or for thanks,
> but out of gratitude and love;
> My reward is that I may do this!
> And if I perish in doing it?
> "If I perish, I perish," said Queen Esther,
> who knew not Him, for love of Whom I would perish;
> But He will not let me perish.
> And if I grow old?
> Still shall my heart keep fresh as a palm tree
> and the Lord shall satisfy me with grace and mercy.
> I go in peace and free from care."

The accusation that his understanding of the office of deaconess with its service of consecration created another order of ministry, like nuns, worried Loehe and his detractors. To refute such an understanding he wrote extensively on how the office was only local and should be at the service of the local pastor (most likely to avoid a free-standing order of women religious without close supervision), but he seemed to hint that the women take vows of poverty, obedience, and celibacy, although he said he was open to married deaconesses. His notions were viewed with alarm by other Lutherans such as Adolf Spaeth who viewed Loehe as "dangerously near to the Roman Catholic practice—if not the theory—of the so-called *Consilia Evangelica*, the three Monastic vows of poverty, obedience, and chastity (celibacy)."[37] Even though Loehe had tried to establish these three vows on completely different bases than the Roman vows, they looked very Catholic to the followers of Fliedner who viewed Loehe with suspicion on this question, as did Spaeth, among others.

From the collection of essays given at conferences over the years when the diaconate was in full flower, it appears that the American Motherhouses associated together in deaconess organizations traced their roots back to Fliedner rather than Loehe. Loehe seemed to have a higher sense of the office than Fliedner, with which the Norwegian deaconess Rikke Nissen agreed. One can read in the Principles of the Female Diaconate (Appendix 1) the care the American Lutherans took to make sure the deaconess office did not conflict with the traditional theology of the one office of the pastor, long held to by Lutherans.

Two sisters in Neuendettelsau garb, which Guldberg preferred to Kaiserswerth

Reading the increasing number of suggestions on how the deaconess houses should be organized and how the individual deaconess should live, one can see the persistent nineteenth century question about a woman in the work place. The women who became deaconesses were single and free to enter the profession, and they got a good education in their training.

While the Motherhouses had been established by pastors' daughters and women of their class who were educated, the large majority of women applying were not. In Norway the candidates tended to be farmers' daughters or women from the cotters' class (*husmænd*), the

Rikke Nissen

unpropertied class, who were accustomed to hard labor. The pastors thought women from the upper classes would be easier to educate, already having received a good education at home, but Mother Guldberg and Rikke Nissen, who, like Guldberg, came from the upper class in Norway, thought it would be easier to form the vocation of a girl who came with fewer expectations. (Florence Nightingale shared that opinion.) Furthermore the work the nurse was to do, although vital to the healing of a patient, was hard, not unlike that of a maid. Given the kind of work expected of these women, it is rather hard to imagine many women of privilege wanting to do such demanding and difficult work, as Loehe seemed to understand.

Deaconess Mother Houses in the North

Because of these developments in Germany, Lutherans to the north who looked to Lutheran Germany as their source of Lutheran practice and theology, began their own efforts to establish Motherhouses where they could train deaconesses. Norway was the last to build such a Motherhouse, but soon its numbers exceeded that of the others. One of the first people in Norway to speak of the deaconess' vocation was Bernt Julius Muus (1832-1900), who would later found St. Olaf College in Northfield, Minnesota, which admitted both men and women. As the editor of *Norsk Kirketidende* from 1858 to 1859, Muus commended the work of Fliedner, printing two articles based on Fliedner's *Report on the Voca-*

Bernt Julius Muus

tion of Deaconesses (Theodor Fliedners Nachricht über das Diakonissen Werk). While few people noticed them, Rikke Nissen in her book on the deaconess work in Christiania saw them as a beginning of the movement and important to mark.

Norwegian Innermission Societies

The Innermission movement in Norway, like many such organizations in Lutheran Europe, also needs some explanation. Ever since Hans Nielsen Hauge's revival, and his "Last Will and Testament" which urged his followers not to leave the state church, but continue to reform the church from the inside, there had been a vigorous lay movement in Norway, but not only there. Awakened Lutherans in every Lutheran land had seen the need for an inner mission in each of their state churches. Wichern's followers in Germany in the 1840s had organized groups that would work to bring a personal Christianity to German Lutherans who were mostly what the pietists called "nominal" Lutheran Christians. The Innermission movement not only urged the evangelization of baptized members of the churches, but had strong philanthropic concerns as well.

A pastor in Norway, Honoratus Halling (1819-1886) had begun a Sunday paper, "For Poor and Rich" (*For Fattig og Riig)* in 1847 which Elisabeth first read in Stavanger. Norway's first Innermission society began in Skien on August 8, 1853, by the pastor Gustav Adolph Lammers, who would be the founder of Nor-

Honoratus Halling way's Lutheran Free Church.

Johnson's Revival

In Norway the leaders of the revival were professors of theology at the university. The revival began after Gisle Johnson gave a lecture in 1854 focusing on the need to bring an awakening to the "spiritually dead masses." It was not long until he, with other colleagues and laymen, founded "The Society for the Inner Mission in Christiania" (*Foreningen for den indre Mission i Christiania*). Its main concern was biblical preaching, Bible study, and edifying lectures pressing what they called "personal" Christianity, distributing Bibles, and edifying literature throughout the country. From this work came revival and spiritual renewal which many of the Norwegian immigrants brought with them to this country, especially those who gathered around Augsburg Seminary, Red Wing Seminary, and later St. Olaf College, United Seminary, and ultimately Luther Seminary.

Gisle Johnson

Johnson's students revered him as did many of the people among the awakened in Norway at the time. Sverdrup wrote that Johnson's influence was so great that students "talked like him, prayed like him, even sighed like him."[38] Because Johnson understood the ability of the laity to speak and carry out Christ's mission in the world, he believed women as well as men could become missionaries and leaders of evangelical movements—such as the women's circles that funded many home mission projects with the poor and sick as well as financed foreign missions. Johnson's significance can hardly be overstated. His emphasis on the work of the laity made a place for devout women to participate and lead the revival, not as pastors, but as proclaimers whose authority came from their knowledge of the Word. As women in Norway began working for their right to vote in the Christian organizations, they used Hauge's and Johnson's understandings as a way forward.

Building Support for a Deaconess Motherhouse

In 1860, Rikke Nissen, by now one of the leaders of the deaconess movement in Norway, traveled to Sweden where she and some friends visited the Stockholm Motherhouse. Two years before, in 1858, she and her sister, Bolette Gjør (1835-1909), also one who experienced a spiritual awakening under Johnson's preaching, had started a Ladies Aid society in Romedal in Hedemark, just west of Christiania, with the goal of improving the education and place of upper-class women especially in things cultural and spiritual. Soon after they started this group, Gjør, an important leader in the Norwegian women's movement both in and out of the church, went to Madeira (1858-1860) to recover her health.

Bolette Gjør

While there she came into contact not only with the international community but also with the medical community, given the number of sun seekers from the north, trying to recover from their diseases. From them she heard about the deaconess movement in Germany, widespread because of the tireless work of Fliedner. Bolette's report caused Rikke Nissen to visit the Motherhouse in Stockholm. Upon her return she began urging that they build such a place in Norway. Not long afterwards Nissen received a package of information from Sweden with a small pamphlet on the idea of deaconesses: "What Is the Deaconess House?" *(Hvad er Diakonissehuset?)* In 1861 she distributed it to members of the Innermission. A theological student translated it into Norwegian and had a thousand copies of it printed to be distributed at a bazaar in Christiania. Sister Rikke wrote later that they were like seeds with wings flying all around Norway.[39]

In her visits to Neuendettelsau and also the Swedish Motherhouse where the Sister Superior ran the house, Rikke Nissen had come to understand the role of a deaconess a bit differently from the Kaiserswerth emphasis on the call to serve, preferring it be more like that of a professional.[40] Sister Rikke, whose poor health (she suffered for many years from severe rheumatism) prevented her from taking a larger role in the Christiania Motherhouse, urged that the deaconess be able to determine her own future, even free to leave the Motherhouse if she felt called. She did take issue with the Kaiserswerth notion that a deaconess should be obedient and disliked the theology of self-denial at the heart of its rules, even the notion that the institution had to be run by a man. She thought a head sister could do it as well, something Florence Nightingale also insisted should be possible. About this she and Guldberg disagreed. Kristin Adriansen, in her thesis about Sister Elisabeth's sense of call, supposes that Fedde was as much influenced by Nissen's thinking as Guldberg's, even if she came to idolize Mother Guldberg and always visited with her when she was in Christiania.[41]

The brochures flying around Norway soon landed in Stavanger. One of those who received the brochure was a woman with a warm heart for the orphans and widows in her city and thought the idea of a deaconess house in Norway spoke directly to the need she saw around her.[42] She had established a home for twelve homeless children, and in that work she realized the most important resource was a book of songs for the children to use in their worship and life together such as the one by Fliedner, *Songbook for Small School Children* (*Liederbuch für Kleinkinderschulen*)[43] This book created in the small group of friends an awareness of the work of Fliedner in Kaiserswerth and made them curious about it. Small groups around Christiania formed to support the work. Nissen says even hospital charwomen (*gangkoner*) who had been moved by the Johnson revivals formed small groups to support such a project.[44]

Kaiserswerth first building, Stammhaus

In the spring of 1866, Cathinka Guldberg and a younger friend went to Kaiserswerth to enter deaconess training. Almost immediately upon her arrival Guldberg was sent to Dresden to help soldiers wounded in the Prussian-Austrian war. This thrust her into a practical situation where she had to learn from the older sisters how to work with wounded soldiers. Her hand became infected during her work so she returned to Kaiserswerth to heal. After she recovered, she was sent to the Charity Hospital in Berlin where she learned more about the spiritual side of the work of a deaconess. From there she was sent to the German Deaconess Hospital in Alexandria, Egypt, established by Fliedner on his trip to the Middle East. She served many Scandinavian sailors who found her care and presence salutary, especially her ability to share God's Word with them in their own language.

News about the work of deaconesses in Germany and around the world came to be more and more well known in Norway. The next notice of Kaiserswerth in Norway appeared in *Norske Kirketidende,* announcing Fliedner death in 1864. This showed his reputation had become well-known in Norway.

With more and more news about deaconesses in Sweden and Germany, two small groups began working to establish a Motherhouse in Christiania. Rikke Nissen was a member of one of those groups. One of her chief converts was the teacher Henriette Bärnholdt (1820-1867) who had lived in England and France and had served as governess in the home of Baron Wedel in Bærum, now a wealthy city and suburb of Oslo. On hearing of the deaconess movement she, with her own funds, traveled to Berlin, Dresden, and Neu-

Wilhelm Loehe

endettelsau to see the Motherhouses there. She also was impressed by the work of Loehe in Neuendettelsau, especially his spirit. To experience life with the deaconesses there, to see how they went about their work, "the glorious liturgical vespers, with the lovely music, and Loehe's moving sermons, made it worth the trip," she wrote, saying it was with "a heavy heart" she left Neuendettelsau.[45] (Most people who visited Loehe remarked on his physical beauty as well as his spiritual depth, especially through his pleasing leadership of the liturgies of the church and his powerful preaching.)[46] She wrote Nissen and said, "Come and see. Stay not six weeks, but six months." From then on she urgently worked to get the Norwegians to see how important such a house could be for them. When she died two years later, in 1867, she left a considerable fortune at the time, 4,000 crowns, for the establishment of a Mother-house in Christiania.

Founding the Motherhouse in Norway

The Inner Mission Society in Christiania began a drive to collect funds for the indigent, estimated to be nearly twelve percent of the population. At the end of 1866, two significant lectures on the deaconess

movement by Pastor Julius Bruun (1820-1899) were also published in *Kirketidende* and *For Fattig og Riig*. In March 1867 the Inner Mission Society established a committee to develop plans for such a house. Bruun became the chair of the committee. The group announced on March 17, 1867, that "the Society for Inner Mission in Christiania announces herein it will establish a place for the education of Christian nurses in the capitol city."[47] For Norway this was a new thing, the first

Julius Bruun

time the term "nurse" (*sygepleierske*) had been used. Bloch-Hoell, the historian of the Motherhouse in Christiania, says this is the beginning of professional nursing in Norway.

Now they needed a deaconess. The Christiania committee, made up of people well known in Norway and among the Norwegian-Amer-

icans such as Johnson, chose Julius Riddervold (1842-1921), son of the Bishop Hans Riddervold (1795-1876). He was elected to the board in 1867 and by all accounts he proved to be an excellent choice. By 1868, the group had gathered 7,000-8,000 crowns for the building of a Deaconess Motherhouse. During the meeting of the board in September of that year, Riddervold was commissioned to write to Cathinka Guld-

Julius Riddervold

berg who was still in Alexandria to ask if she would consider leading the new Motherhouse in Christiania. She accepted but asked for some few months in Kaiserswerth for further training.

In November 1868, Guldberg was named the head sister and Professor Ernst Ferdinand Lochmann (1820-1891) the doctor. Lochmann, one of Norway's most accomplished scientists, was among the first to suppose that leprosy and tuberculosis were contagious, but did not discover how. He promised to assist the establishment of a hospital and the education of the nurses. Now it was time for women who were interested to apply. Riddervold asked that "the congregations in our country" help recruit Christian nurse candidates.[48] Applicants were asked to supply the school with their reasons for wanting to become a deaconess, a short autobiography, a recommendation from their pastor and their local doctor, and permission from their parents. The applicants had to be between the age of eighteen and forty and could not be married at the time. They could marry after their education was completed, although it would mean they had to resign their office. The committee, with the young head sister, Cathinka Guldberg, who had just returned from Kaiserswerth, had a busy time at the end of 1868, meeting frequently through the last two months of the year. They had found a place in what is now downtown Oslo, Grønland, where they could establish their home. They began immediately, interviewing young women who wanted to enter the program. As they were preparing to move into the two-story building in Grønland, Guldberg's friends from the deaconess house in Stockholm arrived and helped her get the house ready for habitation. On November 20, 1868, the program began with Mother (*Mor*) Guldberg, as she came to be

Grønland

called, and her six students. Although there are other dates that could be considered the beginning of the institution, November 20, 1868, is regarded as the founding date of the Motherhouse in Christiania. By December 1 they had taken in their first patient, a little child. On December 26, St. Stephen's Day, they dedicated the building with great festivities led by Julius Bruun, who preached at the event. The building at first was adequate for both the sick, novices and student nurses as they learned the craft of nursing as well as the vocation of being a deaconess. The upper floor had seven rooms of various sizes, along with beds for two of the sisters who would be on night watch. There was a room for children from six months to twelve years, with bedrooms near the sisters so they could hear their patients calling. The first floor had offices for the doctors and the sister superior, dining room, a gathering room for devotions, and classrooms, since the fundamental purpose of the establishment was the teaching of young nurses. In two side buildings there was space for the laundry, a sewing room, a bath, and two rooms with ten sleeping spaces, marked off by curtains, for the sisters. Each sister had a small cubicle with a bed, water basin, and closet. In the basement was a kitchen with more sick rooms and a couple of rooms for janitors. After only four years, the facility was already too small and they had to look for a more commodious building which they would soon find at Ullevålsveien, then on the outskirts of Christiania. In 1888, they moved to the Lovisenberg site where the successors of the movement still keep the tradition alive, training medical students, nurses and doctors in what is now a major hospital in Norway.

As the Motherhouse grew, the reputation of the deaconesses for doing good works spread abroad enough so that they were sought out to help in private homes where family members needed full-time medical care. Frequently they were sent into difficult situations. Sometimes they were called to minister to the mentally ill, although very little was understood about what kind of treatment such patients needed except kindness, exercise, a healthy diet, and a strict routine of daily life. Beside that was the need to care for lepers, of which there were still a significant number in Norway. (Nissen writes a considerable amount on the way

The Motherhouse at Ullevålsveien where Elisabeth Fedde began her studies

lepers should be treated by nurses in her book.) Norway and Iceland were the last countries in Europe to eradicate the disease from their populations; it was the Norwegian doctor, Gerhard Henrik Armauer Hansen (1841–1912), who discovered the bacillus in 1873, proving the disease was contagious, giving it the name Hansen's Disease.

Becoming a Deaconess

When Elisabeth Fedde came to the Motherhouse at Ullevålsveien in Christiania on December 5, 1874, she needed a guide (*sjauer*) to help her find the place. When she rang the bell on the porch, she had little idea what was in store for her. She did see immediately that the sister meeting her at the door was "a long way from being a beauty." It set her at ease because she had always thought of herself as homely. Soon Sister Martha Olsen came to welcome her to the home. Elisabeth thought she was "a friendly, gentle sister, whom I have since thought very highly of, who welcomed me warmly." Sister Martha took her to the noon meal and found her a place to put the suitcase in which she had brought what she needed from home. Then she was registered as deaconess number seventy-one. They entered the dining room, which Elisabeth thought was one of the biggest she had seen. A whole flock of deaconesses gathered for the arrival of Mother Guldberg, dressed in their garb modeled on uniforms in Neuendettelsau rather than Kaiserswerth. (Mother Guldberg had thought the garb that Fliedner had designed clumsy and difficult to wear while working on the floors.) Guldberg came in, tall and erect, with a face Elisabeth thought radiated seriousness and intelligence. Sister Martha presented Elisabeth to Guldberg briefly, "The new sister, who came today. Her name is Elisabeth." Miss Guldberg shook her hand, bade her welcome, prayed the table prayer, and they sat down to eat the meal of soup, herring, and potatoes in utter silence. After they were done, Guldberg gave thanks in the words of the prayer after the noon meal from *Luther's Small Catechism*. Sister Martha then took her to her room which she would share with six other sisters, a spare cubicle with only the privacy of a curtain around her bed which she soon was to discover was not very comfortable. She received a washstand and chair, and was assigned a closet for her few belongings (see Appendix 3). The room, she remembered, was all white and clean. After getting settled, a bell rang and they went to coffee, with sandwiches and a sweet. The evening meal was a bowl of rye meal and milk. At 9:30, after a brief devotion, they retired. For Elisabeth everything seemed foreign. As she lay in her new bed, she remembered thinking:

> Everybody and everything was strange, and I remember how good it was to lie down under the yellow down cover and really cry it out and resign myself to the Lord, praying that he would lead me as he wished just so I would be saved for heaven.[49]

Sister Elisabeth had entered a home, and the idea of a home was fundamental to the Deaconess Motherhouse, where she would be, by her own vow, under the discipline of the institution as she would have been under a father or brother at home. She was to live as a Christian with un-selfish love of the neighbor and show "self-denial, willing obedience, gentleness, friendliness, and kindness."[50] She could do very little without the express permission of the head sister or board—not leave for an extended visit home or even buy clothes for herself. Fedde readily adapted to this system and expected the sisters under her to do the same, but also would ignore it when she thought it necessary.

For Elisabeth the preparation for her vocation was brief compared to what it would become for later applicants. The next morning after she arrived, a Sunday, she remembered, she was awakened at 4:30, taken to breakfast and then to Sister Rikke

LOVISENBERG DIAKONISSE ARKIVET

Elisabeth as a probationary sister

Nissen, who lay sick in bed. She greeted her and beckoned her to come toward her. Elisabeth knelt by her bed and was given a cap by Nissen. It was a brief ceremony in which Nissen wished her God's blessing in her vocation. Later the capping ceremony would take place after the first year to mark the change from apprentice to probationary sister, but for Elisabeth it was immediate. After their morning labors, the sisters rushed to be on time for the noon dinner (*middag*) before Mother Guldberg began devotions. Those who came late had to stand outside the dining room until she had finished reading, usually lengthy selections from a book of German devotional meditations. The meals consisted of plain fare: meat and potatoes, soup—simple nourishing food which most of the sisters were used to from home. At afternoon coffee Mother Guldberg spoke with the sisters, welcomed Elisabeth to the home, and then read a selection by Kierkegaard for their edification. Although she remembered nothing of the Kierkegaard reading, Elisabeth immediately came to admire Guldberg and wished that someday she could be like her. "Never before had I met such a woman! She is the ideal, she is the one I will strive to be like, I thought. Unfortunately, I could not be like her."[51] After their evening chores, they had the traditional Norwegian evening meal, *kveldsmat*—tea, bread, and butter. Guests often came at this time for what Sister Elisabeth called "festive evenings with music and song."[52] Before they retired, Mother Guldberg told Elisabeth she could continue on Ward H where she had spent her first day. The first day had been dif-

Dr. Frantz Kiær

ficult. She had been left alone with seven very ill patients, with instructions on how to care for them while the other sister had gone to church. The next morning she was sent out onto the ward with another sister.

As she took her place, Dr. Frantz Casper Kiær (1835-1893) appeared with two sisters in tow. She described him as a tall, distinguished man, who could be critical, but helpful. The two sisters he brought with him as he made his rounds knew what he was talking about, some-thing Elisabeth admired since she did not understand anything he said. One was Sister Constance Bakke, who had a quill pen and chalk to take down the diagnoses and write them on the blackboards beside the beds as Dr. Kiær called the illness by its Latin name and prescribed treatment. Another, Sister Berit Olsen, the pharmacist, had a basket of medicines on her arm. When Fedde was introduced to the doctor, he called her "Sister Elisabeth." It was the first time she had been called sister. It struck her as a completely new thing. As he taught them, he impressed Elisabeth.

"What were they saying?" Elisabeth asked. Sister Berit smiled and said, "I will explain everything to you." Later when she herself was beginning to initiate an apprentice she would remember her sense of being overwhelmed and ignorant those many years before. On the first Sunday, the meal was a bit more special, and sisters who had positions outside the Motherhouse and Hospital came for the festive Sunday meal, making it a much larger group. Sister Elisabeth felt lonesome among them. No one spoke, and at the conclusion she quickly returned to the patients where she felt more at home. At the afternoon coffee, the sisters, all of them gathered around Mother Guldberg, talked about their various situations. After some time, she read to them again from Søren Kierkegaard's works.

No stranger to work, Elisabeth did the jobs servants would normally have done. She was told to tend the fires in twenty-six stoves in the rooms around the house. Often she had to carry out the night waste from the water basins and chamber pots. Although we might think of it as demeaning today, we have to remember that most everyone was without modern plumbing until around the turn of the last century, and everyone except those with servants had to empty their own chamber pots. Furthermore, it was a medical necessity to keep the wards clean. As Nightingale had recommended, good nursing meant keeping things clean. The waste of the hospital was collected in buckets under the stairs on the second floor, and it was part of her job occasionally during the week to empty them by taking them outside, down a long staircase that in winter was covered with ice and snow. Because it was winter and slippery on the steps, on her first time she fell down and spilled the waste all over herself. "I will go back home," she cried involuntarily. "I soon remembered my promise that I would go where God wanted me to go. That gave me the courage to meet such small trials."[53] Her resolute understanding that because of her promise to God she could wash up and go on with her work is one of the first times we see her steel. This along with more rigorous on-the-job training equipped her for her later work as a founder of two Motherhouses in America. These tasks taught her discipline, obedience, and submission to Mother, as they called Guldberg. In exchange for her hard work, she received both room and board, and a home where she would soon feel a sense of family in a safe place.

As the days went by, she felt better about the work and began applying what she had learned on the first day, giving baths and making the beds, so there was not a "single wrinkle" in them—something Sister Constance had told her was important—cleaning the rooms, opening windows, and keeping the fire going in the stoves.[54] These things she knew how to do from her work at home and as a servant in the Siqveland home in Stavanger. From all reports it seems she was capable of doing these tasks well. The curriculum she encountered enabled the young sister to master the more technical aspects of her specialties as her time went on.

The course of study for deaconesses around the world came from Kaiserswerth and seemed to have been fairly well agreed upon throughout the deaconess communities. Dr. Adolf Spaeth, president of the Annual Conference of Lutheran Deaconess Motherhouses, elaborated on this education in a paper he gave in 1897 at the second conference of the association in Milwaukee, Wisconsin.[55] The first thing a deaconess needed to be was a young woman of strong Christian character. This did not require courses, although it did require certain practices: a devotional life that involved regular use of the means of grace, word and sacrament. Without those a deaconess would not succeed. These were not difficult to master intellectually, but spiritually, they took practice and devotion. Then she needed to be able to "think, to read, to write and express herself correctly, and her manners must be sufficiently refined, that she may, with ease and self-possession, move in different circles of society." Later they would study courses more associated with the liberal arts: Bible, history, music, and especially the history and theology of the office of deaconess.

At first, in Christiania, they subjected the future sister to a practical course, rather like nurses' aid work. If the young novice could not take this work, she would not be accepted into the probationary level of the course. Nursing was the study least familiar to Fedde, although she probably had a rudimentary sense for treating the ill, given the many remedies passed on from mother to daughter in the folk culture in which she was raised.[56] Soon she was alone on the ward because the other sister had been sent to a private home to care for someone. When the doctor came in, Elisabeth curtsied to the doctor. He asked her questions about the patients he was examining, their temperatures, and the like. Of those technical things she knew nothing, but she could tell him whether or not they had eaten well and had good bowel movements, something she knew because she had brought them their food, and taken out their waste![57] She was most

surprised at the exhausting demands of the night shift, which the probationary sisters were required to take every third night. If one worked the
night watch, one had to make sure that the fires in the stoves were tended
and burning before the watch concluded.

One night she watched over a delirious patient who needed close
supervision. She was to answer the door when the sisters living in a
house next to the Motherhouse came for breakfast. When the morning
bell on the ward rang, Sister Elisabeth did not answer it promptly because she dared not leave her patient. The sister in charge dressed her
down and did not allow her to defend herself. She was relieved to hear
Mother Guldberg tell her later that day that she had indeed done the
right thing by staying with her patient. "I understand the situation," she
had said. "You could not have done otherwise; the sick come first."[58]
This would be a lesson Sister Elisabeth took to heart and used many
times later in her own practice.

These first impressions stayed with her for life. She described an encounter with Dr. Kiær as he dealt with a lovely young lady from Christiania,
Emilie Jordan. He bowed to her courteously and spoke gently to her about
her illness, like a father, saying he would do everything he could, all in his
power, to return her to health, but then commented, "But there is so little
we can do." Elisabeth reflected on that line many times throughout her career. "I have often learned that neither science, art, love, nor nursing, can
save us from death, the one certainty for us all. But there is an antidote for
death and that is the assurance of the forgiveness of one's sins for Jesus'
sake. That is the only thing that gives us peace as we die. Nothing else."[59]
She saw the importance of this assurance as Miss Jordan faced her death.
Although her pain was great, she found peace in the words of a Brorson
hymn from the point of view of the women in Luke 7.

O hvor er jeg vel tilmode,	O I am in good spirits
siden jeg min Jesus fandt,	Since I have found my Jesus
da jeg kom og faldt tilfode,	For when I fall at his feet
al min nød med et forsvandt.	All my sorrows at once were gone.

When the young woman died, Sister Elisabeth noted that she
had thought how difficult the work of a deaconess could be, "but
how glorious to be at the bedside of a believer, yes, I said, glorious,"
she repeated, "for that is for the deaconess what outweighs all else."[60]

In addition to her work in the home and hospital, Sister Elisabeth might be assigned to work with the poor in the city. Once she was sent out to serve the poor in a dingy cellar apartment in Christiania:

> One day, a Sunday, just as I was about to go to church, I was ordered to go to a poor place where there was great need. I would have liked to go to church, and thought maybe I could go to the poor after church, but I found no peace from that thought! So I went immediately to the basement in one of Christiania's poorest neighborhoods. When I came in there were two drunk men sleeping it off. I opened the door to another room: inside were three beds, in one lay a man deathly ill from tuberculosis, and in the other, a woman who three days before had given birth to a child and in a third bed, three children, all of them helpless. I wondered how I should begin and asked the women if they had food. "There is a little," she said, "But my husband prefers milk and of that we have none." Therefore, first to get milk. In the meantime, she called, "Petter, you must get up, don't you see we have a 'coness here." Poor Petter was tired and thought little of a 'coness before she came back with milk, bread, butter, and coffee. When the meal was finished, the man and wife taken care of, the child clothed and the laundry and cleaning done, as well as it could be done, I held a service in the basement like a congregation. I thought that was the most festive Sunday I had experienced, and joy and gratitude followed me because the Lord had sent me to care for the suffering. The husband died after some weeks in the hospital.[61]

In this account we can see both the kind of exhausting physical work, all part of the medical treatment she was expected to give, but also the completeness of the work. In order to bring the people in the cellar some help, she had to begin with first things first, relieving the most extreme physical needs and only after that did she hold the service.

With such demanding physical and spiritual work, she needed refreshment. Elisabeth soon learned she could find friends to support her spiritual growth in small devotional groups (conventicles), one of the signal marks of the pietist movement from Spener's book *Pious Desires*

(*Pietatis desideria,* 1675) which helped foster the revivals of both the eighteenth and nineteenth centuries among Lutherans in Europe. One day she received an invitation to the Bible study in Professor Gisle Johnson's home. "It was an unforgettable experience," she wrote:

> With theologians and other Christian intellectuals present, Professor Johnson, Professor Caspari, Bishop [Karl Peter Parelius] Essendrop sat around a table while Professor Johnson presented the Third Article [of the Apostles' Creed;]-Caspari was the opponent. Never before had the Article been explained with such deep earnestness. Then came the lovely Mrs. Johnson with tea and bread and butter, after which the Bishop led in devotions. Such evenings Professor Johnson held every week.[62]

These small groups, whether or not led by Johnson, were staples of her piety and she probably attended such gatherings weekly, as she had in Stavanger, in addition to her private daily devotions and the devotions of the sisters before meals and at night. She remained deeply convinced of the power of prayer and the worth of studying the *Small Catechism* by Martin Luther and Erick Pontoppidan, whose explanations to Luther's brief answers, *Truth Unto Godliness*, remained the central document of the Norwegian church's education ministry for almost 250 years.

Gisle Johnson, like Hauge, stressed a living Christianity, which flowed into deeds of justice and mercy for the neighbor. Although a small, quiet man, when he spoke and read the Bible, his hearers were struck to the heart, "running both hot and cold." The unique thing about his movement, says Ivar Welle in his history of the Norwegian church, was that Johnson attracted both the old Haugians and the bourgeois mer-

The Gisle Johnson family. Mrs. Johnson (Emilie Dybwad 1825-1898) was known for her warm Christianity and hospitality. Their home was unusually happy, according to Ivar Welle.

chants, civil servants and others of the class of educated leaders who had opposed Hauge. Especially important, notes Welle was that "in the women's groups bourgeois wives and farmers wives came together" for mission work of all kinds. Because of his movement, the churches filled up, prayers houses (*bedehuser*) were built to make room for all the seekers, a great number of Christian organizations began, the spirit of the entire country was influenced by the awakening. "Visitors who came to Norway in the 1850-1860s noticed that the people seemed puritanical"—no dancing, drinking, or cards, to name the list of forbidden entertainments.[63]

As a spiritual mentor, Johnson was admired and almost worshiped by many of his students. He and his colleague Professor Carl Paul Caspari (1814-1892), a converted Jew from Germany and professor of Old Testament, held Bible study and prayer meetings on Saturday afternoons

for interested laity and students. Elisabeth's attendance at the Bible study was a powerful spiritual experience for her. These meetings spurred a spiritual awakening that prepared the ground for later para-church movements in Norway, such as the deaconess movement. In any case, the awakened Norwegians and Norwegian-Americans, most of whom traced their new lives back to Hauge and Johnson, sought to live out their faith in obedience to God and service of the neighbor—thus their interest in establishing a Deaconess Motherhouse. Fedde herself was a product of this revival and spoke its language.

Carl Paul Caspari

Practical Nurse

Sister Elisabeth started learning on the job, before she began studying the profession from books and lectures. It was the approach Rikke Nissen had designed and Florence Nightingale endorsed, so Doctor Kiær gradually began to initiate the young woman into her vocation as nurse and sister. It was probably the best way to find out if the student could bear the kind of work a nurse had to do. The day involved everything from the most basic tasks of caring for patients—bathing, cleaning, seeing to their conditions, determining the diet for various patients (which was the major medicine available at the time), making sure they got adequate rest and fresh air, and ministering to them while they were dying. In addition, the student nurses were expected to wash the patients' clothes and bed clothes, among many other chores that today's nurses would not be expected to do, but which good medical practice required. A dirty hospital is not a place in which one can be healed. In very short order Elisabeth began to distinguish herself as one ready to enter into the diaconate.

After about six months, she was admitted as a probationary sister. Before the admittance ceremony each novice met with Mother Guldberg who would admonish her in preparation for her admittance, then pray with her. After that, she would put the cap on the novice's head and then the rector of the house—in this case, either Rector Bruun or the chaplain Pastor Heuch, we are not sure which—asked her if she had ever thought of being anything but a deaconess. Elisabeth thought this a strange question, and she answered honestly: "No, not today; for to-morrow I cannot answer." The pastor thought it a curious response, but added, "Of course, tomorrow is not ours."[64] Elisabeth had received her cap on her first day, but this became the practice she followed later.

Bishop Heuch

With this, she began working as a student nurse, or probationary sister, still not consecrated. According to most of the rules, she would work for about five years until her consecration (see Appendix 3). She received room and board, but no salary. None of the sisters did. Unlike other of the students at the time, Elisabeth seemed to have had the resources to support herself, maybe given to her by the Siqve-lands, and was able to purchase the blue uniform of the probationer. Coming as she did from the land-owning farmers, she seemed to have had more financial resources than daughters of the cotters (*husmænd*). This does not mean she was wealthy, but her reports frequently indicate that she had been able to husband her resources enough to scrape by on her own in difficult financial times.[65]

Not long after she was received as a probationary sister, she was asked by Mother Guldberg to go to help a stroke victim, Sheriff Alme, of Lier, a small town not far from Christiania on the way to Drammen.

It was recognition by Mother Guldberg of Elisabeth's gifts. At first she thought it difficult to leave her new friends in the Motherhouse. After she made her way there, and began working, however, she gained new confidence as she ministered to the old man who died only a few days after she arrived. She returned to the Motherhouse, happy to be back on her old Ward H, but soon was sent again to a private patient, a wealthy old ship captain suffering some kind of delirium. His illness baffled Elisabeth as she watched him command his imagined ship through heavy seas, but she came to appreciate the suffering of mental patients, realizing that physical illnesses most often were treatable, but as yet there was almost nothing to be done for mental illness except send him to the Gaustad Hospital which Norwegians had founded in 1855 for those suffering mental illness. Sister Rikke devoted a chapter to treating such people in her book and essentially says they should be kept clean, well fed, and safe since nothing else seemed to help. Gaustad was well known as a fairly reputable place for such people, unlike many of the hell-holes reserved for people who struggled with mental illness at the time.

When she returned from caring for the ship captain, she was assigned to Ward N in the hospital, where she began to work with the other deaconess. About this time her younger sister, Andrea Andreassen (1853-1875), arrived in Christiania to work as a caretaker for the children of Pastor Anton Christian Bang (1840-1913), chaplain in the Gaustad asylum in Christiania. (He would later become bishop of Christiania and named Extraordinary Professor of History at the University of Christiania.) When Elisabeth heard that Andrea had become sick unto death, she went to Mother Guldberg who promised they could take Andrea into the hospital. She struggled for eleven days before a hard death, on May 17, 1875. She was buried on May 22 in Our Savior's cemetery. The church record indicates she died of tuberculosis. A deaconess who had been unkind to Elisabeth felt sorry for her and helped with the funeral, getting a small choir to sing and arranging the funeral service. Bishop Essendrop led the service, seminary students Johannes Siqveland and Sparre were the pallbearers, and a whole "flock of sisters

Bishop Anton Christian Bang

followed the casket. So my dear sister was laid to rest until the Lord calls her to raise her up on the last day."[66]

After this grief she threw herself back into the work of the hospital. Again Mother Guldberg sent her out to help in a home, this time in Holmestrand, a beautiful city on the western shores of the Oslofjord, where she was to care for Miss Holterman, an invalid who had been the first telegraph operator in Norway. The woman was confined to a wheel chair, and Elisabeth took her on long walks along the fjord. It restored both Elisabeth's soul and body. She would treasure this experience throughout her life. Assigned to work at the State Hospital (*Rikshospitalet*) in Christiania on August 10, 1875, she began the next stage in her education.

Sister Elisabeth served on Wards A and B at the State Hospital where the deaconesses were given charge of the work. There she came to learn more from the doctors. Among her favorites was Dr. Edward Bull, (1845-1925), head of Ward B, a learned doctor in both psychiatric and physical illnesses, who later served as doctor for Henrik Ibsen, the playwright, and Bjørnstjerne Bjørnson, the literary and social provocateur of Norway who came more and more to oppose the church and its attitude toward women. She thought Dr. Bull

> a remarkably kind and accomplished physician [who] tried to instruct me in whatever way he could. He was an unusually cultured man on whom I could confidently rely. I will always remember him with gratitude. The head doctor was very exacting, dutiful, and self-sacrificing in his concern for the sick. Often he came quietly into the hospital room at night to see the very ill. When we learned to know him, we regarded him highly.[67]

While she admired the expertise of the medical professionals and saw their work as necessary for her own profession, she also knew that her calling as deaconess had eternal consequences. In addition to her medical training, she was being taught the care of souls. She took pleasure in leading the sick and dying into a relationship with their Lord and Savior.

Bringing the deaconesses, with their professional sense of vocation, to the wards began to change hospital culture. Doctors unaccustomed to being kind to nurses suddenly had to change their behavior and be chivalrous to the deaconesses. Mother Guldberg and Rikke Nissen both came from the doctors' own class and could not be treated rudely. Elisabeth, while not of their class, quite, found it difficult some times to be subservient to the people above her. If a matter of injustice presented itself, she would be quick to make her feelings clear and seek to remedy the situation. She had already discovered that people whom she served in their homes sometimes expected her to be a maid or servant, which she firmly refused to be, although the line between keeping patients and their rooms clean and being a maid was difficult for some families to understand.

She also had to teach the doctors and professional men in the hospital to treat her with respect. One legendary story involved her encounter with the director of the State Hospital, Mr. Temandus Jonas Løberg (1819-1882), who would scold a young nurse if she broke something that was expensive to replace, most especially thermometers. Sister Jørgine Paulson (1848-) who worked with Fedde on the ward, had broken two thermometers in almost immediate succession. Frightened, she did not want to return to Løberg for a new one. Sister Elisabeth informed her that she would go for another thermometer and brave the expected tongue lashing. When she did and Løberg began scolding her, Elisabeth informed him that she had no more pleasure in coming to him than he did in having her bring more bad news, but if it was necessary she would do it ten times a day. The response surprised the man, and he held back from his usual reprimand. She noticed that his temper changed, and he began to treat her and the other sisters in a more kindly manner from then on.[68]

Once a week they brought the dirty clothes to the laundry and picked up clean linen. The laundry was in a little building beside the house "in a large room with stone floors." An older woman sat there and counted the sheets they brought, which were heavy and foul, Elisabeth noted. "The flock of sisters stood around her holding their noses, quiet as a church, helping those who counted!"[69]

One of the great improvements the deaconesses (and nurses) brought to hospitals was the notion that fresh air and good ventilation was foremost. Having patients breathing in the foul odors of the waste of themselves and others in the hospital contributed to the continued illness, Nightingale and others thought. Keeping the laundry clean and the waste buckets empty was part of the treatment of patients.

Sister Elisabeth enjoyed finding out about people and was curious about their lives. She was amazed to learn that in the hospital laboratory was a chemist who was also Norway's executioner. Fedde was surprised to discover that she knew such a man. To her he was a good and friendly man whom no one would suspect had such an occupation, but he had executed three criminals in her lifetime. She could never forget when he came back after executing the woman Sofie Johannesen, whose sensational trial for poisoning several people made her well known to most Norwegians at the time. "I will never forget when told me how impossible it was to lift the axe after it had fallen. The picture of that scene he took with him for the rest of his life—and what he told me was so gruesome, I will never forget it either."[70]

Increasing Responsibilities

The experience of both submitting to the orders of Mother Guldberg and standing up for herself as she served the patients gave the young Elisabeth increasing confidence as a nurse and a servant of the Gospel. Once again she was chosen by Mother Guldberg to serve in a home, this time in Hamar, a town south of Lillehammer, with the Dr. Mathias Sigevardt Greve (1832-1912) family. There in the lovely home of the Greves she found rest, even as she tended to their teenage daughter who was both physically ill and troubled with a bad case of nerves. The family was kind and caring for Elisabeth, and grateful to her for helping their daughter recover. She remained good friends with the family through the rest of her life.

Elisabeth returned to the Motherhouse rested and ready for more work, this time a dangerous assignment: caring for a young girl in Drammen suffering from typhus which, although they did not know it then, was spread by lice. An epidemic had broken out in Drammen, the port city west of Christiania on the Oslofjord. It would be remembered for many years afterward.[71] Officials in Christiania were fearful the disease would travel to the city, especially since it was so contagious. None of the sisters volunteered to go. Finally Mother Guldberg went to Elisabeth and asked her to go to the family in Drammen. With considerable fear and much prayer, she agreed to go.

When Sister Elisabeth arrived at the station, a wagon came and drove her to a large, lovely villa. Everything in the house and grounds spoke of the wealth and fine aesthetic sensibilities of the family. The father, a grocer, met her in a friendly manner and showed her to his daughter's little room which overlooked the garden. The woman watching over the young girl greeted Elisabeth, obviously glad to be relieved of her job as nurse. The patient was out of her head with fever—the high fever of typhus is sometimes over 105°. The patient had to be kept cool and hydrated while at the same time clean. Elisabeth had to force the young patient to stay in bed. She finally got her to sleep. In the morning, the parents were thankful to find their daughter sleeping and the room spotless. "The lady of the house, a stiff, proud lady in an elegant morning dress and a white morning hat with light red ribbons, came in, looked at her daughter, turned to me, and said, 'Now you can wash and keep this room clean and in order, likewise the hall.'"[72] Elisabeth's mettle showed itself. She told the woman that, although she would keep the room clean in order to care for the girl, she was not a maid.

What she needed, after the trip to Drammen from Christiania, was food. She still had not been fed. After some time she heard footsteps on the stairs outside the room. When she looked she found a tray of bread and butter, with coffee. The next morning when the doctor arrived, she told him how she had been treated and that she needed to be given the necessary supplies to help the girl recover. He assured her she would get what she needed to do her work. Still she was kept in pretty much solitary confinement with the little girl. After five weeks, her patient recovered, and Elisabeth was ready to go back to the Motherhouse. The parents had come to feel kindly toward Elisabeth, although they were not particularly effusive in their compliments to her.

When she returned to the Motherhouse, Mother Guldberg called Elisabeth into her office to tell her the family had sent a large gift of money to the Deaconesses Motherhouse, something that she would not have expected at the beginning of her residency with them. It was a pleasant surprise, like many that Sister Elisabeth experienced throughout her working life. Elisabeth had begun to learn the power of love and service in the lives of people who at first may have resisted it. It is also clear that Sister Elisabeth had to draw a sharp line between being a servant and being a nurse. Sister Rikke had made that distinction clear in her thinking, and Sister Elisabeth came to understand and embrace that premise.

Return to Her Studies

On her return to the Mother-house, Elisabeth continued studying medicine with Dr. Kiær, such as anatomy and bandaging which she found to be very interesting. He would apply a bandage to himself, then ask the students to copy him. When she did not quite do what he wanted, he told her, "Look at me!" He laughed at himself as he stood with his head covered with a bandage and continued to teach them.[73]

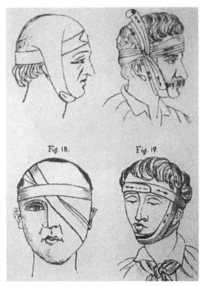

How to bandage from Lærerbog on Sygepleie for Diakonisser *by* Rikke Nissen

Along with medical instruction, she was now taking more courses in theology, such as a course on the history and theology of the deaconess' office from Mother Guldberg and Bible classes from Pastor Julius Bruun, who managed the Motherhouse with Guldberg. Other pastors in the city helped with these studies, including the influential pastor and later bishop, Johan Christian Heuch (1838-1904), whom she valued for his serious classes.[74] Because of Sister Rikke's illness, another woman, Sofie Dedekam (1820-1894)[75] taught the literature courses, but Fedde was not terribly impressed with her. Dedekam made them read *Agnes Elisabeth Jones*, the biography of Jones (1832-1868), the first trained Irish nurse, one whom Florence Nightingale admired.

> "Isn't this wonderful?" she [Dedekam] asked the students. "You have much to learn from her." To that Sister Elisabeth remarked that it was not possible to find such a person, for no one is holy here on earth. Dedekam took her pen in her mouth, bit it, looked into her eyes and said "Elisabeth, you speak like that because you are proud and do so many things wrong, but you must remember, that she was much farther along the road of sanctification than you. You should strive to be like Jones, Sister Elisabeth." She answered, "I would rather be like Mother."[76]

If this is a true account, and we have little reason to doubt it, it gives us a clear picture of Sister Elisabeth's inability to suffer fools or be obsequious. The concern for sanctification gives us a picture of the piety of the sisterhood. It was an important part of pietism to struggle with one's old nature and live more fully in Christ. Oddly enough, while it was a constant concern of Sister Elisabeth to work on becoming more obedient to Christ, another way to describe sanctification, she did not take Jones as a model of sanctification as did Dedekam, who knew nothing of nursing, and Elisabeth gives a rather sharp reply to her teacher with her preference for Mother Guldberg.

Agnes Elisabeth Jones

After her first year on the wards of the hospital, according to Nissen's plan, the apprentice (*læresøster*) would become a probationary sister on her way to becoming a consecrated deaconess. The time until consecration varied and depended to some extent on the progress the sister made. During that time, she would frequently be sent out of the Motherhouse to work in private situations or elsewhere, as Sister Elisabeth had been. However, because of the demands of the work, to her disappointment, Elisabeth did not finish what Nissen called the Big Course (*stor cursus*) as opposed to the Little Course (*lille cursus*) which was something like grammar school, which Elisabeth did not need. It soon became the introductory course which applicants had to take before beginning the regular instruction, after which they could be consecrated.

Elisabeth showed herself to be quite capable in both lines of study, and Mother Guldberg must have quickly marked her as a leader. After Elisabeth's second year, Mother Guldberg trusted her enough to send her back to the State Hospital to reorganize the dispensary ward, Medical Division K. Apparently she had worked miracles there and proved to the skeptics at the hospital that the deaconesses were serious about their service and thus about being professional. She would have preferred to finish her formal studies, the Big Course, but Sister Elisabeth later noted that Mother Guldberg had helped her understand the difficulties of the work and her place in it. "Mother used to say, 'To obey is better than sacrifice,' but this assignment involved both obedience and sacrifice. I went, and after that had no further opportunity for formal study."[77] Self-denial is at the root of this attitude. As Beret Hovland, archivist for the Motherhouse in Christiania has written, "Deaconesses were to embody the Christian ideals of humility, invisibility, and hard work."[78] It was fundamental to the Kaiserswerth culture, and Sister Elisabeth understood it in her bones because it was her picture of an ideal Christian. She did well as a student in every level of the deaconess educational curriculum and might have profited from taking more courses, but she seemed to have been curious and intelligent enough to learn in every situation she found herself. When the Motherhouse asked for her to come back to work for them, the hospital staff would not approve it, so Elisabeth remained with them for two years, until 1878, when she was nearly twenty-eight. One can see her desire to be more educated in things medical. Soon what we know as modern nursing education will emerge from the deaconess institutions and begin the professionalization of nursing.[79]

Consecration and First Assignment

When Mother Guldberg decided to return to Kaiserswerth for a short vacation and spiritual refreshment, she called Elisabeth back to the Motherhouse, asking that she take her place for the brief time that she would be gone. Obviously Mother Guldberg's confidence in Elisabeth had continued to grow. The young woman had been in training for barely three years and already was among the most highly regarded of the sisters. Although she had regretted that this meant she could not quite finish her formal education, she resolved to learn as much as she could about medicine while working with the pharmacist, Dr. Garman-Andersen, and about surgery from the surgeon, Alexander Ludvig Normann Malthe (1845-1928). Because it was summer, there were not many patients, so she could ask the druggist many questions and learn about pharmacology. In the same manner she learned from the surgeon when a young girl came in with a tumor in her stomach. The surgeon, who had not done such an operation before, did it with Fedde in attendance. It went well, and she marveled at his skills, although the girl later died. She remarked many years later, as he became more and more famous for his abilities, it was not his last operation. Nor was it hers.

Tromsø

When Mother Guldberg returned to Christiania, she had plans for Sister Elisabeth. On the first of December 1878, she called Elisabeth in and told her that she was being sent to Tromsø, in the far north, to help with the hospital there. Because it was so far away and she would not be able to return south very often, Mother Guldberg told her she could choose any other sister to go with her so she would have help as well as a companion. Elisabeth chose Sister Elen Iversen (1855-1910) from Haugesund, who trained with Sister Elisabeth before their consecration on December 4.

Consecration was a solemn event that involved making several promises to the pastor leading the ceremony, rather like the vows of a pastor. After this event, they only had five days to prepare and pack for their trip. On December 5, 1878, the day after Elisabeth was consecrated, the two young women boarded the ship, Jupiter, for the long trip north. Soon they were standing on the deck of the steamer waving their handkerchiefs to their sisters on the pier for as long as they could see them. "We knew we were on our way to a place where deaconesses had never been seen before and that we were to be the northernmost deaconesses in the world."[80] It was the dead of winter, not the best time to sail the North Sea, but for them the weather turned out to be relatively calm. For eighteen days they sailed along the rugged Norwegian coastline, until, on December 23, she and Sister Elen arrived in Tromsø. Dr. Johannes Holmboe (1844-1918) met them and took them to the "hospital" a barely furnished room with odds and ends of medical equipment. They took heart only after they were settled in the private quarters of the doctor and his wife, Sofie Jensine, who met them with warm hospitality. Their accommodations, however, the first night were not warm. The room they had been given had two simple beds, a little table, two chairs, with a table for their washing bowl and pitcher and a hanging lamp. They only had one blanket on their beds. They put on all their clothes and were still freezing. Finally, they decided to share a bed and put all the bed clothes they had over themselves. As soon as they could the next morning they went and bought a red table cloth with black roses on it to use for a blanket. When their suitcases came with more clothes they could keep somewhat warmer. With their other belongings they were able to make the room more comfortable. The doctor gave them Lapland moccasins (*finnesko*), especially warm shoes which they appreciated.

The Holmboes, who were also new arrivals, had known from their first day in this very northern city that they needed deaconesses to make the hospital meet the barest standards of quality. Sister Elisabeth reported the joy of their first Christmas Eve. When they went to church wearing their new garb and shoes, they met people who had never seen deaconesses before, attracting attention and comment. As they celebrated Christmas Day together with the Holmboes, Elisabeth observed her twenty-eighth birthday, wondering what lay ahead. The two young women spent the time between Christmas and the New Year getting settled in their small room. After the New Year when they entered the county hospital (*amthospitalet*)

they found it barely habitable. The mattresses and bed clothes were infested with lice and bedbugs. The woman who worked there (*gangkone*), Elisabeth said, was drunk every day, and everything was filthy and crawling with vermin. "On New Year's Day we began immediately to scour, wash

Tromsø Hospital

and every evening strew lice powder around. I had never before seen so many of those kind of animals."[81] When they finished, they had burned all the mattresses with the bed clothes, too ragged and infested to be used. Elisabeth called together the city council and asked them to resupply the hospital with new blankets immediately or she and Sister Elen would take the next boat back to Christiania. There were thirty beds, but only twenty-three blankets, twelve of which had to be discarded. The Council reacted quickly and told them to go to a local merchant, Hans Fredrik Giæver (1843-1905), and buy what they needed, which they did, but they had to sew the material themselves before they could be used in the hospital. People in the community also

Hans Fredrik Giaever

gave of their own blankets and clothing, for which the sisters were thankful, overwhelmed with the generosity of the people, until they discovered that the gifts had not come alone, but were also infested! It took them some time, but finally they had new

Tromsø about the time Elisabeth was there

clean beds and bedclothes for the hospital and were ready to receive patients. Sister Elisabeth remembered that she had taken a course at the Motherhouse on how to make mattresses. She had not liked the course, but was glad that she had learned enough so that they could have the beds ready to make. "How happy we were that our patients could lie in a good bed, clean and free of bugs!"[82]

While life at that time in Norway was never easy, life in the north was even more difficult. The wives and children of the fishermen spent long, anxious winter nights alone while their husbands and fathers were at sea, fishing for the cod they would dry and sell in Bergen. The fishermen faced great dangers. Many were lost at sea, leaving their wives and children to survive on the most meager subsistence. Sister Elisabeth was frequently overwhelmed with how little these people expected out of life, facing their fate with a stoic kind of surrender that was uncommon even for Norwegians. Over the next years, she came to love the people in Tromsø as she worked with them. They helped Elisabeth and Sister Elen build up a medical center much better than it had been when they first

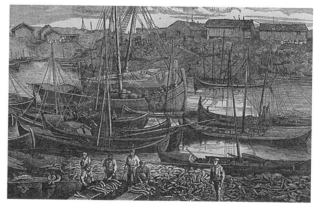

Northern fishing fleet

came, even after a brutal storm—some called it a hurricane—probably on February 4, 1882, that blew in their front windows. It had been so devastating that the palace in Christiania had held a bazaar to raise money for those who had suffered the most in the northern regions of Norway. A terrible thing for the new facility, it paled next to stories others brought to them: of an entire barn falling in on some while they were in it or an avalanche that had buried five people inside a house. A steamer had seen, as it passed by, that the little home had disappeared. They informed the local rescue boat who went out to find four bodies and one nineteen-year-old girl who was still just barely alive. She had been carding wool by the stove, she said, when the avalanche raced through the house and took her family, pushing the red hot stove onto the young girl and pinning her down for five days. She got gangrene in her legs and burns on her back and arms. Her legs had to be amputated, but she lived to tell about it, though crippled for life.

Every day gave them more practice in treating patients and keeping the hospital running. As a nurse and spiritual caregiver, she came to know both the deepest sorrows of people and could also see the humor in even extreme situations. One of her more humorous experiences was when a strong fisherman with pneumonia lay in a fever. He awakened screaming and ran out into the cold and snow. She gave chase and could not persuade him to come back in. Then she got the idea to call to him in her sweetest voice, "Husband mine, come here." On hearing her voice he thought it was his wife, and cried, "Are you there? God be praised! I saw the wrong lady in my bed and would not be in the same bed with her." "No, come now," she said, and hand in hand they stumbled back through snow and ice. She feared that he would have a relapse after the experience in the cold, but to her joy he became well, and they laughed many times at their walk through the snow and cold on that late night.

One of the hardest experiences for her involved a family that came to them for help—a father, daughter, her two children, and the father's mistress. All of them were sick with venereal disease transmitted by the man, who had fathered the two children by his daughter. The younger child was near death, almost rotten, Fedde noted. She wondered if the child had been baptized. The father thought the mistress, Malena, had baptized it in the name of the Father. Malena thought she had baptized it in the name of the Father and the Spirit. The pastor they consulted agreed with them that the child had not been baptized in the name of the Trinity, so the dean of the cathedral baptized it again. Elisabeth fulfilled the duty of many pastors' wives in the Norwegian church and carried the child to the font herself. She could not remember the four strange names they had named the little girl, except for Andrea. The next day the little girl died and was freed of her terrible suffering, Sister Elisabeth said. To her satisfaction both the father and daughter were sent to jail.

Sister Elisabeth noted often that the sick and dying would sing hymns to comfort themselves, and she wrote down which ones. One man who was dying, and had seemed to have lost all his senses, was a fine singer. One day he announced he was going to sing and began singing Luther's hymn on dying, "Even as we live each day . . ."[83] He sang the entire song and then lay down, still and quiet. From that time, she wrote, he rejoiced that he was going home to be with God.

> Shortly before he died, he called to me and asked me to hold him up in the bed. I took him in my arms. "Let us now sing, Amen," he said. We did so, after which he breathed his last. I laid him down quietly and closed his eyes. He was his parents' only son. He should have been a teacher, but God would have it otherwise."[84]

Sisters Elisabeth and Elen became part of society in Tromsø, sharing in daily life, making good friends among the people there. They enjoyed the endless summer days and the long winter nights with the magic of the Northern lights swirling above them in the heavens. One of her favorite families was the Berges who helped to give them some joy in the midst of their many difficulties dealing with such tragedies as those she described. One gets a fine sense of Fedde's eye in her description of Mrs. Berge who sat in her sofa in "her black dress, white collar, and white cap with little violets between them. . . . they made a frame around that dear pale and friendly face. That little thin appearance hid a large and loving spirit, and it was always like a festival to be with Mrs. Berge."[85]

Because Tromsø was on a trading route from Russia and Russia had at one time been able to tax the people in the area, the city had not a few Russian inhabitants and several nationalities beside the Norwegians and Sami. One of Elisabeth's best friends was the Russian wife of the Consul

Christian Dreyer, who once came to the sisters with a basket filled with fruit. The woman had heard it was grim in the hospital and in their simple apartment, so she had put together a basket of many kinds of fruit, even a basket of figs which Elisabeth had never tasted before. Having her come around on frequent visits was like a breath of fresh air from the wider world, Elisabeth said. To her grief, Elisabeth's closest friend, the wife of Dr. Holmboe, died during Elisabeth's last year in the city. Elisabeth had been away when she died, and felt that everything was changed when she came back and Mrs. Holmboe was gone.

By then the sisters had been in Tromsø for nearly four years and had experienced much. One day when a woman arrived at the hospital only to die from what appeared to be starvation, the doctor wanted to perform an autopsy to see what exactly had killed the woman, but the family protested. They did not want such a thing performed on the body of their loved one. Finally, just before burial, they consented, but since the doctor was not there, Sister Elisabeth had to do it herself. She did so, but as she did, she contracted an illness, what she called septicemia, with some kind of stomach infection as well. It almost killed her.[86] She lay near death for some weeks. Although she recovered, she felt weak and could not return to the difficult work in the hospital she and Sister Elen had transformed with their tireless efforts. In the spring of 1882 she resigned her charge in Tromsø and returned to the south, a hard trip in which she had to change boats three times because she could not manage to stay aboard for long periods of time. "The strong, courageous Elisabeth was crushed for a long time," she commented in her *Memoirs*. After she came home, the Greves in Hamar invited her to come for a visit, which she enjoyed. Then she went for some rest to the Gausdal Sanitorium, not far from Hamar, a place where many Norwegians went in the summer to regain their health. The regime recommended there—with its long mountain hikes and exercise in the brisk mountain air—was not appropriate for her at the time, given her still weak constitution. The activities were too difficult for her, so she went to Lillehammer to be with some deaconesses there. Little by little she gained strength and finally received permission to visit her younger sister Olene who lived in Mandal, on the coast not too far west of Kristiansand.

That she felt it possible to do the autopsy on her own in Tromsø indicates her growing confidence as a nurse and medical practitioner. She had obviously observed such procedures as she had assisted the doctors in autopsies, but to have the confidence to do it on her own is something we should mark. She had been learning much from watching the doctors and, we will see later, maybe wondered if she should study further to become a doctor.

Over the summer and fall she remained in Mandal, gathering strength and wondering what she would do in the future when she felt completely recovered. While she was resting, it had occurred to her that Norwegian mission societies who were actively sending missionaries to far-away places, such as Africa and China, seemed to be doing nothing for their own people who had left for America.[87] Many over there could profit from spiritual and physical care, she surmised. "The thought would not leave me. 'Thy will be done on earth as it is in heaven' was my daily prayer, but I did not believe that it would be I whom God would call into that work."[88] Later she would think that these thoughts prepared her to hear the call from America when it came.

Sister Elisabeth had every reason to think of the many leaving Norway for America at that time. The emigration had begun with the sailing of the *Restaurationen* in 1825, a small contingent which numbered some fifty Norwegians, many of them Quakers, leaving Norway to find religious freedom in the new land under the direction of Cleng Peerson (1783-1865), who would establish a colony in upstate New York, and later in Clifton, Texas. It was not until 1838 that the trickle began

The sloop, Restaurationen

to grow. Because of the law of primogeniture which left the undivided farm to the oldest son, the growing population could not be sustained by the land. Extreme poverty drove many younger sons west to the new land where good land was available for the taking after the Homestead Law of 1862. Historians divide up the emigration from Norway into three waves: 1) 1866-1873; 2) 1879-1893; 3) 1901-1910. Norway lost more of its population to emigration than any other country except for Ireland. Between 1836 and 1900 over a half million people had left Norway for America—almost one-third of its population. The emigration upset many of the leaders of the church and state, who for good reason opposed it. While most of the immigrants found their way to the Midwest, many who worked in shipping ended up in New York. During the 1880s the Norwegian fleet of merchant ships was the third largest in the world which included thousands of Norwegian sailors who were only passing through, plus many emigrants needing spiritual and physical care in Brooklyn. People like Elisabeth realized their countrymen needed help in the New Land. She had every reason to hear the call when it came.

CHAPTER TWO

A CALL FROM AMERICA

Elisabeth was still with her sister, Olene Margreth Andreassen (1858-1896), married to Villum Andreas Reiersen (1846-), a tailor, in Mandal, southwest of Kristiansand. On Christmas Day 1882, her thirty-second birthday, she received a letter from her brother-in-law, Gabriel Ånensen Fedde, (1843-1917) a merchant, married to her sister Anna Marie Elene, (1845-1914), who lived in Brooklyn, New York.[89] It was a call to come to Brooklyn and serve the poor and sick. Gabriel Fedde, a former ship captain and businessman, now a settled immigrant and lay pastor—along with several other people, the pastor of the Seamen's church, Andreas Mortensen, (1849-1904), the Swedish-Norwegian consul Christian Børs (1823-1905), and his second wife, Anna Cathrine Elisabeth Schiøtz Collett (1832-1915), who had pledged $150 a year for the support of the work—thought Sister Elisabeth would be the perfect solution to their problem. The idea of a dea-coness seemed salutary, and Fedde knew one they could call: his sister-in-law, Elisabeth Fedde. And so he sent the letter.

Gabriel Fedde

New York, October 6, 1882

Dear Sister Elisabeth,

Yesterday evening Consul Børs sent for me to tell me the news that his wife [Anna Collett Børs] had yesterday promised a contribution of $150 yearly for a Bible woman who would work here with the poor and lost sheep among the Norwegians. The rest of the salary and expenses he will assume in order that the program may be expanded without hindrances. He thought of you as the person who possibly could undertake the work. The Consul's wife also considered our interest in such a mission very worthy and said that she had thought about it for a long time. The consul requested that I write you immediately concerning the matter. He said you could come at once if you *dare, can, and will* undertake this service. For my part, I think I have before expressed my views. I only repeat that Norwegians cry for help. Even yet maybe some of those who have gone astray can be saved. Dedicated to the hearing of his Word and to God.

Gabriel Fedde

Elisabeth regarded his letter as a call from God, and now with her improved health she considered it prayerfully. After a letter to Mother Guldberg, explaining the situation, she waited for an answer. When it came it was positive. Mother Guldberg regarded it as Elisabeth had, a genuine call from God. Yes, she thought, she should go, but only after helping with another situation in Arendal for a month.

Christian and Anna Børs

Christian Børs had left Norway as a young man and made his fortune in America, working his way up from selling books on the streets of

Anna Børs

Boston to establishing a company that exported grain and iron between Brazil, New York, and Europe. He had made a home for himself in America with his first wife, said to be the daughter of Delaware Senator Richard Henry Bayard (1796-1868), until she died. Anna, a widow whom he married on January 9, 1873, shared his passion for helping their countrymen experiencing hard times in New York. Anna was a Collett, one of the most distinguished and famous families in Norway. Her first husband, Søren Daniel Schiøtz (1828-1864), an army surgeon, had died in the war against the Prussians in 1864. Leaders of the Norwegian community in Manhattan, they were also members of New York high society. A typical self-made American, Børs now served as consul for the Swedish-Norwegian government, at the time a dual kingdom. Without their financial support, Fedde's work would have never started.

The Norwegian Seamen's Mission

As Fedde knew when she answered the call, it was not just her brother-in-law and Mrs. Børs who thought her work necessary. The pastors at the Seamen's Mission, especially Andreas Mortensen, also knew they needed help. They had been flooded with requests from Norwegian seamen who needed medical and financial assistance of the kind the pastors could not offer. The Norwegian Seamen's Mission (*Sjømandsmisjon*) had been founded in Bergen in 1864 to care for Norwegian sailors around the world. Sailors, whose lives could be ruined by one careless night of debauchery, needed safe places to gather and resist the temptations of alcohol and the brothels populating harbors around the world.

Fedde about the time of her coming to America

In 1866, over 1,200 Norwegian ships docked in New York, and the growth continued for some time so there were increasing numbers of Norwegian sailors who had need for both spiritual and medical care. In addition there were also immigrants making their home in New York as permanent citizens of the United States. In 1860 there were 539 Norwegians living in the New York metropolitan area, but by 1880 over 2,000 Norwegians made their homes there, especially in the Red Hook area of Brooklyn. David Mauk in his book, *The Colony that Rose from the Sea: Norwegian Maritime Migration and Community in Brooklyn, 1850-1910,* says that officials calculated over 70,000 sailors sought refuge in America either legally or illegally from 1860-1915.[90] Many Norwegians living or passing through the Brooklyn area might have come to the church for help. While the different communities had similar cultural and religious roots, they of necessity had divergent goals and populations. Ministering to transient mariners was rather different from establishing congregations that would be self-supporting and local. Not surprisingly, these groups often found it difficult to work together.

The Norwegian Lutherans in New York

From their first coming to America in the 1840s and 1850s, Norwegian Synod pastors, among the earliest to arrive in America, had been concerned for the Norwegians in New York. Men such as Laur. Larsen (1833-1915), president of Luther College; Pastor Ulrik Vilhelm Koren (1826-1910); Kristian Magelssen (1839-1921); Herman Amberg Preus (1825-1894); and Hans Andreas Stub (1822-1907)—the latter two named as pastors of the church—had worked to establish Our Savior's congregation in Manhattan during their brief visits while enroute to Norway and back. But each time they left the congregation would collapse—not surprisingly, without much pastoral presence.

Herman Amberg Preus

Preus, ever on the watch for opportunities to minister to these needy Norwegian Lutherans, urged the Seamen's Mission Board in Bergen to supply the congregation with a pastor to serve both the congregation and the sailors sojourning in the city. In 1867, during his sabbatical trip to Norway where he gave his *Seven Lectures* on the state of the Norwegian Lutheran church in America, he spoke with leaders of the Seamen's Mission (first known as The Society for the Preaching of the Gospel to Scandinavian Seamen in Foreign Ports,) about this problem, but without much success. Preus appointed Ole Juul (1838-1903) to serve the Manhattan congregation, which he did from 1866-1876.[91] After some consideration and a bit of fretting that in doing so they would be accused of encouraging immigration, something Norwegian authorities worried about given the huge migration of Norwegians to America, the Seamen's Mission Board decided to pay half of Juul's salary. They stipulated that he was not to help the members of congregations in Brooklyn until his work with the maritime people was completed. Juul became aware as he worked among the sailors that the work involved more than spiritual care.

Although Juul's work with the sailors was more than a half-time job, the people in the congregation could not support him in that work nor their own. He and his wife suffered extreme privations in their daily lives because they could not count on a salary from the rather unstable and transient membership of the congregation. In 1876, aware that the

Norwegian Synod needed to do better, Preus sent them another pastor, Carl Severin Edward Everson (1847-1920), a graduate of Luther College and Concordia Seminary in St. Louis, who became the chairman of the Immigrant Mission of the Synod in New York. This, for Elisabeth, was a fateful appointment. Over the years she would be embroiled with him on issues that dispirited and upset her. Both Juul and Everson had studied under C. F. W. Walther of St. Louis, whom Juul praised as a fine teacher and good man.[92] Both

Consul Christian Børs

he and Everson were fierce proponents of Walther's position on presdestination. Everson followed Juul as pastor of the two congregations in Perth Amboy, New Jersey, and then three congregations in Brooklyn while serving as half-time pastor in the Seamen's Mission congregation. Everson's responsibilities would have taxed the strength of most anyone, but he needed to work as much as possible to earn enough to support his family. With the support of the Swedish-Norwegian Consul, Christian Børs, Everson began his work in South Brooklyn, holding evening services which the ship captains supported.

Ole Bugge Asperheim

By 1877, Consul Børs reported to the Seamen's Mission board that these activities had strained the capacities of Everson. He pleaded for the Seamen's Mission Board to raise Everson's salary so he could devote more time to his ministry with the sailors and relieve him of his financial burdens. In July 1878, the Seamen's Mission Board in Bergen called a full-time pastor for the post—Ole Bugge Asperheim, (1846-1891), a Norwegian Synod pastor and professor who had taught at its seminary in Madison, Wisconsin. A typical founder, he saw it was better to ask forgiveness than permission, and did well at that. Without getting permission from the board, he found an American Methodist church building that was being auctioned off. With some brashness, and after some dealing with a ship captain and his banker in New York and Consul Børs, he bought the building with its parsonage where the ministry would be located for many years. It was to be called the Norwegian Seamen's Mission, a link back to the old country. In addition, it was something of a defense against the Norwegian Methodist ministry nearby that was successfully attracting the Norwegian sailors who liked its lively services. Asperheim's presence meant that Everson could devote himself more fully to his congregations. The Seamen's mission came to be as cultural as it was spiritual, providing the sailors the old familiar church rituals along with places to store their chests, receive mail, and look for jobs with the institutions built and supported by their countrymen in the United States. This was to cause problems later with the ever more dogmatic Everson and others as the colony grew and developed.

The church, according to reports, could hold 700 worshipers and it was said to be filled most Sundays. By 1883, the work had grown so much that the pastor, Andreas Mortensen, who had succeeded Asperheim, could not serve it without assistance. Mortensen's book on his time in Brooklyn, *Over the Sea: Stories from the Seaman's Mission* (*Over Havet: Fortællinger fra Sjømandsmissionen*), tells many stories that illustrate how he needed help from someone like Fedde by caring for sick and dying patients whom he had to take to the hospital or the graveyard, almost to the exclusion of any other kind of ministry.[93] What the sailors—many of whom were young teenagers— usually wanted, beside Norwegian services and

Andreas Mortensen

spiritual counsel, was treatment for their diseases. (Moderns can barely understand the scourge of sexually transmitted diseases on the sailors of the day—some have estimated that one-third of the sailors suffered some form of sexually transmitted disease.) They also needed help with their desperate financial situations. It was common for Norwegians, and all sailing nations, to send boys as young as fourteen to sea. Their need for counsel and to some extent parenting made the seamen's mission necessary. It was to these sailors the mission felt most loyal.

On the other hand, as sailors settled in the new land, they created a different kind of population for the pastors to serve. Brooklyn had a unique immigrant problem: Many who had come with great hope to the new world may have been defeated by their experiences on the ships—becoming ill or losing a spouse or child on the way—and they required help that was not in the mission of the home board in Bergen. Pastor Mortensen soon knew he had to have another pastor to help him, and in 1883 Carsten Balthazar Hansteen (1856-1923), an upper class pastor from Norway, was called to the mission. He would serve with Fedde as colleague, friend, and board member until he left in 1889 for a parish in Ulstein. He ended his career as a leader in the Innermission society of Norway.

The seamen's mission may have had many souls to serve, but the record shows very few ministerial acts such as baptisms, weddings, or funerals that would have marked it as a stable congregation. Since the pastors had been instructed by the office in Bergen to serve the permanent residents of Brooklyn only after the seamen, Mauk argues that this created anxiety in the pastors, who found it difficult not to help their needy countrymen now settled in the new land.[94] Although class and situation did play roles in their various disagreements, one cannot avoid the theological controversies that also marked the colony and its pastors. Pastors Hansteen and Mortensen had been affected by the pietistic Johnsonian revival and believed they were called to help their neighbor through deeds of mercy. This was also Elisabeth Fedde's piety, as we have seen. Her brother-in-law shared it as well, with his active work as a lay preacher in Brooklyn. Asperheim, Everson, and Seehus did not share their pietism and had been taught to scorn it by their education in St. Louis which stressed right believing and the confessional documents of the Lutheran church. Although Mrs. Børs seemed to be devout and talked the language of Elisabeth and the Norwegians, she and her husband may have been more cultural Norwegian Lutherans than the Feddes. Gabriel Fedde, who became an important lay leader in the Norwegian American Lutheran Church, had received some training in religion and theology from his education at Holt Seminary in Tvedestrand when he was a younger man. As the congregations of immigrants were trying to figure out their relationships with the Seamen's Mission and each other, Gabriel Fedde had been asked by Hansteen to preach to small groups, to relieve Hansteen of some of his work. Hansteen, a leader in the Innermission society, had no difficulty with Fedde's piety and expression of the faith. Born-again "personal" Christians such as the Feddes would find it difficult to get along with Everson's more orthodox take on Lutheranism. Over and over, Everson came into strident conflict with the devout personal Christianity of the Feddes and their ilk.[95] At one time he would call both Mortensen and Hansteen "Methodists" for their mild confessionalism as Everson saw it.[96] Hansteen later said that the two never were together for long before the debates grew acrimonious and "the fur would fly."[97]

It is more than a little difficult to untangle the various threads which produced almost inevitable conflict while trying to understand not only these strong personalities, but also the challenges of an emerging professional woman such as Sister Elisabeth as they tried to work together to establish a permanent institution of mercy in Brooklyn. That they succeeded, finally, in building a hospital and Deaconess Motherhouse is a tribute to their dedication and grit, especially hers.

It was in the midst of all these sets of circumstances that the need for some kind of institution to deal with the poor and sick in the colony became obvious to the leadership. Not surprisingly the Norwegian pastors and the wealthy Norwegians such as the Børs had come to the conclusion that calling a deaconess might be the perfect solution to their many problems. They knew of the Deaconess Motherhouse back home in Norway. They knew as well that deaconesses were sent out into the communities on various missions, both in private homes and in the cities. Andreas Mortensen and Anna Børs began considering the founding of a Relief Society for the immigrants and seamen whose needs could not be met by the seamen's pastors or congregation. Mrs. Børs had persuaded her husband and his colleagues in the shipping business in Manhattan to fund the project. In order to spread the web more widely and gain future contributors and supporters, they included Pastor Everson from Our Savior's along with Fedde in their plans. While this made the pool of contributors greater, it would also spell trouble for the board as it grew and expanded in ways probably rather different from what they had thought when they started.

Elisabeth's Answer

Elisabeth very quickly wrote the group and Pastor Mortensen, saying she would come to Brooklyn in three months:

> I wrote to Mother Guldberg and Dean Julius Bruun. Mother replied that it was certainly a call from God but that I must give it time. For the present, I should first go to Arendal and organize a small home for some Sisters stationed there. I wrote to Pastor Mortensen that I would come in three months and suggested that meanwhile they in New York should lay more definite plans for the work. His reply was that I must come at once. I stayed in Arendal until the last of February and then went to Christiania. Because the directors of the mother house objected to the letter that was sent to me personally instead of to them, they could not sponsor my going. It should be my own venture. Yes, they said, since you have always been an obedient, kind Sister you may wear the mother house garb. The work, of course, is the same.[98]

After her time in Arendal, a small community on the coast some miles north east of Kristiansand, where she was sent to help restore order in the hospital, she returned to Christiania to begin preparations for her journey to America. The Motherboard's decision that she could no

Elisabeth's letter of call

A Call from America | 87

longer be associated with them baffled and hurt her at first, but she came to see the decision did have some merit. We might find it baffling to read of the legal niceties the board put on the call, ruling that the call to her personally made it impossible for them to honor the request as a board. In some ways it was similar to the dilemma faced by the Norwegian church when it was considering how to or whether to ordain pastors for service in America. While it was clear the need was severe and the immigrants in America remained Norwegian in language and culture, and they needed Norwegian speaking shepherds, the state church had no way to think of itself in the new land where there was separation of church and state. It would not be able to supervise the pastors across the ocean, nor would it have been appropriate to send them under state church auspices. The Norwegian ministers who had gone over to serve a congregation in America did so at the call of a congregation in the new land. Upon arriving, they established church bodies that tried to recruit new pastors from the old country, but they failed miserably. They immediately began to build schools to train pastors who could work more effectively in the new land.

It was almost exactly the same for Sister Elisabeth as she considered the call to Brooklyn. In a way she had prepared for this call when musing about the reasons Norwegians had not sent help to immigrants in America but had been happy to send missionaries to Africa and Asia. There may have also been a slight reluctance to serve the immigrants because the immigration was so huge. Pastors in Norway preached against people leaving home and did not want to encourage it in any way. We see this from the Seamen's Mission board's worry that appointing a pastor to serve the congregations of Norwegian settlers in America would be seen as encouraging immigration. It is also true that the Motherhouse did not have the resources to start a mission or even support a sister in America. So it determined that she would have to be on her own with only the guarantee of the good auspices of her brother-in-law and the others; they regarded her as though she were on extended leave for reasons of health. She was glad to know that the board had determined that she could, however, continue wearing her garb. Later she would design her own cap and garb for the sisters in America.

With the decision from the board, she resigned from the Motherhouse and reconciled with them. At the farewell reception, Pastor Julius

Bruun commended her work and sent a glowing recommendation along with her, as did Mother Guldberg. As she bade farewell to Elisabeth, Mother Guldberg embraced her with the pronouncement that she would always be a deaconess.[99] Wherever she would go, Guldberg said, she would always have the same call and the same Lord to serve. "Now my time as Norwegian sister was ended. I loved them all. But there was only one thing to do. *Where God leads, I will go.*"[100] It was her motto, and she repeated it many times in

Norwegian stamp in honor of Mother Guldberg

her most difficult hours. The young woman prepared to leave, taking only a few things from her home in Feda. Who knew how long she would be gone and what she would need over time? She sailed on March 23, 1883, for America on the *Geiser*, of the Thingvalla line, from Kristiansand, at the southern tip of Norway, to New York.

America

As she watched the coastline of her beloved home land disappear behind her, she thought of all she was leaving behind and the unknown future awaiting her in the new land. God had thus far been faithful to her, she wrote, and for that she was both thankful and aware that such memories gave her the courage to go forward. Soon the routine of life on the ship took hold. The captain, Captain Schierbeck, sought her out and invited her to sit next to him at his table. He cared for her like a father throughout the entire trip, she wrote. The ship also employed a widow who helped serve the people in first class with coffee and conversation. She provided Sister Elisabeth with good companionship and comforted her on the way. They sailed through a storm of hurricane strength that left most of the passengers seasick, but Sister Elisabeth was

Geiser Ship of Thingvalla line

sea strong (*sjøsterk*) and did not suffer any ill effects from the storm. (She remembered this storm later in August 1888 when the *Geiser* sank in a similar storm on the same route across the Atlantic.) As they neared New York, Elisabeth began to wonder about the New World into which she was sailing. On Sunday, April 10, the ship landed in Hoboken, New Jersey, where Norwegian ships generally disembarked.[101] From there all those immigrating were taken by ferry across the Hudson River to Castle Garden, to be processed. Elisabeth, in first class, watched the commotion from the deck. She was not allowed to disembark until a relative or friend came for her. The captain watched especially closely to see that someone met her and told her if no one came to pick her up, he would take her back to Norway. Sending a lady alone into New York City without a male escort would not have been appropriate. As she waited, Elisabeth said, her head was filled with many thoughts. Not until four that afternoon did her brother-in-law, Gabriel Fedde, whose store was on Brooklyn's Water Street, arrive to take her to his home in Brooklyn, where she lived for three weeks. She observed quickly that the area where the Norwegians lived was a poor district with lots of dysfunction: drinking, illness, fighting—so much so that she was frightened by what she thought might have been a murder. During the night, as chaos seemed to reign just outside her window, she wondered what kind of a world she had come to. She had experienced the degradations of a city while in

New York Harbor as it looked when Sister Elisabeth arrived with the Brooklyn Bridge being finished. Castle Garden, the circular building at the bottom of the picture, was where all immigrants were processed.

Christiania, although probably not as daunting as in the much larger city of Brooklyn. In 1880 the population of Brooklyn was nearly 600,000, but in some respects the Brooklyn colony of Norwegians felt like a fishing village in Norway. The Brooklyn Norwegians knew what they needed from her and were ready to provide her with support and guidance. That is a story in itself.

The Brooklyn Norwegian Colony

When Sister Elisabeth arrived in Brooklyn, people were awaiting the completion of the Brooklyn Bridge, the longest suspension bridge in the world at the time. It was to be dedicated on May 24 with great hoopla. Chester Arthur, the president, and many other luminaries were there, as were many sailing ships and thousands of visitors. The sense of optimism

Carsten Balthazaar Hansteen

that built it, and the pride New Yorkers and all of America took in the achievement, gave Sister Elisabeth a sense of what was possible in this new and expanding country. She seems to have imbibed their ebullience. Monday, April 11, her brother-in-law took her to meet the pastor at the Norwegian Seamen's Mission, Andreas Mortensen, who had served there since 1880. They also met the assistant pastor, Carsten Balthazaar Hansteen (1856-1923), who had only recently arrived. The former Methodist church on 111 William Street (now 111 Pioneer) became the center where Sister Elisabeth met with many people during her time in Brooklyn.

At her first meeting on April 11, she discovered that, contrary to the promise in the letter, nothing had been done to build an organization, except Mrs. Børs's promised money was still available. When Elisabeth asked to meet her, the pastor wrote a letter to the consul's wife asking for an audience with her and the consul. They heard back almost immediately and left to call on Mrs. Børs, who soon became someone Elisabeth regarded as a good friend and a fine person worthy of her affection. As Fedde wrote in her *Memoirs,*

> Pastor Mortensen answered that we had to request an audience with her before we could go to her, which I thought sounded promising. He wrote to her and she, as the Christian,

loving, and amiable lady that she was, gave us an immediate answer that we must come! So one day Pastor Mortensen, Hansteen and I went to her. She received us warmly and said she would keep her promise of $150 a year.[102]

The need to request an audience with Mrs. Børs indicated the social difference between Fedde and the Børs, which seemed to become less arch as they grew to know each other, but was always there. Fedde, Pastor Mortensen, and Pastor Hansteen were heartily welcomed by Mrs. Børs when they arrived at her home. As the conversation proceeded, Mrs. Børs, somewhat unfamiliar with the calling, asked Elisabeth what a deaconess really was and what she did. Sister Elisabeth answered that she had received both theoretical and practical training in nursing as well as the art of spiritual care at the Motherhouse in Christiania. It was her belief that God had called her to this work. She said, "I will do what is in my power to help the needy among our countrymen here in America."[103] This satisfied Mrs. Børs, who assured Sister Elisabeth of her support. After lunch they were off to visit another contact, Pastor Carl Serverin Edvard Everson,[104] who lived in Perth Amboy. He ran a Sunday school which Sister Elisabeth visited.[105] He became one of her most frequent companions on her visits to the various hospitals and ships that she regularly visited to find Norwegians in need.

The group, including Mortensen, Hansteen, Everson, Gabriel Fedde, Captain Harris, Mrs. Børs, and several others, decided to meet with Sister Elisabeth on April 19, 1883, in the Hansteen residence at 122 Second Place in Brooklyn to establish the Voluntary Relief Society for the Sick and Poor among the Norwegians in New York and Brooklyn (*Den frivillige Syge og Fattigpleie blandt de Norske i New York og Brooklyn*). The group began its work by establishing a committee and rules for its work. Pastor Mortensen was elected chairman; Hansteen, secretary; and Everson, treasurer. Financial support would come from voluntary contributions and pledges from the community. "We believe that every Norwegian will wish to support this great and important undertaking, according to his ability," the minutes read.[106] It was a momentous day for the young woman: "There I stood without home and without means in this praiseworthy land. Now I had to make myself known. At the Seaman's church I met many kind people and they gave me their addresses and their welcome."[107] A mere eight days after she had arrived, she already had helped establish the society and her work had begun. Fedde's call was to work with Norwegians who needed her help. That she was a nurse and had learned medical practices in Norway at the University Hospital was helpful, but it was only half of her work. The other half was spiritual.

During her first days, she walked about Brooklyn "to become acquainted with the area, visiting homes to help the poor and sick, in all about ten."[108] Although she had lived with her sister and brother-in-law for about three weeks, around April 27 she moved into a boarding house owned by Mrs. Bamber, an English widow, in the hope that she could help her learn English. All the while she went about the area making house calls on the needy, finding help for them, and consoling people tormented by spiritual crises. According to her diary—which was among other things a typical record of a nurse's visits and observations, a skill Nightingale had required—in her first four weeks there she had visited a man she found sitting on his bed, rejoicing in his Savior, found another who was seeking peace with God, and counseled a woman fearful that her family was taking the broad way rather than the narrow way, in the words of Jesus. "God make it so that she will find the way so that she can show them the way herself," she wrote. That same day she found two families where there were two dead, visited an immigrant ship and found a seaman with a five-month-old child she eventually placed with a family. "Thanks to God," she wrote "that the doors of a heart were opened for him."[109] All of these works were exactly what she had been trained to do—help people with both their bodily and spiritual needs.

During this time she and the group supporting her were also looking for a place where she could settle and locate her office and, for the time being, serve as her home. Very quickly they established her headquarters in an apartment at 109 Williams Street, right next to the Seamen's church. It had three rooms which she could rent for $9.00 a month. Mrs. Børs helped furnish them, but the apartment had no stove or kitchen range. To outfit the rooms and make them into what amounted to a clinic, she would need money. Until that time she had used her own supply of cash, but now she needed gifts from her supporters. She was glad to receive five dollars with many supplies from the hand of Mrs. Børs: a bed and mattress, four chairs and a table. Many others came forward with

The Seamen's Mission Church

small things that would appoint the clinic. For that Sister Elisabeth was grateful as she painted her new home and office, sewing carpets and curtains for it. Sunday, May 27, she noted in her diary, she had begun to make the new house ready and would herself lay down carpet the next day. On June 4, 1883, the office at the Williams Street location opened. They now had a nurse and a place to house the Norwegian Relief Society.

109 Williams Street, the first headquarters of Fedde's work, next door to the Seamen's church.

Helping Norwegian sailors and immigrants in extreme situations was an urgent calling for the group who wanted to take care of their fellow Norwegians. At the time, hospitals and institutions for the poor and mentally ill, especially immigrants, were barely habitable, which journalists like Julius Chambers (1850-1920) of the *New York Tribune* and Nellie Bly (1864-1922) were beginning to expose. Like the later muckrakers, they gathered material for their articles and books by feigning insanity to document the ill treatment of the inmates. When Fedde established her Relief Society she was doing so in a context of such scandals and reforms. The Tewksbury Almshouse in Massachusetts was under investigation just as Fedde began her work in Brooklyn. At the time the papers were filled with muckraking articles exposing the terrible conditions at Tewksbury. Originally built to take in the large influx of immigrants streaming into the state in 1852, it had become a hell hole. The insane were chained up, dead infants were said to have been given to the medical school at Harvard, vermin swarmed over patients' bodies, and the food was mere swill. People knew something needed to be done. Politicians like the governor of Massachusetts had made reforming Tewksbury a priority in his state of the state address the previous January.[110] It was in this context that the Norwegians in Brooklyn were working. They felt it was their duty to care for their own people rather than send them off to places like Tewksbury where no one would understand their language and they would be mistreated. There was much to be done and everyone knew it.

In order to do well in the New Land, Fedde had realized from the first that she needed to speak better English, so she began studying the language with Pastors Everson and Mortensen as well as two other men, the engineer Alfred Bryhn and the dentist Dr. Theodore Siqueland (1860-), almost certainly a relative of the Siqvelands in Stavanger.[111] They would meet after church on Sundays and have dinner together while they taught her English. Sunday was her only day at home, she said, so it was good to rest and relax with these men while she learned to speak and write the language with more facility.

Although her days were filled with deeds of mercy, she did take time to visit the sights in New York City. On May 8, after a sick call, she went to visit Central Park, which had been one of the primary attractions of the city since its opening in 1857. During such excursions she realized that she needed to find a way to respond quickly to those in need who came while she was away. To do that she put a chalk board outside the building asking people to leave her their names and addresses with a note as to what they needed so she could help them as soon as possible. Frequently when she came home weary and ready for rest, she would see a request on the board and have to leave immediately to assist whomever was in need. Very shortly after she had arrived in this country, she received a call to help a woman from Bergen, married to an Irishman, who had just given birth to twins. Her story was the first of many Fedde experienced: the woman lay in a basement apartment with the two naked babies. The mother had only some cloth scraps over her to cover her nakedness. Elisabeth quickly bought a basket and her sister, Anna Marie, filled it with food and found some clothes for the poor woman. She visited her every day with a full basket until the woman became well enough to manage on her own. To fill the basket with supplies Sister Elisabeth realized she needed many friends to support her.

Another early excursion came at the behest of a Dutchman who simply beckoned her to follow him to a "sick man" he knew needed help. As she followed him into the worst part of the city, almost to the docks, she admitted to being afraid. Finally they stood before a Norwegian woman with two children who were weeping. They had just come from Bermuda, and her husband had spent the last of their money to rent the room they were in. He had expected he would be able to work on the docks when they got to New

A painting of Fedde from a 1941 calendar featuring famous nurses

COURTESY KAREN FEDDE MAY

York, but became very ill with what Sister Elisabeth diagnosed as pneumonia. Fedde went into the room and began cleaning it and treating the man, along with his family. Things looked fairly bleak, but she stayed through the night into the morning when she went to find a doctor whom she thought would not charge a fee. He came and gave advice. Afterwards he told her that she should not hesitate to ask him to come for help at any time. To her joy, the patient became well and was able to support his family as he had hoped. From these first encounters and her purchase of the basket which was always filled with food and clothes, she would become known in Brooklyn as much by her basket as her garb. Kristin Adriansen in her thesis on Fedde dubbed her "The Lady with the Basket," rather like Florence Nightingale, "The Lady with the Lamp."

While she was getting the house on William Street fixed up, painting and cleaning it to make it ready as a place to meet with the poor and sick, she found it helpful to visit other institutions in the area that she might find helpful in the future. The relationships she established with other hospitals in the area would pay off later when she needed to bring the sick or abandoned to hospitals or orphanages. She and Pastor Everson together made many visits in her far-reaching parish, from Hoboken to Brooklyn to Ward's Island. In their journeys they found every type of need possible. In each case she did with dispatch what she felt was necessary with no regard to the situation or background of the persons she assisted. She helped a Catholic woman who lay sick unto death, and dealt with two drunk Norwegian women with whom she felt it was difficult to speak since they were intoxicated and had never heard or read God's Word, she concluded.

The days before the dedication of the rooms they had found for her, she spent time with both Hansteen and Everson planning the festival, in addition to visits to Mrs. Børs. The day of the dedication, Sunday, June 10, 1883, was hot enough that over 60,000 people went to Coney Island for the first day of the summer season. Coney Island was not far from their new center, but such amusements did not interest Sister Elisabeth at this time in her very busy life. While she did not complain of the heat— Norwegians often found the heat of the city unbearable—she found the day to be both pleasant and serious. They opened the facility in Jesus' name, she wrote, praying she could fulfill her calling there.[112] It was a small effort and attracted very little attention from the press; not even the Norwegian press reported on it until later.

On June 17, she visited a man in Jersey City, dying of pthisis (a kind of tuberculosis) who had denied his [Lutheran] faith to become a Catholic where he thought he would fare better.[113] She came home quickly because she had to finish sewing her own dress, probably her garb, which she finished the next day. Most urgent, something which would plague her until she left the work in Brooklyn, was the need to raise money which she learned how to do very quickly. The first such effort of the Norwegian Relief Society would be a bazaar, the old standby for church women in the nineteenth century who wanted to raise money for a cause. In this they were assisted by Pastors Mortensen and Hansteen. They appreciated that now, finally, someone they trusted could deal with the medical and economic emergencies that confronted them on a daily basis. In her they had found exactly what they needed, and they were thankful to be relieved of these problems. It is not clear if they helped with raising money. Mortensen essentially turned this over to Fedde, who quickly learned the

Bay Ridge about the time of Fedde's arrival in Brooklyn

importance of the women's auxiliary and their bazaars. She was a quick study and began quickly to learn how to beg, as she called it. David Mauk says that by the mid-1880s, forty percent of the money for the seamen's congregation came from the colony and three-quarters of that came from the women's organizations.[114]

Often times Elisabeth went to Hoboken, just across the Hudson from Manhattan, to meet the ships from Norway. From there the passengers, mostly immigrants, were taken to Castle Garden, the Ellis Island of its day. Every Friday Sister Elisabeth visited Ward's Island Emigrant Hospital near Castle Garden. It had been established in 1864 to care for those who needed medical help after disembarking in the New World. (From its founding until 1890, the year before it was sold and Ellis Island became the entry point to America, it took in over 630,000 patients. After 1882 it began charging fifty cents a person for treatment.[115]) At the Emigrant Hospital she would usually find Scandinavians. Most had been judged too ill to enter the United States. To be sent there was a virtual death sentence. If she could not save lives, she could at least offer palliative care to dying patients,

Ward's Island Hospital

Emigrants being greeted at Castle Garden

so she went regularly even if the journey to Ward's Island was a long one involving a trip by rail, then boat. Her first time at the hospital she met a woman missionary from Sweden—of noble birth, she said. When she asked her to help her find out where the sick Norwegians had been sent, the lady had said, rather haughtily, "Sister Elisabeth, you can find them yourself."[116]

Elisabeth's diary shows us how quickly she found her vocation as she was called to help many sick and indigent Norwegians in the city. Between June 1 and June 8, 1883, she made twenty calls on people, about half of them sick calls. By the end of June she had made at least fifty-five visits to those in need. During this same time she continued making acquaintance with the various organizations in the city that had been established to help the poor and sick, where she could place her patients. One of the first people she visited on June 19 was Knud Olsen whom she seems to have known before. They had a good time, but she thought he needed treatment at a hospital. On June 26, she went to the German Lutheran hospital in New York to establish relations with that institution so she could bring patients there, the first of whom would be Olsen. While he found the treatment there to be helpful, he could not understand a word of the German language, so she visited him frequently to see how things were going. She showed no partiality when it came to serving her patients. She visited the Catholic St. Peter's hospital on Henry Street in Brooklyn to find help for one of her patients. Soon she established good relations with them, despite some misgivings on the part of her board about working with Catholics.

Once in the Emigrant Hospital she dealt with a man from Stavanger who was delirious and clearly dying. He had a dream wherein he thought that his mother had been with him, a delusion Sister Elisabeth tried to disabuse him of. Something of a skeptic, he could not believe God loved him. She asked him if he could remember a Bible verse. He said, no, but then when she began quoting John 3: 16, he finished it for her, indicating to her that he had more faith than he realized.[117]

> I taught him a few more Bible verses that he repeated after me.
> We spoke for a while and he asked me to come again soon.
> Yes, today it has been a serious day, but our dear God has told
> us that we must come to him with our needs. I go to him with
> all of these needy sick. O Lord God, help all of them![118]

Often, the death of one of these abandoned souls meant that she would have to find both a way and a place to bury them, at some expense to her.[119] On July 26, 1883, she helped a young girl whose baby had died. She took the little corpse to the undertaker and got a pastor who could officiate at the funeral. In the Ward's Island Hospital most of the very ill to whom she ministered would never leave except to be buried in the graveyard on the island, she said, where the dead of New York were being reburied. It was now receiving the last remains of many Scandinavians. She also cared for them and made preparations for their burial.

In her travels around the cities, she could enjoy the spectacular view of the city from the high promotories of Long Island, with its gas lamps lighting the urban scene at night. She enjoyed the sites of Brooklyn with its over half-million residents and a growing transportation system. Trolleys powered by horses went as far as 25th Street. The city limits ran down 60th Street. One could see truck farms on Fifth Avenue, six blocks from the water. Her parish soon extended from Jersey City to Castle Garden to Ward's Island Immigrant Hospital. Pastor Everson accompanied on most of her rounds, both to help her and to be her escort as she found patients in the most difficult and dangerous of circumstances. Her usual routine, when she entered a home where someone was ill, was to follow the nursing practices recommended by Florence Nightingale: She cleaned the homes of her patients, tried to provide good ventilation and light, found clothes and food for the indigent, among the first recommendations of Nightingale. She also attended those with deadly diseases, helped young women with their babies, nursing those with life threatening diseases, raising money to pay the passage for the immigrant to return home, caring for the dying, washing their bodies after they had died, finding homes for orphaned children or poor children whose mothers or fathers could no longer afford to care for them, even raising the money to pay an undertaker and locate a gravesite. Every day she came into contact with the bad choices people made that plunged them into one disaster after another. Worst she said was that

> the complete darkness of Heathendom broods over sinners, really gross sins, sins against the 6th Commandment [Lutherans count the commandment against adultery as the 6th commandment], committed by children of 4 years and up, until they too experience the consequences of sin.[120]

While she found her work to be consuming, she still took time to be with her new friends and family for Sunday dinners and holidays. On August 8, 1883, she went on a tour with Simon Wright Flood (1839-1895), brother of Mrs. Andreas (Petronelle Flood) Mortensen, and his wife Maria to Fort Hamilton, the old fort near Bay Ridge. Both of the Floods would become good friends of Fedde and serve on the board. On August 10, 1883, Elisabeth made new contacts with the Episcopal Sisters' Home (later merged with Roosevelt Hospital), about what to do with children who needed placement. This hospital and the Deaconess Home there had been founded by William Augustus Muhlenberg (1796-1877), great-grandson of the Lutheran patriarch, Henry Melchior Muhlenberg. While a teenager, William had converted to the Episcopal faith and become a leader in the New York diocese, building the Episcopal Deaconess Home and Hospital beside his church, the Church of the Holy Communion where he housed the Sisters of the Holy Communion. Whether Fedde knew the connection it had with the patriarch of Lutheranism in the United States or not, she felt welcome there. While visiting, she met a man from Trondheim who

William Augustus Muhlenberg

had gone to sea to earn a little money; on the first day he had stepped on a nail and was now in the hospital. At the time he had not been warmed by the gospel, but as they spoke she told him that she prayed every day that God would send her to the people God wanted her to see, and she was certain that their meeting was something that God alone had willed.

> Tears filled his eyes and they said more than words. When I gave him my address and told him that he should always feel free to call me if he needed me, tears ran down his face and the handshake he gave me said more than a thousand words.[121]

From the first Fedde was pragmatic in her relationships with other faith communities. This would become a matter of some concern to the board and some people she met.[122] While most were friendly, not all greeted her with the warm ecumenical spirit she had toward them. The nineteenth century was a difficult time to be open to Catholics, given the feelings many Protestants had toward Roman Catholics especially, and vice versa. At the Ward's Island Hospital, she met a Catholic priest and a German Lutheran pastor who had served at the Gossner Mission in India but was now in New York with his wife who was also a deaconess.[123] The Catholic priest was eager to convert any and all of the people he met in the hospital, including Sister Fedde! She acquitted herself well in her argument with him after he told her that he had been observing her work over the past year and thought she would be able to do well with the sick if only she were not going the wrong way. He offered her a book to read so she could find the right way. When she asked him if he thought she was lost, he said,

Yes, all who are outside the Catholic faith are lost. You believe that God took some earth and created a man and blew his spirit into the man (as he blew into the room while he was speaking!). So it was with the church. He said to St. Peter, "You are the rock, and on you will I build the church. But Luther was a rotten finger on the body and we cut him away. Therefore all of his followers will be lost.[124]

Elisabeth, whose faith and humor helped her through many such encounters retorted, "It is not Luther I believe in, but the Bible, and it was Luther who made it possible for us to have it!" With that she announced that she did not need his help. He placed his corpulent body in front of her so she could not get out of the room, telling her she was a rotten Lutheran, frightening her. The German deaconess, who well knew these arguments, ordered him to let her go, which he did with something of a curse against the rotten and damned Lutherans.[125]

Her many visits to the hospital at Ward's Island and others in the city where the life of a patient was "hardly worth that of a fly" only served to convince Sister Elisabeth she needed to do more for her patients than she was able to do in short visits. As we have seen from the original call letter and her first months in the colony, it had been the original purpose of her call to go out to find the poor and sick in their homes or on the street. She was beginning to consider how she might do this more efficiently.

Soon she organized a Ladies Aid to support her work. The organization began with a meeting in her little apartment on August 13, 1883. There were fourteen in attendance; among them the pastors' wives, Mrs. Ambjør Everson, Mrs. Petronelle Mortensen, with Mrs. Anna Børs, and others. The work began with the resolve to sew clothes for children— pants and dresses, since frequently Sister Elisabeth would find children, even adults, without any usable clothing. The sewing circle decided to meet every Monday. These women would become her core supporters and very helpful to Sister Elisabeth, but soon she began to formulate bigger plans to raise money, not just from donations of handiwork, but also fund-raising events.

It was not just the indigent that came to her for help. Alcohol, a common scourge of Scandinavians, landed people in dire situations that drove them to Sister Elisabeth. One day, she reported, a good-looking man who had walked across the newly constructed Brooklyn Bridge in his slippers, a member of the Swedish-Norwegian diplomatic corps who knew her through the Børs, came to ask for a loan of five dollars. His wife, a pianist, probably in Europe, he said, had been going to send him money but he had not gotten it yet. Elisabeth looked at him and decided to invite him in and made him the best dinner that she could. She gave him advice on where to spend the evening, and the next day he came again, saying that four of the dollars had been stolen and he needed seven dollars more. "You are drunk, Herr Consul," she said, "And what you are saying is not true. You will get food, but no money."[126] She said she never saw the five dollars again, but learned from the experience.

Every day she was witness to "heart-rending scenes." One of the most terrifying was a woman who had come with her daughter to meet her husband and sons who were now in North Dakota. She had gone mad after a fire on the ship. She and her little girl were almost imprisoned in the dark hospital while their husband and father awaited them in the Dakotas. When Elisabeth found them, the mother burst into tears to hear that someone understood her language. As Sister Elisabeth put it, "Think how their bright future had darkened upon their arrival in the new

Norwegian immigrants at Castle Garden

land!" Elisabeth told her she would return in a week with help. The next week when she returned the bed was empty and the young girl was sitting beside it with her face covered in a handkerchief wet with tears. "They have taken away my mother! During the night she died, and they came and took her away. Help me to find my father."[127] She grabbed Sister Elisabeth around the neck and made her promise she would not leave her there. After some finagling with the head nun, she was allowed to take the poor girl home with her, where the young girl stayed until her father came for her some weeks later.

Soon Fedde and her work became well known both in Brooklyn and back home in Norway, since the communication back and forth was sufficient enough to keep them well aware of what was happening on both sides of the ocean. In September she received a young woman, probably from the Christiania prison who had been sent to her from Norway by the founder of the Seamen's Mission who had become the chaplain at a women's prison in Christiania, Johan Cordt Harmens Storjohann (1832-1914). Young girls, seduced by men who took advantage of them and made them pregnant, were sometimes driven to murder their infants out of desperation and sentenced to long years in prison for infanticide. The prison in Christiania had a policy of sending such unfortunate women to America with some money, but usually not enough for them to manage in the New World. Many of them were prostitutes forced into the profession by circumstances like these. From 1879 to 1884, according to emigration records, the Christiania jail sent seventy-one such women to America.[128] Sometimes they could find a new life in the new world but not always.

One such refugee had become ill on the ship and was sent to Ward's Island Hospital where she did manage to recover. Elisabeth helped her find a home. She became ill again, and Elisabeth took her to the Episcopal Deaconess Hospital. She seemed to be doing well and when Elisabeth would visit her they spoke of spiritual things. The young woman rejoiced in the fact that Jesus loved her as he had loved so-called "fallen" women in his time. Sister Elisabeth visited her several times, and she came to rejoice in God's love for her. At one of their last meetings she showed Elisabeth a picture of a man. "What do you think of him?" she asked. "He seems to be a rather good-looking man," Elisabeth answered, "but his eyes have been stabbed out." The woman said, "I have done that. He is the reason for my unhappiness." She then went on to tell of how she had come to Christiania to work as a maid in the house where he also lived. His room was next to hers. He had seduced her with promises of money and jewels. The result was that she gave birth to a child whom, out of desperation, she strangled and put on the porch of the next house. The police soon discovered that she was the mother. When they came to take her she became so ill they put her in the state hospital where she recovered her health, but was then taken to court. The judge brought in the father of the child who admitted that he knew her, but had not known that she was going to kill the child. He was let go. The judge asked her if she had strangled the baby. "Yes," she answered. The judge sentenced her to eleven years in jail. After seven years, the woman was released and given passage to America. Some days after telling Sister Elisabeth this, she died. When she came to take her last effects from the hospital, Sister Elisabeth found the picture of the man with his eyes stabbed out. She tore it up into many pieces and threw out on the streets of New York so the little bits would be trampled under the feet of many.[129] Sister Elisabeth concluded her account: "She was a poor sinner and she came to believe the glad good news of the forgiveness of sins for Jesus' sake." Sister Elisabeth reached out in sympathy to the poor young woman who had suffered from what the man had done to her. As a nurse, especially, she was always eager to help patients recover, not blame them for their suffering.

One day while she was hosting the ladies aid, she had to take in a man who had no other place to stay but her bedroom. "Full house here," she noted.[130] That night she was very restless and uncomfortable, sleeping on the floor, because of the sick man who was in her bed. When the doctor came the next morning, he ordered the man to go to the hospital so Fedde would be able to get some sleep the next night. Soon after, she had to go to wash the body of one of her patients, a Mrs. Johnson, and prepare it for burial. Fedde wrote that she had died after a long struggle, but "she had tasted God's blessed grace here below. Now she was home and singing before the throne the eternal praises. She had been one of my hardest patients, but Jesus gave her the victory, praise him for all eternity."[131]

Wondering how she could get more support to build a larger place kept her awake many nights. She needed money; what she was getting from Mrs. Børs and the Ladies Aid was not enough to do what she wanted. One day she decided to visit a Norwegian opera singer who lived in New York, Lorentz Skougaard-Severini (1837-1885). Skougaard-Severini had been born in Farsund, Norway, son of a customs official. He had gone to Italy for musical training and from there to the Stockholm opera to sing. He had come to New York in 1866 at the behest of his patron Alfred Corning Clark, heir to the Singer Sewing Machine Company, who anonymously supported Fedde with many large gifts over the next fifteen years. She found Skougaard-Severini's address in an address book and went to his apartment on 64 West 22nd Street. When she rang the bell, the door opened. She gave the porter her card and was invited in. As she sat in the room waiting for the gentleman to come, she prayed, "Give me the wisdom to say the right thing." On the wall she saw a picture of Christ and remembered the verse in Matthew 10:19, "Do not worry about what you shall say, for it will be given you in that moment." Just then, the singer burst into the room, remarking on how good it was to meet her and talk with her for he had heard about her. Because one of his students was ill and could not make the lesson that day, Skougaard-Severini had an hour to talk with her, which he did eagerly, regarding the student's absence as God's way of setting aside time for Sister Elisabeth. After much talk about his life as a singer and teacher, he showed her around his apartment and gave her ten dollars, urging her to come to him whenever she needed help. The gift, she said, made it possible to pay the rent and buy food. It was the first of many from the singer who generously supported her until his untimely death in 1885.[132] The meeting had great significance when she looked back on her life and remembered people who had helped her.

Learning how to raise money occupied her incessantly as she realized the urgency she faced every day. She understood that she was really practicing the art of begging. While at first she depended on the generosity of her benefactors, Mrs. Børs and Skougard-Severini among others, she began to realize that she needed other dependable sources of revenue. Their society's finances were in arrears. On October 15, 1883, she reported she needed more money to do her work. The society received about $40 a month from Mrs. Børs and other regular contributors, together with some occasional gifts. Their inventory had cost $41.02; the care of the sick, $34.61; travel, $21.83; and her salary of $205.53. The minutes of November 5, 1883, stated that they had already spent $302. 99 and had only taken in under $300. Someone suggested taking up offerings at local supporting congregations on Sundays. The Lutheran congregations had enough to do with their own ministries and could not share in this expense, they said, so the idea was not adopted. Bazaars were the time-honored way for women to raise money far beyond their own personal resources, along with dinners, fishponds, and other kinds of raffles which the group began to sponsor with regularity. Some months before, the board had a discussion about a bazaar. The conversation grew heated as to whether or not they could use games of chance to raise money. Pastor Everson had been the most worried about this—saying that people who bought chances were more interested in receiving something for nothing than helping the kingdom. This argument would continue for years and grow more and more rancorous. Despite the disagreement, the board voted at the July 18, 1883, meeting to sponsor a bazaar. Sister Elisabeth became the driving force behind these events. One can read in her diary how she would look for decorations, things to sell, and other necessary purchases beforehand, as well as organizing the ladies aid in their sewing and production of salable items. In addition she asked supporters for gifts to sell at the events. After the bazaars she reported on the results of the sale to the treasurer, Everson.

Their first bazaar, held on Atlantic Avenue, October 9-12, 1883, succeeded beyond any of their expectations. Pastor Mortensen, in his book about his time in Brooklyn, described the pains the women went to decorate for the event:

> [T]he tables standing in long rows were covered with snow white tablecloths and decorated with flags. All the gas lights were burning and the spacious room filled with visitors. The taking of numbers was lively and several of the Scandinavians and of the captains let go of one dollar after another.[133]

With the help of Skougaard-Severini, who sang several Norwegian songs and also served as the auctioneer, they raised $400 the first day; with the help of his friend, Clark, they raised $100 the next day. In a day when the yearly pay of a pastor or missionary was $600, this was a great sum indeed. Unfortunately for Sister Elisabeth, Skougaard-Severini died about a year later, on February 14, 1885. She missed both his friendship and generosity. His funeral, on February 17, at St. Peter's Church in Manhattan was gripping, she said, and attended by many who dearly missed him, she wrote.[134]

The Woman Question

We can see in many of the things Sister Elisabeth was doing that her life was in concert with the world-wide movement to give women their rights, although she says nothing about the cause until later. But it is in the air, and she is nothing if not observant. In 1880, Bjørnstjerne Bjørnson, the poet and political provocateur of Norway, had traveled through America, especially the Midwest where he raised a storm of

St. Peter's Lutheran Church

protests against his denigration of the Lutheran faith and its treatment of women. The year before, in 1879, Bishop Heuch had written a critique of Bjørnson's thought, attacking it for being unbiblical and heretical. Heuch had been one of Fedde's Bible teachers, and she admired him. Bjørnson especially criticized the Norwegian Synod during what was known as the Muus divorce case for the way it had treated Oline Muus, wife of B. J. Muus, president of St. Olaf College during the trial. She had scandalized the entire Norwegian American community when she sued her husband for divorce over his mistreatment of her. The issue in question was who had the rights to the inheritance she had received from her father in Norway. Pastor Muus claimed it was

Oline Muus

his under Norwegian law; she claimed it was hers under American law. It was the scandal du jour among Norwegian-American Lutherans, causing church leaders to line up for or against one of the parties. The Norwegian Synod— Herman Preus and others—sided with Pastor Muus, Oftedal and Sverdrup of the Conference took Mrs. Muus' side and even gave her a place to stay at Augsburg Seminary. Bjørnson loudly fomented against the Norwegian Synod and Pastor Muus for their treatment of women, especially Mrs. Muus. He supported her case for divorce and the freedom of women to live free of the domination of their husbands. This was only three years before Sister Elisabeth came to Brooklyn. The scandal was still in the air and surely one that Pastor Everson, a strong supporter of the Norwegian Synod had opinions about, very likely favoring Pastor Muus as had the leaders of his synod. Nor can we forget—in one of those ironies of history—Muus was the first in Norway to present a case for a deaconess Motherhouse in Norway.

Bjørnstjerne Bjørnson

Bjørnson, during his time in America, 1880-1881, had attended several conferences with some of the major suffragettes of the time. They enraptured him. To be at the women's conferences was like seeing a completely new world, he said. "The two hours I was there were, I believe, the finest I have experienced, for I sat as if in the future, and I had difficulty controlling my emotion."[135] Both he and Henrik Ibsen (1828-1906) in particular became interested in this movement, which to them meant freeing women from the claims of the Bible and adopting the new historical-critical methods being developed in Germany. Ibsen's *A Doll House*, 1879, became the most performed play around the world. It raised the issue of what a woman could do, as Nora borrows money on false pretenses to fund her husband's trip to the south for his health. When her husband finds out, it so unmans him he nearly goes crazy, and Nora leaves him to "find herself."

Bjørnson approved of the Unitarianism of most of the women at the convention, especially the preaching of Antoinette Brown Blackwell (1825-1921), the Unitarian pastor. "They wanted to get those celebrations abolished that were associated with the belief that God had lived among us as a human being; these should be limited to the particular church organization concerned."[136] Bjørnson had spent considerable time in Massachusetts with Ole Bull's widow and, incidentally, Aasta Hansteen, the painter and distant cousin of Carsten Hansteen, who had moved to America in 1880 to be free of the shackles women had to endure in Norway.

These ideas were far too radical and unbiblical for someone like Sister Elisabeth to consider, but she surely knew about them. This did not mean, however, that she was not for the rights of women. Despite the criticism of the church by free thinkers such as Bjørnson, ironically it was the women's movement in the church and para-church organizations such as Ladies Aids, missionary societies, and the deaconess movement where women first got the right to vote and occupy places of authority before civil society did. When Sister Elisabeth became a deaconess, she knew well, as she had said in reference to looking for a way to answer God's call, there were few opportunities for women in the public sphere except for that of a deaconess. At the time, however, she knew that she wanted to do something for the Lord. When she spoke in these terms she was expressing the yearning of many young women of the time to find their own Christian vocation by becoming a deaconess, a missionary, or a teacher.

In Norway, at the end of 1883, the same year Sister Elisabeth came to Brooklyn, a small group of women led by Gina Sverdrup Krog, a pastor's daughter from the North, began to foment for an organization

Gina Sverdrup Krog

that would promote the rights of women. In 1884 Krog and Hagbard Emmanual Berner, Hans Gerhard Stub's (1849-1931) brother-in-law, founded the *Kvinnesaksforening* (Women's Rights Society). The next year after a disagreement with Berner, who did not favor women's suffrage at the time, she founded the country's Women's Suffrage Society (*Landskvinnestemmeretforeningen*) which she would lead from 1885-1897. That a woman could achieve such a position was entirely new. Fedde most surely knew about this, no matter what she might have thought of Krog or Berner, the founder of *Dagbladet*, the paper of the left in Norway. *Dagbladet* was no friend of the Norwegian Church or the Bible, and everyone knew it. That same year, Cady Stanton and Susan B. Anthony reorganized the National Woman Suffrage Association, adopting a new constitution which stated that its main goal was women's suffrage. At about the same time the temperance movement, especially the Women's Christian Temperance Union (WTCU), burst upon the world scene. Under the leadership of Francis Willard (1839-1898), it enlarged its program to include women's suffrage. Her theory was, and it was commonly held, that if one wanted to stop demon rum, women needed the vote. They were the morally superior sex and Prohibition could not pass into law without their vote. Willard called it the "Home Protection Ballot." The organization went global in 1883, pressing for total abstinence and women's

Francis Willard

right to vote. In Norway the *Hvite Bånd* *(White Ribbon)* which still exists, was founded in 1889 by Countess Ida Wedel Jarlsberg (1855-1929) and Birgitte Esmark (1841-1897). It grew quickly.

Sister Elisabeth no doubt knew of this movement and its effort to ban demon rum and get women the vote. Whatever her own feelings about the WCTU we do not know. We do know that her experience as a nurse made her hate the effects of liquor on family life and what it did to poor, innocent sailors, but we have no record of her joining the organization. When we watch Fedde trying to negotiate the many different issues she would meet as a strong woman trying to lead an organization in this time, one wonders how she might have addressed the struggle. From the time she arrived in Brooklyn until she left, the country and Brooklyn were alive with suffragettes meeting and pushing for the vote and more respect as equals in the public sphere.

Christians were not of one mind on this issue, even liberal Christians. The reformers, such as the abolitionists, prohibitionists, and suffragettes, had all begun in the church, but it was not long until some women split from the church, viewing it as the enemy of women's rights. Susan B. Anthony, a Quaker, and her close friend, Cady Stanton, disagreed on this tactically: Anthony thought antagonizing the church politically unwise, while Cady Stanton thought the church was the root of the problem.

While Sister Elisabeth did not note it, she probably watched as the yawning chasm between women suffragettes with religious ties and the ones who thought religion was the problem continued to grow and widen. On January 22, 1885, *The Brooklyn Eagle* reported that in Washington D.C. the sessions of the Woman's Suffrage Convention had a lively debate about a resolution that proposed that their organization boycott all religions that did not teach "that woman is as much the image of God as man is." Elizabeth Cady Stanton was the one pushing it because, as she said, "ministers have been stumbling blocks in the way of all reforms and have done more to injure the progress of the temperance movement than nearly all things combined." Her close friend Susan B. Anthony, more politic than Stanton, opposed her, saying that "ministers have aided all reforms, and will, if properly worked with, help on the Woman Suffrage Convention."[137]

One of their best friends for the cause was Henry Ward Beecher, close neighbor to Fedde in Brooklyn, who supported women's rights because of what he also believed was women's moral superiority, as did many men who were for women's suffrage. This argument did not move some church people, like Herman Preus, president of the Norwegian Synod, Everson's and Seehus' synod. He closely followed Beecher's newspaper, *The Independent*, and regularly commented on what he thought of as the outrageous claims of Beecher concerning the rights of women to vote or to preach and lead men in the congregations. He regarded such efforts as flagrant violations of what the Apostle

Henry Ward Beecher

Paul had to say about women keeping silent in church, which he and his compatriots extended to the secular political system. Already in 1870, he had commented on Beecher's position on women: "One of the day's watchwords is women's vote that once again stands in strong relation to women's emancipation and liberation from her bonds, with which God has bound her to her husband and family, and liberation from God and his law."[138] For Preus this was a return to paganism.

While these are written some thirteen years before Fedde arrived in America, they were the considered opinion of many in Preus' camp and likely Pastor Everson, whom he appointed to the post in Brooklyn. Beecher only got more certain of his position as time went on. A column written by him appeared in the December 9, 1886, *Daily Brooklyn Eagle*, clearly expressed these ideas. In it he praised the growing inclusion of women in the

Plymouth Congregational Church, Henry Ward Beecher's congregation

public sphere. In New York City two women had just been appointed to the City Board of Commissioners. He looked eagerly to the day that women would be represented equally with men on boards of education because women were the natural sex to "raise children and run penal institutions." This caused him to note the founding of the deaconess houses by both Episcopalians and Lutherans, which he probably knew also from his own experience of them in Brooklyn, although he did not say so directly. He was proud to note that women deaconesses had been elected by his Plymouth congregation "and it would be difficult to dispense with them," although they probably did not function like the Lutheran or Episcopal deaconesses. They would have been more like officers of the church who took on the duties of spiritually guiding the congregation. He then went on to say that in the past aristocratic women, such as a queen or an artist especially gifted in her field, would have been allowed to speak in public, but "not plain democratic women." He noted that women had been in the forefront against slavery (one of the more important in that struggle, his own sister Harriet Beecher Stowe) and that they were now being admitted to medical schools to become doctors, they were managers of great hotels, they had even been ordained to become missionaries around the world. Now they could enter almost any profession. There were still some battles to be fought, he regretted, especially getting women ordained in more conservative denominations. He looked forward to that day and to further enlargement of the roles women could hold in the public sphere.

In looking back fifty years the sphere of women, her rights and duties, have been enlarging; her rights have more and more been based on equity, not courtesy; her development has not been at the cost of her womanly instincts; she is none the less a refined woman, and fitted for the duties of home, because her enlarged sympathies take in the interests of the whole community. In participating in rights and duties which at one time were committed to men, she has become masculine, and there are a multitude of things that can be and are being done as well by a woman as by a man and in a very large sphere the woman's way is best.[139]

This enthusiastic outburst from the old preacher is well worth some scrutiny for its expression of the typical liberal, but Christian, view of women's emancipation, which he obviously favored. One can also read in it the fairly clear differentiation between men and women. Women have womanly instincts and are morally superior to men. Now they are being asked to take those instincts into the public sphere and become "masculine," a task which seems from this vantage altogether difficult. While the Norwegian Lutherans among whom Fedde worked could hardly be called liberal Protestants—they were by theological persuasion dead set against Beecher—his comment reveals some of the contradictions about the role of the woman in the public sphere. Is she to become masculine in order to fulfill her role into which she brings the "woman's way which is best"? Or will her superior feminine morality be enough? One cannot help but think Sister Elisabeth met such contradictions in her work and had been frustrated by them as she tried to figure out her role as a leader. It may be at the root of the problems that had plagued her in her relationship to her board, especially Everson. Most of the time, Sister Elisabeth's struggles had more to do with the life and death issues that were ever before her as a nurse, but the fact of the women's movement needs to be acknowledged, if only to see her in her context as a woman exploring an entirely new role in a society that was beginning to question the old ways of thinking about men and women.

Ending the Year

From all the things Sister Elisabeth did in a little over seven months since the establishment of the Relief Society, we can see the gifts she had for organization and her satisfaction in giving both the physical care along with the spiritual care. In a summary of her work during December 1883, she gives us a vivid sense for her daily work, and her routine.

> During all this month I haven't written but 1 have made forty-one sick calls and house visits. Have been to the hospital three times, and several different offices to get help, sometimes for our work, or for something else, and distributed a lot of clothing. It has been both a worry and a joy. While often 1 have talked as though to stones, God has still let His Word win through to some hearts and created life. Yes, if there is joy in Heaven when a sinner is converted, then I too have reason to rejoice and it is blessed for me to break through at last. Hitherto has the Lord helped me. In Jesus' name I end this year and pray for forgiveness for my lack of faith.[140]

With these traditional words of repentance and prayer, she ended every year.

1884

Brooklyn greeted the New Year during a rain storm. Most people had stayed home in the morning because of it, but ventured out in the afternoon when the weather improved. *The Brooklyn Eagle* described it:

> A dull grey sky stretched forbiddingly above the earth, lowering to such an extent that the church steeples seemed to perforate it. The wind blew in such raw gusts from the northeast and at frequent intervals rain fell, either in a fine drizzle or in big splashing drops, transforming the gutters into miniature rivers, and the culverts into roaring cataracts as the great masses of snow melted away.[141]

As she began the New Year, Elisabeth put away 1883, and prayed as always, in the language of the Danish hymn, "In Jesus' name let all our work be done" [*I Jesu Navn skal al vor Gjerning skje*].[142] So I begin my work again this year in Jesus' name."[143] With good reason she could start the New Year with gratitude. It had only been nine months since her arrival. She had many things for which to be thankful and proud. Because of the inclement weather, she, like many other Brooklynites, spent the first days of the New Year at home, glad for the rest. On

January 4, she went out on her rounds and came home to find a man with a wooden leg sitting at her door, "hungry, homeless, friendless, and without money." After she had fed him they went to find help, arm in arm."[144] As there had been a great snowstorm on Christmas Day—not all of which had yet melted—it was also slippery where they walked, and they had to be especially careful for him and his wooden leg. She got him help and came home, "weary in body and soul, although I know that 'The Lord is my Light and my salvation, whom then shall I fear, the Lord is the strength of my life, of whom shall I be afraid,'" quoting the comforting language of Psalm 27.[145]

Among other things that first fortnight of January, she went to visit the office of the Thingvalla line, not to look for people who needed her assistance, but to see if there was anyone there who could contribute to her mission, especially the superintendent of Castle Garden. She had grown more and more shrewd in her sense for where she could get gifts of money to support her work, and she did receive seven dollars. She also had to make sure that the pastors she was working with continued to approve of her, so she frequently was with them in their homes and also entertained them in her home—as she did on January 14, happy to see them all there.[146]

When they published the report for the preceding year, Sister Elisabeth could point to many successes. In her *Memoirs* she quoted an article from an unnamed newspaper:

> Not even two years from its beginning it already has its own place. Thirteen dollars a month are assured the home, and with the help of a smart, energetic deaconess, they have made a good beginning. There is only one institution we can compare it to and that is the Francke orphanage in Halle.[147]

Francke's orphanage established in Halle was still in the memory. It had been Fliedner's inspiration as well. The article went on to say how thankful they were for the people who supported the home with gifts of clothes, food, and money over the past year.

> The deaconess has made fifteen-hundred visits, helping both the sick and poor with all night watches, cleaning, binding up wounds, feeding, etc. One hundred and ten have received

Franke's Orphanage in Halle, Germany

clothes, eighteen brought to the hospital, six children to a children's home, therefore saved from physical and moral defeat.
Every week she has visited Ward's Island Hospital to help the
indescribable helplessness of emigrants without the ability to
speak or understand English.[148]

In addition, she had helped those unfortunates who needed passage
home, but who could not afford a return ticket. The article then went on
to say her more important mission was giving the people she met spiritual
help.

But what cannot be counted, but what has much greater significance than all the above: Only on the Day of the Lord will
it be revealed how much comfort in need, encouragement in
the downhearted, how much guidance she has given in difficulties and loving discipline to those in need.[149]

By now she could depend on Skougaard-Severini and the Børs for
support whenever she was strapped for cash. On January 15, she went to
the singer again. He gave her ten dollars which filled her with praise, but
more important to her was the warmth with which the singer had received
her with a generous gift:

Tired from the day's burdens I sit now wishing I had a thousand mouths and a thousand tongues in each mouth so that I could praise God for the good He does me.[150]

That was one day. Some days later she had to find a place for a boy and spent four days looking for the right place. When she found a place to leave him she shed many tears as she had to give him away. "O how hard that was!" she wrote.[151] Experience taught her that she could trust in the Lord to help her in the most difficult time. Such trust made it possible to assure those in need that something would turn up, which it usually did in remarkable ways. She realized this once again when she met a woman about to give birth; neither Fedde nor the mother had any baby clothes, but she promised the pregnant woman there would be some clothes in time. The very next day a woman brought a basket of children's clothing that fit the bill exactly, as Sister Elisabeth had prayed.[152] For this she praised the Lord.

Throughout much of the month of April 1884, she prepared for the bazaar that was to be held on April 17 at the Seamen's Mission Church. Her sewing circle helped her with this task, spending the days before it getting things ready, preparing what was to be sold, buying what they needed for entertainment. She did not record how much they made after all the work of organizing the event and cleaning up after it. She does record, however, that she was ill for several days afterward. Although she did her usual chores, on Sunday she lay sick, trying to recover her strength. Were these minor ailments or is she suffering already from the disease that will ultimately force her to retire? Given how hard she worked, without rest or relief, it is easy to imagine she would become run down and catch cold or other common illnesses such as the flu. Reading her diary and noting that on Sundays she did rest, it is easy to understand how vital a day of rest was for people at the time. Their work was difficult and physically depleting. A good day of rest was something she needed and got partly because of the strict sabbatarian observances of Fedde's pietist convictions which forbade even using a scissor on Sunday. She needed such a day of rest every week simply to keep going.

In addition to finding means to assist each and every needy person who came to her door, to the point of finding them a job, a place to stay, or money to help them with their living expenses, Sister Elisabeth, as a deaconess, frequently ministered to those who were dying. There she demonstrated her full knowledge of Scripture and also her sense for the human condition. If the dying person did not know Scripture, she gave them a verse to cling to. They most always knew John 3:16, "For God so loved the world that he gave his only begotten Son that whosoever believeth on him shall not perish but have eternal life." When that was not enough, she would urge them to remember another verse that she would give them to say as they were dying. As long as they had sense in their heads, they could say it, she would tell them. They would promise to repeat it. It was not always possible for her to be present at each death, given the number of people who needed her offices every day. One dying woman at Flatbush Hospital who knew no English rejoiced to see her so she could talk about her life, which she described as all sin. Fedde remembered the time in her life when she had felt that she was all sin and reminded her of the One who had poured the oil of grace on her sore wounds and witnessed to the Savior who went to his death for all sinners.

> Poor woman! She didn't even know a Bible passage she could cling to, nor a hymn verse, but I do believe she came as a penitent sinner at the eleventh hour. When I left her, she promised that as long as there was a thought in her mind she would turn it to prayer. 1 believe now she will be saved. Next morning she was dead.[153]

Passavant

These were all intense and exhausting experiences for Fedde, and she needed to find some way to relax. Rarely did she indicate that she took any excursions, but on May 31, 1884, around Ascension time, she and Mrs. Børs went to The Wartburg Orphans' Farm School of the Evangelical Lutheran Church near Pelham, New York, now Mount Vernon, in Westchester County. She took something of a holiday to check out the Farm School for children which, just that year had changed its name from the Deaconess Institution of the State of New York. Here they met Dr. Passavant who had founded the institution in 1860 as a Deaconess home. It was established with a generous gift from Peter Moller, who wanted to build a memorial for the son he had lost in the Civil War. Passavant had convinced him that an institution for orphans would be a more appropriate memorial than a statue or park. It was a place where Sister Elisabeth often placed orphans she found. Passavant, a shrewd judge of talent

Wartburg Orphans' Farm School in Mt. Vernon

and character, had noticed the young and energetic deaconess. It was a "great encouragement" for her own vocation to meet Passavant.[154] Passavant obviously knew enough about her work to recommend her to the Augsburg professors and pastors sitting together in Gjertsen's living room that September day in Minneapolis, 1888.

Another Deaconess

Fedde by now was realizing she needed more help not only from those giving money and supporting her with other gifts; she needed another deaconess. Her constitution seemed to have been quite sturdy, but a life of this much work and concern would certainly wear down the strongest person. She often noted without much comment that she had been sick in bed for a day or two. Still she would get up and return to her rounds. Each day she came upon more need and sorrow than most anyone could handle in a lifetime. In June 1884, on her weekly rounds, she visited Ward's Island and met eight Norwegians, two Danes, and three Swedes. One of the Norwegians was a woman alone with two children—one a four-year-old boy who had broken his leg on the ship where his father worked. The father had to return to his job and had to leave them in the hospital. When the mother heard that Fedde could speak her language, she burst into tears, "O how I have waited for you," she wept and told her the entire sorrowful saga.[155]

Immigrants waiting at Castle Garden

Fedde concluded, "There often is such great need that I am sure this is the [right] calling for me."[156]

At the July 30, 1884, meeting, the board discussed two significant issues: whether or not to begin a building fund for a hospital, and how they would get another deaconess. They voted to allow Sister Elisabeth to begin a building fund, which she did with a gift of $35. This was an important moment for the institution and for Fedde. It essentially changed her call. Now she was to build an institution, not operate on her own as an itinerant nurse and spiritual caregiver. She was shrewd enough to know that she had to have the complete support of board and the community before their plans could become a reality. First they had to find a good location and the means to buy the land where they could build a building.[157] Plus she would have to train more deaconesses to do the kind of work she was doing. That meant building a Motherhouse as well. They had written to the Motherhouse in Christiania asking for assistance in finding a deaconess who could help Sister Elisabeth. Prospects did not look good. The Norwegian Motherhouse, while approving of her work, had never really seen its mission one of supporting another Motherhouse in America. It had been with some trepidation that the board began to realize that the Motherhouse in Christiania could not be expected to help them. Still, they needed another deaconess as soon as possible. Their desperation seemed almost critical. Hansteen joked they were breaking the Tenth Commandment's injunction not to covet your neighbor's maidservant . . . or deaconess![158]

After some discussion, they agreed to accept the application of Othilie Marie Olsen (1850-1917) as a candidate. She was from Sandefjord, Norway. Sister Elisabeth had worked with her in Arendal just before she left for New York. Although not yet consecrated, she had applied to work as a deaconess with Sister Elisabeth. Since Miss Olsen had not been consecrated, she would have to finish her training in America. That made for a discussion on what they could do to train her, and whether or not they could consecrate her. Mrs. Børs remembered that Passavant had told them during their conversations that Americans had to train their own deaconesses, something they could begin with Miss Olsen's coming. With Fedde there, herself a consecrated deaconess, they determined that she could both teach the probationary sister the nursing skills as well as the art of soul care implicit in the deaconess calling.[159]

This is the beginning of their actual commitment to becoming a Motherhouse ready to train and consecrate deaconesses on their own. With thanksgiving to God they accepted her application and welcomed her to Brooklyn, waiting expectantly. Sister Elisabeth, using her connections with Captain Schierbeck and the Thingvalla line, negotiated a cheaper ticket for Miss Olsen. Fedde had shrewdly kept the connections with the captain for just this purpose. On May 16, 1885, the young woman was to arrive. To prepare for her they had to decide who and how the sister would be educated. This set up something of a battle among them as to who would be teaching the religion courses. Only after Everson was assured that he could teach the courses with equal status as the others did he support the decision.

Another deaconess was necessary. The needs of the people around Sister Elisabeth had become so demanding that even when she had scheduled a vacation she could not take it; something would come up that made it impossible for her to leave her post for any time at all. In addition, the board was beginning to assert its authority, especially Pastor Everson and his assistant Knut Seehus (1859-1953). Seehus had been called to Our Savior's Church in Manhattan that September. The congregation would move from Monroe Street in Manhattan to Brooklyn in 1885. Seehus also had attended Luther College and Concordia Seminary in St. Louis, since the Norwegian Synod at the time had not yet built its own seminary. While Seehus seemed to be a milder character than Everson, they both shared the same theological convictions and agreed on many things as the board began to establish protocols for working together, trying to establish procedures and rules for the fledgling organization. Over time, Fedde came to be impatient with Everson despite the time they had spent together, day after day, as he accompanied her on her visits. There is little sign of that friction in her summation of this year in her diary, however. What we see are the reasons for her exhaustion and lack of energy to record her daily tasks, while at the same time thanksgiving for what she has been able to accomplish and that each improvement brought more work:

One man sent to Norway, and many, many things that caused my vacation to begin on August 10 and end August 21, because a family's sickness and need were so great that I had to help. The woman full of boils, one child ill and the husband out of work—In the worst kind of need, and ill, so that it meant looking for work for the healthy one, finding a doctor for the sick, finding a hospital for a child, clothes for a lot of old people. Children to Sunday School, which 1 have each Sunday, and several hospital visits each week, always taken up by sick and poor. When one thing improves a little bit there are many new needs for body and soul. Seven patients were hospitalized with the Episcopal Sisters and some were there for a long time, now all are out and healthy. I got the last one placed with a good family. The weekly meetings of the Seamen's Mission, Deaconesses' Association, and a Bazaar in church, and each Friday to Ward's Island 1 have held to regularly, and many sick, poor, irresolute ones have been helped with food, clothing, homes, and medicine.[160]

1885

At the beginning of 1885, Sister Elisabeth began as usual in Jesus' name, praising God for steadfast help: "Hitherto has the Lord helped me." On this day she recorded that she had spent the day on the *Geiser* where she went regularly as it disembarked, finding countrymen who needed assistance, but also to enhance her acquaintance with the captain. The purpose of her visit on this day was to persuade the captain to grant cheap passage for the new Sister Othilie, coming soon from Norway. Sister Elisabeth had been out in the rain and cold the week before to get money from St. John's Guild "for my poor ones" and also to visit a Dr. Gornsey, a frequent contributor at Castle Garden who gave her two dollars and medicine. She continued to go to Castle Garden to find the sick and poor before they could be sent to Ward's Island Emigrant Hospital. This was also a good place to ask for money.[161]

Conflicts

While Sister Elisabeth's work had been growing, it was inevitable that the board would begin to have conflicts with her leadership style and her pragmatic ecumenism. She now began to record in her diary some difficulties with the board, thankful for the time she could spend with Pastor Hansteen, "my only supporter."[162]

At the January 20, 1885, board meeting, Pastor Carl Everson asked whether or not it was necessary to bring patients requiring hospitalization to Trinity Hospital, the Episcopal institution where she had forged an excellent working relationship. He wondered if it was "proper" since the "high-churchly Episcopal Church," he said, "spread its propaganda among the sick, thereby causing a loss of many souls from the Lutheran Church."[163] While this may have been an overreaction to the ability of the Episcopalians to make converts, it was a sensitive point with some Lutheran pastors as there had been a history of Episcopalians appealing to the Scandinavian immigrants to join them as they were very like the Lutherans but used English, the language the immigrants would need in order to flourish in the New Land.

Everson's suggestion, however, irritated other members of the board, especially Pastor Hansteen who objected since the Norwegians had no hospital and Trinity, an Episcopal hospital, generously took in the patients for nothing. The Lutheran Hospital (German) in New York, he implied, had not been welcoming to her. Hansteen suggested that since the Norwegians did not have the means yet to run a hospital, it made good sense to use Trinity.[164] As the discussion continued, it became apparent that the pastors did not like sending their people to the Episcopalians. They may have been somewhat suspicious of Muhlenberg's hospital, given his Lutheran history. Their people needed spiritual guidance as much as physical. It was the pastors' considered opinion that their people could not get Lutheran spiritual counsel at a hospital that was not Lutheran. Mrs. Børs felt that the longer they used other hospitals, the farther away they were from building their own. Sister Elisabeth, whose pragmatic sense was foremost, said "as long as she did not have her own hospital, and while they waited for one, she was happy to find place for a patient wherever she could."[165] Although Fedde thought Hansteen's argument the right one, she did not agree with his assessment of the Lutheran Hospital in New York, saying she had always been "received kindly" there. Her diary records many visits that both she and Everson had made to several hospitals in the area. There was no comment on which hospitals were friendly or not. She went to Trinity Hospital frequently and in fact had just been there with Everson.[166]

He however continued to oppose the idea that their people should be sent to hospitals that belonged to another confession and made a motion to that effect. All but Hansteen voted for it. Then the question was which hospital was available? After much discussion, the board resolved, finally, to empower Sister Elisabeth to judge whichever hospital was best for each situation, and then notify the board at once.[167] That evening in her diary she lamented the conflict on the board. She spent the evening with Pastor Hansteen, a steadfast and trustworthy friend who would comfort her after the conflicts on the board began to take their toll on her constitution. "Sick in body and soul," she wrote on January 20 after the board meeting. "Had to get out. Two sick calls, and am almost despondent, but your Word, my God, will keep me alive. . . . God can help me hold out."[168] The next day she noted that she had not slept much during the night, but then described all that she had done that day: First she had gone to be consoled by Mrs. Børs, and then to a prison, then to see four patients on Long Island, followed by a visit to a dying woman, then to Trinity Hospital to help someone who was sick. She reserved a wagon driver (probably a hearse) for her. "Terribly weary and teary."[169] Her diary does not record the growing tension specifically between Everson and her. Hansteen seems to have been the person to whom she could turn to find refuge from the conflicts. He strengthened her on many occasions as did Mrs. Børs, whom she described as "matchless. God, you must bless her!"[170] On February 22 she was with the single Hansteen for dinner. After their repast she went with him to hear a Salvation Army service which she judged to be a lot of commotion with its drums and loud bands.[171]

She regarded the growing controversies on the board as a nuisance, but heartrending, a grief she shared with the consul and his wife. Once Børs told her when she came to him for a donation that the work was always necessary but indicated his weariness with the argumentative Norwegians. "I have said to my wife that it is all in vain to do anything for the Norwegians here. There will never be harmony. What one builds up another tears down," he said. "There is always something. Just give up."[172] Sister Elisabeth had to agree that it was hard, but would not hear of giving up, remarking how many times his gifts of five to ten dollars had journeyed from his pocket to hers, making it possible for her to do good with it. As she went around on her visits, she often had to go from morning to night without rest or food, doing difficult work. After finishing with the delivery of a child, she sighed, "It has been my lot to function as doctor, midwife, nurse, washerwoman, cleaning lady, pastor, and reliever of the poor."[173] In these few words, she described the vocation of a deaconess at its most holistic—intense, spiritually, and physically demanding.

When she would come home there would frequently be several requests on the chalkboard she had hanging outside her door. These she would answer immediately, no matter how weary she was. One brought her into a cellar where there were several children with a poor mother and husband who was too ill to work. They had nothing but some cold boiled potatoes, so she emptied her pocket, thinking she had more money in her purse, and told the woman to go buy all the food she could with the money she gave her. She would stay with the husband and children and clean the house while she was gone. When the mother returned with food for the family, Sister Elisabeth promised to return the next day. She then began her long journey home. Then she realized she did not have even a nickel in her purse for the trolley. So she began the long walk home, against the blizzard that had come while she was helping the family. Somewhat despondent, she began her walk singing stanza 5 of the hymn, "I Walk in Danger All the Way" (*Jeg gaar i fare hvor jeg gaar*).

> I walk with Jesus all the way,
> His guidance never fails me;
> Within his wounds I find a stay
> When Satan's pow'r assails me,
> With Jesus there to lead,
> My path I safely tread.
> In spite of ills that threaten me,
> I walk with Jesus all the way.

One trolley after another passed her by. When she came to the above stanza, a trolley stopped. The driver told her to get in. When she said, "I do not have the money," the driver said, "Come in. This is not a night for a lady to be out!" When she boarded the car, she told him that this night the Lord had used him as his servant. He replied that he had heard an inner voice say to him, "Take her in." Elisabeth noted in her *Memoirs* that afterward "I felt the Lord was so near and I so strong because I knew that he would always help me in my struggles."[174] She marveled at God's care for her in her most challenging times.

Beginning a Hospital

Although she had become quite shrewd in finding other institutions to take care of the sick and needy, it was not enough. The current site on Williams Street had only two beds, a rudimentary kitchen, and a hallway.

She needed help from another sister to make home visits. With a hospital and Motherhouse, she could educate more deaconesses to help her. This was coming to be a high priority because it not only meant she would have more help, but their work could also be extended with every new deaconess. Although Muhlenberg's Episcopal Motherhouse in New York educated deaconesses, with something of a Lutheran connection, after the conversations with the board she well knew that what her supporters wanted were Norwegian Lutheran deaconesses. One day at the sewing circle, as she finished a pillow case, she held it up and said, "Let us begin sewing such things for our hospital!" The women protested, "We can't start that yet!" But Mrs. Maria Flood, whose husband was a board member, who supported Elisabeth with gifts of money as well as prayer and handiwork, laughed and said, "I think I see Sister Elisabeth's hospital!" Soon they all began sewing for what would become The Norwegian Lutheran Deaconess Home and Hospital.[175]

The fate of women who needed refuge and who had no place to go was always a concern for Sister Elisabeth, who had realized the urgent necessity for a larger building after taking in a girl who had been sent to America from the Christiania prison. Fedde had to take the consequences of the Norwegian law when the women fled to America. Because of her, Sister Elisabeth had no bed on which to sleep except the floor for several weeks. Finding a larger place was urgent. Despite being ill at the beginning of February and experiencing great weariness, she continued searching for a house appropriate for her work.[176] With the help of Pastors Mortensen, Hansteen, and Seehus she went looking for houses to rent, one they could turn into a hospital.

On February 6, she noted that after a visit to Ward's Island, she had gone with Mortensen to look at a house that might be suitable for a hospital. Mortensen had advertised in the January 28, 1885, *Brooklyn Daily Eagle* for a small house that could be rented for two sisters of charity with permission to take in sick, but not contagious, persons. Mrs. Børs and Mrs. Flood were also looking to find a suitable location that could serve as something of a hospital. By the end of February they had found an apartment they could rent at 441 Fourth Avenue. She spent the last days of the month preparing to move and getting the house ready for its new purpose. On February 27, she went to the house and prepared for

Norwegian clock brought by Fedde from Norway to America

the drayman to come. He did not arrive since he had expected rain. She could do nothing but sleep on the floor that night, which understandably put her in a bad mood. "A terrible day!" she concluded. Although she had few worldly possessions, she had accumulated enough that it surprised her when they had to move it: old furniture from Mrs. Børs, a sofa, kitchenware, and other necessary things. She had received a lovely table clock from Pastor Hansteen for the first Christmas in the house, a coffee set from Alfred Bryhn which was white with a green pot. "When one of them broke," she said, at one of the many events where she served coffee, "it was as if she had lost a friend."

When she stood in the empty house looking at the walls which had been witness to all the troubles of the past two years, she was glad they could not speak. While her diary contains many expressions of her sorrow and despair at the conflicts on the board, this is a revealing comment. As many of the tributes say at the end of her life, she seemed to be someone who saw things with good cheer and hope. Either she was good at hiding these feelings and confiding them only to her diary or she had changed so much toward the end of her career that most did not remember these times in that same light.

Years later she remembered the day she had moved as a time mixed with fear and hope. As she was writing her memoirs, at least twenty years later, reflecting on what she thought those times now meant, she gives a more mellow view. What would the future hold, she had wondered, looking around her first home

A moving company advertisement in the Nordisk Tidende, *the Norwegian paper in Brooklyn*

as she left it, thinking, "How many tears had fallen and so many prayers sent up to my heavenly Father who sees in secret. The Norwegian Deaconess work in Brooklyn is living proof his promises could be fulfilled."[177]

The First Hospital

March 1, 1885, was a beautiful day for the dedication of the hospital. Sister Elisabeth prayed, "Oh, God let this house be to your glory and to the salvation of souls!" The larger accommodation had nine beds,

First hospital in 1885 with Sister Elisabeth at the bottom of the steps with a woman, most likely Mrs. Børs

so they could take in several patients at a time. Although it was still very rudimentary as a hospital, this date came to be regarded as the official beginning of the Norwegian Lutheran Deaconess Hospital in Brooklyn. While she had affection for the house on Williams Street (today Pioneer Street), she was glad for the new place, especially now that the old building could be used as a home for sailors run by Magnus Anderson. "Oh, God, let it be to your honor and let all the work be done in Jesus' name and for Jesus' sake. I pray that our house and all in it may be to his glory and that men might praise thee for it."[178]

The new establishment was so lavishly furnished by Mrs. Børs that Sister Elisabeth fretted that the poor might feel uncomfortable there. Mrs. Børs, however, had insisted on red plush parlor chairs to brighten up the hospital. With the money she had received, Sister Elisabeth bought nine iron bedsteads (considered the best way to fight bedbugs because heat could be used to kill the pests). Among other things, she had convinced an American doctor to agree to work in the hospital for free. She was now ready to admit her first patient, an unfortunate woman, Mrs.

Juhl, a sea captain's wife who had sailed with him. Finally her health required that she be sent ashore. The ship's doctor knew of Sister Elisabeth's work and sent for her to come to take the dying woman into her care. Sister Elisabeth brought her to the new hospital. The captain's wife on arriving and taking to the fresh clean bed commended Elisabeth and prayed that God would bless her and her work for all time and eternity.[179]

As the hospital began its work, she happened to be in New York on a visit to the ferries there. Two captains were talking on one ferry as she came from the other one. One, a Captain Hofstead[180] whom she described as a good friend of her Christian work, told the other, "There is our deaconess." "Oh, no," replied the other. "Not another mouth to feed," thinking of her as a parasite, "We have enough with our pastors." Then Hofstead told him all the things a deaconess did for people. "No one can know when one will need her." The scoffer was skeptical and said he wanted to have nothing

Seaman's Mission Church parsonage

to do with such people. A week after she had overheard this conversation, an American woman came to her and said that a Norwegian man who rented a room from her had not been seen for a couple of days. When she went into his room to check on him, he lay in the bed, lame on one side from a stroke and could not speak well enough to be understood. He had lain without help for two days. When he saw her, his eyes filled with tears. He had been the captain of the ferry who had scoffed at having to feed another mouth. She had to change his wet bed and wash him like a little baby. He took his left hand, which he could use and patted her while weeping. She came to him every day for a long time, she said. As he became better and could speak, he regretted his comment."[181]

Meanwhile, they were getting ready for another bazaar. The success of this fundraising activity raised increasingly bitter discussions among the pastors, especially the games of chance that were usually part of the bazaar. Fedde's diary and *Memoirs* begin to lament the conflicts she was having with the board on this matter. She did not suffer fools and much preferred working alone rather than with others. Boards were new to her, and she found it difficult to adjust to their control. In Tromsø she had worked with a board, doctor and another deaconess. Here things were somewhat different. She was alone. Like many people of her energy and vision, she preferred doing it her way and under her own powers, even if her physical work was crushing.

She was beginning to dread the more frequent board meetings. The move to a bigger place also increased her work: more rooms meant more patients, which meant the need for more deaconesses, which meant the need for more organization, which meant the need for more money—on and on.

In the middle of this work, on March 16, she received a letter from Passavant asking her to take over the work at one of his deaconess houses, probably in Pittsburgh.[182] She merely records in her diary that she had received the letter, but says nothing much about what she thought of it or whether she was flattered by it. One wonders if this came out of the blue or if she had been exploring a new call. Passavant, the Davy Crockett of Lutheran home mission, always exploring new places and ideas for Lutheran expansion in the United States, had seen in her someone he could use. She had been in communication with him previously and had written him a letter on February 11 of that year, according to her diary, but on what issue we do not know. Passavant knew talent when he saw it and had encouraged her previously when she and Mrs. Børs had visited him. It encouraged her to know of his confidence in her.

Despite all the tasks involved in settling into the new building, she still continued her usual round of activities. In addition to getting curtains and pillow feathers, buying carpets, sewing them and laying them down, stitching and hanging curtains, she interviewed a doctor with Pastor Mortensen and Dr. Turner, trying to find one whom the home might hire.[183] After such a week, she confided in her diary that she was "exceedingly tired." In addition to all of these extraordinary tasks of settling into a new house, life went on with its ordinary duties such as cleaning her apartment, washing clothes, and hosting ladies aid. That Sunday she enjoyed time with Siqueland learning English. Afterward, at the evening service, she heard what she described as a lovely sermon by her "dear" Hansteen "all about what Jesus has done for us. Later we spent a cozy time with Hansteen."[184] She was also collecting things for the coming bazaar on April 10.

The goal of this event was to help the children. She had heard from many people as she walked around Brooklyn that people wanted their children to have a religious school they could attend. For her the mere suggestion of such a project was a clear call she could answer. She rented a room in a nearby Methodist church where they could meet. She scheduled the Sunday school for Sunday afternoon. To her surprise, thirty-two children came. She gathered them around the small organ, and they began by singing the traditional beginning hymn of the Norwegian church, *"I Jesu Navn."*[185] She decided to teach Bible history and the catechism. After the hymn, she prayed that the school would be a blessing for all. She then gave a little lesson on baptism, for she wanted the children to learn that through their baptism they had come into a covenant with God. They sang another hymn, and she spoke briefly and wrote their names down in a book. Sunday school was also a part of the Innermission program from its beginning in Norway some decades before. Hansteen would later write a book on how to establish a Sunday school with a sample curriculum in it, so her work in this venue was entirely predictable and understandable to the community.[186]

She did it as part of her call, without seeming to think a minute about it, and prayed that the work would be for the glory of God and nothing else. An elderly American woman from the Methodist church heard her praying and the children singing Norwegian hymns. At the end of the session, she told Elisabeth that although she had not understood a word of what was going on, she understood that Sister Elisabeth was bringing the children into relationship with God. For that she gave her $2.00. It was enough for the deaconess to continue this work with the children, as many of the deaconesses did when they chose not to be nurses. When he saw this, Pastor Hansteen wrote to the Seamen's Mission Board headquartered in Bergen and asked them to approve her use of the Seamen's Mission Church for the time being. It was agreed that the Sunday school could meet in its space as long as she was the superintendent. This arrangement lasted until 1896 when she returned home to Norway. Soon there were over 130 children coming to the Sunday school, taught by volunteer teachers. At the time it was the only Norwegian Sunday school in Brooklyn.

Inside the Seaman's Mission Church in Brooklyn

This Sunday school was only a part of her work with children, given what she decried as the failures even of women to raise their children responsibly, mostly because of drunkenness. Children's homes, or orphanages, were also entirely consistent with her Innermission and deaconess background. If parents could not be encouraged to improve their lives and had abandoned their own children or subjected them to abuse that caused them to run away, she tried to find them better homes or place them in a children's home, at least until their parents could care for them. She was most partial to the Staten Island Children's Home, but only those children whose fathers had sailed in an American ship qualified to be taken in. She made good connections with other children's homes in the New York area so she could bring children there from troubled homes. It grieved her when she had to do so if the mother could not support the children and did not want to give them up, but had to. One of the saddest for her was when she discovered a ship captain's widow who could not support her children. She had no other option but to give the boys to the home as her birthday present to them. As they took the ferry back to the city, the mother, a well-educated women, according to Sister Elisabeth, said, with tears falling down her face, that it was her birthday, and her birthday present was to be separated from her boys. She felt that there was a kindly woman in charge of the place and that the boys would be happy. Elisabeth said, "Dear woman, you can come and get them any time" in an effort to comfort her, but could scarcely keep from weeping herself. "Yes," the mother answered, "that is true, but it is so hard." After they left the boys, on their way home, they were both quiet. "It had not been like a trip to the cabin," she concluded. Bringing children to such a place, however, was not always sad for her. Later, Elisabeth noted, the woman got much joy from her boys. Many children found good homes and better lives because of this work.[187]

Recruiting New Deaconesses

At the end of March, Sister Elisabeth attended a Bible study with the seamen's pastors which she thought was very good, but found it troubling to her conscience. "Oh, what a poor Christian I am!"[188] Self-examination was part of her piety, and it is one of the better parts of her; thinking one might be wrong is a good characteristic for one to have, especially one as powerful as Sister Elisabeth. It is important to remember how important Kierkegaard, especially his books *On Self-Examination* and *Works of Love*, was for the deaconess communities. Mother Guldberg had read extensively from his works to the sisters many times.

Fedde's troubles with the board sent her to confide in Mrs. Børs, whom she worried she had upset with her tales of woe. Not only was she sick at heart, but the strain caused by the move had debilitated her more than usual. She spent Easter Sunday with her sister Marie and Gabriel Fedde and their family, whose children, Bernhard Andreas (1877-1955), Adolf Arne Samuel (1879-1954), and Gabriel Martin Nathanael (1894-1953), she enjoyed. (Bernhard would become a doctor at the deaconess hospital and Nathanael a medical missionary to China.) She found the time a rest for her soul, something she needed as she "was tired of everything."[189] Her exhaustion may well have been caused by her having to face another board meeting on April 7, 1885. Despite her good experiences ministering to the poor and sick, the conflicts on the board were becoming more and more stressful as board members and Sister Elisabeth struggled to find a way they could work together. The board realized it needed more organization and structure for its deliberations and elected a committee to write a constitution and by-laws. First the group chose the name: Norwegian Relief Society; second, its purpose—to help needy and suffering countrymen; third, their denomination—Evangelical Lutheran (that they chose not to align themselves with any of the Norwegian

Lutheran Synods that defined Norwegian-American Lutheran life in the Midwest may have been caused by Sister Elisabeth's fear that it would become entangled in theological debates the pastors were having); and fourth, the membership should consist of "communicating" (people who attend communion) members of the Evangelical Lutheran Church.[190] The minutes record that a long discussion ensued on what "constituted a communicating member." They decided it was a person who a) belonged to the Evangelical Lutheran Church and b) lived a Christian life.[191] This was consistent with the Lutheran pietism that drove the deaconess movement and the founders of the hospital and Motherhouse, but it is somewhat different from what one might have expected Everson or Seehus to have agreed to. In some ways they were responding to the success of the Norwegian Methodist mission in Brooklyn that had started a bit before the Seamen's Mission Church had begun. Sailors may have preferred the lively worship of the Methodists, although they yearned for the worship of the Norwegian Lutheran church at festival times, especially Christmas. Here we are seeing what David Mauk has pointed to in his book: the demands from the seamen that the ministry be ecumenical and open to all, with light applications of Lutheran dogma, set against the dogmatic pastors like Everson and Seehus who represented the theological convictions of the Norwegian Synod. Both Gabriel and Elisabeth Feddes' more pietistic backgrounds tended to move in the direction of a genial ecumenism that found unity in Christ, not doctrinal statements. As we have seen in her practices, a common Lord and a common purpose made it possible for her to serve more people and share her tasks with Methodists, Catholics, Episcopalians, and other ethnic Lutherans without insisting on doctrinal uniformity. This was a new issue for Norwegians as well—who had little experience in their homelands with people of different confessions. The American scene tested these commitments as they moved to become a hospital for all people in Brooklyn.

After coming to some agreement on how the board should be constituted, it then discussed Sister Elisabeth's place in the structure of the board. Was she to be a voting member? How did she see herself in the organization? These questions were important to answer. It cannot be forgotten that the work of Fedde in her time was a completely new role for a woman. Watching these people struggle to understand her place and role in the work gives us a unique window into the lives of women trying to move into a public profession for the first time. Sister Elisabeth had a public role. She was the leader of the hospital and soon the Motherhouse. She had to report to the board as any leader of an organization would, but she was also a woman, and dealing with a woman in such a role was a new thing for both the men and Fedde. How was she to relate to the board? How should they "protect her, guide her, even restrict her," and yet give her the authority she needed for the work? It is worth considering their struggles with these new issues as we watch them trying to find answers to these questions. Hansteen, whose distant cousin, the painter Aasta Hansteen, was one of Norway's earliest feminists, favored women's rights. Later in the early 1900s, back in Norway, he would hire a woman to be an administrator of the Innermission society. He thought it was to be understood that Fedde have voting rights as a board member. After her comments as to how she saw her own vocation as the head sister, the discussion continued. Since she thought of herself as doing mission work, she saw things differently than they did, probably because she wanted to do what seemed necessary at the moment in order to enhance the mission, not get caught up in burdensome rules and procedures which obviously irritated her. In addition, she had a different place in the structure because her position kept her closest to the work which she knew better than they.

Pastor Everson worried that it would not be quite appropriate for Sister Elisabeth to be a voting member since she was both management and employee, what we today would call a conflict of interest. After further conversation and information about the management of the Motherhouse in Christiania, and how Mother Guldberg and Pastor Julius Bruun managed to work together, Everson expressed concern about a potential scandal developing if people should hear that the "deaconess, the hired servant, now wishes to be the ruler."[192] Sister Elisabeth not surprisingly took this as a direct and irritating challenge to her authority. One wonders if this is about his reaction to her as a woman or his concern for the appearance of a conflict of interest, language they did not use at the time, but which he seems to be aware of and eager to avoid. Secondly, and this seems to have been a deepening concern, they suggested that if she was going to be a leader in the institution it was incumbent upon her to join a congregation in the city. Since among Lutherans she was considered almost an equal to the pastors with her consecration and her public service being very like that of a pastor, she had to observe certain protocols, they seemed to believe. Did she think of herself as a member of the Seamen's Mission Church, which, she could argue, as a Norwegian citizen she was. Her reluctance to join a Brooklyn congregation could be more evidence of the divisions among the groups represented on the board—whether they were serving Norwegian sailors on their way through New York or Norwegians who were settling in the city and making it their home? This seems to have addressed something that the pastors had been simmering about, but there is very little in the record to help us understand what the problem was. Fedde did not think of herself as an American. She often referred to herself as a Norwegian working in America. She was not an immigrant and thus not interested in joining an American church. Several times she expressed the hope that she could die in Norway and be buried there. Joining a congregation, other than the Seamen's Mission Church in Brooklyn, may have seemed to her to be too much commitment to staying in America permanently— something she did not seem interested in.

This meeting seems to have exacerbated a disagreement which esca-lated at every succeeding meeting. Everson was becoming more and more disturbing to Fedde, especially his insistence on certain well-established protocols which were not unreasonable, but were made in a way that she could only interpret as hostile to her person and work. To their credit, in some way, the men were coming to understand that it was difficult for Sister Elisabeth to work with only one woman, Mrs. Børs, on the board to befriend her and understand her ways as a woman. This is an interesting awareness on their part. Having a woman as a professional colleague was utterly new for them, as being one in an equal relation-ship with men must have been for her. How did men and women work together professionally? Did it mean giving up on the understandings they had for generations about the place of women in relationship to men? Could a woman function in a public role working under the su-pervision of men without her input? The pastors were well aware of the increasing participation of women in the societies that supported them. Hansteen especially knew this from his involvement with both the Innermission and Sunday school organizations.[193] Women at this time were working successfully to achieve leadership and voting rights in mission organizations and other para-church organizations both in Norway and America. They won those rights years before they did in the civil sphere in Norway, winning the right to speak and vote in meetings of the Inner-mission and Sunday school organizations in 1905. This was some before Norway granted universal suffrage in 1913. Something of the same obtained among the Norwegian-Americans as well, especially among the mission circles where women organized national women's organizations to support missions and in several cases even got a vote in the local congregations.

While the deaconess movement may well have been one of the first places women could enter a profession in the society, the pastors on the boards had complete control of the programs and activities of the deaconesses in all the Motherhouses. Although the deaconesses, especially the Sister Superior in each location whom the boards worked with over time, accumulated a great deal of personal and spiritual authority, and the men listened to and respected them, it did not come easy for the pastors and board members of that day to relinquish their authority to a woman, even a powerful deaconess. One can examine the speeches at the conference of the Evangelical Lutheran Deaconess Motherhouses held from 1896-1913 and find not one contribution by a deaconess. All the theological talk about Christian service and how the deaconesses should obey the boards is a one-way conversation without the voice of any deaconess—at least publicly. In all their papers and conferences only men spoke. (By 1904 the Kaiserswerth Principles did suggest that a Sister Superior could be on the board with voting priviledges where possible. See Appendix 2, II , 1.)

The idea that the Motherhouse was a home with the rules of the home began to clash with the increasing sense of independence that women in other Christian organizations were achieving. It would grow continually more difficult and cause several explosions we will see later. The requirement of obedience to the board and the Sister Superior, especially in America where the frontier still beckoned to both young men and women, was difficult to enforce. To criticize the men or women for not quite understanding how to act in this newly developing system is to miss what a moment this was. Kristin Norseth has written about this in her thesis on the leadership of Norwegian women in the Christian organizations of the nineteenth century. The deaconess position was perhaps the most complex compared to the other leadership roles to which women aspired. As Norseth notes, it was clear that the deaconess was under the pastor in her spiritual work and under the doctor in her medical vocation.[194] Neither position gave them much freedom.

The Hardest Meeting of All

At the April 7 meeting, some of these concerns must have surfaced since several on the board wondered if the people of Brooklyn could accept that a woman could have such a position of authority, something the group quickly dismissed. The board in Brooklyn understood something of the problem and chose to deal with it in the best way they could. Among the recommendations they made was to include women on the board, so they could counsel Fedde and help her from a woman's point of view, which they did very soon. In any event, it is surprising that things went as well as they did, given the strong personalities involved. Thus the board appointed three women to the board: Mrs. Anna Børs, Mrs. Marie Flood, and Mrs. Christine Møller. Sister Elisabeth was not elected to the board.

This argument went on for some time. It was not about women voting, it was about Sister Elisabeth's relation to the board. She wanted both voice and vote in the board, arguing that she had been essentially running the institution alone all this time and, with the exception of Mrs. Børs, none on the board had given her any help. (This was somewhat unfair of her, given that they had helped

The Seaman's Mission Church (with parsonage on the right)

her, but in the heat of the exchange it can be understood.) Because she had given much of herself to found the ministry, it "seemed impossible that she would not have the vote."[195] This argument left Pastor Knut Seehus, the Norwegian Synod pastor, cold. In his position as leader of the Board for Immigrants he had never needed to have an official voice in the management or board. Even Mrs. Børs appears to have agreed with this, commenting that Sister Elisabeth already had so much power in the organization it was difficult to see why she could feel that she did not have enough authority. They asked Fedde to respond. She wondered if having the position of manager of the company could result in her being dismissed, which those present reminded her was not allowed in the newly adopted by-laws. At this Sister Elisabeth expressed the desire not to have the proposal that she be given voting rights upheld. The board adjourned, but it is easy to see the relationship with Fedde and the board, especially Everson, was not going well. One of the things we see here also is typical of the life of any institution founded by a strong leader and entrepreneur. Conflicts arise in organizations such as this when boards try to assert their responsibilities to develop the policy of the organization. The founder almost always finds it difficult to give over her ownership of the enterprise to a board because she could see either its lack of vision or its attack on her vision and control. For Sister Elisabeth the April 7, 1885, meeting of the board was a terrible day: "It is the hardest day I have experienced while in America. . . . The entire board is against me, and I have even upset my friend Hansteen. I wish I could die!"[196] After the meeting, the record of the board meetings went silent for some time, although Sister Elisabeth's diary continued. We can see that it was a moment in which the board and Sister Elisabeth had to face difficult questions that changed their relationship in the future.

Her only remedy for these feelings of dejection and weariness was prayer and time away. She wisely chose to spend some time enjoying the advantages of the city.

> Raining out in Nature and in my unclean soul, darkness and gloom so I decided to see Barnum's show, which for the past month I have desired to see. Oh, what a wonder of the Creator to produce all this! Oh, God, how I must thank you for all you have given me beyond that of so many other creatures![197]

At the time the elephant Jumbo, who had created a sensation on tours around the country with the Barnum Circus, was performing in the Old Madison Square Garden. It had obviously filled her with wonder, a good thing for her. The time away from the daily work gave her something she knew she needed: another perspective on her own life. Her expressions of sorrow about her trouble with the board and her sense that she needed spiritual counsel for her despondency caused by her exhaustion show us once again the struggles she had with her own character as she saw her own problems in getting along with others more clearly. How was she to manage these conflicts? She understood the struggle between the old self and the new going on in her own heart, and watched closely to see that she was not always justifying herself. She seems to have been well aware of her own besetting sins.

Board Troubles

The board entered a period of protracted conflict partly because of the way it was organized and the individuals on the board. Mrs. Børs, Hansteen, and the new seamen's Pastor Kristian Sårheim (1857-1909) represented the Norwegian faction, while Everson and the two women from his congregation, Mrs. Flood and Mrs. Møller, represented the churchly faction that believed the settlers were the ones to control the board.[198] While this is superficially the division, and it was profound, there were also the two very different pieties at work here: Everson and his Norwegian Synod, pro-Missourian theology vs. pietism represented by the Feddes which cut in different ways across the board, pitting Everson and his congregational members against all the rest.

Kristian Sårheim

The important thing to see is that this did not stop Fedde, no matter how much grief she felt over these conflicts. The new hospital, which would be dedicated in June, gave her more responsibilities, one of them serving as the attending nurse during surgery. As always, her success caused her to have more work. This is a common problem for many entrepreneurs: When they find themselves to be successful at their initial project, they naturally have to expand what they have to do, only to find themselves unable to manage to do the work they love. Like many people as driven as she was, she could lose herself in her work, but she finally was not physically capable of doing everything that the new institution required.

In addition to caring for the patients in the hospital, she still continued with the original purpose of her call: to help the sick and needy. One job that occupied her now and then was helping some Norwegians with passage back to Norway, a frequent concern of the Norwegian Relief Society. She spent several days looking for cheap passage back to old country for a Mrs. Bernhard, with whom she spent valuable time at the Thingvalla ticket office trying to get her a cheap ticket to Hull.[199] In addition to this their first patient, the ship captain's wife, Mrs. Juhl, was dying and Elisabeth had to arrange for the burial, getting a wagon to take her body. It was their first death in the new facility. Sister Elisabeth had to wash the body, prepare it for the undertaker, make it ready for reviewal, buy flowers for the funeral, go to the funeral, and see to the burial a couple of days later, on April 26. All the while she and Pastor Everson were buying furniture for the new hospital.[200]

With many more home visits and visits to Trinity Hospital in New York with Pastor Everson, she ended the month with a sigh, "Now the month is over with all its troubles past and all in oblivion, though not all!"[201] One might call her frame of mind at this time the result of burn-out. She had overextended her physical powers, partly caused by the successes of her dream and the conflicts of the board. She was exhausted.

On May 1, during the traditional day of prayer and repentance, she found great comfort in Hansteen's sermon with its exhortation to repentance and prayer, but her diary contains a tantalizing comment. While she continued to care for the sick on this day, she also regretted the hard "divorce" from her friend Bryhn, "who is so dear to me. God protect him!"[202] This was Alfred Bryhn who, with the dentist Theodore Siqueland, had agreed to teach her English. Had they had a disagreement? The name is almost illegible as is her entry. He did not leave Brooklyn, at least forever. Did he leave her? Were they beginning a romantic relationship? The record is not clear. While there is no sense she was engaged to her future husband, Ole Slettebø, there are some hints that she and Ole had discussed marriage, but I think those comments are made in hindsight, after her marriage to him. Her comment on losing Bryhn may mean simply that a very dear friend was moving away, and she was losing a good

Mrs. Børs

friend and supporter. The next Sunday, on May 3, she took communion, having prepared for it on the yearly day of prayer and repentance traditional to Lutherans at this time. While she does not record its consolations, she had experienced comfort from Hansteen's exhortations.

On May 13, Fedde visited Mrs. Børs, who was leaving on a trip, to bid her farewell before she left. "There she stood," wrote Sister Elisabeth, "holding out her hand, throwing roses to me. I brought one to a dying patient who rejoiced in it, and said, 'Now found is the fairest of Roses,' (*Den yndigste Rose er funden*), Jesus, who is now all for him, yes, the sweetest Name."[203] This is a reference to one of the great Danish hymn writers, Hans Adolph Brorson (1694-1764), whose beloved Christmas hymn worked for funerals as well as Christmas. The dying man was quoting stanza seven:

> My Jesus will always be for me,
> This rose is my jewel and my glory,
> Forever my keepsake and treasure,
> It fills me with joy and with pleasure.

Brorson was the preferred hymn writer of the Haugean awakening and part of the spiritual furniture of their minds. She quotes his hymns on several occasions and this hymn chosen by the dying man to express his joy in Jesus, the Rose, is the pearl of Brorson's work. These words gave them the language with which to meet the extreme moments in their lives, especially death. Sister Elisabeth frequently attended such moments with both the Bible and hymns and this scene shows us much about the resources they had at the ready when they met sorrow and suffering.

The New Sister Arrives

The next day, Ascension Day, May 14, which was also a day of rest in the Norwegian civil calendar, Sister Elisabeth stayed home, sick again. Although she could not go out, she did have strength enough to write letters. On Friday, May 15, 1885, with joy and relief, Sister Elisabeth met the new probationary sister Othilie Olsen on board the *Island,* the Thingvalla ship with joy and thanksgiving. "God bless her going out and her coming in," she prayed, "from now to eternity for your own sake and make her your servant in Spirit and Truth.[204] Our meeting was joyful." "I embraced her in Jesus' name and welcomed her with a full heart and thanked God for sending her."[205] The day ended happily as the pastors and their families enjoyed a "cozy evening" of mutual rejoicing as they gathered as "God's children." With the new probationary sister, she could now be relieved of more than the basic nursing duties she had fulfilled on her own with everything else, raising money and working in other ways to support the mission of her hospital.[206]

By the beginning of June, she had new sorrows along with her joy at having the new sister with her, and quoted again one of her Great-grandmother Dancke's favorite hymns by Kingo: "Sorrow and Gladness they wander together" (*Sorgen og gladjen de vandre tilhobe*). "It is true that they come together," she noted, "and God has his purposes in all things," but for fourteen days after the arrival of her new sister, she had been so sick she had to stay in bed the entire time. "Now, I can look back and see the bad that has happened and rejoice in the arrival of my dear sister for I have had help the entire time." Because the new sister had arrived, she was able to rest, and it may be that with the coming of Sister Othilie she gave herself permission to be sick and simply get some rest, something she needed desperately. The new deaconess could take care of a patient they had just admitted to occupy one of the free beds the board had approved. "God let it be to the blessing of all!" she prayed.[207]

In addition to the new deaconess who could now help take care of patients, they also needed to find doctors. They had been using the services of Drs. Henry Turner and James McManus. Dr. Turner was considered the head of the medical department at the hospital, and his biography indicates he was a man of many accomplishments. Elisabeth consulted with him frequently. "I went several places to buy things for the home, patients to care for and much to organize and a long talk with the doctor about the home."[208] With the expansion of the work, and the increasing need for funds, the financial accountability of the ministry became more crucial to the board. Because it had ruled that there should be six paying patients for three non-paying, Fedde had to determine how to manage that to the board's satisfaction. Fedde's diary now reports the difficulties of finding free beds for needy people. The board had told her she had to keep track of this and get the approval of the chair, something she disliked having to do. Many people came to her for free help, and needed it, like a young girl whom she had to send away to another place, even if she returned in great need. This grieved Sister Elisabeth.[209] After a trip to Ward's Island on June 5, where she found three sick Norwegians, especially one girl, she came back to a full house, everyone needing her help. Suddenly she had to leave to take care of someone in a private home and did not return until later that evening. She was weary in both body and soul.[210]

Dedication and Sister Othilie

June 14, 1885, was a fine June day in Brooklyn, known as Rose Sunday, or children's day. Most every church in the area celebrated children with processions. Roses bedecked the churches. The children received roses, and the sermons which were reported on in detail in the paper spoke of the importance of raising children well. Henry Ward Beecher in his Rose Sunday sermon attacked the old cruel doctrine, as he called it, of original sin, which said children were born sinners, a doctrine the venerable divine said he hated. He loved the truth, he proclaimed, so he loved God and his fellow man.[211] Across town from where Beecher was dilating on love, the little Norwegian hospital and now Motherhouse was being dedicated to its works of love in the colony. It was also the day they received Othilie as a probationary sister. This was a small beginning for the Motherhouse. Pastor Andreas Mortensen preached to a sanctuary filled with people on 2 Corinthians 6:1-10, "Behold, now is the favorable time; behold, now is the day of salvation,"which is also an accounting of the suffering of St. Paul in his work, a text Sister Elisabeth used in her own spiritual journey many times. He marveled that after only two years the Deaconess House had been established and had grown to what it now was. With between 6,000 and 10,000 Norwegians in New York, they had not only much work to do, but many potential supporters. He continued to speak of the nature of service that the new probationary sister was entering, "Serve, serve, serve!" so that at the final day we would hear our Lord greet us, "Come, O blessed of my Father," he concluded.[212] It moved Sister Elisabeth when the pastor turned to the new sister and asked her the same questions Elisabeth had been asked in Christiania at her admission to be probationary sister. For her, it was a joy to hear Mortensen declare Othilie officially a probationary sister in the name of the Father, Son, and Holy Spirit. Then Pastor Everson spoke on the nature of Christian mercy and its expression in the deaconess' vocation, declaring the Norwegian Lutheran Deaconess Home and Hospital dedicated in the name of the Triune God. After little more than a year of existence, the Norwegian Relief Society was flourishing. Sister Elisabeth had many reasons to be thankful, even though at the same time she was under even greater pressure to provide more adequate funding for the larger Motherhouse.

When Sister Elisabeth reflected on Mortensen's sermon, which she appreciated enough to sum up in her diary, she wrote as one under conviction, using the language of the text to speak of her struggles to be a good servant of God.

> I can with my whole heart say I have tried all longing, but even if I have demonstrated myself as God's servant in everything, I still have nothing more to say than: God be gracious to me a sinner. I have had enough affliction, my honor has also been tested and I have at moments said with the prophet, it is enough, Lord, take my soul!' but I have also at other times been able to say, "even though they take my life, goods, honor, God's kingdom I retain. . . ." [This is a direct quote from Martin Luther's hymn, "A Mighty Fortress Is our God," the second to last line of the last stanza.]

In her *Memoirs,* where she reflects on this entry in her diary after quoting this long section, her tone is different, more mellow, showing that she has grown to think more fully about these times of trial, as we all do, given some distance.

> Many joys and blessings met me in my walking about, often in the poorest home and by the sick bed. I have richly experienced that it is better to give than to receive. When I think of all the times in hospitals, where the sick have lain waiting and gathered everything they want me to say for them, when they themselves could not say it, I think of the light in their faces, when they saw me coming with my basket, I believe that it was

the prayers and thanksgiving of the sick to God that gave the blessings.[213]

Sorrows and Gladness

We can see from her diary entries that Fedde found these times to be as spiritually challenging for her as they were organizationally. It is not simply her conflict with the board, which was very troubling and irritating to her in her work, but we can also see her struggle with her own self as she tried to be more sanctified. "June is over and we are in July. This month is filled with work and tears. We have just consecrated a Sister and the home." While Fedde still remained thankful for Sister Othilie's arrival, there is just a hint—"work and tears"—that the relationship is not going well. She concluded her entry for this day with the observation that even though she had been out much and stayed up nights with sick patients, "several have helped with money and medicine."[214] They had made it known in the community that of the nine beds, three would be free, the other six paid, although she admitted it was more often six free and three paid. The process for determining who got the free beds continued to generate some difficulties with the board which had developed what Sister Elisabeth regarded as an onerous set of procedures. It, however, made her happy that she could offer her countrymen such a place with the help of Dr. Turner who came every day on rounds to visit the sick. She grew fond of him and now enjoyed using the same Latin terms that had so mystified her on her first days with Dr. Kiær in Christiania.

She could leave Sister Othilie to take care of the patients while she tramped from one end of the city to the other, raising money to support the work. All she had for certain was the thirteen dollars a month pledged by Mrs. Børs. Every night, she said, she lay awake mapping out where she would go the next day to ask for help. Frequently people would see her coming and shut their doors, saying they had nothing. On the other hand, where she least expected it, she was given gifts that surprised her. All she could say was, "Our work is built on prayer and faith in God."[215] As she and the hospital continued from day to day she remembered what she had learned as a young girl from the Gospel of John, chapter 11, when Jesus was slow to come to the dying Lazarus and in fact only came after his death. Jesus told the grieving family that he had delayed in order that God who seemed slow to answer prayers could now show his glory more brightly when he would raise Lazarus from the dead. Fedde came to see in her own experience that it was in her hour of utmost need that she would receive exactly what she needed. These miracles would show God's glory even more brightly to her.

The month of August 1885 was equally as exhausting. Despite her weariness, she had to care for a woman, Mrs. Hag, who had been burned in an accident and was dying. She had three children to care for as the mother was dying. After her death she had to prepare her body for burial, get an undertaker, coffin, and wagon to take her body to be buried. What they did with the children after their mother's death is not recorded, but Sister Elisabeth had cultivated those who could take the children and adopt them, or perhaps bring them to the Staten Island Children's Home where she trusted the kindness of the matron.

One day the cash box was completely empty, and she had no idea where she would get the money she needed. The hospital was filled with patients, and the poor waited outside for help, as did the sick in homes she regularly visited. After a fruitless day of asking for help, she decided to go home, weary in body and soul, filled with heavy thoughts, so much so that she hardly knew where she was. When the conductor called out Fourth Avenue, she stepped out of the wagon and heard a voice say, "Silver and gold belong to me" (Haggai 2:8). "Yes, I know silver and gold belong to you, but I need some," she said out loud. When she came to her door, she found three letters. When she opened the first one from an American woman she had met the summer before, she found forty dollars and a note from her saying, "I began to think of you today and thought you might be able to use this." The other letter contained five dollars from a Norwegian woman, the third a request for help. Her weariness vanished, and she spent the evening praising God for giving her exactly what she needed just when she needed it.[216]

On September 27, Sister Elisabeth hosted a farewell party for Pastor Mortensen who left to tour the country, especially the Midwest and Utah, where he spent some time studying the Mormons before returning home to Norway.[217] He had stopped in several places where Norwegians had built institutions that he thought made them likely places for a Deaconess Motherhouse and Hospital. He had visited Minneapolis and the Augsburg Seminary community and kept in close contact with Sverdrup, recommending Norwegian students to him for the seminary. In a letter to Sverdrup on March 3, 1886, commending a student to him, he thanked him for the hospitality he had experienced in Minneapolis the year before.[218] On that same trip he had also visited Chicago, where, on November 1, 1885, he gave a speech encouraging the people there to found a Deaconess Motherhouse, planting a seed that would be harvested some years later through the work of Fedde, among others.[219]

Immediately, on November 3, a Chicago group of Norwegian men and women started a Tabitha Circle to establish either a hospital only and/or a Deaconess Motherhouse to run the hospital. They could not really decide which way to go until some years later. This disagreement did not get resolved, if it ever did, for over a decade and two different hospitals.

The Statue of Liberty

Although Sister Elisabeth's spirit seems to have lost some of its optimism and ebullience, New Yorkers had not. As the year progressed they could see the great emblem of America, the Statue of Liberty, rising out of the New York harbor. It had been designed and built in France and it was during this year that it was brought to America in huge crates so it could be reassembled. The pieces had been put on Bedloe Island while the pedestal was erected on August 5, to be completed before the statue could be put together. Funds were somewhat scarce. Joseph Pulitzer started raising money to complete the task, and by the spring of 1886 enough had been gathered to finish the pedestal. Like the completion of the Brooklyn Bridge, the raising of this iconic statue occupied the minds of Americans, who had contributed over $100,000 in gifts under $1.00 to pay for its completion. New Yorkers took great pride watching its progress. Sister Elisabeth could see it on clear days as she walked around Brooklyn doing her work.

Although Sister Elisabeth confided her feelings of despair in her diary, we cannot tell if her face showed any of it as she

Statue of Liberty being assembled on Bedloe Island

worked with her staff and the board, but the year had been discouraging for her. September 1885 would be an especially difficult month for Fedde. Illness and overwork caused her to take to her bed several times, but the work did not diminish. She reported on September 24 that their two patients were so restless that both she and Sister Othilie had to stay beside them in order to care for them. "Both of us have enough to do."[220] Almost every day's entry began with the word for working hard—"*strevet*" (struggle)—to describe what she was doing that day, whether cleaning her house for ladies aid meetings, preparing for the farewell party for Pastor Mortensen, or working in the hospital. One might have thought that with the new sister there, her work would be less consuming and exhausting, but it seems not to have been; in fact, it probably added to the work. Sister Othilie also became ill, so Elisabeth had to care for her, adding to the burdens of her own ill health and work. The diary seems to be filled with a kind of exhaustion and despondency that is almost overwhelming. On September 30 she wrote, "Heavy days with this sick man who has no hope. He now lies in his bed struggling. He will soon stand before his judge without hope. How hard it is." On October 1, he died. "The suffering was over, although that day it was sad to watch him fight," she commented.[221]

By the end of the month she had served as midwife, arranged things for Sister Othilie to do, gone to Ward's Island and St. Frances hospitals where she observed several patients, all the time looking for things to sell at the upcoming bazaar. It would be held the next month on November 8. After the event she continued her work, weary as usual and needing prayer. "O my Shepherd, only you can come into our hearts and help us for your name's sake. You must now help me or I will not be able to hold out, help me in my journey."[222] On one sick visit with a poor women she heard her say that she had prayed to God to be well and go home, whether she meant Norway or heaven is not quite clear. "*Ak*, dear God, teach her to know you!" she prayed. At times the awareness of what people themselves did to cause their own suffering overwhelmed her. That same day, November 13, 1885, she noted with despair that she had seen a mother who was fifteen years old and a father who was ten. "Terrible to hear, but true."[213] About the same time she met with a patient who had dreamed that a man was standing at the door of her room, waiting to be let in. She wondered if it was God or Jesus. As they spoke she realized that it could as well have been Satan. As she spoke to him, she gave him the weapon of the word: "In the name of Jesus, be gone" that he could use to cast him out.[224]

"What is the world to me?" she asks somewhat plaintively, "It is to me all emptiness."[225] The next month, December, involved even more work what with the need to prepare for the Christmas festivities. Sister Othilie became ill after the board meeting on December 8. Again the board meeting depressed Sister Elisabeth.

Christmas Eve that year involved the daily chores in the hospital with visits from the doctor as well as the typical Norwegian Christmas Eve celebrations and food.

> It was with real Christmas joy that the tree was decorated and our guests had eaten and the patients were brought down and given lighted candles and the Christmas gospel. Praise be to God in the highest. There is nothing better to do than thank God for his revelation in flesh in my soul. Yes, thank you Lord for everything in Jesus' Name!

The next day was her birthday. She was now exactly thirty-five years old, an age once deemed middle age. The community celebrated her birthday as well as Christmas Day with twenty-six children and friends. "Thank you, Lord, for hitherto have you helped me," quoting a favorite verse, 1 Samuel 7:12. On December 31, when she reflected over the entire year, she wrote,

> So it is now the end of this year and it has been one of the hardest, but hitherto has the Lord helped me. Everything is behind me, all that was unknown, my hopes blasted and many things lie beaten down and quite different from what I had thought. But a Friend who never changes is my heavenly faithful Savior who never abandons me. Yes, the heavier the cross, the more my heart longs for heaven with all my mind to see my Savior. The year's last evening and God knows that all was to be to his honor and glory. So, farewell, old year with thanksgiving. Go away now so I forget all my heart wounds during these many days. Amen. Amen.[226]

1886

As always Sister Elisabeth greeted the New Year, 1886, in the name of Jesus. "God, let it be a blessing for those who come to us, that their souls could come into your fellowship, Lord Jesus."[227] The city was coming to life.

> The young ladies of Brooklyn were astir, decking their charms out in the finery of which they had been dreaming, and smiling to see how pretty they looked in their silks and satins and lace and ribbons and diamonds and gold and pearls and rubies, all cast into the shade by their own beauties and graces.[228]

Sister Elisabeth, who struggled to live consistent with the commandments, might have coveted these jewels as she faced the future, always needing money. With her characteristic optimism, now tested by new trials, she hoped that things would be better in the New Year, although things did not look promising. By this time she indicated more clearly that the reason for her despair was the breakdown of her relationship with Sister Othilie. On January 4, she wrote in her diary, "A terribly unpleasant day with Sister Othilie—oh, what pain that is. God show me what I should do with this? . . . Help me God to bear my cross with patience."[229] Sister Othilie again became ill, Sister Elisabeth exhausted. A very sick patient became more and more critical, and she had to stay up the entire night to care for him. "*Ak,* I am weary, but despite that will watch through the night." She expressed grief that he had lost consciousness, and soon it was over. The next evening they were invited to a dinner with the pastors, and when they returned from the party, she had to wash the dead man's body. In addition to preparing his body, she then had to go out in very bad weather to make preparations for his burial. All this time she was caring for a little baby whose two older siblings had died of scarlet fever.

The need for more help, more even than Sister Othilie could give, was becoming desperate. She noted in a diary entry that she had met with a woman who was thinking of becoming a sister.[230] Her only consolation now was Mrs. Børs and her neighbors, and the pastors, especially Hansteen and the Seehuses. With them she found friendship and pleasant associations. It was in the context of this confident and exciting time in New York that Sister Elisabeth was working. The quarrels of the board may have seemed trivial next to her dreams and the expansive spirits of New Yorkers and all America as the great icon of American liberty appeared to be rising from the sea, welcoming many of the immigrants Fedde served.

Fedde's main concern for the first three months of 1886 was how difficult the work had been. The sisters, now with the addition of the inquirer who may have been Sister Bertha, found it difficult to adapt to the strict rules of the Motherhouse. The receipts for September 1885 had been below what they needed: $62 in receipts and disbursements $175.90.[231] Such a discrepancy was unsustainable. Only a gift of $500 from Arthur Corning Clarke in memory of Severini saved them from bankruptcy. The facilities were also in need of improvement: They were too small and in poor condition. She needed more help. Sister Othilie was more and more of a disappointment to Sister Elisabeth and was frequently ill, meaning Sister Elisabeth had to do the work for both of them. She wrote nothing about the upcoming meeting of the board to be held soon. Not only was she down about the board, but she lamented over a trying visit with a family that suffered from drink, leaving the house in what she thought of as a wretched condition. "Many children and sin in everything. . . ."[232]

After this visit she went to see a little girl in Flatbush hospital who lay as though dead, Sister Elisabeth said, with a big cap on her head, but when she saw the things she had brought her, her face shone with joy. The next day she visited more children whose father had abandoned them. "It would be better if he never returned," she concluded, glad the older daughter had gone to City Hall to get some relief.[233] Sin and death all around, she sighed.

Later that day she visited a woman whose husband had just died. This meant she had to wash the body and the next day help the unfortunate widow get her burial insurance and the funeral and burial arranged. Just as she was resting from all this, Pastor Everson came and announced that she had to visit a sick woman on a tugboat, which she did. She found the woman lying in a small berth in terrible pain that no one could help, not even the doctor whom she found to help. It was dispiriting to her. Then she heard, to her horror, that Mrs. Børs was sick. "God, what do you mean with all this? Spare her for your own sake!" she cried out, knowing how important the consul and his wife were to the work.[234]

Two days after that, on January 29, Gurine Nilsen the woman for whom she had been caring, died, which meant Sister Elisabeth had to wash the body and arrange the funeral and burial. As she did all that, a new patient, sick unto death, was admitted. January ended with more work than ever with people whose suffering tore at her heart strings. "Very much to do, with the patients and the washing [of bodies] so there is very little time for anything besides work."[235]

On Sunday, February 7, 1886, she took communion. She found it refreshing and rejoiced in her Savior.[236] It helped her through the next trying days of work from morning to night without relief, caring for the sick, raising money, looking for a lost girl with a child, arguing with her about keeping the baby rather than putting it up for adoption, then a couple with whom she spoke for some time, probably hoping they would hear the Word she brought. "God grant the Word might bear fruit!" she concluded. The month ended with Pastor Everson and Sister Elisabeth trying to find a place for a man sick with tuberculosis, since they did not take people with contagious diseases. They could not find a place, only the promise of a place later. These accounts show how their successes with needy people naturally expanded their work as people came to understand all of the things she could do for them—caring for their ills, helping them financially, burying a family member when the family had no money to do so. One day she had the joy to arrange for a five-year-old boy to be baptized, one of many such events of which she was privileged to be a part. The record of the baptism in the church book is the only time Sister Elisabeth's name is recorded in the Seamen's Mission Church's congregational record book. He wanted to be named Conrad, he told her. At the baptism, when the pastor asked "What is the child to be named?" "Conrad!"[237] he stated loudly, to Sister Elisabeth's amusement.

Just before the March board meeting, she rejoiced that God had given her a new probationary sister, Bertha, to help with the work. Since the minutes of the board did not resume until March 9, 1886, it is difficult to tell whether these conflicts grew more severe, but in this meeting similar issues came up again, this time focused on another nagging question: Who would determine who the paying and non-paying patients would be—something Sister Elisabeth had already fussed about. Chairman Hansteen recalled that the board had determined that the sister-in-charge, in consultation with the doctor, was to decide on the admittance of those patients who had the means to pay, but the admission of a patient who could not pay would require a conference with the board or, if members were not available, with the chair or vice chair. As might be expected from previous meetings, Everson objected to this as not being appropriate for board members to do. He saw it as something we might call today micro-management and a continuing problem for start-up businesses of any kind. The board, according to Everson, who was right about this, was responsible to its public for policies, not the day-to-day management. The process suggested by Hansteen struck Sister Elisabeth as onerous, and she prayed to be free of it. Everson's concern about the public image of the Norwegian Relief Society, something a board member should be concerned about, exasperated Mrs. Børs who said that she could not imagine that their supporters were whispering about the organization, with which several others agreed. Everson, on the other hand, insisted that they must not let go of their authority and cede it to Sister Elisabeth. He moved that the chair and the deaconess come to some agreement about a process for admitting paying or non-paying patients. The board then defeated Hansteen's proposal that the deaconess and doctor determine who should be admitted as paying or not.[238]

Again we see Everson worrying about the corporate responsibility of the board vs. Sister Elisabeth's irritation at the process. She had every reason to be upset. Everson's constant fussing about this seemed to her like a vote of no-confidence. In her diary, Sister Elisabeth wrote, "The Board met. Always opposition. God, is it always so in your kingdom—the way narrow and hard?"[239]

The board, with its increasingly complicated tasks of supporting the deaconesses, doctors, and the workers, had resolved it needed a better structure and began to develop a set of by-laws to organize its efforts.

Sister Elisabeth had been sick for fourteen days at the end of March. Sister Othilie had also been sick, and again Fedde had to work despite her ill health. "God, how great your grace is to me, you took me entirely forward with all that I have and helped me."[240] She could only tell the others what to do. She was grateful, however, for her new helper, Sister Bertha. When she came and from where is not clear in the minutes or Fedde's *Memoirs*. She had not come from the Norwegian Motherhouse, as they do not have any record of a Sister Bertha in their archives. By this time Sister Othilie had become a cross for Sister Elisabeth to bear. "Many pains with Sister Othilie. God have mercy on me! And help me to do what is right in God's eyes and let it be the truth that I will serve you alone."[241] Once again she need to quote her grandmother's favorite old hymn by Kingo, "Sorrow and gladness, they wander together."

Sister Elisabeth did not look forward to the next board meeting. "It will be like all of the meetings with opposition and unrighteousness all on my side when it is discussed." Sister Elisabeth could only confide in her diary that dealing with Sister Othilie had been difficult. "O what a cross she is! Sister O. is almost too great for me to bear, but God has said, 'as your day is so shall your strength be.' God help me to bear it all!"[242]

The board at its April 13, 1886, meeting just as the pedestal for the Statue of Liberty was being completed, something they could watch from their neighborhood, granted Sister Elisabeth a three-month vacation. It then turned its deliberations to finding someone who could run the home during her absence. Sister Othilie had offered to do so, but Fedde, with maybe a little pique, objected to her continuing in any position at the home since she had become engaged—she had abrogated her vow as a deaconess. Marriage meant, to Sister Elisabeth, that Othilie had given up her vocation as a deaconess. Sister Othilie seemed to have been highly regarded by the board who had wanted her to stay until Fedde returned from her vacation.

Fedde's irritation was clear to the board. Everson seems not to have been able to resist commenting that Sister Othilie "naturally has a right to become engaged." It then resolved that "the Board accept with thanks her offer to work with the home but adds that it is the hope of the Board that her work may continue with its usual kindness and diligence."[243] In her reaction to the resignation, we see Fedde's struggling to act rightly. While she may have thought the estate of marriage the highest one, she appears to have been devastated and angry that this young helper was leaving her, despite their increasingly difficult relationship. Coming as she did from the Lutheran Free Church congregation in Arendal, Sister Othilie had been well-trained spiritually by the pastor, Paul Peter Wettergreen, (1835-1889), whom Fedde knew and respected from her time in Arendal. Sister Othilie had appeared to be a perfect fit for the work in Brooklyn,[244] but it was not working out. Sister Elisabeth later, in her *Memoirs*, called her soft (*bløtd*) and perhaps too much influenced by Wettergreen, the Lutheran Free Church pastor in Arendal. This may have been the increasingly bad press of Wettergreen who became more and more radical, leaving the Lutheran Free

Lutheran Free Church in Arendal, where Sister Othilie attended.

Church and beginning to practice rebaptizing. He spent time with the Swedish American mission supporter Fredrick Franson (1852-1908), whose preaching in Arendal sparked a huge revival and interest in the China Mission. Franson was also a supporter of women's rights to speak and preach at the time. By the time Sister Elisabeth wrote her memoirs, the meaning of Wettergreen's life was better understood and she may not have approved of the ultimate direction of Wettergreen's journey.

Frederick Franson

There is also some sense on Fedde's part that she had not acted as she should have in the relationship. On April 22, 1886, she wrote "Conflict on all sides. Now my journey is decided and I have written to [Captain] Sjerbeck [sic], to get a trip home.[245] All looks as if I will go by myself and that is best." This comment may mean that she had been intending to return to Norway with Hansteen who was going home to marry at about this time.

On Good Friday 1886, she wrote, "Painful day today with Othilie."[246] Sister Othilie, despite Fedde's objection and recollections, continued working and resigned her duties for good on November 8, 1886, after Sister Elisabeth's return from Norway. Her resignation, according to the minutes, was accepted, but she was allowed to stay at the home until she found a new place to stay. This was part of the agreement the board had to make with all sisters. Any sister who resigned or was fired had to be sure of a place before the board could in good conscience let her go into the world, so whether she left to marry or not, they had to keep her until she found another place.[247] Her comments seem in this summary more understanding than she had been at the time.

> The joy we had in having her with us did not last long, She was beautiful and loveable and sang well so it is not surprising that we could not keep her for long. A widower from her native city arrived with his ship and "he came, saw, and conquered." She left us when she became engaged.[248]

One day, after Sister Elisabeth had dealt with several needy families, she was tired and hungry, illness seemed to be everywhere, and she did not know how she could last. As she walked down the street, lost in her thoughts, quite upset, she looked down and saw a little page from a book at her feet. On it was a poem that she took to be from the Lord.

> So tired, my friends are gone
> And I am left alone.
> And days are sad.
> Lord Jesus, Thou wilt bear my load
> Along this steep and dreary road
> And make me glad.
> So tired, yet I would work
> For Thee, Lord, hast Thou work
> Even for me?
>
> Small things, which others, hurrying on
> In Thy blest service swift and strong
> Might never see.
> So tired, yet it were sweet
> Some faltering tender feet
> To help and guide.
> Thy little ones whose steps are slow
> I should not weary them, I know
> Nor roughly chide.

So tired, Lord, Thou wilt come
To take me to my home
So long desired.
Only Thy grace and mercy send,
That I may serve Thee to the end
Though I am tired.

As she read it, she said aloud, "Truly, the Lord is in this place." She regarded it a message directly from the Lord. "Yes, a meeting with the Lord gives power for everything."[249]

Respite in Norway

As Fedde was getting ready to leave for Norway in 1886, the board decided not to take in any patients nor admit any probationary students during her absence.[250] In addition, board members began to work on board organization in order to solve some of the problems they had encountered as they moved from a startup organization that had called a deaconess to help with the poor and ill Norwegians in New York, to building a hospital and Motherhouse where deaconesses could be trained. It could no longer be a one-person operation. There had to be protocols for actions, lines of authority, and a structure for the board and its relationship to the Sister Superior. On May 26, 1886, the board adopted articles of incorporation for The Norwegian Relief Society, the purpose of which was to "afford gratuitous aid to poor and suffering Norwegians in the United States and relieve them in their spiritual and bodily distress."[251]

Mrs. Børs had wisely insisted that the name of the society should be something non-Norwegians could say so that when they asked for support from those outside of the Norwegian community they would understand the name and be able to pronounce it. The document stated the regulations by which the hospital would function, what the procedures would be for admitting patients and sisters, and how to elect a board of managers which they did: Henry W. Johnson, Pastor Carl Severin Everson, Knut Seehus, Peter A. Guttormsen, Carsten Hansteen, Kristian Krispinusen Sårheim, Mrs. Anna Børs, Mrs. Maria Flood, Mrs. Henrietta Harris, and Mrs. Christine Møller. By this time the board was also beginning to discuss where and when they should build a new facility. It was the considered opinion of Sister Elisabeth that the people who needed their help were moving further away from their current location and they should investigate the Red Hook neighborhood as being more appropriate for their new hospital, should they build one.[252]

Norway in 1886

On June 5, 1886, Sister Elisabeth boarded the *Geiser* for a three-month vacation in Norway, a much needed rest after three years of constant work and worry. She was returning to a country now in the midst of both a protracted culture war and a cultural renaissance that brought the little country fame and recognition around the world. It would not be too much to assert that one of the major issues was women and their place in society, and what the Bible and church had to say on the question. Henrik Ibsen had made this issue the theme of his greatest works, and this was his most productive decade: *Ghosts,* dealing with the ravages of syphilis on a conventional family, written in 1881 and produced in 1882; *The Wild Duck* finished in 1884; and in 1886 one of his greatest, *Rosmersholm,* which featured characters who had left the church behind completely. Christian Krohg (1852-1925), the painter, and a leader in what became known as the Christiania Bohemians, had just written a novel, *Albertine,* the story of a poor seamstress whose poverty had forced her into prostitution. He and his fellow Bohemians espoused "free love," free of the repressive laws of both church and society. In a sense both the church and the world were trying to figure out what to do for very poor single women who were being taken advantage of by men from the upper classes, whose hypocrisy in speaking against prostitutes while at the same time buying their services scandalized both sides. Christian organizations

Albertine *by Christian Krohg*

of mercy tried to prevent women from such debasement by preaching against such arrangements, establishing the Deaconess Houses, and giving women refuge when they did have babies out of wedlock. On the other hand, the Bohemians, while decrying this hypocrisy, thought the solution should be "free love." Both the church and the legal system were the problems from these artists' points of view. Krohg's several paintings of Albertine, especially the one of her being taken to the police doctor for examination while other prostitutes around her are dressed in their finery, showed the problem in ways thought to be scandalous by church people—but that made its point.

Edvard Munch (1863-1944), at twenty two, was just beginning his artistic career with his first "Self-Portrait" in 1886. He had been raised in a pious family and knew well the language of the Bible and church. His struggle to paint what he saw and what he knew from his childhood home is obvious in his depiction of women and sexuality. Edvard Grieg (1843-1907), at the height of his artistic career, had just finished the "Lyric Pieces" Opus 48 and his Sonata in C for Violin and Piano. While he was Norway's great composer, his religious faith, if any, was a mild Unitarianism. The cultural war between those who held to the Christian faith and those who were abandoning it was growing in intensity, and many of these artists were directly critical of the pious world in which Sister Elisabeth lived and moved.

At the same time, among the devout, interest in missions in the country had rarely been higher. The Schreuder Mission to the Zulu, now led by Missionary Nils Astrup (1843-1919), started in 1842, was a matter of national interest, as was the Santal Mission led by Edvard Munch's boyhood hero, Lars Skrefsrud (1840-1910). Young women were also seeing their chance to serve as missionaries. There was more and more interest in the China Inland Mission led by Hudson Taylor (1832-1905,) who in 1889 on a visit to Scandinavia spoke to over 5,000 Swedes in Stockholm. The Norwegians would soon have a busy and active mission to China pioneered by the early work of two women, Sophie Reuter Smith (1860-1891) and Anna Jakobson (1860-1913) who left in 1884 to serve in Hudson Taylor's China Inland Mission. Their letters home attracted many a young Norwegian woman who wanted adventure and romantic travels in the service of Christ.

We hear very little of these movements and the conflicts surrounding them in Fedde's diary or later *Memoirs*, but whether or not she climbed the ramparts in the struggle, she clearly was a part of the women's movement as it swept through the two countries. As a curious person she without a doubt took an interest in all the conflicts and opportunities rumbling about her in Christiania as she visited Mother Guldberg. While there she also must have learned about the

Sophie Reuter Smith

relocation of the Deaconess Motherhouse and Hospital to Lovisenberg. The time in her home country with her family and a long visit with Mother Guldberg restored both her body and soul. When she left Christiania on September 17, 1886, for New York, on the Thingvalla boat, *Island*, she felt much refreshed and ready to take on her old duties with new zest and dedication. Her travel companions were Hansteen and his new wife, Sofie Charlotte Duus (1864-1946). They had been married in Trondheim September 11, 1886. Their booking on the ship had surely been arranged beforehand and shows the close bonds of affection that Hansteen and Fedde shared, something she frequently noted in her conflicts with the board. He was almost always on her side during the fiercest battles.

It had been clear from the reports of Sister Othilie during Fedde's absence that home visits and other routine tasks of the hospital had declined steeply from over 120 to thirty-eight in one month. Not long after Sister Elisabeth's return, on September 30, New York and the entire country celebrated the dedication of the Statue of Liberty on October 28, 1886. While the statue was exciting to the entire country, Elisabeth realized quickly that the facilities of their hospital were getting worn out and broken down. They needed repair and cleaning. It was as though she had to start over.

Beginning Again

When she returned from her trip, she had to instruct Sister Bertha in the vocation of the diaconate. Soon hostilities broke out. To Sister Elisabeth, Sister Bertha did not appear to take seriously the duties of her vocation. Fedde wrote in her diary that Sister Bertha had left without her permission to help a friend whose child was ill. While a good thing to do, it did not help Sister Elisabeth. "It put me in a bad humor," she remarked. "I have no one to depend upon!"[253] What were God's intentions? She always prayed to be obedient and do God's will, but she was having trouble like this all the time. For comfort she thought of Jesus' words, turning to a little book of sermons and praying for God's help.[254] Five days later Sister Bertha returned from her brief absence and was disciplined for "running away," as Sister Elisabeth called it. A young woman who was about to take the vows of a deaconess should have understood that acting without permission from the head sister would not auger well for her future with the institution. On the other hand, a young single woman in America at the time, while less free than a man, would have found such restrictions difficult or easily ignored. They all knew they could escape to the wide open spaces of the American frontier and leave the strict control of the Sister Superior or board at any time. Discipline was always something of a problem with the deaconesses.

In October 1886, Sister Elisabeth was happy to send Sister Bertha out into the community on visits to the sick and needy. On October 8, Sister Elisabeth visited a man who needed her to sing and bring him soup. He sang hymns as he was dying, which caused Sister Elisabeth to comment, "Blessed are the dead who die in the Lord."[255] Despite that, her feelings of despair and depression had returned. "This morning I am so despondent, although my strength is in the Lord."[256] She soon needed another break. Mrs. Børs and she returned to Mt. Vernon, to the Wartburg Children's Home to place a little boy. They enjoyed the trip and the fall colors on the way as they went. Their trip was somewhat "romantic" she noted, meaning they had taken an old way, via a fish wagon, and did not arrive back home until eleven that evening. Life continued on normally through November 2. Then her entries in her diary briefly end. The minutes of the board, however, tell the story. On November 11, the board called in each sister, Othilie and Bertha, to receive their resignations, which they proffered.[257] They were to leave as soon as they found other positions. It is certainly what Sister Elisabeth wanted.

When we look back at the two weeks between her November 2 entry and the next one, it is not hard to imagine the stress and conflict of those days, especially when we read her comments as she begins again on November 18. Fedde wrote with some small pleasure that since she had last written in her diary, much had changed in the home. "Today, Sister Othilie left, and she could not think anything else but that it was for the best. The next Monday Sister Bertha left." For all this she was glad. "In my need," she wrote, "I cried to God," and her prayer had been heard. "Only the Lord knows what I have been through," she concluded with thanksgiving. "All will work out in the end."[258] Despite her joy, she now had much more to do, but she could do it. The board had authorized her to hire someone to help her with the work because they knew she could not do it completely alone. "It has been a difficult time." She then went on to describe how many patients were left and how much work they would be for her. They had eleven patients; two had died. Somewhere she had found a new help. "With my new nurse it is going well and also with the patients, and now I have peace."[259]

She ended the year as usual with repentance and thanksgiving for God's mercies over the year, counting up the patients they had helped during the past month: 170 sick and 48 children. She prayed that she could be able to forget everything and hold fast to God's unswerving faithfulness and his overwhelming grace.[260] The minutes from December also state that the board had sent a letter to Sister Ingeborg Sponland in Christiania asking her to come, but as of the end of the year she had not answered the letter.

The year 1886 had been a rough one. Things had not been going well. The board had only briefly met while she was on her trip to Norway, and the money was not coming in. The hospital had to borrow money just for expenses, and income remained low. On the last day of the year, Fedde wrote in what seems to be dejection, "Few sick people have been here this year and during this month hardly any. Now the house is empty and all the work is outside among the wretched, where there are enough of them."[261] The hospital seemed to have skidded to a halt and her work as the woman with the basket, bringing help to the forgotten Norwegians on the streets of Brooklyn—the wretched, as she called them—demanded her attention. It felt like she was back at square one again.

1887

The New Year began as always with Sister Elisabeth praying to begin the New Year in Jesus' name. At this time her heavy responsibilities and the increasing conflicts kept her energies, according to her diary, confined to the work. This would be her most difficult year with the board.

Although busy, she was happy to be doing the work she liked: helping the sick and the poor. Still, she knew she needed help. She had been authorized by the board to hire someone new, and she quickly found a young Norwegian immigrant girl to help her with the menial tasks. Apparently she found a Miss Frölich, whom she paid $10 a month. The young woman must have thought the work overwhelming. One day she asked if she could go out to be with a friend. She did not return the next day. Somewhat worried about her, Elisabeth went to the police to see if she had run afoul of the law in some way. She had. She and a man had been arrested for public drunkenness and put in jail overnight. She was going to come before the judge soon, so Sister Elisabeth waited in the courtroom, watching as every kind of nationality and crime made their appearance. When the young girl came out, covered with dirt and vomit, she shrieked in horror to see Sister Elisabeth. When she pled guilty the judge offered her either ten days in jail or ten dollars. Sister Elisabeth paid the fine and then took her out to the trolley where they had to wring out her clothes before she could get on the trolley. "Nothing happened," said Elisabeth. "People were used to seeing me with every kind of person."[262] Sister Elisabeth had obviously made herself known in the community. She seemed to be traveling more on her own and less with Everson or other pastors. In a way, she was becoming a kind of traveling hospital and social welfare institution in her own person, well known and trusted in the Brooklyn area.

At the January 1887 meeting of the board, a new applicant for probationary sister was received from Thora Jensen. They accepted it and advised her she could come as soon as possible to begin her work. The board then moved that it would be helpful if articles inviting young women to enter the deaconess program would be published in both Norwegian and English papers in the area.

The new probationary sister, Sister Thora, seemed to be doing okay, and Sister Elisabeth thought she would be a good deaconess, until she saw almost immediately that the new pastor of the Seaman's church, Kristian Sårheim, was falling in love with her. This upset Fedde, who went to him and demanded that he tell her what his intentions were toward the new sister. If he were going to ask her to marry him, would he say so now rather than have them go through the process of installing her

Kristian Sårheim

into the role of probationary sister. He said nothing, and so "we had the service of admission and we had a lovely party. He gave a very serious sermon and she was received in exactly the same way as the first sister. Now there will be peace, I thought, but no, things just got worse and finally she came to me and said one day, 'Now that I am engaged, will it be bad if I leave you?' I was so upset both because we had to part and that we had to have the same story happen all over again."[263] While Elisabeth once again had

nothing against the marriage, it provoked her no end that the pastor had failed to be honest with her and she was losing another sister.[264]

Although there is no record of the young woman's unhappiness with Sister Elisabeth or the work, it is not impossible to reason from her difficulty in keeping sisters that she, like many founders, was difficult to work with. It is also true that these young women were of an age when marriage was their goal, and they may have viewed the deaconess calling as a way to make provisions for themselves should they not marry. Thora Jensen and Pastor Sårheim did not marry until August 16, 1888, just after Sister Elisabeth had left for the Midwest on vacation.

How God chose to fulfill her needs was always surprising to Sister Elisabeth. One night a small girl stood at her door and told her she had to come immediately to her home. She dressed quickly and went to the house where she found the father unable to walk because he had hurt his foot, but the mother was also in a crisis—she was giving birth. After the baby was born, she swaddled it and gave it to the father to hold while she attended to the mother who feared there was another child yet to be born, but to the mother's relief, there was not. Sister Elisabeth had much to do helping the mother with the little girl. Things improved in the life of the family after that. They became one of Sister Elisabeth's greatest supporters as their economic situation changed for the better. It was from moments like this that Sister Elisabeth knew God was working to bring health and well-being to many through her work.[265]

In March 1887 she taught Sunday school with Mrs. Hansteen on Sullivan Street. Thirty-six children came. Later when she arranged an outing for them, eighty-six children "marched in procession from the Seamen's Mission to the park where we have been the whole day and come home now so tired and with a terrible headache. The trip cost $21.00, all of which I have already received."[266] One might wonder, in the light of the storm that would hit her in the following few months in her relationship with the board, if she had once again bitten off more than she could chew. Having a ministry for children while all well and good and was part of the Innermission program, but the board may have wondered, can we do this much? Can Sister Elisabeth do all this? Perhaps the fact that the times were hard made it possible for her to look for other things to do.

Trouble

Despite her sense that God was blessing her work, the board seemed to be heading for an explosion regarding the matter of using bazaars and raffles to raise money for the hospital. When Pastor Mortensen left in 1885, Mrs. Børs had been named to his place as chair of the board—a rather signal event for an organization at the time, to have a woman chair.[267] Now they needed to raise money for what they called a Children's Home for which they decided to have a bazaar. It was scheduled for January 28-29, 1887. After everything was ready for the bazaar to begin, Sister Elisabeth wrote, Pastor Everson walked in. Although he was friendly and kind, he said very little. He went out just before the event began. Sister Elisabeth could not imagine that so much trouble would come from this innocent event, but sorrow and suffering resulted. At the next meeting, Mrs. Børs came in unusually happy and loving as always, carrying a wallet that she said would make everyone happy. Pastor Hansteen, the secretary, seemed fine, and the business went well. Near the end of the meeting, Mrs. Børs opened up the wallet and announced that it contained a gift of $64,000 from an anonymous American friend.[268] The interest at six percent would assure them $3840 a year. This was good news indeed. She announced that "the interest income stands as long as I live and have my present fortune, and after my death, it is hoped, if that should happen suddenly, for the deaconess home."[269] The gift considerably relieved their problems. They could pay back the money they had borrowed from the building fund and plan a new building. The rejoicing was great. It meant that Sister Elisabeth's daily begging could end and she could do other things with her time. The City Board of Health could now grant them recognition as a hospital which had been denied them. Now they had the money to fulfill the requirements for a permit to operate as a hospital.

Just as their joy peaked, however, Pastor Everson arose and announced that he in good conscience could no longer be associated with raffles and bazaars, especially having children be part of what he regarded as illegal activity. He thought it was even against American law to raise money for a charity with a lottery and wrote a statement of dissent which he demanded be put in the minutes in English so the authorities could read what was at stake. It read:

Carl Severin Everson

To the Norwegian Relief Society of Brooklyn.

The undersigned as citizen of the State of New York hereby respectfully protests against the lottery held in violation of the provision of Table X, Chapter VIII, sections 323, 324, 325, and 328 of the Penal Code of the State of New York at the bazaar in the Deaconess home, 441 4th Avenue, Brooklyn, on the evening of January 28 and 29, 1887. 16 3rd Place, Brooklyn, February 8, 1887, C. S. Everson.[270]

This action struck members of the board as outrageous. Pastor Hansteen disagreed in a kindly way, but Sister Elisabeth lost her temper. "You were here during the meeting where we planned the event. You could have said something. You came before the event and walked around smiling but said nothing. Raffles have always been a part of this!" She thought he was thinking of some Norwegian law, although raffles and other mild forms of chance had been used there as well for good purposes. Even the Norwegian royals had held a bazaar to raise money for the victims of the hurricane in Tromsø, which she had experienced a few years before. After this exchange, she wrote, a great argument ensued, and trouble began that she could only regret. The argument was fairly common between pastors and the ladies aids at the time. Everson's critique, while rather unseemly, was not unusual at the time. Pastors did not seem to understand that women had no other way to raise money than these events in which they could exchange their sweat equity for money. It, however, greatly exacerbated the conflict in the board. His threat to publicize the conflict in the church papers also irritated them. They could not afford bad publicity, something Everson seemed to be doing. The minutes of the board meeting seem to hint that Everson's main concern was that Fedde's work with the children was impinging on Everson's Sunday school program.

Cartoon from Folkebladet *expressing many a pastors' dislike of bazaars and suppers to raise money Jesus is saying, "Know ye not that my father's house is a house of prayer?"*

Hansteen assured him Sister Elisabeth had done nothing of the kind, holding the meetings of the children on Saturday, thereby avoiding a conflict between them.[271] Everson accepted this, but tensions seemed to be growing especially unbearable for Mrs. Børs.

After the meeting Fedde expressed herself in her diary about the meeting:

> A terrible meeting. In peace we gathered and began with prayer, and then the most vehement outbreak from every side. Pastor Everson had to go forward in this connection that the bazaars awakened all his wonderment and he would have to say that it was so evil, it was as if a devil had done it. For myself I will always remember what it was, but for the public, it

should rather be hidden. Went out a little in the evening and am in a terrible uproar.[272]

Fedde did not sleep that next evening. "Lord, let this soon be over!" she prayed.

Board Resignations

The board held an extra meeting on February 15, 1887, led by Mrs. Henriette Harris, the vice chair of the board. She informed those present that Mrs. Børs intended to resign from the board for "as long as the present make-up continued because her conscience would not permit her to remain longer."[274] Mrs. Børs had sent a letter to the secretary explaining her action. He answered saying that the board members shared the opinion that Pastor Everson's behavior at the previous meeting had been such that they agreed he "HAD" to resign. Whether or not this was appropriate for him to say, it was probably the truth. The board seemed slow to act and unable to act effectively to quell the conflict. The board was then summoned to the consulate to meet with the consul. Upon arriving,

Sketch of Anna Børs from Nordisk Tidende

they were told that the Consul and Mrs. Børs' doctor had forbidden her to attend the meetings as long as Everson remained a member of the board. After they received the secretary's report, Everson asked, "What is the question?" Mrs. Harris responded: "A choice between Mrs. Børs and Everson." Everson reacted strongly. For him the issue was whether "right and truth were to prevail or not, and that these were in accordance with the laws of the State." This display of "raw power" could not break him, he said, "his body could be broken, but not his spirit." While it is difficult to know the passion with which these remarks were made, they do seem, at the very least, somewhat melodramatic. When a member of the board, Pastor Sårheim, asked whether Everson wanted to resign or not, Everson answered that was not the right question. His conscience bound him to remain. Finally, he suggested that a Committee on Peace be appointed and he would seek counsel from "pious brothers-in-faith." The board unanimously approved his suggestion and asked him to appoint two members of the board for the

Committee on Peace. He named his two friends on the board—Mrs. Flood, wife of the man Hansteen had begun to suspect was undermining him, and Mrs. Møller—both of whom accepted. Fedde thought that meeting was just as bad as the previous one. "How can people be so awful and still speak of the love of the work?" She prayed for an end to it all and for peace so she could find rest.[275] "God put an end to this trouble soon. I am tired of many plagues and am praying for peace."[276] On February 28, 1887, she wrote, "Now this awful month is over . . . I am weary of fighting and long for rest."

On March 8, 1887, the same day as the venerable Henry Ward Beecher died in his sleep at his Brooklyn home after a stroke, the board met again. Sister Elisabeth dreaded the meeting, but in the meantime had continued her school with the children. The success of it gave her some strength to face the board. The Committee on Peace, however, admitted complete failure, partly because Mrs. Børs refused to meet with them. Everson continued to make his refusal to resign a matter of conscience and told the group that the results of his consulting "pious brothers in faith," some German Lutheran pastors in the area, had been the unanimous support of his stance, as might be expected. That his own congregation supported him was not particularly persuasive to the group; it only irritated them more.

Everson continued to defend his actions, even his conversations about the problems with his congregation. This had made their disagreements public, something that outraged some members of the board, most especially Sister Elisabeth. Everson said he had to speak as it was a matter of conscience, and those who suspected his actions, he raged, were not Christian. Pastor Sårheim said that about this he had his doubts. Everson thundered, "He who doubts, sins!" This was a complete miscontrual of what Sårheim had said. It had nothing to do with faith. It had to do with the character of Everson. Sårheim suggested that Everson's behavior indicated that he was not the type "that could best serve the Deaconesses' cause."[277] This caused Everson to retort that it was not his person that Mrs. Børs found insufferable, but his opinions to which he had a right. For Everson not to speak about what he saw as wrong in the practices of the board would have violated his call as minister, he said. If he did not speak the truth, he "would be finished as a minister of his congregation."[278] The others thought that in his objections to the bazaar he had slandered the entire deaconess project in the neighborhood. Everson had wanted the minutes of this meeting, especially his resolution, made available to the community in English and not hidden in the archives—to protect his reputation, people supposed. Everson then went on to say that Sårheim had accused him of the crime of not having any interest in the society. "This was not true," he maintained. He had in fact been fighting against sin, which was his obligation as a Lutheran pastor. All of this exasperated Hansteen who found Everson's insistence he was acting out of conscience appalling. If it were, "then his conscience was something the like of which he had never before experienced."[279]

As they continued to debate, Everson came to the conclusion that his error, if there was one, was a matter of form—*how* he had done something, rather than *what* he was trying to do. Asking his congregation, Our Savior's, to vote on the conflict meant little to the others since only forty members had been present at the vote. Exasperated, the board told him that a lawyer, Forster, had responded with laughter to the concern as to whether the bazaar and the selling of chances were legal. Another lawyer, Jonson, whom Mrs. Børs had consulted had become so indignant that he wanted to come to the board meeting and confront Everson himself. Everson once again responded that it was, for him, a matter of the truth and needed to be presented again to his congregation for its response. Lawyers, said Everson, "knew nothing about matters of conscience." He raised the rhetorical ante, so to speak, by saying it was for them to decide as to the truth of the matter, between God and a lump of gold. "God owns the gold and silver and bends the hearts of men." History would prove him right, he thundered, since the others were in search of loopholes in God's Word. After more of this jousting, Sårheim moved that the board ask Everson to seriously consider resigning, but after another attempt at peacemaking by Hansteen, the resolution was withdrawn, and he urged that the board write Mrs. Børs urging her to remain on the board. The motion passed, and the secretary directed to write such a letter. Sister Elisabeth simply noted in her diary after the meeting that it was over and "I am going to bed. . . . Only the Lord can help."[280]

The next meeting on April 12, 1887, continued the arguments with the same rancor. They proposed a letter accepting Mrs. Børs resignation with deep regret. (Apparently she had not agreed with their request that she remain on the board.) When that motion passed, Everson moved that at the next meeting they appoint a new member to replace Mrs. Børs. This suggested to the board that Everson was in a power struggle to take over the board. He continued to defend his position because, as he said, it was his plain duty to oppose the lottery since it was against state law. For that reason he felt himself to be doing the board a favor by keeping it from sinning or breaking the law of the State of New York, which the lawyers had already ridiculed.[281] Fedde did not respond much to this meeting in her diary, only to say that they had met and the meeting had brought her much sorrow, but she also had something to bring her joy: The Sunday school now had forty-nine students. She did fear that with Everson being asked to resign, everything would go to pieces, especially the Sunday school, which was obviously a success in her eyes. There had to be an end to the whole effort, she lamented.[282]

Once again Sister Elisabeth took to her bed for another fourteen days. Her assistant, Thora Jensen, was able to do the work while Sister Elisabeth malingered. On May 10, 1887, the board met to discuss other matters, this time finances. Everson wanted to question Mrs. Børs about the anonymous donor whose gift had endowed them with enough money to assure them an annual income of $3,840. Since she had been put in charge of distributing it every year, Everson suggested that she had not been forthright about the gift and could not keep the gift back simply because she disagreed with the direction of the board, although this had been one of the stipulations the donor had made. Hansteen thought this was an insult to the good offices of Mrs. Børs, but others disagreed and thought it was not her call, since the money had been given to them. It was her duty, they said, to continue to see that it was given. Pastor Sårheim, the treasurer, felt this was a reflection on him, and said he had no proof that Mrs. Børs had stopped sending the money, even though they had not received the first quarterly installment of the gift. The donor—whom we now know was Clark—according to Mrs. Børs had explicitly stated that "this gift remains, as long as I live, for *you* to use for the Deaconesses' Home."[283] Sårheim reported that Mrs. Børs had frequently told him, "When I go, the money goes too." Everson observed that since she had disposition of the gift, it was their fiduciary responsibility as a board to find out what the status of the gift really was. The board had to be able to demonstrate to the "world" that they had been financially accountable. The board defeated his motion, four to three, a rather close vote, explaining perhaps the rancor of the fight. One can also read the reluctance of Hansteen to cause a final breech with Everson, despite his behavior. Hansteen's actions as a member of the board at the meetings are fairly mild, but behind the scenes he was working to get a board elected that would be mostly from the Seamen's church and upper class Norwegians in Manhattan rather than the church people from Everson's congregation in Brooklyn.

On August 18, Hansteen's party won, and Everson and his party were defeated. Everson had finally came to the conclusion that in light of all that had happened to him, it was best for him to withdraw for a time from the board, ceding his work as chaplain at the home to Pastor Sårheim, who had been acting as such during this strife. In her entry in the diary, on August 18, 1887, Sister Elisabeth says, "Now it is over, the three resigned from the board and now we are free of them. God, let us keep the peace." When Everson finally did leave the board, after several attempts to pass motions on whether to publish an article or paper on the lottery and its situation at the Deaconess House, Mrs. Børs gladly returned to the board, after being invited back at the November 8, 1887, meeting. All the time she had continued to support Fedde's work.[284] Sister Elisabeth rejoiced that they finally had peace after her three opponents had left, although not for good. Everson would remain in the community and continue to serve the enterprise with Sister Elisabeth.

Everson maintained his good reputation in the Norwegian Synod. As a pastor, he reported frequently to President H. A. Preus about his work among the immigrants and his congregations. One might think that during these very difficult times he would have included at least some details about the conflicts, but did not, except a general lament about the troubles. And later he made a glancing reference to a pastor as being a Schmidt man, a leader in the Anti-Missourian Brotherhood, and an opponent of Preus and Everson on the question of predestination, or election. Most egregious is his failure to mention anything of the deaconess work in his report on the Seamen's Mission Church in Brooklyn in the fiftieth anniversary volume of the Norwegian Synod. [285]

Crosscurrents

There are many strands in this fight which are difficult to untangle, but one of the strands is that this is a full-blown church fight that always involves not only a power struggle, but also a struggle over ultimate things. Everson, a pastor in the Norwegian Synod, would have been somewhat involved in the Election Controversy, a theological skirmish about how Lutherans understood predestination. The debate was searing its way through the Norwegian-American Lutheran churches and causing splits in many congregations. For Everson's side the issue was church dividing. For the others less so, but a battle they had to fight. It simmered under many of these conflicts, for example those between Gabriel Fedde and Everson which continued well into the twentieth century.

It is also a fascinating glimpse into an era and time long removed from our own. It gives us an insight into people trying to understand how to build and run an institution in a new land and a new time. Everson, while unappealing in these accounts, represents the position of one concerned for the policy-making of the board, which is something for which he should not be criticized. His mistake may be that he was thinking theologically about business processes. For him everything appears to have been at stake all the time, and he could brook no variation from his position on gambling and lotteries—which had more to do with using the church building for the raising of money, as per the cartoon, by gambling, not the bazaars, per se. In ridding the temple of the money changers, Jesus had made it clear that no such activities should be countenanced in the church building.

Everson and Fedde represented two different strains of Norwegian Lutheranism. He was concerned for theology and the purity of doctrine; she cared more for her personal relationship with Jesus Christ, not the theology about the relationship. She, like her forebears in Norway, preferred a practical living Christianity that showed itself in deeds of love for the neighbor. Furthermore, the Norwegian church in Norway had never adopted all of the *Book of Concord* as had the Missouri Synod. So one could argue that most of the Norwegian pastors involved in this—Hansteen, Mortensen, Sårheim, all students of Gisle Johnson and Norwegian pietists—were more or less on the same side. Everson's church body, The Norwegian Synod, however, had become more influenced by the Missouri Synod and began to identify more with Missouri than with the church back home. For this reason, among others, it became difficult for these two Norwegian church bodies to come together. It took until 1917 and the merger of the Norwegian Evangelical Lutheran Church in America before the two sides would solve the inborn conflicts by agreeing to disagree on the issue of election.[286] Luther Seminary was the result of the agreement known as the Madison Agreement (*Madison Opgjør*) of 1912 which maintained that one could be Lutheran and continue to disagree on election. It brought the various strands of Norwegian Lutherans together so they could form a new church and seminary, which they did in 1917.

The fact that Hansteen had asked Gabriel Fedde and others to hold meetings of laity in the area shows their implicit agreement on Hauge's notion that laymen could preach (and also women, if pressed), something to which Everson would never have agreed. The organization they founded, the Free Lutheran Mission Society in Brooklyn, helped Elisabeth with her Sunday school. So theologically the pietists from Norway and America got along, but conflicts seethed between them and the Norwegian Synod represented by Everson who called the other pastors "Methodists" or "Schmidt men" for their pietism; they returned the compliment by striking at his colder, more "rational" Christianity.[287]

This went on and on. We can see it in Everson's articles in the paper defending his position against such people as Elisabeth's brother-in-law Gabriel whose pietism offended Everson.[288] Just after Sister Elisabeth left Brooklyn for good, he wrote three long letters to the editor of the *Nordisk Tidende* against Gabriel Fedde, defending his theological position and violently opposing Fedde's, a rather inappropriate attack on a layman of high standing in the Brooklyn Norwegian community.

United Seminary (later Luther Seminary).

Another cross current in the conflicts between Hansteen and Everson was Hansteen's growing concern that Simon W. Flood, by his loyalty to Everson at Our Savior's, had become enemy number one of the Seamen's Mission. While this was not quite germane to the running of the Lutheran Deaconess Hospital and Home, it did not help to have such open conflicts dividing loyalties on the board and in the community.

Added to the theological conflicts are the sexual politics, fueled by the theological disagreements and questions about the management of the hospital and mother house. Fedde obviously found it difficult to be ruled over by a board that disagreed with her rather clear sense of how things should go. Little is said about the fact that she was a woman. Given that she was a deaconess, she did carry some spiritual authority the board could not deny. Were they dealing with her as a woman with superior womanly instincts or as a nurse whose profession they did not understand? Throughout her life we can see the men working with her trying to understand how they should treat her, and we can see in her responses to them that she did not quite understand how to relate to them either. These difficulties reassert themselves when she is in the same position with the leadership in Minneapolis and Augsburg Seminary. Regardless of sexism, one does have to consider how new these relationships were and how they tried to deal with them responsibly. The minutes give us a revealing picture of the times and the difficulties such a breakthrough caused for all concerned.

Or was this simply a personal disagreement in which a strong person found it difficult to be ruled over by a board she thought of as less visionary and more pedestrian than she? All of these reasons might have been lingering in the background of the controversies. Despite all this, Fedde did not give up. She wanted to build a real hospital, the first for Norwegians in America, something they could do now with the anonymous bequest of $64,000. The interest from the bequest provided them almost $4,000 a year. This relieved Sister Elisabeth from having to think about raising money every single day and gave her more time to think of running the hospital. Mrs. Børs gave a beautifully embroidered hand towel to the group which they sold at an auction for $1.50; they used that money to buy the first brick for the hospital. Sister Elisabeth thought it appropriate that a hand towel brought in the first monies for the hospital since towels were used in the care of the sick, both for "drying tears and other things!"

Planning To Build

They began looking for a place to build the hospital, closer to where their clientele had moved. Over the years she, along with other board members, had looked around the city for appropriate locations for their hospital. Then one spring day they found it. Elisabeth reported on it in detail. On "a lovely spring day with fine mist and all the trees budding, some in bloom, as the birds sang and spiritual life seemed to bloom anew, Pastor Hansteen came to me and said we should go out and look

Norwegian Lutheran Deaconess Hospital in Brooklyn, 1889.

at a lot." The lot could not be smaller than fifty feet wide and one-hundred feet deep, they told the realtor. Hansteen and Sister Elisabeth soon settled on lots to suggest to the board. When they found the one they thought most suitable, they were told it would cost $3,000. A lot of money, she thought, but they did have $4,000. All they needed was money to pay for the building. "Now everyone had to work!" she concluded. The board, after much conversation, voted to purchase the lots on the corner of 4th Avenue and 46th Street in June 1887, closer to the center of the Norwegian population in Brooklyn at the time.

As they were beginning to work on the plans for the new building, and gather in money, a deaconess from Norway arrived, one who had been let go from the Motherhouse in Christiania because she was of a religious persuasion—the Motherhouse in Christiania said only that she was unsuitable—other than the Lutheran church, a requirement of all the deaconesses both there and in America. She was able to help Sister Elisabeth through the next year. She had come from Egersund, the town where Elisabeth would go to live and where she had many relatives and friends whom Sister Elisabeth knew. When she had appealed to A. T. Pedersen, a bookstore owner in Egersund, for help after being dropped by the Motherhouse, he had recommended she emigrate to America and contact Fedde. The sister had originally planned to work in a home for a while in America until she found her way, but the family could not pay her when she arrived. Fedde found her weeping on her doorstep one day when she came home from her calls, asking for help. Sister Elisabeth said, "Don't cry, take it easy. You can be here until morning and you will find a place." She could promise this knowing that ladies would come to her for recommendations of Norwegian girls who could serve in their homes. The next day, Sister Elisabeth wrote, "a lady came who wanted a kitchen maid. She took the job and was there for a time. She moved later to another family, but spent her free time mostly with us. After some time she sent in an application to us and was admitted as a student." Is this Sister Mathilde? She fits the description, but Elisabeth does not identify her.

All this time they had been discussing what they needed in a hospital building, so when the time came, they would have a good set of specific plans: a new thirty-bed hospital which would be completed by November 1889. The architect, Gustav Gunsten, was frequently spied in the area with blueprints under his arm, riding in his cart from his home in Blythebourne. At first, when he asked Fedde to give him a drawing of what she thought it should include, she laughed, "I give you a drawing? I can't even draw a straight line!" He insisted and held the paper while she drew on it. "I put down what I had thought the building should include in order to help us do our work. Now we had come so far that it was time to gather money."[289] Here the work of the Børs, especially Mrs. Børs, proved invaluable as they asked their friends in the upper echelons of New York society to contribute. Consul Børs contributed $1,000, as did Cornelius Vanderbilt. John D. Rockefeller gave $250: all told they received $3,110 from their appeal. They now had $7,110, but needed another $8,000 as the hospital was estimated to cost between $14,000 and $15,000.As Sister Elisabeth saw it, that meant, despite their endowment, they still had to beg for more money. The contributions of these non-Norwegians now began to raise the issue of whom the hospital served and whom it could attract as supporters. The question would be answered in another two years when the Norwegian Relief Society reincorporated itself as a hospital open to all, not simply for Lutherans or Norwegians. This question became increasingly important to address as they continued to develop from their original mission of serving poor and indigent Norwegians where they found them, to building a hospital that should serve the same population. Now they began to see that they could not refuse to serve sick people because of their nationality. The institution was at a turning point, and this conversation about its mission would be telling. Its evolution seems natural and inevitable from this vantage point, but Elisabeth could have continued in her first call without changing anything. That she did not is a tribute to her vision and clear sightedness.

Cornerstone of a New Hospital

April 18, 1888, the day before they laid the cornerstone of the new hospital, in the Gowan section of Brooklyn, had been rainy and blustery, threatening the opening game of the baseball season, Brooklyn vs. Cleveland. By evening it had cleared up enough so the game, which Brooklyn won, 10-1, had featured all the ceremonies and rituals of baseball's opening day. The mayor and clergymen appeared as honored guests. The next day when the Norwegian Hospital and Deaconess Motherhouse community gathered to lay the cornerstone for its new building on 4th Avenue, it was a typical brisk April day, the temperature in the 40s. They had chosen April 19, 1888, as the day because it was the fifth anniversary of the founding of the Norwegian Relief Society, begun a few days after Sister Elisabeth's arrival in New York. Although it had not been her dream to

Life aboard ship was difficult, and many arrived in ill health.

build a hospital on that day five years before, now it was. She could hardly believe their blessings as she watched the service unfold. To think they had come this far! She was both thankful and exhausted. Not surprisingly, she was ready for a vacation. Unfortunately, because she stopped keeping her diary, we have many fewer contemporary accounts of her work in Minneapolis and later back in Brooklyn. From this point on, we have to rely on her *Memoirs* and occasional letters as we seek to discover the rest of her story. Her last entry in the diary is in May 1888 when she bids farewell to the diary for good. "Now I will lay you aside, you old book . . . but you will remind me of the many things that have happened in these years and in these months in which the Lord has richly blessed our work. . . . Yes, Lord, be praised for all that has happened in your blessed name!"[290] It was with some sense of accomplishment that she looked back over the past five years. The hospital was being built with the support of many more people than she had thought possible when she first arrived; she had other sisters working in the hospital. Several doctors were now on staff. The board and a larger group supported her efforts. She was thankful, and exhausted.

Rest and Relaxation

Sister Elisabeth, who had worked without respite since her trip to Norway in 1886, needed a vacation. She and a friend, Marie Holmboe Iversen, very likely a relative of her friends the Holmboes in Tromsø, traveled to Chicago together. There they parted ways, Iversen went north, Fedde went south to visit an uncle of hers, John Hanson (1833-) in Missouri. He had married her mother's sister, Olene Sofie (1830-) who had emigrated in 1854. Fedde's aunt had died, but her cousin was still living in Chariton. She was curious to see them and this new and different part of America. There for the first time she saw conditions south of the Mason-Dixon line. The farm she came to visit was in Chariton, quite a distance from the depot, and she had to get there by horse and buggy. The place had several white stucco houses. She would stay in one of them with her cousin, Marie. Missouri seemed almost tropical to her. She became, almost instantly, she said, a banquet (*festmåltid*) for mosquitos. Although she had some experience with them, it was nothing like what she experienced in Missouri. "It was worse than anything else."[291] Her relatives lived among Germans and African-Americans on a former plantation where there had been slaves, something about which Sister Elisabeth was curious. She viewed the plantation with its slave huts and the owner's mansion with dismay, her moral sensibilities keen and sharp. She and her cousin rode around the farm, asking questions about all they saw in the empty slave quarters and the new little homes the former slaves had built for themselves. They heard a black preacher preach in a church the former slaves had built after the war. She thought it was the wildest and most restless service she had ever attended, but remarked with interest on the way the preacher led the congregation to give of their worldly goods. He would send the plate around and then count it, and when it was not enough, would send it around again, something he did four times, until they had collected five dollars, enough to support their work as a congregation. When a large woman stood up to sing, "Gonna' put on my golden shoes and walk all over God's heaven," she and her cousin got up and left. As something of a professional fundraiser herself, she was clearly impressed by the preacher's technique!

Her interest in the physical appearances of the people made her wonder about why there were so many light-skinned and light-haired people among the former slaves. When she asked a woman why that was, she told her that when the slaves did not bear enough children, the slaveholder would come out to the cabins and impregnate the women so there would be more slaves. Elisabeth found this difficult to hear, especially the fact that the woman who was telling her this had two children by the master. Much of what she found there, the results of slavery, appalled her. She would never forget it.

One of the most interesting foods she discovered was watermelons at the home of a millionaire, whom the neighborhood called "Kaiser Wilhelm," who looked the part of a Kaiser on his full-blood horse. At his home, they were invited to come in and sit cross-legged on the floor, something she had never done before. As they were sitting one of their hostesses got up from the floor and went to an organ in the room and began to play "Yankee Doodle." As they left the house, they saw many black sharecroppers standing around on the tobacco plantation. Later they were taken to a German couple who owned the land worth millions now. They had come before the Civil War and now were old and sick. Their current situation made Fedde wonder whether they were rich or poor. She did note that they had *Luther's Small Catechism* on the table and obviously used it daily. "Kaiser Wilhelm" had to leave for an errand in Kansas City. She and her cousin returned to her house, deciding it was the better place to be. Her uncle told them many stories about the Civil War, escaping with money in his boots which was never found by his captors when he was imprisoned by the rebels as he tried to escape into the North.

In the tropical climate and rich vegetation, which she said she could almost see growing, she had hung her clothes line beside grapes, sugar cane, and walnuts. As a typical Norwegian from the northern climes, she loved it, but found it too much. The mosquitos were unbearable, she said, and it was time she left. While she had been able to rest there, she was glad to come north. We can see from her description of the trip, long after she had been in Missouri, her curiosity about different experiences and places which she enjoyed with her fine sense of humor. In addition, we see her moral outrage at the poverty and results of slavery. While we could attribute this to her hindsight and not how she felt at the time, the experience as she described it seems to be an accurate memory. We can mark here both her curiosity and interest in all that she sees, her willingness to have new experiences, and her clear sense for what is right and wrong—not surprising at all from what we have come to know about her thus far.

It was from Missouri that she traveled to West Salem, Wisconsin, near LaCrosse. Coming from Missouri, she had to change trains many times, boarding a train near Dalton, probably the train from Kansas City to Mason City, and from there to LaCrosse. Because she could not catch a train to LaCrosse that evening and it was chilly, she needed a room. She found a hotel in Mason City, Iowa. Something had made her fearful, so she kept the lamp in the room burning. It was a wise move. During the night a man broke into her bedroom and tried to molest her. He had locked the door behind him and stood in the way, but she remembered there was a back passage so she ran to it, up the back stairs into the room of a startled couple who protected her through the night. She said she suffered shock from the incident for some time afterward and, for the first time, was glad to be homely ("grim").

CHAPTER THREE

MINNEAPOLIS

When Fedde came to the Twin Cities, many different church groups had gathered there: the annual convention of the General Council of Lutherans, the 250th anniversary of Swedish immigration to America, even the Women's Christian Temperance Union (WTCU), were all meeting in Minneapolis at the time, making it profitable for the railroads to offer cheap tickets. After she had been in Minneapolis for two days, Gjertsen found her and invited her to meet with the group he was assembling. Whether she had attended Spaeth's speech on the diaconate or not, we do not know, but it had spurred the men to gather together to discuss building such an establishment in Minneapolis. Now she was sitting in the room hearing their ideas and telling them about her own work. As Gjertsen and the others made their proposal to her that fateful day in September 1888, she did not have to think for long. The Brooklyn hospital at the moment was being built. Things seemed to be going well, and for the time being they did not need her. The Brooklyn Board of Man-

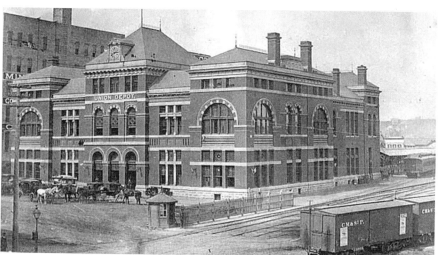

Union Depot, St. Paul

agers knew what needed to be done. She listened closely to Passavant and Gjertsen: What should she say? She thought for a bit, then nodded, "Yes." She decided to accept the challenge with some caveats, mostly having to do with her responsibilities in New York.

Sister Elisabeth wrote a letter to the board in Brooklyn and explained everything to them, promising to return as soon as the house in Minneapolis was established and on its own. It would take about two years, she supposed. Mrs. Børs wrote back, much upset at the news, but also willing to accept that God had called her to the work in Minneapolis, at least for the meantime. She said that they, probably the Board of Managers of the Motherhouse in Brooklyn, had decided, on hearing this surprising news, to write to Norway to call two women, Sisters Dorothea Zeiffert (1842-1915) and Karen Sodnak (1846-1901), to work in Brooklyn, help they had to have whether Sister Elisabeth remained there or not. The work had gotten to be too much for her alone. The Brooklyn board had received a telegram from Norway saying the two deaconesses from Norway had accepted its call and would be in Brooklyn by the end of March. This relieved Fedde somewhat of her responsibilities in Brooklyn. She promised to return after she had organized the work in Minneapolis.

Sister Elisabeth began, "full speed ahead!"[292] Gjertsen and Oftedal launched a fund drive to raise money; she bought medical supplies and furnishings for the Motherhouse and the hospital. After a meeting at Trinity Congregation, two women, Mary Alnæs and Martha Langaunet, came forward wanting to be deaconesses. (These names with their biblical references were oddly common among applicants to the sisterhood.) The speaker at the meeting is not mentioned, but it would not have been surprising if it had been Sister Elisabeth herself, as Gjertsen and Oftedal supported the rights of women to vote in the congregations, if not to speak. But we do not know.

Almost before they knew it, there was a Deaconess House ready to open. The October 31, 1888, issue of *Folkebladet* reported that Banker Sunde had offered his house in the loveliest and highest part of the city looking down on the Lake of the Isles. The Minneapolis Health Department had been quick to promise that the doctors, nurses, and probationary sisters would all have speedy access to two of the city's hospitals—the hospital intended for infectious diseases (pesthouse or lasaret) and one

for the poor where they could send patients and where the probation-
ary sisters could receive further training. On November 2, 1888, Sister
Elisabeth and her two colleagues began preparing the house for habita-
tion. Four doctors offered to serve the hospital: Doctors Tønnes Anton
Thams (1848-1912), Frederik F. Laws (1849-1917), Salisbury, and
Due. The board included Sunde, Oftedal, State Senator Lars Swenson,
R. Nilsen, R. Iversen, Han Bottelsen (a lay preacher), and Gjertsen.[293]
They were expecting a big celebration.

Dedicating the New Motherhouse in Minneapolis

The weather in the Twin Cities that November was typically bright
and cold for Minnesota. It had put roses on the cheeks of the girls in
town, the *St. Paul Globe* reported. Sunday afternoon, November 11,
1888, barely two months after her arrival, the Motherhouse at 2731 Hennepin Avenue was dedicated.[294]

The board and Fedde had scrambled to prepare the home so it could
begin its work quickly. Now it needed to prepare the community to support its plans. Many in the city had never heard of deaconesses, although
the idea of a hospital for Norwegian Lutherans was not difficult to sell.
The city was bustling with new building projects, railroads, and a system of horse-drawn city trams which made travel more convenient in the
city; the skyline of the city quickly changed as more and more impressive
buildings rose from the former hunting grounds. The previous Tuesday
Republicans had won the national election and were basking in their
victories in Minnesota. Heading the national ticket was the Republican
Benjamin Harrison who had defeated the Democrat incumbent Grover
Cleveland with the enthusiastic support of Northeastern and Midwestern Republicans. They gave Harrison a landslide victory in Minneapolis.
While the Augsburg leadership were liberals from Norway and had some
tendency toward the Democrats in America or the reform movements
such as the Prohibition or populist parties, a large majority of Scandinavians supported the Republicans because of Lincoln and the Civil War.

Both Sverdrup and Oftedal had brothers (Jakob Sverdrup and Lars
Oftedal) serving in the Norwegian Parliament at the time, both clergymen
on the left. They were close friends and fought together on the same side
in the political battles of the time in Norway. Sverdrup's uncle Johan
Sverdrup (1816-1892) had been prime minister until 1884. As the al-

liance between the left and the church became more and more strained in Norway, it was also being strained among Norwegian-Americans for the same reasons. Georg Sverdrup and Sven Oftedal both supported several reform movements, especially Prohibition and Women's Suffrage, although Oftedal was the more vocal in his advocacy. He thought of it as his cause and had agreed with the wife of his colleague at Augsburg, Elise Welhaven Gunnersen, that it was the major issue of the day. Oftedal's favoring of suffrage put him in a tight spot, especially when he had to speak against the increasingly anti-church proponents of suffrage such as Bjørnson whom he could abide no longer.

Oftedal was also a member of the Minneapolis library board and supported the idea, for example, that the Franklin Avenue Library purchase books in the Scandinavian languages to serve the Scandinavian immigrants in that area, a policy the Minneapolis library board has continued for other new immigrant groups. Augsburg Professor Theodor Reimestad (1854-1920), the musician at these festivities, had been the candidate for lieutenant governor on the Prohibition Party ticket. This meant he had also signed the pledge not only to stop liquor, but also to support women's suffrage. The male quartet he led for Augsburg had Prohibition as one of its missions, as did *Folkebladet* and many at Augsburg.[295]

Prohibition and women's rights were on the same page in this election. Frances Willard, the leader of the Women's Christian Temperance Union had made sure of that. Still, the uneasy bond of women's rights and the church through Prohibition seemed to split church people right down the middle: those in the church who favored women's suffrage and Prohibition, and those who opposed women's suffrage, but not Prohibition. The suffragettes were also split between those who thought the church was the problem and those who did not. Susan B. Anthony counseled Cady Stanton to desist from opposing the church because it drove many who would support them away. She thought, rightly, that offending church people was politically unwise. Those who opposed the church because they favored women's suffrage, like Cady Stanton, thought the church was the problem. The Augsburg professors and Pastor Gjertsen, who favored the vote of women, were often caught in this bind: Whether to be associated with the women's movement, half of which was against the church, or to oppose suffrage because the proponents were so critical of the church. It grew to be very difficult.

By the middle 1890s, women of property in both Norway and America could be elected to local committees like school boards, partly because they were seen by worthy divines such as Beecher to be the morally superior sex. As a newly elected member of the Minneapolis School Board, Gjertsen had sought endorsements from both Democrats and Republicans in his effort to be non-partisan. As a strong advocate of Prohibition, Gjertsen would push for women to vote in his congregation in the next decade.

Service of Dedication

The service of dedication began in the afternoon at 3:00 p.m. at the Motherhouse on Hennepin Avenue; attendees enjoyed the view from the house overlooking Lake of the Isles. The festivities commenced with the congregation singing a Pentecost hymn, after which Missionary Hans Bottelsen, also the sexton at Trinity, read Psalm 103 and prayed. The service continued with the singing of the first six stanzas of Paul Gerhardt's hymn frequently used by Lutherans for such events, "Commit Thou All that Grieves Thee" (*Befiehl du deine Wege*). Gjertsen, as the chairman of the board, the chief mover of the project, spoke briefly on the mission of the Institute: to provide peace in the midst of suffering, away from the tumult of the world, a place where people could receive both physical and spiritual help. Lars Swenson, treasurer of both Augsburg and the deaconess organization, prayed a closing prayer, and then the group sang Martha Clausen's closing hymn, "And Now We Must Bid One Another Farewell." Space was at a premium, so the festivities continued at Trinity church that evening.

Trinity Lutheran Congregation at the time was situated on 10th Avenue and 4th Street, a good walk from the Mother House. A capacity crowd had gathered to celebrate this new venture, both Norwegian Lutheran church officials as well as the Yankee Minnesota politicians: Former Governor John Sargent Pillsbury (1827-1901), among the richest Minnesotans; Captain Samuel Prather Snider (1845-1918), a popular Civil War veteran and a Republican representative from Hennepin County to the state legislature, newly elected to the House of Representatives; and Mr. George Augustus Brackett (1836-

George Augustus Brackett

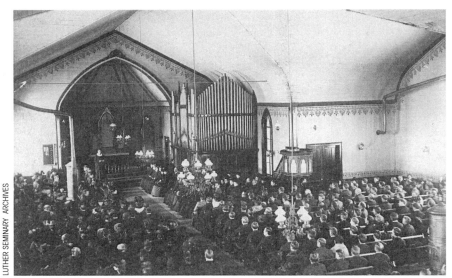

*Inside Trinity Congregation at the final service in the building in 1896.
Several deaconesses are sitting across from the pastor in the robe—very likely
M. Falk Gjertsen. Fedde was long since gone by this time.*

1921), a former mayor of Minneapolis, an industrial leader of the city,
and one of the founders of Lakewood Cemetery.

The service began with the singing of a hymn. Professor Sven Oftedal
followed with a sermon in Norwegian in which he considered the duties a
Christian had to help the sick and the poor. His speech took cognizance
of the fact that at last the Norwegian Lutherans in the city had established
a place where the poor could find shelter and food in the hard winter that
was about to descend on Minnesota. Because the pastors had seen more
of these problems than most others, he concluded, this effort would be a
blessing for them, as well as for the ladies aids such as the Tabitha Circle
of Trinity who, with their small gifts of nickels and dimes, had already
made a significant contribution, pushing as they had for several years
to get a deaconess house established in the city. Oftedal understood the
power of these women's groups and knew they should be thanked. He
had printed in his paper a small announcement inviting women to come
to the house on the following Friday to sew pillow cases and sheets. If
they had extra bed clothes they should bring their gifts either to the Motherhouse or to Pastor Gjertsen's home at 941 14th Avenue South, between
the hospital and the church, now a location over which freeways howl on
their way into Minneapolis.

Reimestad followed Oftedal's remarks with a solo. After that, Gjertsen gave a short talk in English on how the Deaconess House had come to be and thanked those who had brought them so quickly to this moment. It was an amazing thing, and something about which to give thanks. The Augsburg Chorus sang, giving the event an especially festive

Augsburg Quartet in 1888, standing left to right: Frantz Norman, Martin Havdaln, Johannes Nydahl; seated: Thedore Reimestand

feeling. Congressman Snider then spoke. A well-known veteran of the Civil War, he told of the suffering he had seen during that conflict and noticed, as had many before him, how the nurses on the battlefields and in the sick wards had brought peace and comfort to the sick and dying, like angels of mercy—the same work that the deaconesses were embarking on now in the city. As the Civil War was still vivid in the memories of most of the people sitting there, his remarks gave a special solemnity to the occasion. In his comments about the nurses on the battlefields, he was repeating a realization of many soldiers around the world as he remembered the women who had had served on the battle fields in Crimea, where Florence Nightingale gained her fame.

Most interesting, however, was the speech of ex-governor Pillsbury who expressed his amazement at the growth of the city. Minneapolis had been on the north side of the river in St. Anthony, and now it was growing on the south bank. Most amazing to him, and he knew whereof he spoke since he had lived there for many years, was that where Trinity now stood had been Indian hunting grounds a mere thirty-five years earlier. No friend of the Native American population, he regarded this as a good thing. Now Minneap-

Governor John Sargent Pillsbury

olis was a flourishing and growing city, with more institutions of mercy than any other city he knew. Brackett, in an expansive speech, prophesied, rather accurately, that soon the house they had just dedicated would be far too small for its mission and supposed that they would have to build a new place that cost not just thousands, but hundreds of thousands of dollars. He could see hundreds of deaconesses going forth from the house into the booming Northwest with their skills and earnest prayers to help the sick and needy. He was quite impressed that these immigrants, not long in the city, who, with their small gifts of nickels and dimes, had collected enough to begin such a work. Small stones can build a large building, he concluded. With that the congregation stood and sang the mission hymn most beloved by the Norwegians of the day, "O Happy Day When We Shall Stand" (*Tænk Naar Engang*).

The *Folkebladets* editor, quite pleased with the event, especially noted how impressed the English were with the sound of their choir and the large crowd. Such events, well attended by the Yankee politicians, gave the Minneapolis establishment at the time a sense for what these new Americans, largely unknown and speaking a foreign language, were doing in their midst.

Minneapolis Public Library on Hennepin Avenue with tram line

Oftedal concluded the service with a "gripping" appeal for money. As a former pastor at Trinity Congregation, he told a moving story of one such appeal he had received while serving the congregation. His speech had the desired effect: The offering they received totaled $103. While these numbers may seem small (the average pastor's or professor's salary at the time was about $400 to $600 a year), the offering could be reckoned to have been in today's dollars about $15,000. Merely eight weeks after they had met with Sister Elisabeth and broached the subject of a Deaconess Motherhouse in the cities, they were now dedicating one with a deaconess in their midst. One reads in these accounts an excitement and optimism at what had come to be so very quickly. It seemed almost unbelievable to read in *The Minneapolis Journal* the announcement that the Deaconess Institute, as it was called, was ready for occupation by both the sisters and the sick. Its founders and supporters had every reason to be pleased with the progress they had just made toward building a major institution of mercy in the new city, one that would endure for a century before it was taken over by Fairview Hospital, another Norwegian Lutheran hospital built up some years after Deaconess had started.

Beginning

The Motherhouse and Hospital on the northeast corner of Hennepin and 28th Street lay on the new horse-drawn tram line from the city center via Hennepin Avenue to Lake Street, still almost rural with enough green grass to pasture grazing animals. The tram lines had just recently been built to provide smoother riding over the bumpy and often muddy, nearly impassable, streets of the day. It made the Motherhouse easier to reach from both downtown and Augsburg. The next day after the dedication celebration, on November 12, 1888, the young women began their work. Sister Elisabeth later remembered their amazement when the three of them walked into the 2731 Hennepin Avenue building, ready to start. The Institute now included a Sister Superior, two probationary sisters, four rooms for their patients, one for the two probationary sisters, Mary and Martha. Sister Elisabeth took a suite of rooms in which she had an office, a sofabed, and a tiny living room. In addition to that the house had a small theater for surgery and place for a kitchen. A young woman from Eau Claire, who was only sixteen, applied, and had been accepted. Later her application was set aside until she was eighteen, but two others applied and were accepted. The records are not clear on who this applicant was. She may have stayed and worked at the hospital until she came of age because Sister Elisabeth refers on occasion to help that she got from someone working for them.

Martha and Mary began their education as nurses and deaconesses immediately. Sister Elisabeth taught nursing practices, and Professor Anders M. Hove (1859-) from Augsburg taught English; Pastor Nils Iversen (1843-1907), a pastor from North Minneapolis, taught religion. Hove, a Luther College graduate briefly became a part of the Augsburg faculty since many Norwegian students were learning English as a second language. As the seminary necessarily expanded its offerings in order to give its students a good and useful preparatory education, it realized that not every student's future would end in ministry. Soon the preparatory department would develop and become the college. The deaconesses also needed medical instruction and rudimentary science in the preparatory department, which later would become the early science division of the college.[296]

Suddenly articles began appearing in the church papers explaining why and what the deaconess movement was about and why Minneapolis needed such an institution. *The Lutherans*, (*Lutheraneren*), at the time edited by Sverdrup and Oftedal, in its November 10, 1888, issue explained why the institution had been an answer to prayer. Pastor Gjertsen, the article said, had seen the poverty in the community, especially when new immigrants appeared at his office with their heart-rending need. For this reason they were especially thankful that Fedde, on her vacation in Minnesota, had agreed to take a short leave from the work in New York to establish a Motherhouse and Hospital to serve Norwegian immigrants who needed such a refuge.

The first patient they took in, on November 17, was a young Swede with nerve fever. It had resulted in gangrene in his extremities and sores over his entire body. Fedde reported that it felt good to have a patient. She was glad to begin doing the work she was called to do as deaconess. However, because his condition resulted in a noxious odor, he could not be kept in the house. Sister Elisabeth took charge of him. Gjertsen indicated the young patient was put in a private home nearby and treated lovingly by Sister Elisabeth. Although Gjertsen noted they had done everything they could, the doctor knew from the beginning there had been little hope for the patient's survival. Sister Elisabeth remembered that, despite their best efforts, he died. His death came to him as liberation from unbearable pain, she wrote. Nerve fever, a diagnosis difficult to understand today, was frequently associated with the aftermath of typhus, but Sister Elisabeth in her *Memoirs*, written a quarter century later, remembered the gangrene as being caused by the young man being trampled by a horse.

About the same time another patient was admitted, also suffering nerve fever that had become gangrenous. His arms were black with gangrene, and the infection was spreading quickly throughout his body. The doctor suggested that his arms be amputated. These two difficult cases, according to Gjertsen, put the young probationary sisters, Martha and Mary, face to face with the worst diseases and the terrible sufferings of their patients. They worked faithfully, but it was not long before Sister Martha Langaunet contracted typhus and became deathly ill, as did Sister Mary Alnæs a few days later. Sister Elisabeth was the only one left to attend to the young man. She did have the help of the younger woman who had not yet been admitted to the training program, but the work was intensely exhausting to Sister Elisabeth who had to stand night and day over the two patients, attending to each of them alone. Her weariness caused her to doubt not only whether she could hold out, but also whether God was there. The board realized they had to get her help in the kitchen—one wonders if Sister Elisabeth was also cooking—but about that time Sister Martha had recovered enough to return to the work. Both of the patients now were covered with infected bedsores and died, one after the other.

In his article in *Folkebladet* some weeks later, Gjertsen grieved their deaths, but also rejoiced that both had come to the knowledge of salvation through the ministry of Sister Elisabeth. As the second patient was dying, she reported, his face filled with light, and he exclaimed, "Now I am going home; now I am going home!" Because he loved music and singing, he wanted Sister Elisabeth to play the organ for him. As he died, she was playing "Home Sweet Home."[297]

Church Unity

The coming year, 1889, would be a time of intense planning and organization as the pastors and professors worked to build a new united church which would bring together three smaller groups of Norwegian American Lutherans in the new country. The pastors and professors on the board of the Deaconess Institute had many other things besides the Deaconess Motherhouse to think about at the time. The occasion for this quickly realized merger had been a theological battle over predestination, or election, that had broken out in the Norwegian Synod, centered at Luther Seminary at the time in Robbinsdale, Minnesota, rather distant from the center of the young city.

Younger pastors and theologians such as Peter Andreas Rasmussen (1829-1898) and Ludvig M. Biørn (1835-1914) came to disagree with the older Norwegian Synod pastors' theological stance, and in 1887 they decided to break with it. They called their small rump group the Anti-Missourian Brotherhood. Not quite able to support a college or seminary, they realized they needed an institution of higher learning and gathered around St. Olaf College in Northfield, Minnesota. Their numbers were not sufficient to support a college and seminary. So the Anti-Missourians called the Norwegian Danish Conference (Augsburg Seminary) and

Ole Jensen Hatlestad

Norwegian Danish Augustana Synod (those around Augustana College) to merge with them.[298] The two previous churches had been together at the Scandinavian Augustana Seminary (1860-1870) in Paxton, Illinois, which included Danes, Norwegians, and Swedes. The Norwegians, under the leadership of August Weenaas, decided they needed to train their pastors in Norwegian, not Swedish, so they sued for peace and left in 1869 to build a seminary in Marshall, Wisconsin. After some disagreement, in 1870, some few of the Norwegians decided to leave the Conference to found the Norwegian Danish Augustana Synod led by Ole Jensen Hatlestad (1823-1892), Andreas Wright, and David Lysnes. Because they wanted to adopt the entire *Book of Concord* as their basic document and the Conference preferred only the Augsburg Confession and the Small Catechism, these pastors broke away from the Augsburg group and set up their own seminary which started in Decorah, and then settled in Beloit, Iowa. Now they were being called back together. The resulting merger would create a church of Norwegian American Lutherans of greater numbers than the aging Norwegian Synod. This merger prepared the way for all of the Norwegians to merge in 1917 in the Norwegian Evangelical Lutheran Church in America (NELCA). It may have been one of the reasons the board for the Deaconess Hospital seemed so confident it could build such an institution at the time, and so quickly. By the time the summer of 1888 rolled around, things were well underway. On August 15-23, just three weeks before Fedde met with the group in Gjertsen's home, twenty-eight leaders of the three Norwegian Lutheran churches had gathered in Eau Claire, Wisconsin, to work out the final agreements on the merger. It was a heady time. Anything was possible with their combined efforts. Just before the first board meeting of the Norwegian Deaconess Institute in Minneapolis, on November 15-23, over 300 delegates had met in Scandinavia, Wisconsin, to fashion their final agreements. One of the most encouraging parts of the agreement, to the Augsburg party, must have been the resolution that Augsburg Seminary as the seminary of the new church would gain an endowment of $150,000, from new gifts and existing monies, the *Minneapolis Journal* reported. Sven Oftedal, the fundraiser for the school, said he doubted the figure, knowing as he did that what they had counted as part of their current endowment was worthless paper. To his mind, it could not have been much over $50,000, if that.[299] Times, however, had been good for the seminary in the past several years and looked to be even better after 1890. Many said these two years were the most peaceful and productive years for Augsburg.[300] It is no wonder the Augsburg Seminary professors and friends were confident they had the means to establish the Deaconess Motherhouse in Minneapolis. They were going to be richer and bigger.

Just after the gathering in Wisconsin, the Deaconess Board had its first official meeting on November 26, 1888, in Dr. Laws' office in the Scandia Bank Building at 2021 17th Avenue South in the Cedar-Riverside area. Present were Gjertsen, Oftedal, Bottelsen, Swenson, Drs. Thams and Laws, with the banker Sunde. They began immediately by approving necessary medical purchases at the Scandia Drug Store on Riverside Avenue for medicines that would be necessary for their work, approving arrangements for the teaching of the young women (which textbooks to use and which teachers they would hire), commissioning Gjertsen to recruit religion teachers. They then authorized Sister Elisabeth and treasurer Swenson to buy an accounting book appropriate to the work. In addition they voted to repay Sister Elisabeth the $20 she

Lars Swenson was named treasurer of the board.

had spent of her own money as they readied the home for patients. While these were prudent and expected actions for the running of home, the issue of how to handle the finances would come up many times, given the shoe-string on which they operated. One does have to marvel that these leaders were able to think of this new venture in the middle of these myriad of church activities. It is a testament to their youthful vigor and maybe too much optimism. They resolved to meet the second Monday of every month at 3:00 at the Deaconess House.[301]

The board met, however, the next week on December 3 for what appears to have been a brief meeting in Dr. Tham's office at 1805 South 4th Avenue. Only two issues came up: approving the payment of a bill from a local business and appointing Dr. Thams as a committee of one to investigate the price of a telephone for the home, then report back at the next meeting. The next week they met at the regularly scheduled hour in the Motherhouse. The question of how to manage the finances

Deaconesses in Minneapolis after Fedde left

took up most of the time—as well it might for a new venture as big as this. The first motion set up a process for reviewing, approving, and paying the bills. All of the expenses for the home were to be approved by the Board of Directors and signed by the president of the board before the treasurer would pay the bills. Sister Elisabeth would present the monthly bills for each month to Gjertsen, the chair of the board. It voted to reimburse Sister Elisabeth for a variety of expenses she had incurred in the past month: $25 for groceries, $17.18 for diverse expenses. Swenson, the treasurer, recommended that the board buy insurance for the home in Sister Elisabeth's name. In addition, they discussed issues having to do with building outhouses in the city. They heard in the treasurer's report that they had received $853, spent $101.30, and had $751.70 in the bank. Oftedal then reported on the faculty they had already hired to teach, Hove and Iversen, adding that Pastor Gjertsen would teach one hour of soul care (*sjelesorg*) every week.

Although nothing is stated in the minutes, the need to meet on Christmas Eve to approve one bill for $36.64 for building materials looks odd, even if the minutes do not indicate anything out of place. It was an extraordinary meeting, outside of the normal schedule. There must have been a number of issues discussed that did not make it into the minutes, nor did they need a formal meeting for such discussions. Since most were members of Trinity Congregation and saw each other in both business and church activities nearly every day, we can assume many conversations and decisions transpired over the Christmas holidays. One can infer from the resolutions passed at the January 7, 1889, meeting that much had been decided before the meeting. Not all of the board members were present, not Sister Elisabeth or the doctors. Most of the business of the meeting was receiving and approving the payment of bills. In addition to these actions, they also resolved to pay Sister Elisabeth $200 a year in quarterly installments. Another resolution dealt with refining the process for the receipts of the bills: They were to be approved both by the president and, at this meeting, they added the secretary of the board to the list of people who had to approve the bills before they would be paid.[302] This recurring concern is never explained, but it seems to indicate there were already some disagreement between the board and Fedde concerning her financial management.

At the next meeting, on January 21, 1889, most of the board members, including Sister Elisabeth, were present. She reported on the two patients who had died. After these two deaths, and the illness of Sister Martha, the Minneapolis Health Department ruled that the house had to be disinfected (fumigated) after Sister Martha became well enough to move. For seven weeks she had been so ill they were not sure she would survive. They could not receive any more patients until the house could be disinfected. At the time of the meeting, however, they were glad to report that she was recovering and even able to walk some, but they knew she would not be able to resume full activities for a while. Although at the time they did not know lice caused typhus, they did know they needed to fumigate the building. The city's Health Department had been helpful, allowing them to wait until Sister Martha could be moved. This meant that for a brief period their work had to be halted.

Included in their deliberations was a resolution asking Gjertsen to write to Dr. Adolph Spaeth in Philadelphia to get some information about the rules for running the hospital at the Motherhouse there. While there is no record of the conversation, one can imagine that the group, despite its boundless optimism, was wondering what they had started and how they could continue running the institution wisely, especially how to handle the standard business practices necessary for the institution to flourish. In addition they wanted to see what the rules were for the deaconesses in the Philadelphia Motherhouse. To help publicize this work begun so quickly, they recommended that Gjertsen write articles in various church papers about the Institute, articles that would make the community aware of the Deaconess Institute and tell young women about this new calling available to them now. At the next meeting on February 4, 1889, the board heard the news from Sister Elisabeth that the hospital had been successfully disinfected and could now admit new patients. Among other actions taken, the directors heard Sister Elisabeth's report, with her expenses, and voted to pay them. They then scheduled an extra meeting for February 7, at 5:00 p.m., in Dr. Laws' office.

Gjertsen's article appeared in *Folkebladet* on February 6, just after the February 4 meeting. He spoke of troubles and difficulties not recorded in the minutes of the board meeting. The situation appears to have been dire, much more dire than the minutes indicated. With his characteristic optimism Gjertsen reported many of the activities and decisions the board and home had made over the past few months, but they had need for funds. Even though the home was now fumigated, they could not begin the work again, Gjertsen wrote, without having more money. The board had authorized an ingathering of money by distributing to their supporters little books to fill with nickels and dimes, a common way of asking people to give at the time. Given the many Norwegian Lutherans in area, they were hoping that this would assure that they would have enough money to pay their bills without which they would not make it. He concluded by noting that the work they were doing should win support from most everyone, urging all who were friendly toward the work to save their small coins to build up a fund that would help them reopen the hospital and house. Those who agreed to do so should contact him.[303]

Difficulties All Around

From Gjertsen's pleas, one might think the Motherhouse seemed to be in danger of never reopening. The board in an extra meeting on February 11, heard the report from Dr. Thams saying that he could no longer work alone and needed other respectable Norwegian doctors to help him, suggesting Drs. Knut Ørn Høegh (1844-1925) and Karl Bendeke (1841-1905) as other Norwegian physicians who might be able to treat the sick.

Karl Bendeke

It was at this meeting that Sister Elisabeth asked for five weeks off so she could return to Brooklyn. As she wrote in her *Memoirs*, the deaconess she had left in charge at the Brooklyn site had become more and more "unchurchly" (meaning probably not Lutheran). She returned to wait for the new sisters.

Sisters Dorothea and Karen, who would be traveling to Brooklyn in March on the S/S *Danmark* nearly lost their lives in a shipwreck. The *Danmark*, a ship in the Thingvalla Line, had sailed from Copenhagen on March 20, 1889, with a large number

Knut Ørn Høegh

of emigrants on board. From there she went to Christiania where the two deaconesses had boarded. Her crew was fifty-nine with 665 passengers, all but twenty-six in steerage. Many of the passengers were women

Abandoning the Danmark *for the* Missouri

and children going to America to find their future with new husbands or new jobs as domestics. When they had abandoned the *Danmark* for the *Missouri,* no life was lost and all were taken to the Azores where they could get water and food, something the overburdened *Missouri* needed desperately. With more than 700 people on the *Danmark,* the *Missouri* needed to land quickly.

In the accounts of the struggles of the ship, the deaconesses, described by the American papers as

> sisters of a Scandinavian religious sect in New York went about among the terrified passengers calming their fears, giving them religious counsel and endeavoring to cheer them up. Their efforts had a very marked effect, particularly among the women.[304]

The newspaper account praised the work of the sisters as they helped calm the passengers and held services for them, especially the children as they met the fearful waves and storm in the life boats and then arrived at the Azores. The rescued passengers spent the last Sunday, as the voyage was ending, in worship and prayer.

> They were aided in their devotions by the peaceful-faced sisters and preachers who had risen among them since their peril. That evening, their last to see the sun sink in the sea, a sound of great harmony and beauty went out from the ship *Missouri* far across the water. The children of Denmark were singing hymns.[305]

This account gives us a sense for how the deaconesses were seen by the public, strange as they may have appeared in their garb to many, but praised for their calmness in the face of peril. When the *Missouri* arrived in Philadelphia it was escorted by other boats and met with great crowds praising the captain for his heroic resolve to save all of the passengers on the *Danmark* which, to the amazement of many, he did.

This near tragedy had delayed the arrival of the two sisters who had been expected in Brooklyn at the end of March. Fedde decided to stay in Brooklyn until they got settled.[306] They arrived on April 22, 1889, in Philadelphia, so it was some time before they could begin working at the hospital. Fedde took the time in Brooklyn until they reopened the hospital in Minneapolis. She very likely was exhausted from all she had done in Minneapolis.

The Minneapolis board met again on March 17 to respond to the request of the Deaconess Home in Brooklyn that Sister Elisabeth's leave from Brooklyn be extended by fourteen days.[307]

A week later at their next meeting they authorized the payment of some bills and discussed what they would do with the Motherhouse if Sister Elisabeth did not return from Brooklyn—whether it should continue or not.[308] The future did not seem clear to them, especially without Sister Elisabeth, which they were beginning to fear might happen.

Only a few months had elapsed since their confident beginning. Now they had to face the prospect of not being able to continue. On April 25, 1889, the board met in Dr. Law's office to discuss the future of the organization. The minutes report

> That after discussing the work of the Deaconess home and
> its future work, it was decided to write (*tilskrive*) Sister Elisabeth. A committee composed of Pastor Gjertsen, Professor
> Oftedal, and Bottelsen were elected to write the letter.[309]

The meeting adjourned to meet again at noon the next day. The board seemed to be aware that they should be looking for a way to continue without Sister Elisabeth, a likelihood they would have to face some time in the future, in any event, but this was sooner than they expected. They had asked Sisters Marie, Martha, and another unnamed sister whether any would be willing to continue as nurses in the home if Sister Elisabeth did not return. Sister Marie said she would, but the others could not give their answer at the moment. The board voted to go no further with its deliberations until it had heard directly from Sister Elisabeth as to her plans.[310]

The board, it can be inferred, was worried about whether the work could continue and had some inkling Sister Elisabeth might not return, and they were not a little annoyed with Sister Elisabeth. Several things were at issue now: Sister Elisabeth's position with the board, her ability to run the hospital to their liking, and her independence.

She received the letter soon afterward, but there is no record in the minutes of its contents. It left her confused, so in a cry for help on May 4, 1889, she wrote Professor Sverdrup asking him for his honest advice. Marked strictly confidential, Sister Elisabeth poured out her heart to Sverdrup saying of all the men she had met in Minneapolis, he was the only one whom she could trust unconditionally. Along with it she included the letter of call and the letter of acceptance or resignation she intended to send after she heard from him. Gjertsen

Georg Sverdrup

apparently had said in his letter of April 17, 1889, that they would pay for her trip to Brooklyn, but what else he had to say, she did not tell Sverdrup. Her main question at this time was which call to take: Brooklyn or Minneapolis. The board in Brooklyn had allowed her to work in Minneapolis because they had a new sister, probably probationary Sister Mathilde Madland (1859-1923), to take her place, and the two coming from Norway. In the meantime, the Brooklyn house needed a leader, especially now that they were building a hospital. What should she do? She did not feel well. What was God's will for her? In addition, she wrote, her health did not allow her to do as much as she had before. She no longer had the strength to do the physical labor required, nor face the strife. "Oh! What conflict there is in this valley of tears!" she concluded. "Please answer me as soon as possible," she concluded, giving her address as 31 Stone Street, New York, the home of Gabriel Fedde and her sister.[311]

Sverdrup answered her immediately, but what he said we can only infer from her next letter. She expressed her gratitude effusively: "You do not know how thankful I am to you for your dear heartfelt letter. During such a time of distress it is good to know a safe place to go." She then went on to say that she would soon send her letter to the board regarding its call, and would have resigned immediately if she had not been so worried about the sisters and the work of the Institute in Minneapolis, especially since they had done so much to get things going. Now, it was all in God's hands, she said. She would come back to Minneapolis if Sverdrup thought she should, but she did not trust Gjertsen, fearing he would oppose her. She then made a remark about Gjertsen that may explain some of her feelings about returning, but she does not give the reason for the comments. She had come to understand that Gjertsen had an entirely different spirit—"poor man, for his own answers, thoughts and expressions." Her eyes had been opened to his character, she said, and she wondered what God meant by all this. She went on to say that she wished that she could be with the sisters in Minneapolis and expressed her frustrations with the work, saying she had asked God to be free and quit of the deaconess vocation, wondering whether she should change her vocation.

She confessed that she had been so weary that many times she had wondered if the door was opening for her to become a doctor. Doctors she had worked with had counseled her to do so, and "I believe it could happen in spite of my being thirty-eight years old. Could that dream even with all the work come to be?"[312] This dream of Fedde's was attainable, even at her age. There were by this time a number of women physicians in America. Sister Elisabeth may have wearied of her place in the pecking order of the hospitals and disliked having to take orders, obediently, from the doctors and the other men on the board who assumed their authority over her, something we can see had rankled her. She may very well have envied the almost unchallenged power of the doctor and thought it might be good for her to have such power. It was clear from her love of the medical instruction in Christiania that she had a gift for the medical side of the deaconess vocation.

Actually, it would have been easier for her to become a doctor in the United States than a nurse since at the time the nursing profession was still rather inchoate and somewhat undefined. The first woman to become a doctor in the U.S. was Elizabeth Blackwell (1821-1910). The Woman's Medical College of Philadelphia had been built so that women

Elizabeth Blackwell, first woman doctor in the U.S.

could be admitted to medical studies as early as 1860, some fourteen years before Bellevue Hospital in New York and others opened nursing schools for women which were based on the Florence Nightingale plan. Sister Elisabeth was well aware of the fact she could have become a doctor in the United States. In Norway women could not become doctors until 1893 when Marie Spångberg graduated in medicine from the University of Oslo. One Norwegian woman, Ragnhild Botner (1868-1955), had come to America to receive a medical degree so she could serve in China, since Chinese women mistrusted male doctors. When Elisabeth writes this to Sverdrup, we can see a mid-life crisis in full bloom.

She then abruptly changed the subject and proposed that the Deaconess Home should also have an orphanage, something she thought could be done soon, not in the distant future. She concluded the letter with the fear she had wearied him with her complaints. She hoped to hear that he and his children were doing well which would make her very happy. She was now living with her sister and doing well. "Please receive my heartiest well wishes."[313]

The record goes silent for a few weeks at this point, but we can assume that the board deliberated many times informally as to what to do about the hospital and Motherhouse: whether it could be continued without Sister Elisabeth. Obviously she had wearied of Gjertsen's bombast and found him untrustworthy; in fact, his great oratorical powers

Sven Oftedal

seemed to be off putting to her. She rarely mentions his name without some slightly denigrating description of him: "well speaking (*veltalende*) Gjertsen." What Sverdrup thought is not clear, but she had decided he was someone she could confide in. She had determined she could work with him, not Gjertsen or Oftedal, even if Sverdrup at the moment was not on the board. Whether or not he advised her to answer in the following way, we do not know, but her letter does make clear both her willingness to continue her position in Minneapolis, but also her unwillingness to be treated the way she felt Gjertsen, Oftedal, and Bottelsen treated her.

The letter she wrote to the board is undated, but it is an answer to Gjertsen's letter of April 27.

To the board of the Deaconess Work in Minneapolis:

After I have tried "myself and the case" before me, I will now give the board my answer. When I lay the two letters before me, my letter of call and this last one, the case stands clearly before me: what I was called to, namely to manage the hospital and the Deaconess Institute which the honorable committee will begin and run. To that I was called and with much persuasion and many promises I was asked to leave the position I was currently bound to with such strong bonds and which was my home.

They [in Brooklyn] promised that the sisters would come from Norway so I saw in that God was persuading me with my own exhausted strength to begin anew [in Minneapolis]. So I took the cross upon myself and went, not for the sake of my flesh, but out of my own obedience. Following the wisdom and the ability God has given me, I decided to manage and educate the sisters and get the hospital and deaconess work going as well as I knew how to. Now there is an emergency in my old home [where I must stay for now] and I claim it is one of the promises to be fulfilled if I am to travel back [to Minneapolis] in time. It was decided, although not by all, especially those who have made the promise that I could go. The goal for my travel [back to Brooklyn] was to restore life in the home I had left and which had suffered great troubles with my leaving before the sisters came. The Board here asked the Board in Minneapolis to lengthen my stay here [in Brooklyn] until the sisters arrived and for that purpose they answered yes. Now the sisters have come who were saved in a wonderful way so I am a lot more willing [to come to Minneapolis] than before now that this place is in the sisters' hands. Then I received the command that I stay until I received the letter.

Now I have the letter.

My answer is this: I am willing to do all that is in my power to run the hospital and the Deaconess house to which I was called on October 11, 1888, and which I accepted. But if the Board maintains its decisions which are recorded in the last letter of April 27, 1889, signed by Mr. Gjertsen, Oftedal and Bottelsen, then I must regard the agreement between the board and myself broken and I am consequently removed from my position.[314]

When the board received the letter is not clear. When did she send it? The fact that the letter is filed in Sverdrup's archives causes one to wonder who else saw the letter. They all knew about it because when she returned things appear to have changed, at least from the record of the next meeting of the board. What was obvious to them was that she was not warmed by any of the three she called out by name in her answer. All of them were preachers and fine orators, but it was Sverdrup she preferred. He was known for his trenchant wit and fine preaching, but not his loquaciousness. Sister Elisabeth knew the reality of life as a nurse and also as an administrator of hospitals where people at the edge of life met with her daily. What mattered was the plain truth. Eloquence did not help much in these situations, and it is easy to imagine she would come to distrust Gjertsen and Bottelsen, especially.

Although Gjertsen was very much for women in politics and public life, that was not a guarantee he treated them well. He wanted them to have the vote in the congregation, but how did he treat them personally? His character is something of a mystery that has never been resolved. There is an odd coda to the story: Ten years later Gjertsen would be accused by Pastor Carsten Hansteen, Sister Elisabeth's close friend and colleague at the Seaman's Mission in Brooklyn, now returned to Norway, of having an inappropriate relationship

M. Falk Gjertsen

with Esther Paulson, wife of Michael Paulson, an employee of the Inner Mission Society, and young enough to be his daughter. Gjertsen had been traveling on a preaching vacation with Hans Bottelsen, also on the Deaconess Institute Board. They visited several spas for their health on their trip. Hansteen wrote Sverdrup with the accusations, thinking he could deal with them as Gjertsen's superior, which he was not.[315] He was only a member of Gjertsen's congregation. During Gjertsen's efforts to recover his reputation, rumors swirled about him as a lady's man with several inappropriate liaisons, none of which was proven, although Fedde seems to have heard something of them. Tantalizing, they are also common accusations against charismatic evangelists. Was Fedde reacting to his careless flirting, empty words, or did she see something that had caused her to think Gjertsen was not as he portrayed himself? Something had happened, and she would not return if she had to work directly with him. She did not include Oftedal, in this instance, maybe because she knew Sverdrup would not brook any criticism of him since he and Oftedal were so close. Oftedal's brother, Lars, had been helpful to her in Norway, but later in this same year of 1889 confessed to an inappropriate relationship with a woman that led to his downfall. It was more serious than the one Gjertsen had to defend himself against a decade later. Sverdrup, who received Hansteen's letter against Gjertsen, tried to deal

Fedde with Minneapolis deaconesses (left to right) front row: Martha Langaunet, Sister Elisabeth, Agnette Fagerlie; back row: Ingeborg Birkeland, Amalie Kittelsen, Lina Strøm, Marie Langaunet

fairly with the pastor, but came to believe the accusations. Gjertsen had to resign as pastor of Trinity. He did so, leaving with a flourish, walking down Franklin Avenue with other disgruntled Trinity members to establish Bethany Lutheran Church. Did this fracas in 1889 between Fedde and Gjertsen produce results unforeseen a decade later? It is difficult to know, but without a doubt if the work was to continue with Sister Elisabeth, Sverdrup would have to be the chairman of the board, not Gjertsen. They all appeared to know this.

While she waited for an answer from Minneapolis, Sister Elisabeth was putting things in order at the hospital in Brooklyn, getting ready for the ceremony of laying the cornerstone. On May 29, 1889, to the joy and astonishment of the community, they had arrived at this point. Mrs. Børs laid the cornerstone for the new building in the name of the Triune God. Pastor Hansteen preached on Genesis 32:10: "I am not worthy of the least of all the deeds of steadfast love and all the faithfulness that you have shown to your servant." Fedde's dream had come true.

There is an interesting report on this event in *The Bergensaddresscontoir* of June 22, 1889. Norwegians were proud of the accomplishment of the Norwegian colony. The write-up, which had been sent to the paper via a letter of someone who attended the event, included Pastor Hansteen's sermon along with the remarks by the Danish pastor, Andersen. The writer focused mostly on the charitable work of Mrs. Børs, without whose financial support the project would never have been completed. The correspondent gets some facts wrong: saying that the hospital has been open for one year, since 1888, missing that it had been operating since 1885. Then the correspondent muses some about the fact that while the colony was well served by the hospital, it had also been the occasion for rather strong conflicts and declining interest from its supporters. He told of the work during the

COURTESY MINNESOTA HISTORICAL SOCIETY

Minneapolis deaconess dress from 1889 to 1893

past year, which included treating sixty-four patients, forty-two of whom were treated without payment. Twenty-eight families had received help with their rent, 126 had been helped with food, fifty-seven with clothes, etc. He regretted that Norwegians were not very generous with their private gifts, and then listed the many contributors to the building, among them an anonymous gift of $4,700. All told, he concluded, "we should be thankful for the warm interest the hospital had kindled in many in the New York area." Not one word about Sister Elisabeth. To be fair, she had been gone from Brooklyn for a year, but she was at the dedication, in fact, had come back for it. Leaving her name out of the letter seems inexplicable. The troubles that the colony had experienced over the years because of the variety of little interest groups always came bubbling to the surface at unexpected times. Despite the pride of the entire Norwegian colony in this achievement, the leadership of the Seamen's Mission in Bergen had made the ruling that the pastors at the mission should not perform any ministerial functions for Norwegian settlers. This simply exacerbated the tensions between these various groups. One's suspicions that this could have been a report from Everson have to be considered. He, however, should have known that the hospital had started in 1885. Whatever, the omission of Sister Elisabeth's name in this long and expansive report is something at least to be noted.

Back in Brooklyn

While Sister Elisabeth had been sojourning in Minneapolis, the board in Brooklyn had been working not only to complete the building of the new hospital, but also to make its procedures more applicable to the current situation. Increasing the endowment meant meeting the requirements of the City Board of Health so they could be incorporated as a hospital. It was no longer simply a relief organization for Norwegians, with a sister walking around Brooklyn with a basket on her arm looking for poor and indigent Norwegians. Now it was an institution prepared to serve any and all who came to it for help. The Brooklyn board had to rethink completely its by-laws and articles of incorporation. Several things made for such a rethinking: Attracting non-Lutheran philanthropists would be easier, as Mrs. Børs had insisted from the beginning, if the name were not in Norwegian and easy for native English speakers to say. The requirement that all members of the board be Lutheran also had to be discussed. Another requirement that caused concern was the notion that the institution existed only for needy Norwegians. As late as 1891 a Swedish woman was denied admittance because of her ethnicity, and another woman was admitted only because her husband was Norwegian.

Another question was who could admit patients. At the beginning, when the patients were not so numerous, it had been Sister Elisabeth and the board who admitted patients. Doctors should also have that right, something they realized after they learned that Dr. Turner, the head doctor, could not admit his own patients, not only because they may not have been Norwegian, but also because he himself did not have the authority to do so. As the organization moved toward becoming a hospital, the notion that all the patients should be poor no longer worked. The medical staff was also increasing, which meant that the voices of these new doctors also began to shift the mission. People of all sorts, rich or poor, Lutheran or non-Lutheran, Norwegian or non-Norwegian, needed medical attention, now the main purpose of the institution.

Finally, the question of whether or not to keep the Deaconess Motherhouse became something of an issue. Although the deaconess movement was still growing during this decade, to build a school to teach and train them, and a place to house them added expensive burdens to the organization. These questions became central to the board as it worked to build the hospital, now in the absence of Sister Elisabeth. (By 1892, they revised the Articles of Incorporation and By-laws to take into account their changed circumstances.) Meanwhile, Sister Elisabeth remained in Brooklyn, trying to figure out what to do next.

Starting Up Again in Minneapolis

On July 2, 1889, Georg Sverdrup wrote a friendly letter to Sven Oftedal about things having to do with the annual meeting of the Conference which had been held, as usual, in June. In it he added that he thought things had settled down regarding the Deaconess Institute during the summer heat and the empty campus. Things would clear up over the summer with a little moderate work ("*lidt maadeholdent Arbeide*"), then strength would return. "The pastor" (Gjertsen?) was by "the lake," probably Lake Minnetonka where he and many other Scandinavians owned homes in what was called the Saga Hill area.[316] The deaconesses had moved out of the Hennepin Avenue location for the time being. He thought things would be more clear "when she was here and there was no other advice than to try to keep it going" (*naar hun først er her og der ingen anden Raad er end at prøve at holde det gaaende*) which was necessary."We do have a patient yet to care for." He was obviously expecting Sister Elisabeth to return. Had he heard from her privately?

She did return by the end of July or early August because she was there for the signing of the Articles of Incorporation on August 17, 1889. With his good sense, Sverdrup thought that Sister Elisabeth's presence would put them back on an even keel, partly because she would not be able to avoid doing what was necessary. This was a shrewd measure of her character. In addition, Sverdrup seems to have been aware that he had some responsibility for the work.[317]

It may also be that with the new church he would have fewer obligations and could turn his attentions to the Deaconess Hospital. Plans for the new denomination were now proceeding with what could be almost called lightning speed. Høyme, president of the Conference, would become the president of the new church, and in that capacity would be more involved with the board of the Deaconess Home.

One can infer from the minutes of the next meeting of the board on July 30, 1889, that many of the solutions had been agreed to before the gathering. Later Sverdrup noted that Fedde's being gone for a longer period than the board had agreed to had caused the Minneapolis work to fall apart.

> Of the three consecrated sisters [this is not correct because there were no consecrated sisters in Minneapolis until after Sister Elisabeth left] one left, the other two had to be let go, the treasury was empty, and some of the committee's members resigned. But the Deaconess House should not die in Minneapolis in that way.[318]

Andreas Helland, in his biography of Sverdrup, notes that "when several of the members of the committee had given up in despair, it was he [Sverdrup] who stepped in and carried the plan through to a successful realization."[319] Sister Elisabeth's *Memoirs* agree with the assessment of Sverdrup and Helland: She had returned ready to work but she found everything at a standstill. All that was left "were sisters and furniture and a large debt."[320]

From the board's motion to collect money from one of the patients for his care at the home, one can assume they were still operating minimally as a hospital. They also voted to pay a small salary they owed to the two probationary sisters who had been let go temporarily. More significant, however, were the resolutions which recognized Sister Elisabeth as more of an equal. They named her as a member of the board, as well as the treasurer for the contributions that came in from the "dime books" they had distributed to their constituency. In addition to this, she and Pastor Gjertsen were selected to look for a new location for the hospital. Sverdrup was asked to nominate men who could be members of the new board. Many of them had been on the board before, but Sverdrup encouraged them to begin anew, probably thinking, rightly, that his taking of the helm might persuade them to try again. Articles of Incorporation were filed on August 17, 1889, with the State of Minnesota. The new articles required a board of nine members with staggered terms and allowed members to join the corporation with a small annual contribution of one dollar. Soon, Fedde said, everything was going full speed and Tabitha, Trinity's women's organization, was once again helping with its support.

That the Articles of Incorporation were completed is a tribute to Sverdrup's organizational skills. At this time he was also leading the seminary, editing *Lutheraneren*, the paper of the Conference, and would go on to edit several other such journals, among them *Gasseren*, the magazine for the Malagasy mission. The most significant change in the Institute's operating procedures was the change in the status of Fedde. The Notary Public for Hennepin County, Adolf Edsten, recorded the names of all who appeared before him to make the corporation legal: M. Falk Gjertsen, Elisabeth Fedde, A. C. Dahl, Ingvald Eistensen (1843-1901), Olaf Hoff (1859-1924), John H. Hove, Lars Swenson, Endre Eriksen Gynild (1859-1928), Bottelsen, Georg Sverdrup, Anton C. Thuraas (1851-), and Fredric F. Laws (1849-1917). These people had

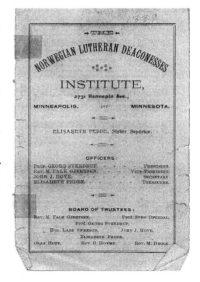

been handpicked by Sverdrup and most had been on the previous board, now assured that it would be led by Sverdrup whom they trusted. It did not include Oftedal, who may have been traveling at the time, but Gjertsen is there. Fedde's status in the organization had been much improved.

As per the Articles of Incorporation, they elected officers to be in place for the first meeting in September: President Sverdrup, Vice Chairman Gjertsen; Secretary John H. Hove; Treasurer Sister Elisabeth Fedde. Fedde now had equal status on the board with voice and vote. After they dealt with their financial situation, they voted to print 500 certificates of membership which they could sell, plus 1,000 copies of the Articles of Incorporation to send to the pastors and congregations who supported them. They hoped this would raise enough money to pay their old bills. To take charge of this, they elected Olaf Hoff. They then voted to send the letter of call to Sister Elisabeth, now referred to as Sister Superior (*Forstanderinden*) Elisabeth. In English the name became Sister Superior, probably to avoid the Catholic practice in the convents of calling their leader Mother

Olaf Hoff

Superior. They also needed to continue looking for another locale for the institution since the lease for their current property would soon expire. They reelected Fedde and Gjertsen, adding Dr. Laws to the committee. They also voted to lower the price of a hospital stay from $7 a week to $5. The next meeting would be at President Sverdrup's office at the seminary. Her letter of call laid out her responsibilities clearly as well as the responsibilities of the board:

> On the resolution of Board of Trustees of the Norwegian Lutheran Deaconess' Institute, passed at the meeting on the 17th August we call the undersigned to be the director of the Norwegian Deaconess Home and its connected hospital to which end we need from you [assurance]that you will faithfully lead the education of the sisters in their holy call into which they have shown themselves, that you will administrate the home and the hospital budget so that the patients will receive

orderly physical and spiritual care . . . and so that there can be good order in the home and hospital.

On our side, we commit ourselves as an organization to pay you $200 a year for your life's work. We also agree to care for the Deaconess home and its associated hospital including your tenure at the deaconess home and the connected hospital, organization and movement. If it is necessary on both sides to end the call, three months' notice must be given.

Sverdrup brought steadiness to the board and the entire project. After the flurry of official tasks required by the new Articles of Incorporation and paying off the debt, they had to plan for the annual meeting on September 3, at Trinity Church. The minutes show the regular meetings proceeded with dispatch. Part of the reason Sverdrup had more time now was that his future wife, his sister-in-law Elise Heiberg, who had been trained as a deaconess in the Motherhouse in Christiania, had arrived from Norway ostensibly to take care of Sverdrup's children. Whether they had planned to marry before she came is not sure, but it was not uncommon for a sister of a deceased wife to come to help raise her sister's children, and then marry the widower.

When Elise Heiberg arrived in New York, she was met by Gabriel Fedde, Sister Elisabeth's brother-in-law, who hosted her and got her on the train to Minneapolis. In a brief letter to Sverdrup, Fedde included receipts for the expenses he had incurred in getting Miss Heiberg a ticket to Minneapolis on a sleeping car to Chicago. He had been in contact with Sverdrup for a while, trying to get a pastor for the new congregation he was a part of and with whose piety he agreed. He concluded the letter with a note on Sister Elisabeth. He was glad that Sverdrup was now the chair of the board and hoped that the work would go well. He did not, however, think it was good that she was the treasurer for several reasons: "Very unfortunate" (*Meget uheldigt*). He thought time would change many things.[321] What he meant by this is not self-evident, but Sister Elisabeth had spent the summer with them in Brooklyn and he had very likely heard a great deal about the situation in Minneapolis. In addition he was on the board of the Brooklyn Norwegian Relief Society and had dealt with his sister-in-law as a member of the board. She was probably along with the group as they had begun rethinking the mission of what they

The house may be the Deaconess Hospital on Hennepin. We have no known picture of the first house, but one can see a lake behind the house and the picture was found in the Lutheran Deaconess Institute materials in the Luther Seminary Archives.

would soon call the Norwegian Lutheran Deaconess Home and Hospital. Nothing in the record indicated Fedde was not doing well in her new position, but the constant uneasiness with finances continued. Her own *Memoirs* record how things began again. The hospital work grew quickly, so fast that they soon realized it would be necessary to find a larger facility to hold the patients who came to them for help, plus more room for several applicants to be deaconesses. Unfortunately diphtheria broke out in their hospital among both patients and students. Because the hospital did not admit people with infectious diseases, they had to find another place for their students. There was a lasaret—where people with infectious diseases were sent for a kind of quarantine—south of the city where some of the students went to recover. Most often it had meant a place for those with leprosy, a disease at the time still endemic among west coast Norwegians, who brought it to America with them. Dr. Hansen, the doctor who had discovered the bacillus, had come to Minnesota the summer before, in 1888, to study the immigrants and see how many of them had brought the disease to America and whether any had contracted the disease here. In the paper which he gave in Rochester in May 1888, he noted that he had found 160 Norwegian immigrants in Wisconsin, Iowa,

Minnesota and the Dakotas, who had leprosy, but only thirteen were still alive with the disease at the time of the paper.[322] Elisabeth may well have known Hansen and his work from her time in the hospital in Norway. It is difficult to find any record of this lasaret in Minneapolis today. Very likely none of the patients at this place of refuge were leprous, but it was not entirely impossible given actual cases in Minnesota.

During this time Elisabeth had gotten to know the State Board of Health inspector, probably a Dr. Grønvold, who had come to the hospital several times to inspect it. One day Grønvold invited her to drive in his sled out to the lasaret so she could see it. On their way, she reported with some trepidation, the horses went very fast and, while it was an enjoyable excursion, it was somewhat dangerous, especially when he took a short cut across a newly frozen lake. The ice was not quite thick enough and the sled rocked and rolled and threw them out of the sled—he on the bottom, she on the top. When they got on the sled again, the horses, frightened by the thin ice, ran quickly over the ice as it rocked up and down. She was glad to be back on land and commented drolly, "I did not wish for any more such tours."[323]

The Union

The late fall and winter of 1889 were busy times for the leaders of the three churches involved in the new church union, working to get the organization up and off the ground, ready for the big celebration of the merger in Minneapolis the coming June. Also with the start of the new church, they hoped they would receive much more support from a larger church so they could do more charitable and educational work. Children had always been part of Sister Elisabeth's concern in her work in Brooklyn and with the merger she saw her opportunity to establish such a place in the Midwest. Sister Elisabeth's dream of founding an orphanage, or children's home, became more and more likely as she realized the buildings in Beloit, Iowa, where the Norwegian Augustana Synod had its seminary, would soon be empty. She was not one to miss this opportunity for her children's home.

The meetings of the board proceeded routinely, as can be seen from the November 5, 1889, minutes when it met to oversee the expenses, accept new women for training as deaconesses, deal with a troublesome student, and give the treasurer authority to buy insurance for the home which they valued at $500 with another $500 for the head nurse and $50 each for a couple of nurses, a total amount of $1,150. The cost of that insurance was $9.73 for three years, which they approved and otherwise tended to the condition of the Institute.[324] A slight note of warning can be read in one decision: The board wished to hear a letter from the president of the Tabitha Circle (a major supporter) to Sister Elisabeth. Had she written to commend her or to complain? We do not know.

The December 1889 meeting dealt with several of the same issues, but this time the admittance ceremony of several sisters needed to be planned, a sign of the Institute's progress. While this was not a consecration, it was treated with great seriousness as it was the first step of the young woman toward consecration. It probably became the capping ceremony in later nursing education. The board appointed Professor Sverdrup, Sister Elisabeth, and Pastor Gjertsen to arrange the program for the Fourth Sunday in Advent, December 22, at Trinity Congregation. By this time, seven probationary sisters worked in the home, and through-

Ladies Aid supporting The Deaconess Institute in Minneapolis (left to right), standing: unknown, Sister Elisabeth, Mrs. Laws?, Mrs. Bredesen, Mrs. Olaf Hoff; seated: Mrs. Vetlesen, Mrs. Lovtang?, Mrs. Sven Oftedal, Mrs. Gregory?, Mrs. Gjertsen, Mrs. Egeland, Mrs. Nydahl

out the church interest in the work was returning, Sverdrup remembered, and it was a sign things were improving. That they had to look for a new locale because they were growing and the lease with Sunde was expiring was good news as well. They needed more support, however, and were looking to increase their annual gifts from members of the larger church. In accordance with a resolution of the board to publish more articles on the project, in journals such as *Luthersk Kirkeblad, Lutheraneren,* and *Folkebladet,* an article appeared in the December 14, 1889, *Lutheraneren* by Henriette Eggen, giving a brief history of deaconess' work from biblical times to the present, especially the development of the movement in Norway and how it had come to Brooklyn. Now the tradition had also come to

COURTESY MINNESOTA HISTORICAL SOCIETY

Minneapolis deaconess dress from 1893 to 1900

Minneapolis via Sister Elisabeth. Although Miss Eggen claimed to know little about the whole idea, she gave a fairly concise history of the movement and then appealed for help from rich and poor, ladies' aids and girls' societies. Those who wanted to know more about the work, she suggested, should ask Professor Sverdrup or Sister Elisabeth. While Sverdrup was very well known in the community, Sister Elisabeth was still quite new, as was the vocation of deaconess. Sverdrup had already written on the topic and would continue to write more as the hospital and Motherhouse became more and more successful. Although there were both Episcopal and Methodist Deaconess Houses in Minneapolis and deaconesses were not unknown, Fedde in her garb must have attracted attention in the city as she traveled around the city on the new tram system, gathering help and support. She remembered this as a time of relative peace and quiet, with many happy memories, partly because there was less to do in Minneapolis than in Brooklyn, she said.

220 | Sister Elisabeth Fedde: To Do the Lord's Will

When they celebrated Christmas Eve, a most holy family time for Norwegian Lutherans, with the traditional dance around the Christmas tree and the Christmas foods and carols, Sister Elisabeth had reason to be proud of her accomplishments and thankful for God's continuing guidance. After the festivities, the night before her thirty-ninth birthday, a time restless with questions and thoughts about how things were going in her life and work, she attempted sleep, something she had some difficulties with, given all her worries about the home, the finances, and her work. "A thousand thoughts flew around me," she wrote. The clock struck twelve, and it was her birthday. Her bed, a sofa in the parlor was close enough to the window, so she was often disturbed by noises on the street below. Just as she was going to sleep, she heard the voices of two children serenading her with a Swedish lullaby: "She's sleeping quietly, may the angels protect her" (*Hun sofver ren. Maa englar henne skylde*). Sister Elisabeth immediately was fully awake and looked down to see two neighbor boys whose father had died in November, the day they moved into the home and whom she had comforted in their grief. Now they were comforting her like two small angels. She never forgot these two young boys and was always thankful to them for this lovely memory, although she lost track of them over time.

The help she had given the boys in their sorrow was the kind she had given to many as they faced their own death and the death of dear

Augsburg Seminary building where the board would meet with Sverdrup

ones. She wanted to assure that patients could meet their final hours in faith. One of her most heart-rending memories from her time in Minneapolis was of a woman from the Trondheim area who needed help and came to them. They cared for her, but then she became angry and left for a while. She may have been either suffering some mental illness or delerium. Soon she returned, wailing that she had always felt unhappy and damned throughout her life—a cry, Sister Elisabeth wrote, that seemed to come out of the depths. It was terrible to hear. After this outburst, which horrified both the younger probationary sisters who heard it and Fedde, the woman seemed to have been emptied of something and lay down to die. Quietly, Sister Elisabeth told her about the thief on the cross who repented at the last moment. It was for people exactly like her that Jesus had died on the cross to save, she told the dying woman. She appeared to have heard Sister Elisabeth's words and folded her hands, while Sister Elisabeth knelt by her bed praying, "from the depths of my own heart, that the poor unhappy sinner would be saved." She wrote many years later that she believed the woman died in faith, that the merciful God who alone knew her heart would receive her. Such experiences made Sister Elisabeth remark that after such wrenching experiences she felt the need to cry out to everyone she met, young or old, "Take care for your salvation while you are young, before you come to a place where you can no longer hear these words or repent." Today's Lutherans may not recognize this scene or Elisabeth's burden, but it was common language in the nineteenth century among our forebears who did not believe baptism was enough. This process was what the Pietists called the Order of Salvation which always involved a personal confession of faith after a struggle and conversion or reawakening, which gave one assurance of salvation.

Buying a Cow

The New Year, 1890, began with hope for the Norwegian Lutherans who were going to merge in June. The Deaconess Home seemed to be running well and with little conflict. As could be expected, raising funds was the major concern. At the January 7, 1890, meeting the board asked Sverdrup, the chair, to give a report on the work of the Deaconess Home along with its financial position, always a worry.

In order to keep expenses down, at the March 4, 1890, meeting, the board voted to let Sister Elisabeth buy a cow if she could manage it, which she did. Along the way she had an experience which she called in her *Memoirs* the "adventure with a cow." Because the home on 2731 Hennepin Avenue was at the edge of the city at the time, and the home was surrounded by grassy fields that could be used for pasture, she decided that buying a cow would be to the benefit of the institution. Since almost everyone at the time had been raised near animals, it was no problem to keep it, although the sisters were too busy taking care of the patients to feed and milk a cow. They bought a snow white cow with lovely horns, she wrote. Immediately the night after they got it, it gave birth to a calf, freshening it. This resulted quickly in what she thought was twenty-two liters of milk.

While it was wonderful for the hospital to have fresh milk and have it so nearby and without much cost, they realized they needed help to care for the animal. One can suppose that she, the old farm girl from Feda, had done a lot of milking. (In Brooklyn she would also show herself a quick study when she bought a horse for the ambulance they needed and learned how to care for it.) Then a Danish man stopped by and asked for a job. He was well educated, but could find no work. His wife, a pianist, had studied with Liszt, he said, and was now in Copenhagen waiting for him to get work so she could join him in America. He was in such need, he told her, that he would do anything to have a place and food. "Have you ever taken care of a cow?" she asked. "No," he had not done that, but given his situation, he thought it would be possible to learn. Sister Elisabeth and he agreed that he would try the job. "Then I went in to the other sisters and told them that we were going to have help with the cow." Relieved to hear it, they were still uncertain. "No! An academic in the barn?" Another remarked that when one needed a job, then it wasn't so unusual to see such a thing.

The Danish gentleman ate, left to get his clothes, and came back. I rented a little room next door. It was modest, but pleasantly appointed and satisfactory. Now he began his dirty work. The cow was both cleaned and washed, the floor was scrubbed and strewn with fresh sawdust. The animal had certainly never had it so good! There was no work we could not ask him to do, he would never say no. He also treated us like the gentleman he was, and we paid him as much as we could. After some time he got better work and his wife came over. They were a loveable couple, and were always friends of mine. When he left our employ, we sold the cow. That was my first and last cow in America!"[325]

This episode reveals Fedde's sense of herself, her capacity to see possibilities, and her keen sense of humor—and her willingness to do what was necessary so that life could flourish on all sides.

The board, at its next to last meeting as a committee of the Norwegian Danish Conference, on May 6, 1890, planned for another service of admittance and the acceptance of another trial sister. Sister Elisabeth and Pastor Gjertsen were to plan the service. It would be the last admittance service held by the Norwegian Danish Conference. After this meeting, things would be quite different as their supporting churches were coming together organizationally. They would have more resources, something Fedde was hoping. It had been difficult work, she remarked, to get all the rules approved and allocate funds to the various schools and missions of the prior church bodies, but it had finally been accomplished. The joy with which the agreement was met made the celebration a great moment among Norwegian Lutherans in the Upper Midwest.

The United Norwegian Lutheran Church in America

June 13-18, 1890, the annual meetings of the preceding church bodies and the newly united church were held in Minneapolis in the Swedish Augustana Church on the corner of 7th Street and 11th Avenue. Later, it would be said of the event that it was the largest gathering of Norwegian American Lutherans up to that time.[326]

On the morning of June 13, at 10:10, after meetings in which they dissolved their old churches, the Anti-Missourians marched from St. Paul's Hauge church on Franklin and Portland to Trinity where the Conference delegation waited. The Norwegian Augustana delegation gathered at Augsburg Seminary and then marched to Trinity. As the Anti-Missourian Brotherhood arrived, the entire congregation stood and sang "God's Word Is Our Great Heritage." Then the Norwegian Augustana group entered to the singing of Kingo's hymn, "Praise to Thee and

Interior of Augustana Lutheran Church, Minneapolis

Adoration." When all had arrived, the entire group sang the Te Deum. Commentators remarked on the glorious sound of nearly 2,000 male voices raised in praise and thanksgiving to God. From there they processed to Augustana Church on 11th Avenue and 7th Street, entering to the organ prelude by John Dahle, who later would be Professor of Church Music at Luther Seminary, on various Reformation hymns. Here they would continue their business meeting. Bells were said to have been rung throughout the Upper Midwest as the churches became one. The event concluded with a service on the evening of Wednesday, June 18, in the Coliseum at the University of Minnesota. More than 5,000 people were in attendance. Høyme with his usual poetic eloquence urged the delegates:

> to return to your homes, pastors and lay delegates, and let the
> church bells ring from every steeple—let them ring so their
> sound will echo among Norway's mountains and will declare
> to the mother church that her emigrated and separated sons
> and daughters have found one another. [327]

It was moving to everyone, including Fedde. She was caught up in the optimism and excitement of the new day.

Fedde is, to my knowledge, the only woman who has left a personal account of the event with her typical detailed sense for both sorrow and gladness. Ever on the prowl for a new way to build more resources for the needy, with a children's home high on her list, she had come to know Professor David Lysnes (1832-1890) of the Norwegian Danish Augustana Synod, probably through negotiations about establishing a children's home in Beloit, Iowa. Professors from each seminary and school were to be elected by the new church convention, and it was a matter for the entire convention. These negotiations had involved quite a bit of deliberation by the union committees and he had, according to Fedde, been left out. One could not become a seminary professor without the vote of the church in annual conference. "Lysnes was a warm Christian," she noted, "whose [convention] devotions at the beginning of the day were a bit too long, but not TOO long," she commented. She had watched the march of the delegates into Trinity and shared the excitement of the day. Her report seems to confuse the first gathering with the last, but she did observe one of the most important matters of business—electing the professors and teachers for all of the various schools—and then the electing of a president, or bishop, as she called him, Gjermund Høyme. "All the professors and teachers had place in the church except for our dear professor," she remembered. "He was not considered appropriate for the most educated school now." The high lords, she

Gjermund Høyme

recalled, had talked over where they would put him, but found no place for him. (These kinds of hurts are familiar to many Lutherans from small synods who can never forget the pain of merging and losing place in the larger body.) Fedde is actually slightly wrong about this. She may have seen that he was left without a place to sit in the gathering and may have heard remarks disparaging his qualifications. Lysnes had been elected Theological Professor from the Norwegian Danish Augustana Synod. He may have been treated rudely by the assembled professors, but he was one of them. She concluded with the note that the "Lord of Lords called him home to himself" shortly after that, where there was place for him. "I was glad that he could die and be free of all the strife that followed this and destroyed so much energy."[328]

David Lysnes

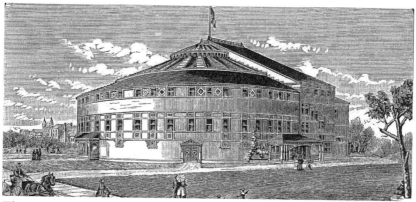

The University of Minnesota Coliseum, where celebration of the merger took place

There are probably not a few swipes at the Augsburg professors in her comments which we must remember were made several decades after this happened, after she experienced the schism of the United Church caused by the Augsburg professors. Somehow she had gotten to know the Norwegian Danish Augustana community leaders during this time of negotiations and seems to have taken their view of the union. In a brief time, the Deaconess board would start the orphanage in Beloit, where Lysnes in fact had been. Lysnes' seeming disorientation at the meeting may have pointed to a mental decline, but the pathos of Fedde's description is moving. Some years later in a conversation with President Høyme, very likely during the dedication of Trinity Lutheran Church in Brooklyn in 1894, she said that he told her, "All the conflict we have had, took all of my strength. He did not live much longer, either," she concluded. Høyme's death in 1902 while the church was about to dedicate the main building at its seminary, what is now Bockman Hall at Luther Seminary, shook the young church to its core.[329]

Sverdrup's Defense of the Diaconate

No one could argue for the work of the deaconesses with the clarity of Georg Sverdrup. At this first convention of the United Church he gave a lecture making a case for the deaconess calling, which was now the responsibility of the new, larger United Church. The lecture was given with the aim of informing new congregations about what the Conference had done to establish a Motherhouse, something he recalled happening as the idea of the Motherhouse was spread abroad throughout the church via its magazine, *Luthersk Kirkeblad*. He argued, as he frequently did, that wherever Jesus went he brought both the forgiveness of sins and physical healing to the people thronging around him. It was the care Christians took

Number of Sisters in USA	
1897	163 Sisters
1899	197 "
1903	205 "
1904	220 "
1905	238 "
1907	294 "
1908	305 "
1910	313 "
1912	353 "

Table on deaconess numbers for American Lutherans

for their neighbor's earthly situation as much as their preaching of salvation that converted the early Roman empire to Christianity. Sverdrup then explained the history of the renewal of the deaconess movement in Germany, under the leadership of Fliedner, which he said came as a result of the awakening there after the Napoleonic wars when the needs in Germany, particularly, were particularly tough. It called for sisters of mercy to help the poor and sick, which they did to the enrichment of many. Now there were over 6,500 sisters and sixty Motherhouses in the Lutheran church around the world. They were a blessing to any whom they helped.

Sverdrup then went on to explain what a Deaconess House was and laid it out with his characteristic clarity: First of all, it was a school where the future sisters were educated. They must be living Christians and willing to work hard and be educated in two branches of study: 1) God's word, and 2) nursing and helping the poor. A deaconess had to know how to deal with those sick in bed and those dying. And that meant she had to know the Gospel. Although she might have time to call the pastor for help in this regard, or a doctor for one in physical pain, should she be called on she herself could minister to the person with the help of her spiritual training. Therefore the Bible should be first and last in

Cover of Sverdrup's lecture on the deaconess movement

her education. Although she was not a pastor, she could share the power of the Word with her patients. To be a deaconess was more than nursing, it was an art that could be learned. For this reason, the deaconess needed a school to be trained for all these occasions. Second, the deaconess house must be a hospital where the young woman could be trained to work with the sick. "It is not easy to learn to care for the sick without having sick people around." Third, the Motherhouse was also a home where the young woman could live with her sisters and enjoy Christian fellowship with them. They should not have to be on their own: they should be a society where they lived together in love and respect. Should this be thought of as a cloister? he asked. No, he answered. The woman in the cloister is trying to make her way to heaven, it was the only end of her life, but the deaconess was using her work as a means to bring salvation to others. Careful not to be too clerical, he wanted to be clear that neither all women nor all men with religious talents needed to be clergy; there is one Spirit and many gifts, he reminded his hearers. It is the call of our church to build such a house. There are many reasons to say yes to this call, he noted.

He then addressed the question he knew was next in his hearers' minds. What about women's rights?

> We live in a time when the cry is lifted up, that certainly is right in many ways: Give women their rights! Make a place for her own ambitions, work and her strengths, give her a way to move forward. That need has often been exaggerated and often has resulted in many sorrowful results, and has ruined many. Also it is true that in the congregations, some here and there, have made mistakes in an attempt to help women's work. All the same, there is work that women can and ought to do, and it is not done because some cannot bear that women should have their work. Christianity shows the way for all to come forth where it is said, those who will be great, should be least, and those who will be greatest, must be servant to all. Here we should rightly say: give women their rights; give place for her ambition to serve, let her find her way to the farthest place that her service leads her to! Give women work in God's congregation and do not stand in her way. It is also for us to make way for women's work in God's kingdom.[331]

Sverdrup's response to the feminism of the day, with its cry for women to get the vote and be treated equally, is like the responses many Norwegian American clergy gave to this question and a bit more liberal than others who opposed the movement entirely, such as Vilhelm Koren, who some years later in his speech at the dedication of the Red Wing Ladies Seminary, found the idea of women's rights and their public vocations laughable.[332]

Sverdrup does not quite buy into the notion that women were morally superior, but he seems to have a decided sense for what women could do and saw the congregation as the place where the gifts of women should be used. What he thinks about women's suffrage in the civil world is not entirely clear from this piece. All of these leaders were well aware of the women's movement both in Norway and America and that many supporters of suffrage were critical of the Bible and the church. In Norway, the debate was probably more virulent, with its leaders such as Ibsen and Bjørnson attacking the church, clergy, and Bible with sharp and vitriolic arguments in a culture war that has lasted for over a century. Sverdrup had watched these debates in Norway closely and labeled Bjørnson and his ilk "free thinkers." He saw them as being from the same group of rationalists who had imprisoned Hauge.

The place of the deaconesses in the running of the deaconess organizations got to be a source of uneasiness if not conflict between the Sister Superior and the male boards in several of the Motherhouses. When one reads the rules concerning the life of the deaconess communities, it is clear that these women, while proud of their vocations, had no power over their own lives. While the matron did work with the board and later came to have a vote, she could influence the board only with the power of her person, which over time would grow considerably; on her own she was essentially powerless. In addition, when the pastors spoke to them about their vocation and used biblical references like Sverdrup used to talk about the service of women, it began to irritate the women. They could hear the men using scripture to keep them submissive and to maintain their own place above them. While Christ says this to all Christians, it became very easy to use it to speak particularly to women and thus keep women down, some deaconesses began to think. The difficulties Sister Elisabeth had with the board in Minneapolis may have been caused by this implicit attitude. That they made her a member of the board, in their restructuring of the institution, as well as an officer of it is a credit to them, though it would be seen as a conflict of interest by today's standards. It however did not stop the "anxieties" as Sverdrup would call them later.

Beloit

With the new church starting up, and its greater resources, both in congregations and leadership, Sister Elisabeth saw her chance. While she enjoyed Minneapolis and was pleased to note the work of the Institute was growing, not surprisingly she made plans to do more. She had been hoping to found an orphanage under the auspices of the Deaconess House in Minneapolis. At a meeting on June 3, 1890, just before the first meeting of the United Church, which now included new members Høyme and M. Saterlie, who was voted secretary pro tem, money was still an issue. Sister Elisabeth read her report to the assembled board: The balance in the bank was not encouraging; Dr. Laws had not been paid a bill he was owed. Sister Elisabeth was ordered to take care of the bill as soon as possible. Later it became clear that tension between Fedde and Laws was increasing and about to reach a boiling point. Several other tasks were assigned to her as well. The committee to find a new location for the home had problems because of the necessity of finding water and sewer conveniences in the city. Furthermore they needed to find a man, maybe a pastor, who could administer the Deaconess House. They decided to

Beloit Children's Home. Notice the children on the front steps.

begin such a search. Was this more help for Fedde, or someone who would be in charge over her? They also voted to assure that the lecture given by Sverdrup on the deaconess work at the convention be printed in the record of the annual meeting and in pamphlet form so it could be distributed easily among "our people." In addition they empowered Høyme, Sverdrup, and Swenson to organize a drive among the women's organization to gather money from members of the United Church. One of their main objects was to raise money to support a children's home in Beloit, Iowa. Pursuant to that drive, they voted that the chairman of the board travel to Beloit during the summer to see what was going on there and how the board could relate to it. Sverdrup went there in August 1890 and renewed the relationship with Augustana's president, Anthony G. Tuve (1864-1918).

Andreas Wright, (1835-1917) one of the leaders of the Norwegian Danish Augustana Synod, a man of many talents, who had been president of the synod from 1885-1888 while the negotiations for the new church were going on, had urged the new church to open a children's home in Beloit where Augustana Seminary had been, on its way to Sioux Falls where it became Augustana College. There was a professor's home and several other buildings that would be left empty. When the school moved to Sioux Falls, across the river and north of Beloit, these buildings could be used by the new church. Wright had also pushed for there to be an old people's home on the site as well. That did not come to be, but the children's home did.

After the first annual meeting of the Deaconess House Institute and the election of Marcus Bøckman to the board, the first board meeting was held. Sverdrup was reelected chair of the board with Gjertsen as the vice chair. They then considered a new property on 23rd Avenue and 34th Street. It would cost $6,000. They voted to continue considering the deal. Then Sverdrup gave his report about his journey to Beloit. He had been very impressed and strongly recommended that the Institute take up the work. The board resolved to authorize beginning the work for a children's home in Beloit, but Sverdrup suggested that there was only one building suitable to be used over the winter. The chairman and Sister Elisabeth were asked to choose which of the sisters should be sent to Beloit to run the home. At the same time they needed to find a better house in Minneapolis to serve the needs of the Motherhouse.

Sister Martha Langaunet

Sister Agnette Fagerlie

In November 1890, the children's home in Beloit began its work under the leadership of Sisters Martha Langaunet and Agnette Fagerlie. Their charge was to receive children between the ages of two and twelve from Iowa, South Dakota, and Minnesota, after thorough inspection of the child's situation. The home accepted children nominated by those who were aware of a bad situation in a family. This was not an uncommon practice at the time as Sister Elisabeth knew from her work in New York, when she took a mother with boys to a home where they would receive better care than the mother could afford to give them. Sometimes people used these homes as places of temporary relief and placed their children in these homes to be taken care of until they could be taken back home.

The Beloit home started with one boy; by the next spring there would be twelve children in the home. This meant that Sverdrup was now, as chairman of the board, helping to run an institution far away from Minneapolis. In order to do this he needed advice from Augustana College's president, Anthony Tuve, who wrote him several letters about his perceptions of what the facility needed before it could be functional: plaster, repairs, etc. The work was done, and the home in Beloit began smoothly. On October 4, 1890, the board received a report from Sister Martha about the work in Beloit with the usual request for money. They sent her $20. One of the better things about the home was that it was far away from Minneapolis and had local supporters who could fund the home without taking money from the Deaconess Motherhouse or hospital. It would be a concern of the Deaconess Institute until 1892 when it would be taken over by the United Church and operated until it was closed in 1944, when the Iowa Board of Examinations determined it was no longer an adequate facility for children.

A new issue came up at this meeting, something that would also intrigue Sister Elisabeth and cause her final difficulties with the Minneapolis board. The board received a letter from Pastor Nils Christian

Brun (1846-1919), pastor of Bethlehem Church in Chicago, and its Tabitha Circle, asking Sister Elisabeth to come to speak with them in October or November about starting a Deaconess Home in Chicago.[333] This was too much for the board to consider, given its own situation, although we will come to see it interested Sister Elisabeth.[334]

That they knew they were stretched too thin is to their credit, or at least it shows they are a bit more aware of their limitations. What they had already done in taking on the Beloit project must have seemed a bridge too far at this time. It, however, intrigued Sister Elisabeth who never gave up on her interest in the Chicago project—too much interest for the Minneapolis Deaconess Institute board. This began what finally resulted in the separation of Fedde from the Minneapolis house.

The work proceeded as they accepted new sisters more and more often. Pastors, such as Theodor Halvorson Dahl (1845-1923) in Stoughten, whose brother-in-law was Gjertsen, requested that a sister be sent to his congregation to help. Such requests became more frequent, and they needed to establish processes and payment for these requests, determining that the congregation should pay $150 a year for such help, plus all travel and room and board for the sister. The need for a larger facility became more urgent as they had to rent the upper floor of a neighbor to the Deaconess House for $7.00 a month. At the next meeting they appointed Gjertsen and Sister Elisabeth to find a man who could work in the home, something like a janitor. More families were requesting sisters to help in their own need, such as an Augsburg student who needed someone to help care for his wife who was ill and needed assistance he could not give her. In addition, Fedde and Sverdrup had to find more teachers to help in the instruction of the probationary students, and not only for the spiritual dimensions of their calling, which the seminary could provide. They needed the requisite courses for nursing as well. All these were encouraging signs of hope and growth in the community. In answer to the pleas of Sister Martha in Beloit, they received both her request for funds and voted to accept her recommendations concerning the children who were brought to the attention of the home.

A recurring matter that the board seemed to be reluctant to take up was the resignation of Dr. Laws. For several meetings in a row they had tabled it and refused to accept it.[335] While the reason for his resignation was not expressly stated, the board minutes seem to indicate it concerned something else, more in the nature of pay or his working relationship with Sister Elisabeth, who spoke poorly of him and Gjertsen in a letter to Sverdrup.[336]

This was not news to Sverdrup. In mid-December 1890, during a private conversation with Sverdrup about the state of her health and her job, she had discussed her attitude toward the doctor. At the time she was ill and needed medical attention and was probably not in a good frame of mind. Her story, told many years later, was that while she was assisting with an operation, she fainted. The doctor told her that she needed surgery, for what condition we are not told, although it sounds rather like gallbladder. As she was recovering from her fainting spell and probably suffering from whatever condition for which she needed surgery, Sverdrup had come to her to tell her that Dr. Laws had said that he could no longer be the doctor in the home if she no longer had confidence in him. Apparently this was the reason he wanted to resign and the reason the board kept tabling the matter. Sverdrup was fairly confident Elisabeth was about to resign. During the conversation, Fedde showed Sverdrup a letter she had received from the Brooklyn board. Until then his words, according to her *Memoirs*, had been rather sharp. After that, he became still.

Dr. Laws

> The letter, she said, was short, like a prayer that I would return, for they could not continue without me much longer. Sverdrup asked what I wanted to do, and I said, as he could see I was too sick to do anything now, as soon as I could, I would return to Brooklyn. You can comfort Dr. L. that I will no longer be in the way, for if I were well, I would write my resignation. After that visit, I became very sick, almost unto death.[337]

Troubles such as this with Fedde could not have come at a worse time for Sverdrup. He was facing troubles all around in his work as seminary president and professor. His level of stress must have been very high at this time. About this same time, letters appeared in the *Skandinaven* newspaper purportedly by an Augsburg student that by its ungrammatical and poorly written style besmirched the quality of Augsburg's educational program. It would deepen the split between Augsburg and St. Olaf so that ultimately Augsburg left the new United Church. One can also posit that

Fedde's growing discomfort with the Augsburg leadership is another sign that things would one day come to a head. She wanted to serve patients, not be mired in theological or church political debates.

Immediately, after this conversation, Sverdrup wrote to Kaiserswerth to get some resources for their work from the Mother-house and began to recruit deaconesses from the Motherhouse in Christiania where his new wife was well acquainted. She may have recommended several potential candidates to him, among them, Ingeborg Sponland (1860-1951). She regarded his wife, Elise, as a sister, who must have highly recommended her. Sponland wrote in her memoir, *My Reasonable Service*, that she spent some weeks with the Sverdrups upon her arrival in Min-

Sister Ingeborg Sponland

nesota that spring before traveling to her parents who lived in Park River, North Dakota.[338] When Sverdrup asked her about becoming Sister Superior in Minneapolis, she told him that since she was on furlough, it was not in her power to accept the offer, He would first have to write her superiors in Christiania, which he must have done, because when the call was sent to her in May, she accepted readily. Fedde also approved of Sponland. Sponland answered Sverdrup in the affirmative on December 23. Sverdrup had probably received the letter by the end of the year. It does not appear, however, that he shared the response with the board since it was a private letter. She would not figure in their deliberations about finding a matron at least until May 3, 1891, when they determined it was now possible to call "the recently arrived from Norway" Sister Ingeborg to be the Sister Superior (*fosterinde*) of the home.[339]

These letters show that Sverdrup was obviously aware they needed to be thinking about a new head sister long before Sister Elisabeth resigned.

Resignation

The first meeting of the board in 1891, on January 6, Sverdrup himself knew that the conflicts had been resolved. Fedde had sent in her resignation on January 3. She was not at this meeting because she was ill and sent a letter to Sverdrup with her monthly report on the state of the hospital. She had resigned, but had not yet left for Brooklyn. Correspondence from her at the time says that she had resigned because of poor health, and that may well have been the case, but there is another disagreement with the board that can be seen in its response to her. The meeting had many things to deal with, mostly the resignation of Fedde. The board preferred that she receive a year's leave with full pay ($200) unless she "takes up another position in the meantime" (*hvis hun i mellomtiden overtager nogen anden bestilling*).[340]

They had good reason to be suspicious that she had started to correspond with Pastor Nils Christian Brun in Chicago about the dreams of the Chicago Norwegian Lutherans for a deaconess hospital and Motherhouse there. Chicago's Norwegian Lutherans had been dreaming of such a house since 1885 when Pastor Andreas Mortensen, the Seaman's Mission pastor who had also worked with Sister Elisabeth in Brooklyn at the time, gave a speech on November 1, 1885, at Bethlehem Church encouraging the congregation to

Bethlehem Lutheran Church, Chicago

start a Motherhouse there. Immediately, on November 3, 1885, a group of men and women had formed a Tabitha Society with the goal of establishing a deaconess house and/or hospital in Chicago. They could not quite agree on whether it should be only a hospital or include a deaconess house. Under the leadership of Pastor Brun, pastor at Bethlehem in early 1891, they did succeed in establishing a two-story hospital and Motherhouse on Humboldt Street in Chicago. This was an institution of the new United Lutheran Church and its leaders were increasingly bitter about Sverdrup and Oftedal's insistence on making Augsburg Seminary the chief school of the United Church.

Things grew even worse when three sisters from Minneapolis, Martha Bergh, Amalie Kittelsen, and Marie Langaunet left, to work at the

The first Deaconess Hospital in Chicago

Deaconess Home and Hospital in Chicago. Later the board of the Institute would accuse Fedde of encouraging these sisters to go to Chicago, against the explicit instruction of the board, to work with Brun. The accusation appears to have been well-founded. Elisabeth left behind in her diary a copy of the hymn sung at the opening service on March 8, 1891, in Chicago on Humboldt Street where the new house would be built. On November 3, 1891, the institution was dedicated with Brun as the chair of the board.[341]

The feelings between Sverdrup and Brun never improved and only got worse. Brun had been instructor in English at Augsburg Seminary when it was still in Marshall and was in the same era as Gjermund Høyme. Although the break would begin in 1893 with the founding of the Friends of Augsburg, by this time both Høyme and Brun were becoming a thorn in Sverdrup's side in church matters.[342] Although Brun remained on the Augsburg Seminary board until 1899, he became a strong champion of the United Church, opposed to Sverdrup.

Fedde, however, kept her interest in the new institution in Chicago. After a fire in 1893, the Chicago Deaconess Home regrouped to start up again, laying the cornerstone for a hospital on June 3, 1894. The hospital, The Norwegian Lutheran Tabitha

The Norwegian Lutheran Tabitha Hospital in Chicago

Hospital, was formally opened. The deaconess side of the old fight re-emerged and left to found its own Deaconess Motherhouse and Hospital. Once again the fight between the Norwegian Synod and the pietists, this time represented by the United Church, broke out. The Norwegian Synod did not want a Deaconess House and preferred a hospital for Norwegians; the United Church wanted a deaconess house. (Later, in 1910, the Tabitha hospital would abandon the adjective Lutheran in its name and the hospital did well as a secular, Norwegian institution.) Those in the United Church, however, wanted a deaconess hospital and Motherhouse as an arm of ministry for their church. It was not up and running until 1896 when Pastor John N. Kildahl (1857-1920), pastor at Bethlehem and later president of St. Olaf College, guided the project to completion. It would later become the most successful Deaconess Motherhouse among Norwegians in America, graduating some eighty-one consecrated deaconesses while the Minneapolis house consecrated thirty-seven, and the Brooklyn house consecrated only twenty-nine. (Several more may have attended the school, but had not been consecrated.)

On January 14, 1891, an article by Sverdrup in *Folkebladet* reported on the situation at the Institute. While things seemed to be going well and more women were applying to be deaconesses, Sverdrup confided in the readership that they had a problem that was not small. The head sister had been sick for some time and needed a period of rest to recover. The board, he said, had granted her one year of rest or sabbatical. While it was necessary, that made the work that much more stressful for everyone else. The women's organizations to whom he was writing needed to pray for them and help in whatever way they could. Nothing was said about Fedde's resignation.[343] On January 30,1891, the board met and this time Fedde made her final appearance. They passed the motion that she

should give instruction and council about running the home to Gunde Thoresen (1844-1935) before she left. Thoreson would not be consecrated until 1893. She, according to Nil Nilsen Rønning's book, *They Followed Him*, had been serving at the Episcopal St. Barnabas Hospital in Minneapolis.[344] She must have been in charge, because at the next meeting, on February 7, 1891, Sister Gunde was

Sister Gunde Thoresen

present in Sister Elisabeth's stead. A correction to the previous minutes was made about the "former" matron, Sister Elisabeth, and her instruction of Sister Gunde. In the correction to the minutes one can see the recommendation that Sister Gunde become the interim Sister Superior scratched out. The change in the minutes of February 7 is also difficult to read because of the revisions in the text, but it looks as if Gjertsen and Oftedal had made a written report on their examination of the home in order to find out whether or not Sister Elisabeth had left with another sister, Sister Lina Strøm, without getting permission for her to leave. This had as much to do with the board's concern for the fate of the women as it did with its sense that it had been disrespected. Deaconesses were not to leave without permission, according to long-established rules, and one of the reasons those who recommended them to the vocation had to promise, as Siqveland in Stavanger had, they would take the young woman back if she did not work out. Women on their own without a means of support were in danger. Sverdrup had realized the board needed better rules for the sisters and had written to Julius August Gottfried Disselhoff (1827-1896), the rector at Kaiserswerth, on December 20, 1890, to get some resources.[345] When they had received them, sometime in January, they presented them to the sisters as the new rules. The response from the sisters was outrage. Seven of them tendered their resignation in the following letter:

> To the Board of the Deaconess Home:
>
> In response to the rules, which were read to us today, all of the undersigned find it necessary to resign our Deaconess' calling as it is completely impossible for us to follow them. We had thought to work together with all our life and soul in this calling, in spite of all the burdens, but this change in the rules is something we cannot agree with. We are willing to work under the former rules if you can find a matron for the post who is experienced and whom we can obey and respect as our leader.[346]

The signers of the letter were Elise Tonnig, Martha Bergh, Amalie Kittelsen, Marie Langaunet, Ingeborg Birkeland, Ingeborg Weltzin, and Inga Bøen. The letter contains some pique at the board, and maybe Sister Gunde and even Sister Elisabeth ("finding one we can respect"). This was a blow to the board, but it responded in kind, resolving that the sisters who had signed the letter be asked to leave immediately, giving up their garb and rooms in the house as soon as possible. What most upset them was the idea that the sisters found the rules, "which were accepted by Motherhouses around the world," to be onerous. Sverdrup's letter to the Motherhouse in Kaiserswerth asking for advice on how to organize the sisters and the procedures for running the Mother house had been answered by the head, who sent along several books on their work and protocols. This was perhaps the source of the greatest outrage of the board against the sisters, that they would not accept the rules used by all other Motherhouses around the world.

The letter they wrote to each sister contained much of this information. Their strongest response had to do with the sisters refusing to follow the rules "under which the entire Lutheran church operates." There had to be some reckoning financially, and the treasurer needed to be paid for their room and board if they could not leave immediately. The letter closed with the wish that "the Lord might lead you into his right way." Sverdrup and Olaf Hoff, the secretary, signed the letters. Although nothing is said about their emotions in the minutes, the language and dispatch of the letter is filled with outrage.

Sister Elisabeth, however, had left Minneapolis on February 5, before all the fireworks went off. Her *Memoirs* contain a lengthy report from a newspaper on the farewell party at the Union Depot in St. Paul. Sverdrup and Lars Swenson were there along with many others, she remembered. The February 11, 1891, issue of *The North* reported on it at great length:

> Last Thursday night Sister Elisabeth, the Sister Superior of The Norwegian Deaconesses Institution of this city, was seen at the Union depot surrounded by a large number of friends. She was leaving Minneapolis for Brooklyn, N. Y. in order to recuperate after the sickness that she has been suffering from during the last two months. It is to be hoped that she soon will do so, and her many friends in Brooklyn who repeatedly have requested her return, because the work, which she so successfully had started there, has suffered a great deal during her absence, would be but too glad to see her resume her work there.

But her loss will be felt as severely here as it was at Brooklyn. That the Norwegian Deaconess Institute has grown to what it is now, is only due to her zealous application and to her ability and love for the work to which she so long and so nobly has devoted her life.

In Minneapolis as wherever she comes she has gained many devoted friends among healthy and sick, among poor and rich alike. The doctors, who have had patients in the hospital at the Institution, cannot praise her skill and ability [enough] as a nurse and manager of a hospital.[347] The patients, that she has had under her care, love her as their mother. It seemed hard for the sisters to take leave of her.

Sister Elisabeth left with the most earnest wishes of her friends for a rapid recovery; they would all be still happier if they could entertain a hope of her speedy return.[348]

It is somewhat surprising, given the fury of the board at her behavior, that both Sverdrup and Swenson came to bid her farewell as she left. Although Sverdrup was a fierce polemicist, his reputation for being kind and attentive to others is supported by his understanding that as the head of the institution it was important that he do the right thing for her. More surprising, however, is the failure of this article or any other to state the truth: Sister Elisabeth had resigned from the work and would not return.

Even more surprising is that *Folkebladet*, the paper edited by Oftedal and sometimes Sverdrup, reported, very briefly, that Sister Elisabeth of the Deaconess House had "left on a vacation to Brooklyn the previous week. She may also take a trip to Norway before she comes back. In the meantime Miss Gunde Thoresen is serving as the current manager."[349]

The failure to tell the story of the conflict, or at least to say that she had resigned and that there was no hope Sister Elisabeth would return, and Sverdrup's very public farewell as though nothing had happened indicates that the men knew this news would shock their supporters or at least cause them some unrest. Were they protecting themselves or Sister Elisabeth? By this time Sverdrup had been in serious correspondence with several deaconesses in Norway about taking over the Sister Superior position in Minneapolis. To be fair, the board did not accept her resignation until its April meeting, and protocol may have demanded it not divulge this news, but it does seem odd.

At the next meeting, a week later, on February 18, the board was astonished to hear the report from Gjertsen that three of the sisters—Sister Marie Langaunet, Martha Bergh, and Amalia Kittelsen—had indeed received letters of call from Pastor Brun in Chicago. This hurt, especially when Gjertsen told them that in a letter he had received from Sister Marie that much of it had to do with Sister Elisabeth. The board voted to write up a complaint against Sister Elisabeth for trying to lure the sisters away to Chicago. This document would be read at a later meeting. After dealing with a few more housekeeping details having to

Nils Brun

do with hiring instructors in English and how to furnish the home, they adjourned.

The board had reason to be upset about this. While we do not have much proof of what Sister Elisabeth actually did for the Chicago deaconess effort, the testimony of the sisters is pretty clear. Her copy of the hymn sung at the opening of the Chicago Deaconess Home on March 8, 1891, is good evidence that she was well-apprised of the Chicago effort, and very likely supported it.[350] We cannot know, either, if she went directly from Minneapolis to Brooklyn. All traveling that route would have to pass through Chicago. I can find no record of her having spoken directly with Brun, but she went through the city about a month before this service. Although she was quite ill—and if it were gallbladder, the pain and symptoms of that would be occasional rather than constant—it would have been very possible for them, at least, to meet and have a talk.

By this time the news about the need to find a new matron for the Minneapolis Motherhouse was public. During Fedde's absence and before they could find another Sister Superior, three women came to help Sister Gunde: Christi Olson, Jensine Eriksen, and Lena Nelson. They were not yet consecrated, but hoped to be in a few months. They kept things together over the summer while receiving instruction in their vocation.

On March 11, *Folkebladet* announced that things were going well at the home; there were eight patients being treated, and a three-year-old boy had undergone a very difficult operation performed by Drs. Laws and Sanve, and he was improving quickly. In addition, it noted, Mrs. Elise Sverdrup, "who had been a deaconess in Christiania for five years had started teaching the deaconess office and nursing. Sister Gunde the new head deaconess is doing well, going forth with strength and calm."[351]

Although the Deaconess House archives in Oslo do not have a record of Mrs. Sverdrup being consecrated as a deaconess, the community and tradition treated her as one. The note that Gunde Thoreson's leadership was effective and especially that the work was going forth calmly is significant. Is it implying that the former sister had been restless and erratic? It is a tantalizing clue, but once again, it leaves us only with hints and suppositions that are not helpful. To be sure, Sister Elisabeth with her strength and sense for what needed to be done immediately could have been difficult to manage as the Board of Managers in Brooklyn had discovered. Those working for her may well have found it a turbulent and distressing experience. On the other hand, the sisters did express loyalty to her in their eruption against the board.

We can see that after these events, things moved quickly. Sverdrup received a letter from Pastor Guldseth written on February 20, 1891. In it, he regretted what had happened and hoped that the will of God would be done, asking about a drive to support the Motherhouse by distributing little boxes to collect coins at each ladies aid in the area. Then, he asked Sverdrup to send him the rules for the sisters, which had been a matter of dissent with the sisters at the home just before this. He was going to show them to potential applicants for the sisterhood. He then hoped that Ingeborg Sponland would be among the new sisters, remarking that Sister Elisabeth had told him she was coming. For him that was good news. These intimate and knowing letters show us the tight-knit community surrounding the deaconess communities stretching from Minneapolis to Christiania. They were in close communication, especially now, through Mrs. Sverdrup.

Conversations about the fate of the Motherhouse in Minneapolis must have gone on after the previous meeting of the board and later as the board realized it had to find a deaconess to run the home temporarily and deal with the after-effects of the resignation of both Sister Elisabeth and the seven others. At its next meeting they discussed both Sister Elisabeth's leaving and her recommendations for an interim Sister Superior.

Fedde had recommended they call Sister Gunde, of whom the sisters who resigned did not approve for some reason. Sverdrup commented that when he had discussed Sister Amalie as a probable Sister Superior with Sister Elisabeth before Christmas, when she was recovering, she had told him that Amalie should be kicked out of the house when Fedde left. Why, she did not say, but this was persuasive enough for the board, so they settled on Sister Gunde because she had a much longer experience in nursing than the others. They then heard the letter Sverdrup was prepared to send to Pastor Brun who had what they thought of as the effrontery to call the sisters there. They approved the following letter to be sent to Sister Elisabeth.

Copy of letter to Sister Elisabeth Fedde

Minneapolis March 7, 1891.

From the Board of Trustees for Norwegian Lutheran Deaconess Institute (NLDI)

To the Matron Sister Elisabeth Fedde

In our meeting of the 3rd, the Board of the NLDI authorized the Chairman and Secretary to write you with the decisions and the decisions we have made regarding your situation with the following points.

The Board of Trustees for the NLDI has learned through the chair and one of those named in the connection with this committee (Profs S. Oftedal and Pastor M. Falk Gjertsen) have received the report that the matron has, without the permission of the Board or the Chair, taken with her to New York one of the sisters of the home Sister Lina Strøm and has paid her travel to New York without getting any permission from the Board as to whether Sister Lina Strøm can come back to the home.

It is also come to the Board's attention that the matron has contributed to the reasons for the sisters' resignation.

It has also come to the attention of the Board that the matron has given information and advice about the Deaconess home in Minneapolis to Pastor N. C. Brun and the Tabitha Circle in

Chicago; and that they have, without addressing themselves to the Board, since called three sisters from the home in Minneapolis either just before or just after they resigned.

The Board wishes to have an explanation from you concerning each one of the points, how you have addressed yourself to the Board and in which case what right you have to this kind of behavior which we can see has not served to build up and protect our Deaconess home.[352]

Sverdrup and Olaf Hoff both signed the letter on behalf of the board and sent it.

Soon, Sverdrup received a letter from Sister Elisabeth written on March 11, explaining herself. It is in some ways a pitiful letter, but also sharp. She began by noting that she had not heard that the board wanted a letter from her.

What should I say? Pain, pain, from the beginning to the end.

She could not understand that it was right to be treated in such a way as they had treated her. Because of her illness, she had decided to remain silent, nor could she understand how they could treat her as they had. Then she explained why she had taken Sister Lina with her:

In reference to Sister Lina, who herself had already told the two who called themselves the "committee" that she intended to leave with me which I also greatly needed, but after the gossip of your wife who knew more than I and thought it would go the way it would go. What could I do, sick and hurt as I was if I had not had a sister and brother-in-law to go to? It was frightfully handled altogether. Sister Lina was sick when she came from Pettersens, and when we came here [to Brooklyn] she had to go to bed, I have her here and she has been sick

Sister Lina Strøm

such a long time. We realized it was nerve fever so I took her to the Deaconess hospital. She has been very bad and near death, but now she is recovering. There was a thought that she should begin school here and stay with my sister. Now

I do not know when she will be better and what she will do then. She will remain with me, naturally.

What has made me marvel much is that your wife slandered me to the sisters, as she has done, saying I once disparaged my life in Norway, she who has never known me there [in Norway] and whom I believed would never say what she was not certain about. My recommendation from Pastor (Julius) Bruun can show who I was when I was there. I am myself not convinced that I have done or wanted to do to her anything other than the best I could. I am very upset with the thoughts she has shared about me—but one thing she can be very sure about—one day everything will be revealed in the light.

I would rather have spoken with you personally instead of by letter, but the slander has been great and Gjertsen and Laws have had much to say, poor folk. It is amazing, all of the sisters will be scattered so who will be left at the home? S. Ingeborg B. has written to me and I have also heard from Elisa and Miss Bøen has written me as well and Ingebor Weltzin I do not know.

A friendly greeting, Yours faithfully,

Sister Elisabeth

While not all of this is clear, what is clear is that Sverdrup had gotten himself into a conflict the likes of which he had never experienced, although he was well-acquainted with strife and professed to love it, saying he "enjoyed nothing better than to walk against a snowstorm."[353] This was new. Watching women quarrel may have been part of his experience at home, but now for the first time watching them quarrel as professionals with whom he was working was new to him and the other men around him. Not only were the sisters quarreling with him and each other, but now his wife was involved. What she was saying about Fedde is not stated, but it comes from her time working with the deaconesses at the Motherhouse in Christiania. Sverdrup had good reason to be mad. He must have come to believe that nothing would be possible until they were completely rid of Sister Elisabeth. In the meantime, on March 17, 1891, he had written to another deaconess in Christiania, Sister Sabine

Georg and Elise Sverdrup with children (left to right), front row: Ragna, Harald, Gunhild; back row: Inga, Else, George

Leschly-Hansen, another very good friend of his wife, asking her to consider coming to work in the Motherhouse in Minneapolis. She did not reply until April 23, 1891, begging forgiveness for waiting so long before answering him to tell him she could not consider his invitation to come to Minneapolis because of her brother's refusal to grant her permission, given the uncertainty of the Minneapolis call, especially that she had not been admitted as a sister in Minneapolis.[354]

"It has given me great sorrow to hear about the situation in the deaconess home there." Her brother would let her go to Brooklyn, where she had applied. Mother Guldberg, with whom she had consulted, had agreed with her decision to apply to Brooklyn before going into a much less certain situation in Minneapolis. She praised God for leading in the right direction and kept her from coming over to Minneapolis "in the middle of all of these complications and maybe the home's closing."[355] Obviously she had heard of the difficulties with Sister Elisabeth. Through Mrs. Sverdrup, most likely, the news of the troubles had made it to Norway. She concluded the letter with the hope that when things resolved themselves in Minneapolis, it might be that she could find her way to Minneapolis if it were God's will. With that she thanked Sverdrup for

all his help and confidence in her with "many greetings to your wife, my dear sister Elise." This letter
leaves little doubt that Sister Sabine knew many
things about the situation in Minneapolis from Mrs.
Sverdrup as well as from his letter to her. Fedde's
outrage at the gossip she well knew was coming
from Mrs. Sverdrup and her connections in Norway is not surprising. It could have been about many
things, but her reference back to the recommendations she had received from both Julius Bruun and
Mother Guldberg seem to point to some accusation
about a flaw in her character, or something she had

*Sister Sabine
Leschly-Hansen*

said. Given that Sverdrup's letter to Sister Sabine was written after the
blow up over her leaving with Sister Lina without getting permission and
also encouraging three sisters to go to Chicago, the issue could well have
been what the board and Sverdrup especially would have thought of as
Fedde's insubordination. She would have thought of it as responding to a
new call that needed to be answered, we can only suppose. It is clear that
the Chicago opportunity attracted her greatly.

New Troubles

At this time, in addition to the conflict over the head sister at the
Motherhouse, Sverdrup had other problems with the new church that
also were beginning to heat up. The sense of betrayal the Institute board
expressed in its letter to Fedde also can be seen to be played out as the
conflict between the Friends of Augsburg and the United Church finally
ended up in court. Brun is named as the leader of those suing Augsburg
Seminary to recover its publishing house and buildings. He remained as
one of the leaders in the United Church, publishing its twenty-fifth anniversary book, *Fra Ungdoms Aar*, in 1915.

At the next meeting on April 7, 1891, the board accepted Fedde's
resignation and seemed surprised that Høyme had also resigned. They
resolved not to accept his resignation, but let his term run out. While
Høyme may have been busy and thought the responsibilities of the board
too much for him as president of the United Church, it is also true that
the church was beginning to experience the beginnings of a schism, centered around Augsburg and the discussion about which would be the

primary school of the church. Høyme may have felt it first, but Bøckman as professor at Augsburg would also soon be gone from the Augsburg faculty as the opponents of Augsburg formed the United Seminary in Minneapolis. Although those church-dividing difficulties are not mentioned in these minutes, there had to have been some ruptures in the relationships on the board. Høyme, Marcus Bøckman (later president of United Seminary, then Luther Seminary), Swenson, and Hoff would resign from the board of the Deaconess Institute as the church split and Augsburg went its own way.

Sverdrup was asked by the board to inquire whether Sister Elisabeth had received its letter. Then they decided to say that her place on the board should be considered vacant. For the most part, this was the ending of Sister Elisabeth's position at the Minneapolis Deaconess House except for determining how to pay the rest of her salary. As the board dealt with these questions, it was also preparing the home it had bought so it would be ready for dedication at their annual meeting on September 1, 1891. On May 3, they approved a motion to call Sponland as the matron for the Motherhouse. She accepted the call. On September 1, after the annual meeting of the Institute, they both celebrated Sister Ingeborg's arrival and dedicated the new home at 1417 23rd Avenue in Minneapolis, a block off Franklin, about three blocks from Augsburg Seminary. Gjertsen gave a celebratory speech on the veranda and afterward the gathering was invited to enjoy the garden on the west side of the home. In the evening,

Minneapolis Deaconess House, dedicated in 1891

Deaconesses at the Hillsboro, North Dakota, Hospital

the festival moved to Trinity Congregation where Oftedal and Bøckman spoke; President Høyme did not appear. Ludvig Marinus Biørn spoke in his place.[356]

Things seemed to be settling down with Fedde gone. Ingeborg Sponland would serve at the Minneapolis Deaconess Institute until 1904 when, broken in health, she joined her brother in Thief River Falls and staked a claim to a farm there. Her work in Minneapolis, built on the foundations Fedde had laid, resulted in the establishment of hospitals in Grand Forks[357] (which came as a direct result of Fedde's time in Minneapolis), Hillsboro, Fargo, and Grafton, North Dakota; Crookston, Fergus Falls, and Austin, Minnesota; also a children's home in Poulsbo, Washington. Two sisters went to Madagascar, one to China. These were great accomplishments and to her credit, but the board, now much reduced in supporters after the split in 1895 when the Augsburg professors finally left the United Church to go on their own, simply could not provide a larger facility. In 1906, Sponland was called to head the Chicago Deaconess House where she stayed for thirty years until 1936, when she retired. This became the most successful of the Norwegian deaconess institutions in America, educating and consecrating more than eighty deaconesses. Without stretching too much, Sister Elisabeth could be credited with its beginnings as well as the Brooklyn and Minneapolis Deaconess Hospitals.

CHAPTER FOUR

BACK IN BROOKLYN

When Sister Elisabeth came back to Brooklyn, she could see the finished hospital on 4th Avenue, a dream come true. Instead of resuming her work as Sister Superior, however, she went to stay with her sister and brother-in-law, Gabriel Fedde, who had worried in his letter to Sverdrup about her capacities as treasurer. Whether he had been exactly right about her potential as a treasurer, he did seem to sense that she might

Etching of Sister Elisabeth from the Brooklyn Daily Eagle, *April 5, 1891*

have difficulties in the financial area. When she arrived in Brooklyn it was clear she needed immediate medical attention. The new chairman of the board, Captain Carl Ullenæs, visited her and told her to go to the new hospital where she could be treated for her illness. She agreed. When she got there she was immediately sent to bed. While there she experienced the hospital as a patient rather than Sister Superior which was a new perspective for her, something from which she would learn. The doctor told her she needed surgery, which she feared. She had never gone under anesthesia, but since it was necessary she would brave it. As she was being put under, she said, "I am going to die," and then she heard a voice saying, "No, you will not die." It was the voice of the sister assisting the doctor. She knew the voice. "I knew nothing more until I awakened in my bed." Although she healed soon and was back on the wards doing her work, the full recovery took some time.

Sister Elisabeth in her *Memoirs*, many years later, remarked that her time in Minneapolis had been filled with happy memories (*lyse minder*) in comparison with her Brooklyn memories, partly she said because Minneapolis was more peaceful than Brooklyn and partly because there

Brooklyn Deaconess Hospital in the 1890s

was less to do there.[358] From the letters and other documents we have seen, that is a remarkable statement, given what appears to have been a turbulent and fractious time for her and the Minneapolis board. During her convalescence she had time in which to reflect on her experiences in both Brooklyn and Minneapolis. For her first five years in America, 1883-1888, she had confided in her diary about various events and happenings, especially her relationship with the Brooklyn Board of Managers. After 1888, we do not have as many contemporary accounts to peruse in order to discover her immediate feelings about board meetings, the other sisters, her experiences in the wider community, only some newspaper articles, yearly hospital reports, and church documents. Her *Memoirs,* show her to be somewhat mellowed by time and a bit inaccurate as to times and locations. While she does remember the problems she had and reports them accurately, she is in a different place in her own self-evaluation of the struggles she had. She could use her diary for the period from 1883-1888 in Brooklyn, but after that she had to rely on her memory. We can ask, however, if the time she had resting after her surgery and her return from Minneapolis changed the way she saw herself, maybe even how she acted, as she began the next four years of work in Brooklyn before she returned home to Norway. From what we can see, after the operation and resumption of her position as Sister Superior in Brooklyn, she seems more settled.

While Sister Elisabeth had been working in Minneapolis, the Board of Managers in Brooklyn had organized itself and the hospital. Consul Børs and his wife now lived in Paris; the president of the board, Captain Carl Ullenæs, seemed to have understood how to keep things running well and with much less conflict than had marked the workings of the previous board. There was still a significant debt of $8,000, however, left to pay on the hospital mortgage. It may have been to the benefit of everyone that she had been gone for those two years, even though she kept close watch on the work in Brooklyn while in Minneapolis. The Board of Managers in Brooklyn, however, was desperate that she return after it became apparent to them they could not recruit a deaconess from Norway to become the Sister Superior. When Brooklyn sent the letter of call to her in Minneapolis, as we have seen, she was deathly ill. She could not quite accept their offer, which she regarded as a prayer from them, because of her health. She replied that her condition was such that she might have to give up all her work, so she could not give them a yes or no. She did say that she would take the call if her health improved after surgery and she got some much needed rest.

Despite her illness and exhaustion, and the Minneapolis board's irritation at her encouragement of the group in Chicago, we can see that the situation there continued to interest her. The Minneapolis board and now the Brooklyn Board of Managers adamantly refused the request of the Tabitha Circle in Chicago for some sisters to help them build its hospital. The Chicago committee slowed its progress toward a Motherhouse when it realized that it would have to provide a yearly salary of $200 for each

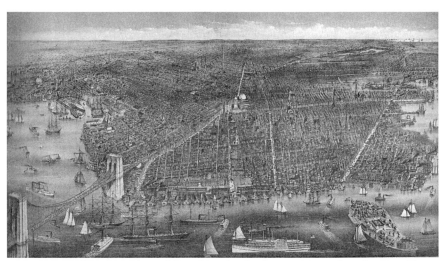

A Currier and Ives etching of Brooklyn in the later 1880s after the Brooklyn Bridge was built in 1883

deaconess, although it had already installed three sisters—Sisters Amalia Kittleson, Martha Bergh, and Marie Langaunet—from Minneapolis in a ceremony on March 8, 1891. When the Chicago board appealed to her again and asked her to send at least two deaconesses from the Brooklyn Motherhouse, she brought it to the Brooklyn Board of Managers, which strongly objected, saying that "Chicago with its forty thousand Norwegians and several large, rich congregations could supply its own deaconesses."[359] Brooklyn's Motherhouse did not have enough of its own sisters, a frequent concern of the board. Even if Brooklyn had enough sisters to share, they would not have sent them to another institution that far away. Although the numbers of applicants to be deaconesses were still going up, there were not enough to fill the needs of the many new immigrants who had settled all across the upper tier of states in the United States.

Recovery

Sister Elisabeth must have enjoyed her recovery in the new hospital finished during her absence. *The Brooklyn Daily Eagle* printed a story about the work of the deaconess community on April 5, 1891, written before Sister Elisabeth had returned to her work as Sister Superior sometime in March. (A letter from Pastor Martin Hegge of Trinity in Brooklyn to Georg Sverdrup on the situation in Brooklyn presumed that she would take up her work again in March.)[360] The article told the history of the Norwegian Relief Society, Mrs. Børs' concern for the poor and indigent, the calling of Sister Elisabeth, her coming to Brooklyn, and especially the recent building of the hospital:

> . . . on Forty-sixth street and Fourth Avenue—an elevated and healthful location. A building was erected at a cost of $15,000, a frame house consisting of three stories and basement, containing in all eighteen rooms. Large, airy halls run through the middle of the house. In the rear of the third story a hall, provided with windows throughout its length, affording a cheerful and extensive view of Brooklyn and New York bay, serves as a sun room, a pleasant lounging place for convalescing patients. The house is heated by steam and is well ventilated. It has facilities for accommodating thirty patients. One sister acts as district nurse, visiting among the families

of the poor. The institution is under the immediate charge of Sister Dorothea and her band of assistants. An additional feature for the winter is a soup kitchen.[361]

Sisters Dorothea Zeiffert and Karen Sodnak who had come from Norway to take Elisabeth's place while she was in Minneapolis were bound by their agreement with the Motherhouse in Christiania to return after two years. Sister Dorothea, who had been one of the first deaconesses to be admitted to the Motherhouse is Christiania, was celebrating her twenty-third year since her consecration. She would soon leave for Norway. Sister Karen got an extension and would remain another year to serve the neighborhood as Sister Elisabeth had done when she first arrived.

When Sister Elisabeth reassumed the position of Sister Superior in March 1891, she appeared to have found a better and more effective way to relate to the board and her staff. *Nordisk Tidende* printed a brief column on the 1890 annual report, noting that in the previous year, the home had doubled the number of patients it had served from the year before, to eighty-five, twenty-four of whom had paid in full. The sisters had increased their visits to homes to 1131. In their visits they had helped their patients with a variety of problems: paying the rent, having enough food, clothes, and meals. One patient had been sent back to Norway, six to other hospitals in the region, and eleven patients had died. One of the hopes of both the paper and the hospital was that the work could become better known in the years ahead. The Sunday school had continued with about the same number of students as before, with the summer excursions to Staten Island well attended. During the Christmas holidays, Sister Dorothea had treated over a hundred poor children to a meal and given them a party on New Year's Day. The board was glad to report that it had received an anonymous gift of $316.72. In addition the bazaars had raised between $300 and $400, something to be proud of in the difficult times, the paper noted. The board also expressed its thanks to its doctors, as well as its gratitude for the assistance of Consul Christopher Ravn (1849-), who served as treasurer of the Board of Managers. He had been especially helpful. His report on the financial situation indicated the expenses and income of the home had left a positive balance on hand of $1,351.29. All told, the paper said the colony had been thankful for the two Norwegian sisters' faithful service, adding its hope that the sisters' trip home would not be as stormy as their coming had been, referring to the shipwreck that had delayed them in the Azores.

While these compliments seemed to be unopposed, Fedde commented in her *Memoirs* that she had not known Sister Dorothea in Christiania. Sister Elisabeth did observe that according to some board members the enterprise under Sister Dorothea's leadership had been in steady decline.[362] The best thing that had happened over her time away was that a young probationary sister from Egersund, probably Sister Mathilde Madland, had been accepted in 1888 and would be inducted into the Motherhouse on April 10, 1892, the next year. A capable woman, she would take Sister Elisabeth's place when she resigned. One other woman had applied and was there when Sister Elisabeth returned, but she "left a short time after I returned."[363] With Sister Karen Sodnak and the other two sisters, she now had three sisters to help her: Sister Mathilde and Sister Elise Tonnig, who had resigned along with the other sisters in Minneapolis in protest when the board had imposed its new rules. The minutes of the April 13, 1891, board meeting recorded the mutual joy shared by the both board and Sister Superior at how things had developed over her absence. However, along with their successes, the same problems emerged. With the new facility, even if they could take in many more patients, they could not treat them without raising more money and training more deaconesses, an old cycle Sister Elisabeth knew well: Any improvement meant more money.

They still had a debt of $7,000, so they had to live within their income (*sette tæring efter næring*). Despite these privations, they had established an operating theater on a long kitchen table and the doctors, whom Sister Elisabeth described as outstanding, were most often successful in their operations. In the basement they opened up four more rooms and added a pharmacy. With all these new facilities, Sister Elisabeth noted, they could take in more patients, up to sixty in the emergency rooms, but they also could have employed more sisters. Sister Lina Strøm, who had left Minneapolis with Sister Elisabeth without the Minneapolis board's permission, had recovered from her nerve fever and was approved by the board to study in Brooklyn, plus another sister who previously had been with Fedde. The hospital was pleased to have in its employ "a whole flock of sisters."[364]

Sister Elisabeth remembered in her *Memoirs* that with the higher number of sisters she had to raise even more money.

> It was often my night labor to think about where I could go to get help. It became almost a belief of mine that if I was going to be successful in my requests, it would have to be either Tuesday or Thursday. If I went out on Friday, I never received anything. Even so one Friday I thought I would try and went to an office where I had once gotten $50. The servant took my card and went to see if I could speak with the gentleman myself, but he came back with the message, "No, I cannot see you today." That was the same as telling me to leave. I had nothing more to expect.

> After such visits I was often very worried, but not without courage for I knew that the Lord, who had sent me the poor and sick, would help me as he had done before.[365]

Sometimes, despite her prayers and worry, she did not think she would be able to pay the deaconesses in her charge their small monthly allowances. In her *Memoirs* she recalled that one of the Brooklyn sisters (most likely Sister Mathilde, who returned to Egersund several times after her retirement) remembered how once, as they were sitting around having their coffee, Sister Elisabeth had come in to their living room with bad news. She had been out trying raise money all day and was very weary and very disappointed.

> We sisters sat around the coffee table and it was toward the first of the month. You said, "Sisters, you will not receive your pay this month—it was $10 a month—for I cannot manage any more with what we have than pay the hospital bills, but as soon as I have enough, you will get your pay. Will you be okay with that?" "Yes," they responded. At the evening meal, you came in beaming with joy with some letters in your hand saying, "Now, Sisters, you will all get your pay and I have even more!"[366]

One gets a sense from the routine of the work, even if it was still financially at risk much of the time, it was now an established institution and a significant member of the world-wide group of Motherhouses.

That fall the Deaconess House in Kaiserswerth hosted the tenth general conference of the Motherhouses in the world. Although Sister Elisabeth had not been able to attend, she had sent a greeting to the group. In answer, she received a letter from Dr. Disselhoff, the rector in Kaiserswerth.

September 24, 1891, Kaiserswerth on the Rhine

Dear Sister in the Lord,

With pleasure I received your letter dated August 28. I had the honor to read it to the Tenth General Deaconess' Conference here assembled on the 16th and 17th of this month. The members of the Conference enjoyed your kind salutations and begged me to repeat them together with many thanks and good wishes for the progress of your work. May God bestow his Holy Spirit upon all your workers and make them a salt among the Evangelicals [Lutherans] of North America. We hope that from this conference will come new life and inspiration for the church of Christ.

Believe me in the Lord,

Yours faithfully, Dr. Disselhoff[367]

Educating Deaconesses

Now that they had admitted some more probationary sisters, they had to educate them into the office of deaconess. This meant developing a formal course of study for the deaconess candidates under their tutelage. A curriculum, similar to the other Deaconess Homes, was prepared and begun in the fall of 1891 with all volunteer teachers, most of them women: Mrs. Groth taught grammar; Miss Rosenqvist, English and history; Miss Sthyr, singing; Pastors Martin H. Hegge and Carl Severin Everson taught Bible; and Sister Elisabeth with the doctors, taught them nursing and other medical studies needed for nurses.[368] Everson and his wife were still heavily involved with the raising of money via bazaars. An announcement printed in the February 13,1891, *Nordisk Tidende* by Mrs. Ambjør (Carl) Everson instructed people giving things to sell for a bazaar on February 27-28, 1891, to leave their contributions with the Eversons. Had he changed his mind about bazaars or games of

chance in church? While he may have accepted the need for bazaars—
they were the main method for raising money that all the Brooklyn
charities used at the time—had he also accepted games of chance? That
is not clear. Although he was not on the Board of Managers when Sister
Elisabeth returned, he did lead the annual meeting of the corporation on
January 1892 as president. His teaching of the students along with Martin Hegge meant that he was still heavily involved with the Motherhouse,
although in this same year Hegge took the office of rector, replacing
Everson. In 1894 the board would commend Hegge for his work as a
chaplain: "In spiritual matters he [Hegge] had done more good for the
suffering than anyone can tell except those who have received his care."[369]
This sounds like a subtle dig at Everson, but not obvious.

Meanwhile things continued apace as the ministry expanded. Although she wrote in her *Memoirs* that she healed quickly from the
operation, it appears from the records that it took Sister Elisabeth some
time to get her energy back after her surgery. By the end of the year her
health seemed to be fine. At the annual meeting of 1892, which reviewed
the previous year, Sister Elisabeth thanked the board for its work and
said that the past year, 1891, had been her best year yet. She hoped the
board would express its thanks to the doctors, both in the annual report
and in other venues, for their "unusual interest, skill, and success in the
treatment of patients." The board agreed and determined that during the
past year the "home had undergone a complete change for the better."[370]
It had patients in the hospital for over 5,000 nights—a figure they arrived
at by adding up how many nights each patient stayed, a useful figure for
them to see how much their work had grown or not—and 2,844 visits to
homes in the area. The sisters had distributed clothes to 184 people, food
to over 300, found passage home to Norway for three, and placed eleven
children in the Staten Island Children's Home. It had found a place on
the property for a small morgue, added a pharmacy on the third floor, as
well as buying more equipment for the surgery ward. It also created an
emergency room in the basement, where it constructed two new hospital
rooms, with place for sixty patients. All these improvements helped serve
the increasing number of patients as well as made it possible to give the
probationary sisters a better education. Sister Elisabeth also wanted to
build a birthing room, but the funds were not yet available. (In 1943, the

hospital would name its maternity ward for Elisabeth Fedde.) The Sunday school continued with seventy students and twenty-one teachers. The annual trip to Staten Island and the Christmas party remained the high points of the year for them, and Sister Elisabeth rejoiced that this ministry continued. The board was proud to announce that each day the hospital's work improved and could be favorably compared with any hospital in Brooklyn or New York, even those in Europe. This report by Dr. Henry Turner, the head doctor; Carl Ullenæs, the president of the board; and Sister Elisabeth concluded with many thanks to their supporters in the community. The board commented that it was under Sister Elisabeth's practical leadership and experience, begun while she was a patient herself, that the work had experienced a complete change for the better. She had returned somewhat more focused and better able to restore a new sense of purpose and order to their efforts.[371]

The Seamen's Mission

The relationship with the Seamen's' Mission Church needed attention as well, now that the hospital and Motherhouse were becoming successful independent institutions on their own, especially since the Seamen's Mission board in Bergen had declared the congregation could not serve permanent Norwegian residents in Brooklyn, but could only serve Norwegian sailors. The congregation, with the help of the consulate, contracted with the hospital to serve the Norwegian sailors who landed in the New York harbor. The Seamen's Mission Church paid the hospital twelve dollars a month to take in all the sailors who were ill.[372] It was like an insurance policy. If there were no sailors to treat, the money was still paid. If there were many who needed treatment, the money assured the sailors' treatment, even if it might have cost much more than twelve dollars to treat them all. When Norwegian ships arrived, Dr. Volkmar, Examining Physician to Steamships, would go on board the steamer and decide which of the sailors, if any, were ill enough to be hospitalized. Sister Elisabeth appreciated the chance to be in a closer relationship with the Norwegian seamen. At the same time, she knew they could bring with them highly contagious diseases which had to be treated with great care, such as the sailor who came with yellow fever—a viral disease for which there is still no treatment, only prevention through the eradication of mosquitos carrying the disease, something the medical community did not discover until a few years later in 1900 while the Panama Canal was being built. Although it was thought to be communicated person to person, it was Walter Reed (1851-1902) and others who discovered infected mosquitos were the culprits. The incidences of the disease came mostly from sub-tropical and tropical areas of the globe where many of the sailors had been. Many came with scurvy, a common disease for sailors who lived for long periods of time without sufficient vitamin C. Although by the 1890s doctors were coming to see that certain foods could stop the disease, they were not quite sure why. The British Navy required that British ships carry Rose Lime Juice to keep the illness at bay, which is why British sailors were known as "limeys." Fresh meat also had enough vitamins to help, especially liver. Sister Elisabeth did not record how they treated scurvy, but it could have been any of these cures.

Perhaps one of the reasons for the success of the Seamen's Mission Church was that it offered sailors a place of refuge from destructive entertainments. There had been a strong wave of religious revivals among the Norwegian merchant marine during the last half of the nineteenth century. It had the effect of keeping the sailors away from the bars and brothels that could be so deleterious to their health. Pious Christians opposed these vices not only because of their obedience to the Ten Commandments, but also because they realized that the commandments helped people live lives that were more healthy. Sister Elisabeth often told stories of young boys who had been warned by their mothers before they sailed not to be led astray by drink. Many were the stories of the very young teenage sailors being taunted into getting drunk and being taken into brothels where they contracted syphilis or other venereal diseases for which there was no cure. While they did not die immediately from syphilis, for example, they well knew the progression of the disease. One young man had succumbed to temptation and the next day had gone back to sea where he soon realized he had contracted the disease. He tried to hide it, but its typical symptoms of pustules on his body began to appear: "When the ship returned we received him just as he was." The worst for her was having to stand beside the bed of the young man and translate for the American doctor treating him exactly how he had contracted the disease. "I will never forget the young boy's tearful eyes as he told me everything. Poor thing, he had to undergo a difficult and long treatment for his forced excursion. O what horrible consequences such old seductions cause!"[373]

If these sailors died, Sister Elisabeth took the responsibility to prepare them for burial, buy a coffin, find a pastor to officiate at the service, and locate an appropriate place to bury the body, normally with the help of the Norwegian Consul General's office and captain of the ship on which the sailor had arrived. Before, she could count on the good graces of Consul Børs and his wife. They had left while she was in Minneapolis and been replaced by Consul Christopher Ravn and then Consul Karl Woxen, with whom Sister Elisabeth found it difficult to work, although she realized she had to. For example, the death of a fine young man who had come on shore from a boat importing fruit greatly affected her. He had a disease they could not treat. When he died, she grieved that such a handsome man now had to be carried away as a corpse. She wanted him to have a proper burial. Because it was so warm, they needed to bury the body as soon as possible, before decay set in, but she did not have the resources to pay for such a service, and the ship where he had served had sailed, meaning they could not help pay for the funeral. She went to Consul Woxen and asked for support. Given the young man's position in society and family, she wanted the consul to give her money for the burial. She explained the situation to him, certain the ship, on its return, would reimburse them for their expenses. The consul was unmoved. "Bury him for $10, as you usually do, for you cannot know for sure the ship's captain will reimburse you."

This raised her ire. "You can't believe that his shipmates or his family would want him to be buried in a black box, driven to Potter's Field, so he can never be found again? It can't happen. We must bury him nicely."

"No, no," he replied. "It must be as I have said, and I will not support anything else for him. Forget it."

She retorted, "No, he shall be buried in the customary way. If you do not, I will."

Sister Elisabeth went to a funeral parlor, found a casket, a shroud, and a hearse, because "it was so terribly warm that it had to be done immediately." She organized the funeral and got a pastor to speak. Many sailors attended, and the seamen's pastor followed him to the committal service at the grave. Even if it was sad to have to bury such a fine young man, she took comfort in the fact that she had given him a fine funeral. The conflict with Woxen, however, did not subside. The next day, according to Sister Elisabeth, a long article appeared in a paper about the argument.[374] Sister Elisabeth was suspected as the source of the article which she denied. Woxen later sued the editor, Nielsen, for slander. After that she could not visit him without, as she said, feeling as though flames and sparks streamed out of him whenever he saw her. "I had done nothing, nor was I afraid, which made him even more angry. When I came and stood outside his office among the sailors, my concerns were handled speedily; he was not happy to see me. And he became even more angry when the ship came back and the captain both paid her for the funeral and thanked her."[375] Such encounters made her wish to have the Børs return to the consulate. As she knew this was not possible, she wished that Vice-Consul Ravn would be promoted, which he finally was. Consul Woxen fled New York in 1898 under suspicious circumstances, proving her sense for his character was fairly well founded. Ravn reported to the authorities, after looking through Woxen's accounting, that he had been pilfering the consulate's treasury ever since 1896 and had written several bad checks, for which a warrant for his arrest was issued. Those stories may well have explained to her why Consul Woxen's behavior concerning money was so rude. Her memory of the actual event is without a doubt true. She knew from personal experience that it was important to have a good person in the consulate as so much of their work with the Norwegian sailors had to go through the consulate.[376]

Consecrating New Deaconesses

On April 10, 1892, the Brooklyn Motherhouse consecrated two probationary sisters, Mathilde Madland, and Elise Tonnig. The officiating pastor was Pastor Hegge, now the hospital chaplain or rector. It was a time of great festivity. Over a hundred people attended, among them, the rector of the Deaconess House at the Mary Lane Drexel House in Philadelphia, Karl August Seth Cordes (1859-1936). The new sisters wore the new garb Sister Elisabeth had designed—white woolen uniforms instead of the dark blue from Norway.[377] She thought it more festive and better looking. During the lunch after-

Martin Hegge

ward, Captain Ullenæs, the president of the board, spoke, as did Pastor A. Sommerfelt, assistant at the Seamen's Mission Church, as well as Sister Elisabeth and several ship captains. While it may not have been the first time that she spoke publicly in a church, it is the first time it is recorded.

Daily Life

The routine she had learned in Christiania became the routine of the Brooklyn Motherhouse. The day began at 6:00 a.m. and ended at 7:00 p.m. From 6:00 until 7:00 in the morning, they ate breakfast, had devotions, and sang hymns in the hospital corridors. At 7:00 the night watch left. The uniforms of those doing bedside care were white-dotted blue (seersucker) in which the nurses worked until noon. For noon dinner they changed to white uniforms which they wore for the rest of the day. They sat together in the dining room according to when they had been admitted as probationary sisters, the same order as in the Christiania Motherhouse. After the evening work and light supper, they went to the living room where they had devotions while sewing things for the coming bazaar. If they were out of clean linen for the operating room the next day, the sisters had to do the laundry themselves.[378] During this time Sister Elisabeth began looking for new opportunities to expand the reach of the institution beyond Norwegians. Going to the poor and indigent Norwegians she found in the streets or in their own homes was one

Brooklyn deaconesses in new white uniforms designed by Fedde

Brooklyn deaconesses gather in the living room. Sister Elisabeth is seated at the desk.

thing; to build a place all could see and all could use was quite another. The Seamen's Mission Church and the pastors had found it difficult to serve only Norwegian sailors, and ignore the other immigrant Norwegians with needs. Now that they had a hospital building, Sister Elisabeth's problems became even more complicated, but her pragmatism helped her handle the problem. Even though they had refused patients who were not Norwegian as late as 1891, such a practice could not endure for long. If people saw a hospital and needed one, their nationality should not matter, except perhaps for needing a common language. They were quickly becoming an institution that served everybody who came to them for medical help without regard for nationality or confession.

Ambulance

In order to serve the community better and increase their visibility, Sister Elisabeth realized that the hospital needed an ambulance. The Board of Managers authorized its purchase. Elisabeth asked the city if it could support the project. The city needed help and was glad for her offer. The ambulances from other hospitals found they were too far away to serve the area where the Deaconess Hospital was. The city offered to pay $1,200 yearly to assist her in getting an ambulance up and running. Its area of responsibility would be from 24th Street to the city line on one side and from the water's edge to Greenwood Lane. Sister Elisabeth immediately began looking for both an ambulance and a horse to pull it. The board agreed. "We thought that an ambulance would be a representative of our little Norwegian undertaking and would make it recognized throughout the city as it came clattering by on its often sorrowful errand."[379]

She engaged Denigan and Nilsen's Wagon Factory on 3rd Avenue to make the body of the ambulance according to her exacting specifications. She wanted it to be both effective and attractive, making certain the bed was soft enough so that the injured they were transporting would not be further hurt by the ride over the rough streets to the hospital. She went many times to the factory to make sure they followed her instructions. They must have been quite exacting and thorough! When it was completed, she thought it both serviceable and lovely, painted white with the name of the hospital on both sides in gold letters. The inside was russet brown with all of the necessary equipment. It cost $500. *The Brooklyn Eagle* described it as very pretty, along with the uniforms of the surgeon and ambulance driver designed to go with the colors of the ambulance. The black horse, it said, made a nice contrast to the colors of the ambulance.[380]

Now she had the wagon. What she needed next was a horse and stall to house it and keep the wagon sheltered from the elements. She also had to find someone to care for the horse and drive the ambulance when it

A horse-drawn ambulance extended the reach of the hospital.

would be called out on an emergency. A sailor, Olsen, had been to the hospital for treatment, and Elisabeth asked him if he knew anything about horses. "No," he said, "Where do you think I am from?"

"The sea," she replied. "And I know there are no horses there. But now you will be a coachman and drive our new ambulance. You will have a uniform in the summer and leather coat in the winter. Now just come and see."

"No," answered Olsen, in his friendly manner, she wrote. "No, Sister Elisabeth. You can get me to do many things, but not this."

"I will teach you how," she answered. It would work she thought. "We already had the coachman's material ready." Where to house the horse and wagon was another question. She thought they had a suitable veranda where the horse could be quartered and where they could store its food. They also had spring water and a cement floor where the horse could stand. All she needed now was the horse. She knew that with the coming of the electric trams, there would be many horses on sale. So with her usual dispatch, she went to a horse dealer. While she was not particularly used to horses, she understood animals well enough to be able to make this transaction shrewdly with a horse trader in the neighborhood.

> I told him that he had to know I was not well acquainted with horses. He realized that and then began to show her one horse after another. She stood there as she criticized each one, "That one does not lift his hooves high enough. This one's back legs are not straight. Uffda! That one is not attractive!" Then came a black one with lovely marks and a white nose. I thought he was lovely. "What does he cost?" she asked. "Fifty-eight dollars," he said. "We will take it for eight days to test it," she told him.

Then she went on. "Mr. Superintendent," I said, "I am only a sister and do not know horses, but you do. If you try to palm off one that is no good, when you know what we are going to use it for, then you are not being chivalrous. But I trust you."

"That you can do," he replied. She then called her newly hired coachman whom she asked to come and take the new horse. As the stable boy led it out to them, he confided in her, "Sister, you have gotten our best horse."[381] They took the horse home. With her usual purpose, she went to someone who had many fine horses and asked to be taught how to care for the animal. The course lasted from morning until evening, she said. Afterward the man gave her a list of things to do every day. The next day she went to the nearest fire station and asked the saddlemaker there to make the horse a good harness, which cost sixty dollars, more than the horse, which she persuaded the man to give them a good deal on. She came home, put the instructions for the care of the horse on the wall, and, with the reluctant coachman and a kind doctor in the hospital, they were set to begin their ambulance service.

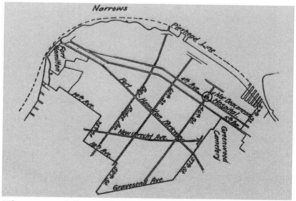

The map of the ambulance district

The next day, a Sunday, she said they took several rides around the area, and many came to the hospital to see our horse which was "radiantly fine." When the bill came for the horse, she took the fifty-eight dollars in cash to the horse dealer and said, "The Norwegian Deaconess' Hospital has bought this horse for its ambulance service and here is the money. But I am wondering since your trams are involved in the most accidents and you have the most use for our service, I am thinking you could give us a horse." He looked at her and agreed there was something to what she said, so he reduced the price to fifty-five dollars. She left with three dollars in her pocket, remarking that it was their first horse and a trusty servant for them until it met with an accident. "Everyone was happy with 'Freya' as they called the horse."[382] It was to begin its work January 1, 1893.

Although this is related by Sister Elisabeth many years after it happened, and she has had a chance to think it through, the account seems trustworthy. She enjoyed telling the story: her success in buying the horse, her shrewd horse sense and dealings with the men, plus her ability to drive a hard bargain. The story also reveals a great deal about her as we read it. She was confident of her powers, nor was she afraid to learn how to do new things when they had to be done. She was well known in the area and expected the men she was dealing with to respect her and treat her well. Furthermore, the skill with which she writes the story is to be admired. It is clear, concise, and very funny.

Complaints

Sister Elisabeth always evoked strong reactions from people. The strength of her personality may have made her the kind of person who was either hated or admired. Several articles appeared in the *Nordisk Tidende* about this time reporting on complaints made against the hospital and especially Sister Elisabeth. One complaint involved the treatment of Severin Hansen, a man from Arendal, who had died of nerve fever at the hospital and, according to a witness, had received less than kind treatment from Sister Elisabeth. The witness praised the other sisters and doctors for their good care. He wanted it to be clear: The complaint was against Fedde. Because of the seriousness of the complaint, the paper sent a reporter to interview her and others at the hospital. After some small talk, the reporter asked her directly about the accusation. She answered quickly that this kind of a complaint was nothing new. She encouraged the reporter to visit with other patients in the hospital who had shared the room with Hansen and ask for their opinions.

The reporter did. He interviewed some ten patients, six of whom had been there when Hansen died. He printed each one of their names with their home city in Norway in his article so they could be checked out. All agreed that her care for the dying man had been exemplary, as had her treatment of them. One sailor remarked that the person who said otherwise should be whipped (*jules*). The reporter concluded that as he went around "asking several the same questions that the results were always the same, and so I bid them farewell and left with the impression that their remaining patients believe the entire home is in an entirely and completely unimpeachable position."[383] On December 23, 1892, however, the same paper published an editorial on a new rumor about the conditions at the hospital, this one believed to be far more serious. It had to do with a Swedish patient, Johanna Nordström, wife of a painter in Brooklyn. The complaint involved the way the sisters, especially Sister Elisabeth, had handled a strange incident. Nordström had a very serious operation on the stomach. During the operation she had gotten hurt in the arm, and the bandages for the wound were said to have been inappropriately applied. A friend of Nordström, according to the report, came to visit and when she related the problem to Sister Elisabeth she was, reportedly, met with an unfriendly retort, something to the effect that someone with "dirty hands" shouldn't say anything. When the husband made the same complaint and said he was taking his wife home to recover, Elisabeth had become angry and made disparaging comments about his wife, but he did not take her home. A week later, the friend of the woman returned and this time took off the bandage and treated the sore with oil, whereupon the doctor on call yelled at her to "get out!"

The next month in January 1893, *Nordisk Tidende* again addressed this issue since the rumors about the event had spread to other papers in the Norwegian community. Now they heard it described as "vandalism," not the work of a friend. They could understand why a doctor would be angry at someone, almost like a vandal, as they described it, who threatened the life of a patient with the application of a strange balm to the wound. She should have been forced out of the hospital immediately. What had really happened, however, was still not clear. The paper felt its own integrity had been impugned, and the editorial said it had learned the facts from good reporting. While the issue never was well described, it is obvious the matter was much discussed in the Norwegian colony, and many rumors and suspicions of the hospital had arisen, for which Fedde herself was always concerned.

On the other hand, articles seemingly unsolicited by her or the hospital also appeared in the paper and praised her. A shipmaster, O. N. Hendrickson, had sent a letter on August 17, 1892, to the *Sailing Times (Sjöfartstidende)*, warmly commending both the hospital and Sister Elisabeth for their kindness toward Norwegian sailors who needed care. By offering their countrymen a refuge, they were doing a work that Norwegians, especially, should value. He appealed to his countrymen to support the work since the need was so great.[384]

Incorporation

The board decided it was time to reincorporate as a hospital, no longer as a relief society. Now the question had to be asked again: Did they exist only to serve Norwegians? Could only Lutherans be on the board?

What was the place of the Deaconess Home or Motherhouse in the future of the organization? This called for much conversation and thought. After some time they came up with some decisions: First, they agreed to use the word Lutheran in the name of the institution, but allow non-Lutherans to be members of the corporation. Second, they stated directly that they were there to treat any person who came to them. Third, they agreed that the Motherhouse should be under the direction of the Sister Superior and that she would be appointed by the board. This was something Florence Nightingale had recommended in other contexts. One of the reasons they decided to keep the Motherhouse going, an expensive process, was to assure that there would be more deaconesses to do the work. On November 15, 1892, they reincorporated as a hospital under the name The Norwegian Lutheran Deaconesses' Home and Hospital.[385] The annual report explained the reason for the new name: "Said name signifies to us the duty which we as Norwegians and as Lutherans owe to the community and the country in which we live. If we share the blessing of our adopted land, it is certainly also our duty to help carry its burdens and to shrink from no responsibility resting upon us."[386] (See page 348.)

1893

The January 1, 1893, issue of *The Brooklyn Eagle* had on its front page a report on the hospital. The headline "Norwegian Lutheran Deaconesses Doing Good Work Here" may have been in answer to rumors sweeping through the community. The object of the institution, it said was to provide both spiritual and physical care for suffering humanity. The writer praised Sister Elisabeth for her "untiring perseverance" in building not only the Brooklyn facility, but also the one in Minneapolis. Most impressive to the journalist was the good rapport between the staff, sisters and doctors. He then reported favorably on the number of doctors employed by the hospital: Dr. Henry C. Turner, the head doctor of the medical ward, and Dr. H. Beeckman Delatour of the surgery department, known throughout the city for his ability to save wounded limbs from amputation along with his other gifts as a surgeon. Over 100 surgeries had been performed in 1892, the article noted, now

H. Beeckman Delatour

that the hospital had a doctor, Dr. Robert E. Coughlin, who resided on the premises. They also were beginning to realize the good the ambulance could do. It had just been put into service on December 24, 1892, when a woman in the Bealty's Drug Store on 3rd Avenue had suffered a lacerated forearm.[387] The ambulance had brought her in quickly for treatment.

Because of her confidence that the work would continue to expand, Sister Elisabeth had convinced the board to buy two lots next to the hospital when Trinity Lutheran Church, just across from them on 4thAvenue, put them up for sale. Although they could not build immediately, all agreed it was wise to buy the lots, even though doing so put the hospital in some financial jeopardy, the paper concluded. The Board of Managers hoped that members of the community, whether Norwegian or not, would help support the institution because it served all in the community without distinction now. "The addition of the ambulance, the increase in the number of patients, and the expected continuation of the hospital . . . are all proof positive of the good work being done by this Institution."[388] It also congratulated the hospital for the ambulance design and appearance with its russet leather upholstery and exterior white sides with gold lettering making its appearance "very pretty."[389]

The article ended with the statement that the hospital needed to be supported by the wider community. While the hospital had taken in $1,202.08 more than it had spent in the previous year, more gifts from the community would be good:

> It might be well to state here that the Board would very much like to have the general public take an interest in it and help it along as it is a great help to the city in many ways. All sufferers are admitted to the hospital. It may be added that at press time owing to the increase of service the funds in the treasury are low. The yearly report of the institution will be issued in February. The additions of the ambulance, the increased number of patients and the expected completion of the hospital are all proof positive of the good work being done by this institution.[390]

The Brooklyn Eagle story may have been some kind of response to the slightly scandalous story printed in the *Nordisk Tidende* of the woman who had walked into the hospital and torn off the bandages of a patient recovering from surgery.[391]

As they expected, after the ambulance had been purchased, the hospital began to receive more patients from farther reaches in the community. With them came even more sad stories. One of them Sister Elisabeth could not forget. A widow had a son, who was quite ill, on whom she had spent much time and money, hoping he would recover. Nothing seemed to work, and he died. After his fine funeral and burial at the Greenwood Cemetery, his mother

> purchased a revolver, dressed herself up very well, bought a large basket of chrysanthemums, and went to the grave. With the basket in her hand and the revolver in the other, she tried to shoot herself so she would be lying dead over her son's grave. The gun went off, but the entire bullet remained in her upper jaw and nose. Fainting she was brought to us by the police. (Suicide is counted as attempted murder in America.) One did not have to keep watch over her while she was recovering from the wound. When she was well, she had to be taken to court and I came with as a witness. Poor person! She told them everything and when she promised never to try it again, she was set free. It appeared to me that it was a great enough punishment to be kept among the murderers and warriors [the brief time she had been incarcerated]. She recovered from her sorrow over her son and became well. She lived in New York, but soon moved to where no one would know her.[392]

The Women's Exhibition in Chicago—1893

The activities of the hospital and its board seemed to have gone quiet in 1893. The doings of Fedde seem also to be muted. What was exciting, despite the hard times of the 1893 panic, was the Columbian Exposition in Chicago. Many Americans thrilled at the exposition celebrating 400 years since Columbus. Chicago had very quickly built what was called the "White City," a marvel to all who attended it. It opened on May 1 and featured exhibits from around the world. Norway had an exhibit hoping to prove that Leif Ericson had discovered America long before Columbus. Many Norwegians eagerly rushed to see the Norwegian exhibit and also may have stopped by the Women's Building, designed and filled by women. It featured the stories of the progress women around the world had made over the centuries. The controversies that swirled around the planning and building of it showed the very many different concerns and political opinions of the women participating. Exhibits ranged from how to bake and how to cook Iowa corn to a mural, now lost, by Mary Cassatt on the modern woman.

The old suffragettes were coming to the end of their reign; both Susan B. Anthony and Cady Stanton were now giving way to their younger sisters and daughters, but the issue of women's rights, especially now the vote, continued to grow and gain support among women in the United States. An honor roll of the suffragists appeared in the hall, among them, Susan B. Anthony, Lucy Stone, Julie Ward Howe, and Helen Gardner. The crush of people there to see them became almost frightening to the speakers, except for Anthony, the old warrior, who cleared a way for them to walk through the thronging crowds.

Elizabeth Cady Stanton and Susan B. Anthony

They had been fighting for their rights since the 1848 Seneca Falls meeting. Because of Stanton's ill health, Susan B. Anthony read a speech from her to the assembled women on May 18. Anthony focused exclusively on what she always referred to as The Cause: getting women the vote, a cause appealing to Yankee women more than to immigrant women. It was no secret that the leaders of the women's movement tended to be Yankee blue-bloods, quite unfamiliar with the lives of immigrant farm women, the new class of factory working women, and women of color. Susan B. Anthony's view that the only issue that mattered was getting the vote seemed to be one of the few unifying forces at the Conference.

The rest of it seemed to be a potpourri of causes, a few of which were opposed by some of the leaders. Even with the national exhibits from Scandinavia it was a difficult thing to get Scandinavian women involved in this cause. Why that was has not yet been fully examined, but the language barrier had to be one important reason. Since a large percentage of Norwegian-American women at the time were on the farm or working as maids in the city, they occupied themselves with causes that maybe were more immediate to their language and culture: if they were church members, raising money for their own church buildings, for missionaries, deaconess houses, orphanages, and the like. If Norwegian church women worked for the vote, it was to get the vote in their congregations. The only important Scandinavian Lutheran woman who would get involved publicly in the fight for the vote at this time was Swedish Augustana's Emmy Carlsson Evald (1857-1946), daughter of the early Swedish Augustana pastor, Erland Carlsson. As president of the Swedish Augustana's Women's Missionary Society, she could lead.

Emmy Carlsson Evald

If one looks closely, the major question beneath the swirling controversies at the fair was how women should enter the public sphere. Lucy Stone summed up the progress of the past fifty years with gratitude by noting that the laws had been changed so that a woman now had her own property rights. "In regard to the personal and property rights of women they have been greatly changed and improved, and we are very grateful to the men who have done it." Property rights had been the pressing issue at the Seneca Falls meeting and it was Frederick Douglass (1818-1895), the former slave and fighter for abolition, who convinced them to add women's suffrage to their Declaration of Sentiments.

For our purposes most important is the continuing debate about the kind of woman's vocation nursing was. At the time, 40,000 nurses and midwives were listed on the 1890 census, but only 500 of the nurses had been trained. That same year there were fifteen American programs to train nurses. The profession seemed to be growing, spurred on by Florence Nightingale and Clara Barton's heroic work. By 1893, the year of the exposition, nurses were asking for the profession to be formally accredited. Women in the medical community had campaigned to have a working hospital ward at the exposition to show people what they could do. After much discussion and many funding problems, an emergency ward and drugstore were finished on April 28, 1893, two days before the exposition opened. Over the time of the exhibit the ward treated over 3,000 people for injuries and illnesses. Hospitals in New York and Philadelphia featured scenes from their nursing programs. The most impressive exhibit in this part of the Women's Building was the exhibit of Philadelphia Women's Medical College Hospital. It was favorably reviewed in the *Woman's Journal* for its smart use of design to tell its history. It had produced 170 nursing graduates out of 282 candidates.[393]

Clara Barton

It was clear to all that nursing had been radically changed by Florence Nightingale in England and in America by Clara Barton (1821-1912), the heroine nurse of the Civil War, founder of the Red Cross and worker for women's emancipation. The fair showed to all the question concerning the role of a nurse and her training. What should she know and do? Nightingale thought the moral character of a future nurse was most important, maybe even more so than her intellectual abilities. She should be able "to learn personal cleanliness, hygiene and proper diet, as well as sobriety, gentleness and the keeping of accurate records."[394] The Americans, however, disagreed with Nightingale on that point and began requiring more and more education in order to make nursing a respectable profession without the religious line of schooling. While removing the religious component resolved some of Nightingale's growing problem with the diaconate and its vows of obedience and less-than-complete nursing education, it still left nurses—all women—on the lower side of the equation, below the doctor who was almost always male.

The vocation of deaconess seemed to be that of a minor doctor and a minor pastor. As the office of deaconess became less attractive to women who wanted to be nurses without having to take the vows of self-denial and obedience, the diaconate began to lose support from women like Nightingale. With the coming of the professionalization of the nurse, it became difficult to figure out what the nurse could do that the doctor could not do. Florence Nightingale once said the doctor was brutal, tearing apart the body to get at the problem, while the nurse watched as the body repaired itself—once again a woman's natural role vs. a man's natural role.[395] This impacted the understanding of the deaconesses' role as well. They all had to deal with these questions. What were they: minor doctors or minor pastors? Was theirs a public profession or not? Earlier in the century they had taken up this new vocation to find a way to serve their Lord and neighbor as women devoutly hoping to make a difference and find their voices. At the time it had been revolutionary, but now it was beginning to seem old-fashioned as women began taking up more public roles. Should or could they be both Martha and Mary? Many of these initially pro-women beginnings seemed to be at cross purposes with each other and in some senses were never resolved. These various streams and eddies in the women's movement continued to swirl as the deaconesses were trying to figure out who they were in society. To Anthony's dismay, not even all the women in the exposition wanted the vote, although she said in her speech that they would one day. The messy nature of the planning of the women's building and the controversies that threatened to undo their event were an emblem of the many different convictions among the participants.[396]

The Panic of 1893

A mere four days after the opening of the exposition, the stock market crashed and a deep depression hit the American economy. It began, experts say, with the bankruptcy of the Philadelphia and Reading Railroad in February of that year along with bank failures in Argentina that spread around the world. Railroads had overbuilt, and the panic that ensued when their stocks fell caused people to make a run on gold. While the causes of it are complicated, the effects were not, especially for institutions of the church who began to feel immediately the collapse in their support. Farmers in the Upper Midwest, the backbone of the Norwegian American churches and their institutions, could not ship their crops to market and many lost almost everything. This made it difficult to collect money for charitable causes. Colleges and seminaries of the Lutheran churches in America, like many other similar institutions in other traditions, were all affected in one way or another. The construction of the Red Wing Ladies' Seminary built by the Norwegian Synod as its way to address the question of women's edu-

Red Wing Ladies' Seminary

cation and place in society slowed to a crawl. The Norwegian Hospital in Brooklyn did not escape the consequences of the panic either.

In the advertisement of the June 17, 1893, *Nordisk Tidende* for the hospital bazaar, people were urged to be generous since the number of its patients who could not pay had increased rather suddenly. In all they had treated nearly 500 patients during the first part of the year, and a great majority of them could not pay, the announcement said, especially in the month of May during which they had to treat over 100 non-paying patients. The panic and depression which had begun that month made things difficult for everybody in the country, especially the religious institutions that counted on charitable contributions to survive.[397]

1894

As Sister Elisabeth pondered how to fund the hospital with its increasing needs after the panic had set in, she was approached one day by an old Dutch man, a Mr. Blees, whose wife was a friend of Elisabeth's. He would donate a horse for the hospital ambulance later. One day he called her in to his office and suggested that, like other American hospitals in New York had done, she should petition the state for a grant. If other hospitals could receive state funding, why not the Deaconess Hospital? He then told her to go to his lawyer at Bergen and Dykman, 189 Montague Street, and get help in making a case for such a grant from the New York State Legislature. She immediately went to the lawyer with the proposal that New York State could give them a yearly grant of $4,000, as it did for other American hospitals in the area. He kindly received her and then said he would think about the case. After some time he advised her to take his letter and go to Albany to speak with members of the legislature there. He gave her a letter of introduction to Mr. Hamilton Fish II (1849-1936), the chair of the committee. It would be to him and his committee that she should make her request for funding. She demurred, but he advised her

Hamilton Fish II

to do so. After some consideration, she resolved to go. On a day in early February, 1894, she took the 8:00 a.m. train to Albany, arriving at the capitol building at 10:30. It loomed before her with its massive wings. When she entered the building, the meeting had begun and the doorkeeper asked her with whom she wished to speak. "Mr. Finnegan," she answered. "He is in a very important meeting just now on the question about New York, Brooklyn, and the cities around it, whether to unite them in one city," he responded. Did the sister want to observe the meeting? "Yes," she said that it would be a great pleasure. She entered into a very fine room and took her seat.

"Here I sat, like a queen in New York State's Capitol and had never before been in such a formal place." The discussion fascinated her, and she never forgot that she was at the meeting where the cities of New York, Brooklyn, Staten Island and Hoboken discussed becoming one city, The Greater New York. Soon it was 1:00 and time for a break. Mr. Finnegan and Hamilton Fish came to speak with her and tell her about the meeting where she would

New York State Capitol building

speak in about a half-hour. She asked to stay where she was as she was completely unacquainted with the place and did not want to get lost in it. They left her there alone. She sat quietly in the room, all of a sudden remembering how hungry she was. Yes, she thought, it is possible to be in all this finery, a beautiful room on a fine chair, and still be very hungry.

When the meeting began, Fish gathered them together at a long table, and took charge. He introduced Sister Elisabeth and told the committee that she had something to tell the group. Then he asked her if she wanted to stand or sit. She stood. The entire group stood in her honor.

> There I stood. I had never thought of myself in such a situation. The room grew still. I began to speak in my quaking manner about the situation of the Norwegians. By the time I had explained everything about our work and its growth here, I could have easily spoken before the king.

> What I explained was that we admitted the sick of all the nations, if they came in our ambulance; in the same way the state should help support our work as it did other hospitals in the area. What I sought was $4,000 a year. After that they began to debate the proposal. When I had to leave to get home in time, I was promised that they would do what they could so that the bill would pass. When I came out in the hall, I was surrounded by reporters, but I had to run from them in order to catch the train home. I ran into the first class car for once. Now I would be upper class [fine] for an entire day. But I was still hungry.[398]

Some days later a newspaper, thought to be the *New York Herald*, described the event.

> The bill to give the Norwegian Hospital an annuity of $4,000 will probably pass. She [Fedde] came up before the Assembly cities committee to Albany to speak in its behalf. She was very kindly received and Assemblyman Finnegan introduced her to Mr. Hamilton Fish, the chairman of the committee, and to the Senator, who will have charge of the bill in the Senate. She spoke for some time before the committee and impressed them so with justice and righteousness of the bill, that they

said they would give it all their power, report it favorably and push it through. Sister Elisabeth was the only lady present among so many men and she is to be congratulated upon her courage, firmness and forethought.[399]

Soon, the papers were reporting that Governor Flowers would sign the bill which had passed, thanks to Assemblyman Finnegan and Sister Elisabeth. The *Nordisk Tidende* featured the story in much the same way. What they marveled at most was her speech before the committee: "She made a clear and able talk for the high gentlemen in the room." The paper emphasized that Fedde had gotten her request, remarking on the stunning results of a single woman's energy and talented presentation, a woman who deserved to be more well-known in the area. "When the level of our men in Brooklyn reaches the level of this gifted woman, then we will be well blessed in our colony."[400]

Høyme and the United Church

On April 6, 1894, Trinity Lutheran Church (which had been formed in Fallesen's Hall, in Brooklyn on July 29, 1890) dedicated its new building. The church had been built because the Seamen's Mission board in Bergen had ruled that the pastors of the Seamen's Mission Church could not minister to the Norwegian immigrants in New York, only the sailors. Gabriel Fedde had been shocked when Pastor Sårheim had announced from the pulpit in 1889 that from that day, "none of the permanent residents could get any pastoral service in the Seamen's Church!"—not even communion. Sårheim and his assistant, Pastor Sommerfelt, then tried to assure that those permanent residents of Brooklyn attending the church would transfer to Our Savior's Church, Pastor Everson's church. This was completely unacceptable to the lay preacher and leader Gabriel Fedde and many of his group. Carl Everson's personality and theology did not appeal to them. Fedde wanted a more pietistic Lutheran church and had asked Georg Sverdrup for a candidate to be pastor from the United Lutheran Church, one who would know their kind of piety. Sverdrup had suggested Martin Hanson Hegge from Willmar, Minnesota. So Trinity Lutheran Church on 4th was built. Pastor Hegge, a good friend of Sverdrup, got on better with the deaconess board and Motherhouse than Everson, probably because he shared Gabriel and Sister Elisabeth's piety. *Nordisk Tidende* in its announcement of the dedication explained that the congregation belonged to the United Lutheran Church in America (*Den forenede norsk lutherske kirke i Amerika*) which had its headquarters in Minneapolis. It had been formed, the article said, "the year before in 1890 when the Anti-Missourians, a part of the Norwegian Synod, had broken away from it."From this short sentence sharp observers would know that Hegge's church disagreed with Everson's on some fundamental issues, especially the election controversy. The ecclesiastical conflicts of the Norwegian Lutherans in the Midwest were lively even in far-off Brooklyn, with Everson and Hegge representing the two sides in the debate. Two Norwegian Lutheran churches side by side, a feature of many a small town in the Upper Midwest, were not confined to Midwestern states. The conflict on this theological point raged from one end of the continent to the other as one side split from another and built a second Norwegian Lutheran church next to the other. We see it from Brooklyn to Astoria, Oregon.

In a curious note at the end of an interview in 1896 with Sister Elisabeth, *Nordisk Tidende* commented that Sister Elisabeth from the beginning had resisted the notion that the hospital should be under the church's control or, more specifically, the pastors' control.

> At that time, as always in this kind of situation the clergy stretched out their hands to take over the operation. But on this matter Sister Elisabeth stood firm. With the people's help she had begun the deaconess work and with the people's help and situation that was the way it should continue without being transformed into a particular church's use.[401]

This may explain why the institution was not affiliated with any of the brawling Norwegian Lutheran churches in America until the creation of the Norwegian Lutheran Church in America, formed in 1917, which included all of the Norwegian Lutheran churches except for the Lutheran Free Church (1897) and the Lutheran Brethren (1900) whose large congregation at 59th Street became a lively part of the Norwegian American Lutheran debates in Brooklyn. Fedde's convictions may have strengthened in this regard after she had observed the difficulties with Deaconess' Hospital and Motherhouse in Minneapolis as the church supporting it left to be on its own. This lessened the support it could get. It should be noted that the Fairview Hospital nursing school was established by several of the same pastors who gathered to found Deaconess Hospital in Minneapolis—M. Bockman, T. H. Dahl, etc. They wanted to provide nurses and hospitals for the United Church. There was also the Norwegian Synod's hospital in St. Paul—built in 1902 to serve the Norwegians in the Cities, since as Hans Gerhard Stub, the chairman of that committee noted, there was no hospital for Norwegians in the entire city—something to which the Deaconess Institute might have taken exception.[402] Fedde cared mostly that she be given enough support to do her work among the people who needed help, not which synod or group gave it.

Gjermund Høyme, the president of the United Church, came to Brooklyn to dedicate the building. During his time in New York, Sister Elisabeth and Høyme had a long talk. By now the United Church and the Friends of Augsburg had almost permanently parted ways as the Friends of Augsburg began the Lutheran Free Church in 1897. The acrimony between Høyme, Sverdrup, and Oftedal had become irreversibly bitter. Høyme, who had been on the deaconess board in Minneapolis when Sister Elisabeth had been interviewed, knew Sister Elisabeth well. He talked with her, according to her *Memoirs*, about how the conflict and debate around the issue who should own Augsburg Seminary and which school should be the primary college of the United Church, Augsburg or St. Olaf, had debilitated him.

What the two said about Sverdrup, Oftedal, and Gjertsen we do not know. Their opinions could not have been positive. Even if she later did count her time in Minneapolis as a happy time, she had not had a good experience with the men on the board, not even Sverdrup. She may have also by this time understood her role in the unpleasantness and said less than she might have in her own *Memoirs* simply to let the past die. From her account of the merger celebrations in 1890 and her quick agreements with Wright and Lysnes of the Norwegian Danish Augustana Synod concerning the orphanage in Beloit, it is obvious that she got on with them better than the leaders of the Conference, probably because she had not worked with them as much or as intensely. In any case, she ended her report on this conversation by noting Høyme had died young, in 1902. This was a surprise to her as well as the young church which was to dedicate the United Seminary (now Luther) building in St. Anthony Park (midway between Minneapolis and St. Paul) that summer.

A small squib under the report on Sister Elisabeth's success in Albany revealed that Sister Elisabeth would be leaving on May 5, 1894, for a long trip home to Norway on the *Hekla*. As she said, "all of the spiritual and physical work took my strength away" and her health seemed to be in constant decline. "To live among the sick, with the sick, and by the sick could weary the very strongest of natures with the most iron will." She needed rest again. The paper wished her a good journey and a restful time so she could return refreshed and ready to work again. In her *Memoirs* she also noted that she needed a time with Mother Guldberg in Christiania.[403] By now, with the leadership of Captain Carl Ullenæs, the hospital and Motherhouse were doing very well. The number of sisters had grown to ten, two of whom devoted their time to helping the poor, as had been the original intention of the board. They had two doctors who worked from six in the morning until eight in the evening when the sisters gathered in the living room for singing and handwork, getting things ready to sell at their profitable bazaars. One gets the sense for a cozy evening, like a family in the parlor, sitting around working, talking idly, writing letters, having devotions in the time-honored family way that Luther had recommended in his *Small Catechism*: singing hymns and reading the Bible together. Frequently, though, they were interrupted by the sound of the ambulance clattering and clanging as it brought in one or another injured person. Many of the ones who came in the evening and at night were the victims of violence in the neighborhood. "Often it was murder, suicide, fights. That meant some were brought in to die, others for stitches, or bandaging."

At the time, she said with thanksgiving, the board and the staff were in complete harmony, as were the deaconesses with each other. For Sister Elisabeth, as she remembered it, "It was my best time, for it was as if all the nations stood protectively around us and the stone had been rolled up the hill and it was important to keep it there so it did not roll back down again."[404] She was clearly remembering the strife of the previous years when they had begun the work. She treasured this time for good reason.

Sister Elisabeth enjoyed the diverse communities around the hospital and the different nationalities they served. The hospital treated many Italians who were their close neighbors. She thought they were a bit too quick with their stilettos, but she enjoyed their vitality and love of music and flowers. One day a little Italian girl came in, with third degree burns, without much hope of surviving. While they had worked to bandage her and did all that they could to relieve her pains, which were excruciating, they knew it was hopeless. Sister Elisabeth tried to be with her as much as she could to encourage her in her last days, playing and singing for her. Nothing helped. Then one day she brought the little girl a great big American Beauty rose. "*Rosse, rosse,*" the little girl cried joyfully as she reached for the rose with her scarred and bandaged hands. "With it she died, and it went with her to the grave."[405]

Mixed Marriage

Toward the end of her *Memoirs,* Sister Elisabeth told a humorous story which reveals both her difficulties in running the hospital and the Motherhouse along with her own sense of human foibles. As she worked to increase the number of deaconesses, or at least nurses and doctors in the hospital, because the number of patients was increasing, she often had to hire people about whom she was not always confident. The physicians recommended a doctor of French descent, a Catholic. She had no problem with him as a doctor in the hospital. For a while he did well, and she had no complaint until a new sister came to work. She was from the northern part of Norway. According to Sister Elisabeth, she was dark, with dreamy brown eyes. He was soon smitten with her. Not only was she attractive, she could play guitar and sing. The doctor could often be found wherever she was. One day the young woman came to Sister Elisabeth and said that the doctor had been courting her, and "I have said yes. What do you think?"

Sister Elisabeth said, "What does it matter what I have said, if you have already said yes?" She then asked if she had thought whether or not the two could be happy given their very great differences, culturally and religiously.

The young sister replied, "Oh, he isn't a very serious Catholic."

"Even worse," said Sister Elisabeth. "That is nothing to bank on. Ask him to come in and speak with me."

She did, and soon the young man came in so she could question him.

"Is it true that you and Sister L. are engaged?" she asked.

"Yes, it is," he answered.

"Have you thought it through? You have come here, a stranger and become engaged to one of our sisters from another country, of another religion, and another class. Not that her class is lower than yours, it is simply different. You are a worldly man who has lived in Paris and had Parisian girlfriends over the years, even if you think those loves are over. You must know that she is young and alone in this country."

He interrupted Sister Elisabeth's long speech with the words, "That is true, Sister Elisabeth, but I have considered all that and I love her so much I will overlook those differences for the sake of love!"

Sister Elisabeth answered, "About love I cannot say anything respecting you two, but I will simply say that if you do anything to hurt her, you have a great responsibility. Remember, Sister Elisabeth has told you this today!"

They were engaged and she was about to give up her garb and go civilian as they called it. When she met him in her new dress, Sister Elisabeth wrote, "It was as if his love vanished at once. He reluctantly took her for a walk, but did not take her to his family living in New York. So it went. I thought it was going to end badly.

One day he came into my office and told me very impudently, "Will you go into the living room and comfort L. I have told her I no longer love her anymore and have broken our engagement."

"What are you saying?" Sister Elisabeth exclaimed. "Are you crazy?" She then went into the living room and found the poor thing loudly sobbing on the sofa. The ring he had taken off her finger lay on the floor; she was heartbroken. From her side it was true love.

I went back to him and called him both a murderer and a knave. He had to immediately pack up and leave as quickly as he could. He had ruined her honor and would pay dearly for it. (At the time breaking an engagement was tantamount to a divorce.)

"No," he said, he had not done that. He packed as quickly as he could and went over to the Catholic church for confession and was forgiven. So it went with our first house doctor.

My great grandmother Maren Dancke Eiberg, used to say many times, "Sorrow and gladness, they wander together, fortune, misfortune, they come side by side." After that experience I sang the song yet again![406]

To Sing-Sing Prison

Despite her increasing focus on the administration of the hospital, she still continued to work for the poor and helpless as had been her original call. Because of her earlier successful conversation with political leaders in an effort to get a grant from the legislature for the hospital and her reputation of fearlessness before other American authorities, members of the colony asked her to help them get a Norwegian man pardoned from his sentence at Sing-Sing Prison. He had been sentenced to life imprisonment for murder, something he claimed not to have done in cold blood. Some weeks before she left for Norway in 1894 and after her visit to Albany to ask for money, she went to see him. A number of Norwegians in the colony had gathered money together for his defense, but to her it seemed impossible. Despite that, she took the trip up the Hudson to visit him. She wrote in her *Memoirs* that she had thought she would wait to seek a pardon for him until a new governor was elected. She was thinking politically about her task and what it would take to persuade the powers that be to pardon the man. She described it from memory, in considerable detail.

> After receiving permission to enter, I came through an iron gate and then through another, and then came into an office, where three men sat with several guards. I had a basket of fruit and other edibles along and it was searched thoroughly. An iron gate opened and out came our unlucky Norwegian in his striped prison uniform followed by a guard. Around the walls there were benches and since it was visiting day there were many sitting there waiting for their visit. There were large, fat men, small thin ones, some with glasses, others without, but all had short hair and were clean shaven, all clad in striped pants and shirts. Here were no ranks, all were equal.[407]

As they spoke, Becker explained his story. He had been married to an Irish woman and owned a tavern. One Sunday morning he stood on his deck cleaning his revolver, which he did not know was loaded. A man came in, the revolver went off, and the man fell dead. Becker's wife accused him of murder in cold-blood, and on the basis of her testimony he was sentenced to life in prison in 1889. Since then he had sat in prison. Now that a group of Norwegians was seeking to get him pardoned, he had some hope again, especially with her as an advocate. Although she apparently tried to help, nothing seemed to work. She had done what she could. After she returned from Norway, she found nothing had been accomplished. To her it was hopeless.

Brides of Christ?

On April 22, 1894, the Deaconess House in Brooklyn held a consecration and admittance service at Trinity Lutheran Church for two new deaconesses and eight probationary sisters, a sign the enterprise was growing, but who these women were is never made clear. It was a festive time for her and the entire Norwegian American colony in Brooklyn. The paper of the Norwegian Synod, *Evangelisk Luthersk Kirketidende,* to which Our Savior's Lutheran and Pastor Everson belonged, printed a long story describing the entire service in vivid detail, from the hymns the congregation sang, to the texts for the sermon and the three questions Pastor Hegge asked the candidates: "Were they becoming deaconesses of their own free will?" "Would they as long as they held the office to which they had been called devote themselves to God's honor and do the best for their neighbor?" Finally, "would they with prayer and self-denial seek to win and protect souls for God's kingdom?" After their answer, "Yes," while the young women knelt at the altar, the pastor declared over each one, "In the name of the Father, Son and Holy Spirit, I consecrate you to be a Deaconess of the Lord. Amen!" After that the pastor prayed and gave the blessings to the newly consecrated deaconesses who remained kneeling. While the congregation sang a hymn, the ten women—two deaconesses and eight probationary sisters—all went to the table to receive communion. None of the assembled congregation joined them at the altar. After this, the article continued, the annual meeting of the deaconess community was held, at which they sang a hymn written especially for the event.

Newly Sisters now are clothed
In their pure white garments.
See them take the bread and wine,
Filled with holy gladness.
Praise be to our Lord and God
What we see now happen
As we now his Churchly brides
Send each other forward.

The author of the article, after this rather objective description, then editorialized rather sharply against the service and the office. "Where in Holy Scriptures does it say that young girls should be consecrated into a half-spiritual unmarried office, and that they should be celebrated by giving themselves completely to Christ to be his church's bride?"[408] The writer, whose initials E. P. were the only attribution of the article, was Pastor Emil Johan Petersen (1854-1919), a Dane who, like Everson, had studied at Concordia Seminary in St. Louis, and then later at Fort Wayne Seminary. He had found his way to Luther College where he taught religion, Latin, and German. At the time of the writing, he had moved to New York to work alongside Everson as a missionary to the immigrants. Although Everson had seemingly supported the work of the deaconess establishment, one wonders if he and the Norwegian Synod ever really accepted the idea of the diaconal office or of Fedde as a leader. This may have been at the core of her difficulties with Everson.

Home to Norway for a Conference and Medical Treatment

On May 5, 1894, Sister Elisabeth set out for Norway on the *Hekla* ship, in the fleet of the Nordvalla Line. Because she had maintained her good relationship with Captain Schierbeck, who was now the director of the line, she got a deal on the ticket. Schierbeck had been generous to the deaconesses, often giving them free passage back and forth. The fourteen-day trip across the Atlantic seemed long and tedious to her, someone who was always busy, but she could endure it without too much trouble by watching what happened on the journey. During the trip she observed a burial at sea, something she found intensely moving. She titled a little piece she wrote about it in her *Memoirs*, "The Norns (Viking sorceresses) Spin While the Ship Sails On." She watched closely as

. . . the body was covered with wreaths made of flowers brought along on board. The bells on the ship ring slowly; the sailors, dressed in their best uniforms gather slowly around the flag-draped casket which is very heavy so it will sink to the bottom. The singing of the hymns sounded and the pastor prayed and spoke to the gathered people. The ship slowed down. A box of dirt was brought out and three handfuls were thrown on the casket. Then the flag was taken away, and with a splash it sank into the deep, to wait until the Lord returns and the Lord's voice calls to the sea to give up its dead. Then the ship resumes its normal speed. The noon bells ring and life goes back to its normal speed."[409]

Sister Elisabeth had returned to Norway at the invitation of the Motherhouse in Christiania to celebrate its twenty-fifth anniversary. The actual day of the anniversary should have been November 20, 1893. It had been quietly remembered by the sisters and Motherhouse. For their big celebration they called a conference of Nordic deaconesses and their leadership. It began on June 7, 1894, and went on for five days. All the founders of these original Motherhouses were still alive. They had been in "lively" correspondence with each other during their years as Sister Superiors: Lina Snellman from Finland, Clara Eckerström and Louise Fryxell from Sweden, Bring from Denmark, Fedde, and Sponland, who did not attend the conference. A sister from the Minneapolis house, Martha Langaunet, who had been sent to Christiania by Sverdrup, may have been there. It is possible she represented the Minneapolis Institute. Someone did, but the record simply says someone was there, not who.

The festivities began with a celebratory worship service in the Christiania cathedral at one 1:00 on June 8. Pastor Julius Bruun, the longtime rector at the Christiania home, preached. The choir performed a cantata whose text was written by the Trondheim pastor, Sigurd Skavlan (1839-1912), with music composed by Christian Cappelen (1845-1916), the organist at Vår Frue church, the cathedral, *"Min Lodd falt mig liflig,"* ("My lines have fallen in pleasant places"). It celebrated the deaconess calling.[410] At the festive banquet, many spoke in honor of the work of Mother Guldberg. Gustav Jensen, the liturgical maven of Norway, professor and pastor, read a hymn he had written in Guldberg's honor. "It is good to give, so one gets many friends. Yes, blessed to give, God gives us back again" (*Godt er det at give—saa faar man mangen Ven. /Ja, saligt ret at give, Gud giver rigt igen*).

The house received over 100 telegrams, an especially congratulatory one from Julius Disselhoff, rector at Kaiserswerth, as well as a telegram from Queen Sofie (1836-1913) of Sweden and Norway. The Norwegians took great pride in the fact that even though they had started later than the others, they now had consecrated more deaconesses than

Christiania Cathedral, Oslo, in the 1880s

any other house in the region. The speaker believed the success of the movement in Norway, which now numbered 334 deaconesses, could be attributed to the Johnsonian revival. It had created good soil for the work in Norway. For the next few days, the conference addressed important issues. At the conference, there was already some hint that the leadership knew that the deaconess movement could not sustain itself in the future without beginning to adjust to the education of nurses who did not want to take the vows, but would be educated to do the medical care.[411]

This becomes more and more of a neuralgic point. In 1899 at the Motherhouse conference in Omaha, W. A. Passavant, Jr. addressed the question of "The Deaconess and The Trained Nurse." The main thrust of his argument was that the deaconess had a sacred vocation, the nurse a secular one. While acknowledging that deaconesses were not always well trained nurses, they were trained to deal with the soul—nurses not always. Passavant, heir to his father's concern for the diaconate, makes that clear in his address.

> The selfishness and love of gain, demoralizing servility toward the rich and the disdain of the claims of the poor, the

substitution of worldly expediency for truth and Christian consistency, so frequently found among them, threaten to sap the strength of her genuine womanhood and rob the trained nurse of the moral power she ought to exert both as a most valuable member of society and a confessor of her Lord and Savior Jesus Christ.

This is an unfair argument, to put it mildly, on Passavant's part, but its tone reveals the growing problem for the deaconesses who were also nurses. Their training left much to be desired from a medical standpoint, as Nightingale saw. Attacking "secular" nurses for being selfish was not a winning strategy. Christian nursing would soon develop out of the deaconess programs in Brooklyn, Chicago, and Minneapolis. One can hear in this argument, however, that the deaconess community was threatened by the rise of nursing programs. They seemed to know that, by the end of the century, their time would come to an end even if they continued to educate and consecrate deaconesses with some success until the 1920s when the movement, as a nursing program, faded.

We can see this concern in a side comment by Bloch-Hoell on the gathering in Christiania. In discussing the future of nursing, he marks the concern of Mother Guldberg to introduce the sisters to contemporary literature and finds in the library of the Motherhouse the works of many writers who were, if not anti-Christian, at least not pious Christians—writers such as Henrik Ibsen, Bjørnstjerne Bjørnson, Alexander Kielland, a particularly virulent critic of the pietists. Mother Guldberg even allowed these to be read to the sisters for devotions, even if she would smile at their arguments.[412] Sister Elisabeth must have listened carefully to these conversations as well as the readings, then spoken with Guldberg about them. We can see in her later writings she took that advice to heart and did not shrink from these ideas even if she understood them to be anti-Christian. She needed to know what they were saying in order to be a leader and educate nurses in the future.

The Baths

After the festivities, Sister Elisabeth repaired to the Sandefjord baths for five weeks to rest and seek treatment for her growing problems with her malingering illness, probably rheumatoid arthritis. Dr. Heinrich Arnold Thaulow (1808-1894) was the first doctor in Norway to investigate the theory of baths which were becoming more and more popular as a medical treatment in Europe and America at this time. The treatments involved drinking the sulfur water, sitting in warm salt water baths, and putting the sulfuric salt clay on one's body. A treatment called *"slambad"* involved lightly striking the skin of the patient with a branch or towel in order to bring the blood to the joints where it could rid them of their poisons. Whether any of this worked ultimately, it

Sandefjord baths and church

must have felt good to bathe in these waters and receive loving care from the attendants. A pamphlet advertising the baths shows that the most common disease they treated was rheumatism. The statistics on the improvement of the patients said about half felt relief from the treatment.[413] A five-week cure was recommended, something Sister Elisabeth reported that she had taken.[414] It was here, after the long periods of treatments and rest

Heinrich Arnold Thaulow

and consultations with the doctors, that she probably came to realize the prospects of a cure were not good and began to make plans for her retirement.

Home for a Death and Burial

From there she went to Egersund, where her future husband, Ole Slettebø, made his home. She would marry him two years later. One wonders if their marriage was discussed while she was there. Nothing of course is said about that in the article. She did go to Bergen, for what reason the article does not say, but very likely she met with the leaders of the Seamen's Mission headquartered there. I would not be surprised, given her friendship with the Hansteens, that she met them there for a bit. (Hansteen, now an envoy for the Indremisjon, had just moved to a parish in Ulstein, quite a bit north of Bergen, but he could have been in Bergen for some time talking with the leadership of the Seamen's Mission.)

She then returned to Feda to attend her sister-in-law, Anne Cathrine Jacobsdatter (1854-1894), in her final illness. Anne died of tuberculosis on September 7, 1894, and was buried on September16, just before Elisabeth returned to Brooklyn. Her husband, Elisabeth's late brother, Willum Andreassen (1856-1888), a skipper of a coastal sloop, had drowned in a shipwreck off Mandal six years earlier, so their young children were now orphans. Elisabeth took responsibility for the four children, whom she placed with other relatives. When Elisabeth returned for good to Norway, she cared for two of the children, Jakob (1885-1949) and Ida Marie Willumsen (1883-1919), until she died.

Back to Brooklyn

After the funeral, she left for America. In the middle Atlantic they met another storm, rather like the near hurricane she had experienced on her first trip to America. The passengers had to confine themselves to their cabins. If one had to go out, there was a rope that they could hold onto so they would not be pitched into the sea by the wind and waves. The first mate came to her room and told her to follow him to the doctor's office. Together they crept toward it, clinging to the rope for dear life. Finally, they arrived at his office where they found the doctor lying on the floor trying to read a book for midwives. For some years he had served as ship's doctor on a navy ship where, she noted dryly, "there was little use for a midwife." As she was sizing up the situation, sailors came bearing a shrieking woman from Østerdalen and put her on the floor. Her husband was creeping behind her the best he could. There was no way she could lie anyplace else but the floor because of the terrible heaving of the ship.

The crawling and reading doctor cried out, "God help me to remember some of these things! What shall I do?"

> "Just be calm," she told him. "I will manage the woman." He was so glad he prayed God to bless both me and the woman. They left the two of us and after a bit a baby girl was born. But not a stitch of material could be found to swaddle her. A handkerchief and a shirt became the baby's first dress. Now people sprang into action on board. Women sewed baby clothes out of shirts which the men brought. The captain came with some old handkerchiefs and soon we had a complete layette.[415]

Sister Elisabeth now had a patient to care for. Every day she visited the mother and child. She told the husband to wash the baby clothes. The next day when she returned, however, he had not done so. Impatient, she told him that if he did not wash the clothes for his own child, she would not return to check on the baby and its mother. That was the least he could do. "And you must do it nicely," she ordered. "That helped." The next day the baby's diapers hung on a clothes line in the bow of the ship.

Now the mother wanted the baby baptized and arranged for the service with the ship's pastor. The salon was decorated appropriately with candles and many sponsors. "I asked to be excused." But when the baby was to be named, the doctor and I and the Atlantic were named. For a baptismal shawl they used a bridal veil that belonged to a young woman who was to be married when they arrived in the new land. Then they took up an offering for the family which got them ninety-five kroner. When the little family arrived, everything went well and in addition they had money in their pockets.

Whether Sister Elisabeth thought it was as humorous at the time as she did later in life when she recorded the event for posterity, we cannot tell, but her ability to take stock of the situation quickly, to see the humor in the ship's doctor praying to be relieved of bringing the little girl into the world, her demands of the husband to wash the clothes, show the typical view of a practiced nurse who has seen just about everything life and death have to offer, fully capable of meeting it with aplomb and good humor.

Sister Elisabeth arrived back in Brooklyn on October 6, 1894, just about the time that the board put an appeal for funds in *Nordisk Tidende*. While everyone knew the hospital had a great future, it had to be supported now. The paper interviewed her and in that article we get a glimpse of her thinking as she took up the work again. She said that the hospital would now be her main focus, almost as though she had decided to concentrate especially on the administration of the hospital rather than many of the other things she might see to do around her. She was especially concerned that the ambulance service continue to receive the necessary funding—and implied that the work of the Deaconess Hospital was more than most others of the same size. The state hospital, she said, everyone knew, had only one ambulance, "a black one, with an ugly inside, where a patient could die of old age before it came, and then have to ride a long while before arriving" at the hospital.[416]

She would continue to care for those in the prisons whom she regularly visited. The interview concluded with her musings that her trip had been good for her health. When it came time, however, she said she could think of no better to place to return to than Norway when she was done with her work. The time on the fine ship with its soft chairs, kind waiters, and the finest menus had been restful and restorative, but now it was back to the Deaconess Motherhouse with its "seriousness, need, sickness and death."

Although she said it felt good to be at home in Brooklyn, she wondered if her strength would hold out. She began to think it would not. One can sense that her co-workers saw this because she remarked that the other sisters, doctors, and board were doing all they could to relieve her of many of her duties and make the work less exhausting. It still seemed to be too much on both sides, the spiritual and the medical. Their pastor held weekly[417] devotions and came for emergencies, but the daily spiritual care was the responsibility of the sisters. Even this seemed exhausting to Fedde. If my suspicion is correct that she was beginning to suffer much more intensely from her rheumatism, then it is not just that she needed rest, but she needed rest from the weariness pain causes, especially the intense pain that comes from this kind of debilitating disease. All she could do was concentrate on the administration of the institution.

It is as if her illness and increasing awareness of her condition had focused her efforts toward what she could do well. "All in all," she concluded, "my trip was unusually pleasant, restorative and I have no other wish than to live in Norway when I will no longer have to worry about how things will work out [financially]" (*Slap at sørge for udkommet*). This might have been a sly reference to her upcoming marriage which would relieve her of any financial concerns. We also see that she considered herself a Norwegian and not American. She wanted to be buried at home.

As usual she found the hospital desperately needed money because its ministry was expanding so quickly. The ambulance had indeed gotten them much attention, but also more expense than they could bear. On October 22, 1894, the chairman of the board, Ullenæs, made an urgent appeal to his fellow Brooklynites, not just the Norwegians, for $5,000 to pay for incidental costs to keep the ambulance, especially the horse, going. The institution needed not only to build a stable for the horse, but also a building that could house both deaconesses and servants. For many reasons they were "obliged" to build the stable. For one, the work was too much for one horse. Their area of responsibility was enormous—"embracing all that section south of Twenty-third Street, which means New Utrecht, Bath Beach and Blythbourne"—so they needed to purchase another horse. Ullenæs then made an argument that became more and more important for them as they had to raise funds to support their work:

> The hospital, notwithstanding its name, is strictly non-sectarian and knows no difference in creeds and nationalities, where it is a question of relieving suffering humanity. The name indicates the duty we consider that we, as Norwegians and Lutherans, owe to the community and country in which we live. If we share the blessings of our adopted land, it is our duty to assist in bearing its burdens and not to shrink from any responsibility resting upon us. In accordance with this view, we have invariably admitted patients of all nationalities and creeds who have been too poor to pay for treatment.[418]

Ullenæs went on to give an accounting of the many different nationalities and creeds they had actually admitted over the past year. There had been 815 American citizens, 416 Norwegians, 104 from Sweden, 93 from Ireland, and so forth—even one Syrian. Of these only sixty-nine had paid in full, so they had to raise money to continue their charitable work. Because of the financial panic of the previous year, 1893, donations had fallen behind and more patients needed free treatment because they were unable to pay for it, given their financial exigencies.

Pastoral Counseling

One of Sister Elisabeth's more interesting observations on soul care came when she heard that Pontoppidan's *Truth Unto Godliness* was being abandoned in favor of another, shorter, version. She remembered how frequently she had used it in times of spiritual need with patients facing terrible pain or facing death. Because all Norwegian youth had to memorize it (few pastors demanded its 700 answers be completely memorized!) before they could be confirmed, it was a common language they could use in such cases. She thought it was the best resource, with the best wisdom, she had ever been able to use during spiritual counseling. Many times she would ask a dying patient questions from the *Small Catechism* which they could, with some prompting, call forth from "the treasure chest" of the book to use as a guide. "It gave comfort in life and death."

One elderly man who was suddenly faced with death told her he was not afraid to die, but feared what would happen when he met the living God "for now I see clearly all that I have done from the time I was little." She asked him if he remembered anything from his catechism. He did— the sentence on conversion, "Unless you are converted you cannot come into the kingdom of heaven." Elisabeth then asked the next question from the book, "What is conversion?" He answered in the words of Pontop- pidan without missing a beat, "To heartily repent of your sin, be sorry for it, and in faith seek after God's grace in Christ." "Yes, there you see that is all you have to do." He burst out and said, "God knows that I am sorry and I can do nothing but pray for grace, for grace." She concluded, "Erick Pontoppidan's *Truth Unto Godliness* is the best book I have used in soul care." She was not alone in thinking that.

Pastor Everson, a Good Samaritan?

On December 14, 1894, two months after her return, Sister Elisabeth must have read with interest an article in the *Nordisk Tidende* with the head- line, "Pastoral Love for the Neighbor: Pastor Everson as Samaritan." In it there were three accounts of Pastor Everson's failure to be a good and lov- ing neighbor. The worst, according to the paper, was his failure to support the petition asking the governor to pardon Andrew Becker whose life sentence in Sing-Sing Prison was, the paper said, really a death sen- tence for him, both spiritually and physically. Pastor Everson had re- ceived the petition and it had come back unsigned, the paper reported. After some time, the pastor came in to the newspaper office to submit an announcement of Thanksgiving services. The editor gave him another petition asking him to sign it and get other pastors to do so as well.

Headline in Nordisk Tidende: *"Pastor's Love of the Neighbor"*

Although he did not say he would support it, he took the paper, stuck it in his pocket and left. When it came time for the governor to receive the petition, they asked Everson about it, and he sent it back, once again, unsigned, saying he knew little about the case. The paper concluded without much comment except to say that abandoned people who may not have access to heaven at least tried to do what they could here on earth while the preachers of the word stick their tail under their feathers and slink away saying they don't understand the case![419]

The picture the paper gives us of Everson's character here is not flattering, nor did they mean it to be. Emil Nilsen, the editor of the paper, could be quite controversial and was not afraid to take sides, but still this was a pretty direct attack on Everson. This story gives us a sense for his reputation in the colony and why he was difficult to work with. That a paper such as this would feature on its front page this long and uncomplimentary article about the pastor of one of the largest and oldest Norwegian Lutheran churches in Brooklyn may not be surprising if this kind of behavior was typical. Editor Nilsen clearly had the pastor marked for some kind of comeuppance. Sister Elisabeth had done her part in visiting the poor man in Sing-Sing. The rest of the colony had tried to help, but the pastor found it easy to ignore the petition. He may also have continued to oppose Sister Elisabeth in other ways, less obvious to her and us. Pastor Everson questioned the paper's veracity on its reports of his failure to be a good Samaritan a few weeks later. The paper would have none of it. "We can, for our part, assure the public that we have not removed a jot or tittle of the report. If what the pastor says is true then we should be put on trial. Lying should be punished."[420]

Ultimately, as Sister Elisabeth had expected, nothing happened with the prisoner's case. In 1904, Fedde did receive a letter from the prisoner, Andrew Becker, who was still in Sing-Sing Prison.

Andrew Becker, Consecutive no. 50,069

Sing Sing Prison, N. Y. May 1st, 1904.

Dear Mrs. Slettebø:

I have read of you in the *Brooklyn [Nordisk] Tidende*, that you are on a visit in this country as an honored guest to the

Norwegian Hospital in Brooklyn. Yes, it is now many years since the time I had the honor to be able to speak with you and probably never again will I see you in this world so I will take this opportunity to write some words to you and thank you from the bottom of my heart for what you did for me, although I am much troubled that nothing came of it. I have now given up all hope of a pardon and help in this world for I have no friends or acquaintances who can help me. I know that you have married and wish you happiness and blessing on the life's path you have in this world and in closing give you a friendly greeting from a poor man in prison suffering a terrible and unrighteous sentence.

Andrew Becker

Sentenced October 28, 1889, for life

1895

At the beginning of 1895, *Nordisk Tidende* printed a little filler on the situation of Lutherans in Brooklyn. There were thirty-six Lutheran congregations in the city and thirty church buildings; 15,000 members belonged to these congregations which were served by forty pastors. Over 1,100 children attended Sunday schools taught by over 180 teachers. The value of the property these congregations owned was estimated to be worth $1,360,000. With that many Lutherans and that much wealth, they could support a hospital, an old people's home, and a Deaconess Motherhouse, it concluded.

On April 5, 1895, the paper printed facts from the 1894 annual report of the hospital. It noted that the sister charged with visiting people in their homes had made 1,808 visits and the ambulance had been called out 441 times. Of the 1,174 patients they had served, only 67 had paid in full, 63 had paid part of their bill, and 1,044 had paid nothing. There were eleven deaconesses working in the hospital which made it possible to serve this many people. The report also announced the retirement of Dr. Theodor Siqueland from the board, with the hope that he would return in some future date. Pastor Martin A. Hegge of Trinity Lutheran Church had been retained as the rector. The column also printed the nativity of the patients served by the hospital. From the United States, 410; Norway,

363; Iceland, 118; Sweden, 82; Germany, 60; England, 44; Italy, 25; Denmark, 28; Finland, 16; Canada, 10; France, 5; Scotland, 5; Russia, 4; Austria, 1, Spain, 1; Mexico, 1; Africa, 1. This gives us a good picture of the wide variety of patients who came to the hospital that year.

Women's Suffrage

The question of women's role within the church was growing for Norwegian-American Lutherans more within the church than in the public sphere. Their record of supporting women's work and causes within the church was impressive. It had started with the Ladies Aids formed in nearly every congregation. They had begun their work generally around the 1880s, and first gathered together to work for the local congregation's needs, such as buying a bell for the church, or other such necessities. Then they turned their attention to the mission of the church both here and at home: they supported the colleges and seminaries and finally missionaries. They were among the first to call for and support the deaconess movement in America. Their small gifts of nickels and dimes had raised enough to send out several single women missionaries and two deaconesses to China, Madagascar, and to the Zulu. The colleges had hired women to teach at the coeducational colleges such as St. Olaf and Augustana (Sioux Falls); they had supported the deaconess communities and their numbers were growing. The Norwegian Synod had just built a finishing school for young women in Red Wing, The Red Wing Ladies' Seminary. The one question that began to be raised about this time had to do with women's suffrage in the churches: Could women vote in their congregations? Some were doing so, much to the consternation of others. The Norwegian Lutheran church press began to notice it in 1894, about the time of the twenty-fifth anniversary of the colorful M. Falk Gjertsen's pastorate at Trinity Congregation in Minneapolis, who agreed with his colleague Sven Oftedal, the editor of *Folkebladet,* on the issue. Both had caused Sister Elisabeth many tears of frustration, resulting in something like disdain on her part. Gjertsen tried to get Trinity Congregation to allow women to vote in the congregational meetings. The idea shocked a good many people in the church, but Trinity was not the first congregation to do so, according to reports, especially closely watched by the Norwegian Synod. In August, the *Evangelisk Luthersk Kirketidende* reported that it had heard that the Kvams congregation in Ottertail

County, Minnesota, had granted women the right to vote in its congregational meeting that year. The editor, Johannes Thorbjørnson Ylvisaker (1845-1917), long-time New Testament professor at Luther Seminary, criticized the report: Such a "reform means ruining everything. What God says in his Holy Word means nothing to these people."[421] Ylvisaker, in a speech at the dedication of Red Wing Ladies' Seminary made his thinking about the issue more precise, but while it was thoughtful and typically brilliant, it strongly opposed women getting the vote either in the congregation or society. His editorial comment in the *Evangelisk Luthersk Kir-*

Johannes Thorbjornson Ylvisaker

ketidende caused readers to react rather proudly to the record of their own congregations in regard to women's suffrage. Pastor Heiberg of the Hauge Synod wrote to say that the first Lutheran church in the world to give women the vote was in Barnes County, North Dakota, in 1893. Pastor Knut Birkeland (1857-1925) of the former Conference disagreed, reporting that he had organized many Lutheran churches and in each of those congregations the women were given the right to vote. He claimed the first church to grant women the right to vote was the St. Olaf Congregation in Fort Dodge, Iowa, as early as 1883. This provoked an angry comment from the editor, "these are the first Lutherans to overthrow God's Word!" Pastor Ole Hermundsen Aaberg (1844-1935) of the Norwegian Synod and founder of the Aaberg Academy, wrote an angry letter to the editor questioning whether these people could read the Bible at all, once again appealing to the traditional proof texts against women speaking in the churches.[422]

The topic became even more heated as the bitter controversy concerning Augsburg and St. Olaf came to a head when Gjertsen may have had more than the emancipation of women on his mind. He was also a leader in what would become the Lutheran Free Church (and maybe not coincidentally would lose his pastorate at Trinity for an inappropriate relationship with a woman in Norway). As the Friends of Augsburg were joining together to prevent the loss of Augsburg as the only preacher's school precipitated by the St. Olaf forces in the new United Church, the papers noted that when the Friends of Augsburg (*Augsburgvenner*) tallied the number of attendees, women were included in the numbers. That seemed an unfair tactic to the reporters who regarded the use of women in the meetings as simply a technique to swell the numbers of voting members—or worse, as an absolute disregard of God's Word.

After the United Church took control of the *Lutheraneren,* which had previously been edited by Sverdrup, the new editor, United Seminary Professor Frederick A. Schmidt (1837-1928), wrote, "It can be reported as an oddity that at the Augsburg Friends' meetings, there were gathered together 35 from the Willmar congregation alone, not counting women and children."[423] In a column commenting on Sverdrup's theology of the laity, Schmidt, now completely estranged from the Augsburg party, reminded his readers of what Paul had to say about women speaking in the congregation. As Schmidt considered what Sverdrup's position on women and men in the church was, he did understand the logic of his position that both men and women should have the same access to God's gifts. Who can forbid God's spirit from working where it wills? Still, Schmidt could not quite stomach the idea, as he concluded, but what does Paul say to women, he asked? "Be quiet in church."[424]

In the *Lutheraneren* of December 12, 1895, there was an announcement of Cady Stanton's eightieth birthday and her speech on that occasion. Why the editor felt it worthwhile to print it is difficult to tell. The editorial comment at the end of the note on her speech remarked that some old crones (*kjærringer*) are like that.[425] There was some grudging respect for the old suffragette, but certainly her thought was not to be taken seriously. On the other hand, predictably, the editor of the temperance paper *Afholds Basunen*, Pastor Knut Birkeland, a proponent of women's vote, was reported by the *Lutheraneren* to have said that "one would think in these days that Christians would not be so old-fashioned (*gammeldags*) as to refuse women as preachers or delegates."[426]

The strong relationship between the forces for Prohibition and women's rights is apparent in this comment. Support for women's suffrage tended to come from the pietists who often opposed drinking and saw it as a women's issue. It should not be forgotten that Hauge did not proscribe women from preaching if they had the gift. His followers almost always tended to be more open to the possibility of women's full participation in the work of the church than the Norwegian Synod could be. It is perhaps the one way that the immigrant women were able to partici-pate in the suffrage movement. The strong connection between suffrage and temperance caused the *Evangelisk Luthersk Kirketidende* alarm at the beginning of the next century when one divine wrote that while he un-derstood the reason for temperance, having to sign the pledge also meant supporting women's vote.

A few snide comments were made in the periodicals about the way the emerging Lutheran Free Church formed in 1897 (formerly the Friends of Augsburg 1893-1897) conducted its meetings. F. A. Schmidt noted with disdain that the new church body, if it could be called such, had an in-credible kind of congregational freedom: noting the lopsided numbers of delegates at the meeting: forty-eight were from Minneapolis, twelve from Willmar, ten from St. Paul, and among them a good many women, most likely, he added dryly, because of a new-found apostolic word.[427] Another writer in the *Lutheraneren* also had noted that with such a strange way of organizing, the group could hardly be called an organization (*sam-fund*). Anyone can come, he wrote, professors, laymen, and women.[428] By 1897, Trinity Congregation had finally decided to give women the vote. It was duly reported in both the *Evangelisk Luthersk Kirketidende* and the *Lutheraneren*. The note read, in both journals, that when it was passed, someone asked if women could hold office in the church as trust-ees, or treasurer, or deacon. The question, according to report, was met with universal laughter.[429]

The Friends of Augsburg were the people with whom Sister Elisabeth had worked closely in Minneapolis and for whom she had a complicated set of reactions. While she very likely agreed with their political and theo-logical reasoning on the rights of women to vote in the congregation and in the civil society, it is interesting to think of how she got on with the men by self-description most pro-women. As we have seen, it had not gone well, and she seemed to carry some resentment against them and the Lu-theran Free Church as we can sense from her comments on Høyme and the United Church conflicts with Sverdrup and Oftedal. Then there is my lingering suspicion that she had some small connection with Hansteen's accusation of Gjertsen's misalliance with the Norwegian woman in 1900. While there are absolutely no bits of evidence that she collaborated with Hansteen, since we have no letters of hers after she retired, it is hardly possible to imagine she and Hansteen never communicated with each other again after they returned to Norway.

The Black Sheep

Elisabeth's reflections on a particular case of a young man, probably the black sheep of his family, also give us an account of how intertwined her work with body and soul were. For her the health of the soul had direct implications for the health of the body, since many of the consequences of bad choices came from what she understood to be sin. It was her feeling that every large family, especially, always had a black sheep, many of whom were sent to America to find their way, escape some shame, or simply escape a bad situation at home. Although they often were lost to their families, they could find their way to the hospital, a kind of home for the lost, which many did as a last resort. Many would come, recover their health and then leave, promising to do better, and just as hope began to seem real, the nurses would see them return cast down in sorrow and pain in the same situation as before. The young man whose story she told came from a rich, upper-class family well known in a city in the western part of Norway. He had wandered for years, lost to all. He would come to her, usually in the middle of the night and say, "It is I." Over the years, she came to know him well and would not be surprised when the bell rang late at night. "It is I," he would cry out. He usually came with sores all over his hands and legs. Sister Elisabeth would wash him carefully and tend to his wounds. Once, after she had finished tending him, he told her that he was going to change his life and go to work on a ship. "Do that," she said. "When you come back, let me see you." He agreed to do so. One month later they heard the bell ring and there the young man stood, a good-looking sailor in a blue hat and marine blue shirt. He looked so good to Sister Elisabeth that she stood there, taking in the picture of health he gave her. "I could hardly believe my eyes," she wrote. To celebrate his return in good shape, they prepared him a banquet, and rejoiced in his recovery. Fourteen days later he returned again, this time having drunk up all his money wanting to hide himself away. "It was heavy," Sister Elisabeth said. "Here he was in poverty and need, and his family in Norway one of the richest in Norway."

This behavior continued for several years. He would go out promising to do better. Then he would appear in the middle of the night, ringing the bell and announcing, "It is I." One day, an ambulance came clattering into the hospital. She asked the doctor who it was, and the young man lifted his head up and said, "Sister Elisabeth, it is I."

"Dear me," she said. "Are you sick again?"

"Yes," he replied, "I am sick." They treated him as well as they could, both spiritually and physically.

> In the time he lay there God's grace for poor sinners was told to him daily. And when his illness began to take its toll, he received the word with a childlike simplicity. He now was suffering from pneumonia, and after much suffering, he was freed of everything that had made his life so sad. I believe that the "black sheep" has now been made white for Jesus' sake. We washed and cared for his body for the last time as though he were our brother, and put him in his casket. Sister Olette played and all the sisters were gathered. Pastor Sommerfeldt spoke. Now I will never more hear him say, "It is I." When his final days and his death were announced to his rich parents we received a card framed in black with thanks for all we had been and done for him.[430]

Many of the people Sister Elisabeth served were desperate and driven to desperate solutions by their problems. Usually the worst were sailors who, as she said, had long ago left home and had not informed their parents where they were, many times because of shame for what they had done to themselves or what had happened to them.

The pastors of the Seamen's Mission were said to have regarded many of the sailors, having gone to sea as young boys, to be rather boyish even as they grew old, having never had parents to help them through their adolescence. Elisabeth often found this to be true. One man came to them, lame and half blind, completely helpless. Because of his situation they took him in, rather than let him lie outside the hospital alone and untended. He stayed with them for several years, during which time he became completely blind and they had to care for him like a child. In the summer, because of the heat, they put up a tent in the back yard where he could be during the day and then carried back into the hospital at night. Sister Elisabeth read for him every afternoon, if she could. During these conversations, she would remind him of God's great love for him and the glory God had saved for those who believed. She cared for him and tried to help him as much as she could.

Then one evening as they were finishing supper, an orderly began calling out, "K. has killed himself!" Elisabeth ran out and got to the man first. "O what a sight!" There he lay, bleeding profusely after taking a rusty barber's blade and trying to cut his throat and hands. He had thrown a blanket over himself. Elisabeth lay down beside him and yelled into his ear, "K. what have you done? Pray to God for forgiveness!"

"Despair, Sister," he whispered. "Despair."

The doctor came and sewed him up and bandaged him as he could, but there was little hope for him. He lived another fourteen days, but died of pneumonia which came as a result of his wounds. "O how upset we all were. We had wished and worked so that all could believe and be saved. But this is not really a human work," she concluded.[431]

Accident at Woodlawn Station

Labor Day afternoon, 1895, Sister Elisabeth received a call. "From the police. An accident at Woodlawn Station. Send two doctors." Apparently an old locomotive, No. 6, had been taken out of mothballs to serve the many Coney Island visitors on the last holiday of the summer. It had to pull the cars up the hill to Bay Ridge. After helping the Sea Beach train, the engineer went down to get the next cars. The locomotive going full steam ahead crashed into a train continuing on to Woodlawn Park Station. Although 2,000 passengers were involved, only 200 were seriously hurt. Sister Elisabeth immediately went to work, sending the ambulance on its way, ringing and clanging through the city street, which aroused concern among the city folk as it sped toward the station. She then called together the doctors in the hospital, found the sisters so they would be ready to receive the injured. The first to be admitted was a Jewish man who had been nearly scalped in the accident, and two women with broken legs or otherwise maimed or disabled. They bandaged them and cared for them as ambulance after ambulance arrived with more and more injured. Even police wagons brought some in. The hospital was already full, so they had to find place for the forty-one new patients they received at the time. Both the doctors and sisters worked through the night to save the lives of many, doing emergency surgery on twenty-two patients. The entire hospital filled up to capacity, even her own bed was occupied by a patient. For Sister Elisabeth it was rather like being at the front of a war. She remembered what Mother Guldberg had said during her service in the Franco-Prussian war, that it was worse to stand outside a room and hear the screaming of the patients' family than to stand beside the bed of the patients and hear them weeping. Now it was her own experience as she watched the daughter of an actor whose toe had been shoved back to his heel screaming while he lay perfectly still. Many other relatives came shrieking in to visit their family member who lay in bed groaning.

As she, the doctors, and the sisters grew weary unto death, the press arrived and wanted to know more than she could tell them. She thought the reporters were almost the worst of all, but it was to her benefit to be gracious to them. They all had something to say, and she patiently let them speak and ask questions. The hospital staff needed to get food for everyone, plus make sure the workers who were exhausted got some help. She was most proud, however, that not one limb had to be amputated. When they had sent home those they thought able to manage on their own, they still had many left, some who had to convalesce for a long time. Finally, she was thankful none had died, and all had some use of their arms and legs, although they may have been somewhat crippled, and one man had lost both ears. She concluded her reflections on this event by saying something a good public relations person would say: The Deaconess Hospital's good reputation increased and all praised it. For that she was especially grateful, even if it did not fill their treasury! Only one of the forty-one paid for the care.

The *Nordisk Tidende* published an article praising the efficient work of the entire hospital in handling the disaster. "This institution has borne the heaviest burden in the heavy work, and for the most part, it can be said that because of this hospital, the death toll was so low.[432] Dr. H. Beeckman Delatour received great commendation for his organization of the process to take care of the worst. He had decided not to amputate quickly, the way many doctors at the time might have, and thus saved many people's limbs, about which Sister Elisabeth had also bragged. The paper then urged the readers to remember the need of the hospital for funds and attend the bazaar to be held on September 24-27, hoping that the readers remembered that the hospital had needed money to build its own stable and housing for the sisters. It would be a blessing for all, both spiritual and physical, the sick and suffering, especially those of our own nationality, it concluded.[433] The story of the disaster ran in papers all around the country, from New York to Arizona to Washington State. Sister Elisabeth's hopes for good publicity were fulfilled.

Christmas Endings

As Christmas 1895 approached, she found the many obligations to provide a merry Christmas for the 110 children in the Sunday school, the patients, the sisters, the staff, the doctors almost overwhelming, as many do on facing the holiday. She knew they had to have something to give each child at the Christmas tree program and it had to be made, not bought with funds from the hospital budget. That meant a lot of work for the sisters, and Sister Elisabeth especially. Mrs. Børs, in Paris, always remembered them with a gift of $20. The gift helped with the festival. As was the custom, they put up a tree on Christmas Eve. At 4:00 the pastor arrived and the festival began. The Christmas tree stood in one of the largest sick rooms, the pastor spoke briefly in both Norwegian and English, and the group sang Christmas carols, walking around the Christmas tree as is the tradition, singing both sacred and secular songs. Many wept to be celebrating the traditional holiday in a foreign land yet with familiar hymns, customs, and food. The patients all found little presents under the tree that would remind them later of the time they lay sick in the Norwegian Deaconess Hospital one Christmas. They were then served porridge and spare ribs, a traditional Norwegian Christmas Eve meal. After that the sisters took the tree into their own living room. When all had been done for the patients, it was the sisters' turn to have Christmas Eve. When they had eaten, they also danced around the Christmas tree, took their presents, many and lovely, from the sisters to each other and from the friends of the home. Weary but happy they went to bed to rest. "It was good to get some rest, for we had to be up early for Christmas morning."[434]

The festivities continued the next morning, but as usual for Elisabeth it was a time of special joy as it was also her birthday. She was forty-five. "At five o'clock that morning, I heard the sisters breathing outside my door. Soon they came in singing with gifts, cakes, and coffee." After that beginning they assembled on the stairs in their white dresses, each with a candle in hand, and went around to the sick rooms singing, "Rejoice, rejoice this happy morn" (*Os er Idag en Frelser født*) and "A Child is Born in Bethlehem" (*Ett Barn er født i Betlehem*) To hear and see the nurses singing in the early morning darkness, each holding a candle, brought many patients to tears. One, however, an American who wanted nothing to do with the Christian faith or God, threw a blanket over his head in order that the nurses would not see him. But still they stood around his bed and sang a Christmas carol said to be by Fanny Crosby:

> Where is the King, the new born King,
> Whom angels proclaim today, today.
> We unto him our gifts would bring
> But how can we find the way?

> *Refrain:*
>> Star ever bright, grant us thy light,
>> Star ever bright and fair.
>> Open your eyes where the Savior lies
>> And stay while we worship there.

> Where is the King, the promised King,
> In years of the past foretold.
> Where is the babe of Bethlehem
> For him we would now behold.
> *Refrain*

> Sweetly there comes a still small voice
> And gently we hear it say:
> Ye shall behold the new born King
> And faith shall direct your way.
> *Refrain*

The man lifted the blanket from his face and in tears thanked them all. After they had given the patients coffee and cakes, they once again gathered in the living room for morning prayer. "I always concluded morning prayer with the Creed and the renunciation (*forsakelsen*) of the devil," she remembered. "I renounce the devil and all his work and ways."

That same Christmas something happened, she said, that had never happened before. A male chorus from the youth group had gathered in the hall to sing a song by Captain Carl Ullenæs, the chairman of the board, written especially for her.

As Christ's own bride you consecrated
Your life to human benefit.
Each year on earth you have lived
Your field of work has grown
And that is to care for the Lord's little ones
Is all your heart's desire.
Thanks for each sick and wounded
You have cared for with great kindness
Our Father will repay you surely
What you have done for heaven is sure
Where the palms of victory will be poured out
In the light of peace.

Thanks for every year you have struggled here
And fought the fight of faith
Thanks for every pain and every breast
You have soothed.
Thanks for every comfort
You poured out into the sickest mind
And wiped the tearful cheek.
We greet you on this day
A doubly high festival
And pray that you will find
Full many a year of happiness.
In this world's fight and conflict
And joy for all eternity.[435]

She had said many times that she did not think she could hold out much longer in her current position; seeing these young men filled her with a joy she could not express, but it also caused her to think. When they had left and she was alone in her room, she began to wonder, "Did it mean that this was really my last Christmas here at the Deaconess home in Brooklyn?"[436] Was she picking up something they were telling her? Or were they responding to her remarks that her health had been such that she could not continue her work with them? One can infer from her comments that her own death was something she was thinking about more frequently.

In her *Memoirs*, Sister Elisabeth reflected on her visit to identify bodies in the morgue on Ward's Island. She had been there many times before, but in these musings death seemed more present than ever as she thought of her life in New York and her own death. She tells about riding

> . . . on a large ferry which came daily to take the dead to the large cemetery that lay on Ward's Island. As I stood in the morgue, filled with decomposing bodies the question, "What is a person's life" became more lively to me: One strives for knowledge, education, careers, and joys of various kinds and here lie, side by side, a man and woman, some in fine clothes, others in rags, all are alike, they receive the same treatment. If no one comes to find them and claim the body, they are carried away in a box and thrown in to a large, common grave, where many lie together. I prayed to God that he would allow me to die and go to my rest in my dear fatherland. We went home, quiet and thoughtful. The busy life of people on the streets of New York made no impression on us—we had seen life's denouement.[437]

Her own death seemed to be haunting her as well as her wish to be home in Norway when she died, so she could be buried there. It was

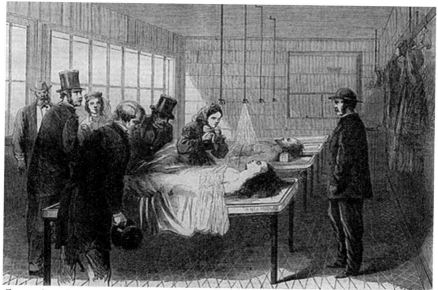

Scene in a New York morgue, 1866

something about which she was thinking and praying. It is not surprising the men's chorus serenaded her. They all knew, as she did, things were about to change.

1896

Sister Elisabeth continued to manage the hospital for several more months into 1896. She could look back over the past year of 1895 and see the successes the hospital had experienced. They had treated 1,678 patients with a total of 20,578 nights in the hospital, a remarkable growth. One sister had made 1,744 home visits outside the hospital, making it possible for the poor to get free doctors, medicine, food, and clothes. It was a worthy set of numbers, and one that gave the entire hospital and Motherhouse a sense of achievement.[438]

Camilla Collett

There is little in the way of news about her in the *Nordisk Tidende* after 1895, except for a letter to the editor she wrote in the April 10, 1896, issue, urging that Norwegian-American women donate money to fund a statue honoring Camilla Collett, the sister of Norway's greatest poet, Henrik Wergeland, and Norway's first great feminist writer. Collett had written some of the first novels about women's place in Norway and had grown more polemical

Camilla Collett

as she grew older. Her death became an occasion for the suffragettes in Norway who were fighting for the vote to honor her and keep the struggle before the people. Fedde indicated in her letter that she had been contacted by an international committee, one of them her old friend Mrs. Børs, a cousin of Collett, asking her to help with the project. Sister Elisabeth in this letter appeared to have no problem with the drive and the cause.

> At the initiative of the Norwegian women's emancipation organization held on June 21, 1895, in Christiania, it was decided that Norwegian women should work to support a statue honoring Camilla Collett. A committee was organized and the

hope is that women all around the country will gather money to support this project for Norway's most important woman author and the first to fight for women's rights. After the organization of the committee and the recognition that here in this country [USA] there were many women that would be interested in this cause we are asking all women who wish to contribute to it to send money to the following undersigned women.

The invitation of the Norwegian women in Christiania said, "In respect for the gratitude our land owes Camilla Collett for her battle for women's spiritual and social liberation and her fruitful work for our culture and our spiritual life we Norwegian women have decided to raise a worthy memorial to her."

The invitation is signed by hundreds of Norwegian women from all societies and representatives of groups together with many Norwegians living abroad: in Berlin, Mrs. Betsy Gade; in Boston, Selma Loontz; Dresden, Laura Budde; London, Lilly Gude; Paris, Mrs. Børs; Stockholm, Antoinette Gram and here in New York Mrs. Magelssen Groth. A national ingathering from invited colleagues such as these will assure her importance to our literature and her entire life. Every Norwegian woman, regardless of political party or conviction, owes a great deal to this woman and her struggle for women's rights.

Fedde had been reading the culture both in Norway and in the Norwegian American community where she was. She had apparently come to some convictions on the issue of women's rights. Fedde was aware that Collett had become increasingly radical on the issue of women's rights. We know that her mentor Cathinka Guldberg did not support the program of the Norwegian suffragettes, but did vote in 1913 when women finally got the vote in Norway. Did Sister Elisabeth break with Mother Guldberg on this issue? Did she attend the unveiling of the statue in 1911? There are no records of that, but it could have been entirely possible as she was active in some community activities past that time in her life.[439]

Ending

Sometime early in 1896, as she always did at the beginning of the year, Sister Elisabeth reviewed her life and all that she had done. Two sisters were now devoted to helping the poor, as she had originally done upon arrival twelve years earlier. Several ladies aids had been founded, and the deaconess school was going well. Twelve sisters worked at their jobs faithfully. Peace and unity ruled in the entire endeavor. Sister Mathilde could take over the work and do so competently. All of the difficulties with the enterprise seemed to have passed. It gave her hope and satisfaction. Now they could devote themselves to the education of those probationary sisters who had been admitted. To see with her own eyes all that had been accomplished made her feel thankful and somewhat amazed.

Sister Mathilde Madland

Fedde knew that her health would not improve, and she would not recover with more rest or another vacation. "The board wanted me to take a long rest and travel back to Norway," she wrote after she had spoken with them about her future. It was doubtful she could return if she did not feel well enough. With the strength she had now, she did not think it possible to be the Sister Superior much longer. Chairman Ullenæs thought she should at least try to get some rest and see if that might help her, even restore her health, but they both understood that there was not much chance she could return. After this conversation, she began a struggle within herself. She described it as a great battle between flesh and spirit. They could not agree. Her love for the work and her interest in it remained strong and fresh, and her will to continue great, but her nerves and her body said, "Quit." Without her health, she knew she could not continue.

Her sense of duty, however, made the decision difficult. "I had to do what the chairman had suggested. I knew that until this time I had been led and guided by my heavenly Father who would now also make things clear to me." It made her somewhat depressed, but she never complained. For her to quit working, to give up her calling, felt like a separation from everything that meant anything to her, almost like death. There was still much to do in the hospital. After much prayer and thought she made the decision to do as Ullenæs suggested: go home to Norway and then decide about returning. Before she left, she gathered together the hospital staff, patients, and friends, for a last devotion in the "home which had cost so much to build in this foreign land."[440] While they were gathered, she was told of a young Norwegian man who had broken his back. He was poor and alone. He needed to be brought in for medical attention. She sent the ambulance after him. That was the last patient she admitted to the hospital.

Going Home

Earlier in January 1896, she had written a letter to Anders Sever-in Slettebø, her future brother-in-law and her cousin, telling him that a friend Einar had sent her books by Ibsen and Jonas Lie (1833-1908).

Jonas Lie

Lie's book *The Family at Gilje* had strong impulses towards women's causes showing the few options open for bright young girls at the time. Any educated Norwegian at the time would have read these authors, two of the four greats of their era—Ibsen, Bjørnsøn, Kielland, and Lie. The letter she wrote, however, makes one think she has just opened her eyes to what has been going on around her outside of the hospital. Before that she had been far too busy to read and take in the cultural opportunities of New York. While she had been curious and interested in most every situation she had met, this sounds a bit different and also causes us to wonder, was she beginning to think about her place in the world as a woman?

The letter seems to be an answer to someone who has welcomed her into the family. It is also a brief summary of her life in New York with both regrets and resignation. She thought no one in Egersund had as nice a place as she did in Brooklyn. Of earthly things she had all she could ask. As she thought about leaving, she gave herself over to the will of God. She always prayed to do the Lord's will. Although nothing was said about a marriage to Ole, she seemed to hint that something was afoot and he had asked her to marry him, based on her remark that she has always thought well of him.

I know that God who searches the heart also knows mine and knows what is best. He will also let everything happen as he

knows is best wherever I am, either in Egersund or Fedde—
or wherever. I have always thought well of your brother [Ole
Andreas Danke Slettebø, her future husband]. But you know
well that a long life in a large city among the highest classes,
makes it not so easy to bid farewell to all that, but it is strange
with this struggle, sometimes in spite of all. This winter I have
been out a little more and enjoyed myself at operas and concerts. Here one finds all of the important people in the world,
since everyone wants to come to New York. Last week I was
out with one of the doctors and, my, it was so lovely that I
had to think of Brorson's hymn, "It is like many sounds when
they play of joy." (*Det gaar som mange Lyd . . . naar de slaar
om Fryd*) it was almost heavenly. When I am weary there are
so many things here that can change that and I have many
friends, in any case as long as I do not need any help.

It is very pleasant to hear from my friend Einar that it is always best to stay as long as one can in one place. I had two of
the last books of Ibsen and Lie sent to me and they are from
him, I believe. I will soon write and send him the money for
them as I have asked him to send me the latest new books.

Greet all of yours from and in Slettebø, please. Say to Theo-
dora that it would be wonderful to get a letter from her and
also greet Anna and Ingeborg.

Sister Mathilde Madland greets you and says that the next
time you write, you must tell us much more about Egersund.[441]

Sister Elisabeth noted that she had been out in New York City to hear
concerts and operas. She could hardly have been there at a culturally
richer time. That December she could have heard Wagner's *Lohengrin*, or
earlier in the year a concert conducted by Anton Dvorak, or that fall Hans
Seidl conducting the "New World Symphony No. 9." It was, as she said,
an exciting time to be in New York, but she needed to return to Norway.
The records are not entirely clear exactly when she left, but working back
from her letter of resignation in October it must have been in the middle
of summer.

CHAPTER FIVE

SISTER ELISABETH GOES HOME

Outside the hospital, an elegant carriage with two white horses waited for her, sent by the local undertaker. She stepped in, looking back. The sisters, doctors, staff, and patients waved to her, white handkerchiefs fluttering in their hands. She looked back as the carriage clattered off to the German steamship that would take her to Bremen and then to Hamburg, from where she would return to Flekkefjord and then her childhood home in Feda, which she had left twenty-two years earlier. She rested for two months there in her family home which she would buy. As the leaves began to turn and the blue skies over the sparkling blue fjord filled with harbingers of autumn, she wondered what she should do. After prayer and much thought, and maybe Ole's urging, she decided that her work as a deaconess had come to an end.

On October 14, 1896, she sent her resignation with thanks to the board for all their love and help. It was her prayer for them that God's name would always be glorified in that place, in the work which had begun and had grown by God's unspeakable grace and mercy. On November 17, 1896, Sister Mathilde Madland was installed as Sister Superior. She had been Sister Elisabeth's right hand person ever since she had arrived from Egersund in 1888; she had served as head of the Motherhouse whenever Sister Elisabeth had to leave for a time.

Back in Norway

Not long after Fedde sent in her resignation, she received a warm letter from the board written by Captain Ullenæs.

Dear Sister Elisabeth Fedde in Flekkefjord:

Your dear letter of October 14 has been received for which you should be thanked, likewise the letter to the board with your resignation as Sister Superior of the deaconess home. Under the circumstances we could do nothing else but accept your resignation, even if it caused much sorrow over the loss of you as the Sister Superior. I have been asked by the board to express to you our most hearty thanks for our work together over the many years in which no disunity has disturbed the good working conditions we have shared. With only good feelings and love which have eased the work and made our duties and burdens lighter. You have now gone into a new life work after maturing here and we wish you the happiest and most blessed future. A rich Lord's blessing both to your body and soul, with as many true joys as possible and as few sorrows and difficulties as possible, all in the Lord's time, and by his grace and wisdom which he may find necessary and serviceable to prepare you more and more for his glorious Sabbath rest that is prepared for all of God's people. At the same time, as we regret the loss of your help in the deaconess work, and that you after your explanation in your letter have come to the conclusion that because of your poor health you must resign, you should also know and understand that you are heartily welcome back—despite your poor health— you know that your being here would have a great meaning for the sisters and the entire work in all. It would have been a great pleasure and heartily welcome even if you had been much worse than you now are. The deaconess home and its leadership are convinced of the great worth you have given us for your many years work—well blessed work—that many years of heavy responsibility and often trouble at the same time at the deaconesses home—always with admiration, gratitude and thanks which will remind us of the founding of this great work, so you will also with joy and rightful pride look back on a solid and well done work which you have borne and with God's help it will also continue to bear its great fruit to God's glory and many suffering fellow human being's gifts and welfare for all time and eternity.

All has now come to a good end and we have great hope that Sister Mathilde, who has been chosen as your successor, will keep things going in the same track and with a good sense for your experience and insight into the work and will also in the future come to do well for us in the coming critical days. The Lord bless you in both your physical as well as your spiritual life and a hearty greeting to you from each and every one on the Board of Managers and also to Mr. Slettebø. My family and others you know also greet you with the heartiest of greetings and also with the best well wishes.

In addition to this letter from Ullenæs on behalf of the board, the corporation also wrote her a letter

Mrs. Elisabeth Slettebø, Egersund

At the last meeting of the annual meeting of the Norwegian Lutheran Deaconess Home and Hospital the members wished to send you a hearty thanks for all you have done now that you have chosen to leave Brooklyn and your work at the deaconess home. A hearty thanks for your effective and faithful work. You did much for the sick and poor here and the love and interest for your work that never flagged and which has brought it forth into the place it is now—

It has made the members here glad to hear that you have felt stronger and fresher during you stay in Norway; in connection with your marriage the members send you the best well wishes and wish you and your husband a happy and bright future.

Repectfully,

Gundersen, secretary

Marriage

On November 5, 1896, the Egersund church book records, Tonette Elisabeth Andreassen Fedde, deaconess, and Ole Andreas Pederson Slettebø, farmer, were married. The book also notes that they were first cousins: The bridegroom's father and the bride's mother were siblings. Egersund, on the southwestern side of Norway, near Flekkefjord, where

Ole owned a farm, is one of the best natural harbors in Norway and at the time one of the busier fishing ports in the country. Still, as Elisabeth had said when writing her future brother-in-law, it was a much less exciting place than New York with all of its cultural

The church where Elisabeth and Ole were married

blandishments which Elisabeth had come to enjoy, perhaps on the advice of Mother Guldberg.

Life in Egersund

The arc of the known and more public life of Elisabeth Fedde ends in 1896 with her leaving the Norwegian Deaconess Hospital and Motherhouse, but there are details that need telling to give us a more textured picture of Sister Elisabeth. Her life and records of it disappear into the local history and family memories.[442] We find her on a list of winners in a lottery raising money for an orphanage in Stavanger, an irony not to be missed by those still wondering about her conflicts with Everson concerning games of chance.[443] A book about Egersund written in 1937 provides us some hints: She was elected to the Health Council (*Verjerådet*) in the community in 1900 and then again in 1911. Its work was to oversee the health of the district's chil-

Ole Andreas Pederson Slettebø

dren, something she would be well qualified to do, especially given her long interest in them. Family members and neighbors continued to consult her on medical issues, and she was always glad to help anyone who came to her. She was on the planning committee for the celebration of the 100th anniversary of the Norwegian constitution in 1914.[444]

Her husband, Ole, was on many boards and committees in Egersund and served as mayor and vice-mayor several times after her return. She has left us very little data on this time, except for letters and the testimony of relatives, especially nieces and nephews who grew to be very fond of her. She liked to work on the farm. She enjoyed handiwork and embroidered a dramatic tapestry for the Brooklyn hospital depicting her life on the farm, which she sent just before she died. She did write her *Memoirs*, without which this book could not have been written and for which posterity is grateful. Given the degenerative nature of her disease, most of this work probably caused her pain. When she returned to Brooklyn for the dedication of the new Deaconess Hospital in 1904, she was glad to be there and watch, but took no public part from the records we have. Women rarely spoke in public at this time, no matter who they were, so that is not surprising, but a little odd. It should be noted here that at this celebration, Pastor Everson, her old nemesis and still difficult to understand, gave a brief history of the beginning of the project, from the time Sister Elisabeth came until 1904. *Nordisk Tidende* commented that in his reminiscences he had the entire audience with him as he spoke.

> Twenty-one years ago the work received a gift of $150 a year which it accepted from a kindly disposed person [Mrs. Børs] eager to help. Sister Elisabeth who is now sitting here with us was the one who came from Norway to help us with the difficult work. Why she had to leave her work most of the people present here tonight will understand, but the fruit of her labors will always be remembered.[445]

This gives us a more gracious and generous picture of Everson than we had from him before. He praised her for her hard work in the beginning and rightly noted that what they were celebrating was largely a result of her labors. There is no parsimony of spirit in his comments such as one might have expected.[446]

The comment that "most people present here tonight will understand" why she had to leave the work seems to indicate that her illness by then was fairly obvious to all. I take this to mean they could see the consequences of her illness in her appearance, in the way we can see the crippling effects of arthritis.

In 1908, one of her early colleagues, Dr. Robert E. Coughlin, the first ambulance doctor, wrote:

> Elisabeth was a remarkable woman and one was fortunate to know her. Her one idea was to help the poor and distressed. Her energy knew no fatigue. Her executive ability rivaled that of any man. Action followed quickly upon the thought. Her powers of observation and judgment of character and human nature equaled that of George Eliot. Her sympathy and interest in her fellows left a lasting impression. She had all the womanly traits. She and the other sisters demonstrated the moral principle of the Home.[447]

This shows that her public image was one of strong character and conviction and good humor, along with the language about a strong woman who had a public leadership role—the notion being that women are kinder and gentler, but also that a woman in charge needs to have some of the capacities of a man.

In 1915, Mauritz Brekke (1878-1951), assistant to the Seamen's Mission Church, brought Fedde a gift from the Brooklyn Norwegian Lutheran Deaconess Home and Hospital: a silver bowl filled with artifacts and memories from America. She put it in a room in their home where she kept mementos from her time in Brooklyn. When she received it, she gallantly presented it to Ole, saying, "You are the one who shall have this because you accepted me when I was worn out and gave me a good home."[448] Later she would say more. "I was an old bride, but now I can be happy about the bluebells by the roadside. They are my wedding bells."[449]

Although she never used the word *arthritis* to describe her disease, she did speak of her body as being worn out and in pain. In the church book, the cause of her death is simply described as *"gigt"* or rheumatism. She seemed to have had longer and longer periods of illness as her time went on at the Motherhouse in Brooklyn. We have no pictures that I know of after her time in Brooklyn, so we cannot see if she was stooped or arthritic. Nor do we hear from her of the pain which comes with the disease, but it would have been possible for her to continue with some activities. We know that she enjoyed life on the farm and lived always interested in those around her and full of curiosity and good humor.[450]

The Slettebø farm

Final Honors

On her seventieth birthday, Christmas Day 1920, telegrams and letters poured in to her home in Egersund praising her for her life and work. At their annual meeting in January the Norwegian Lutheran Hospital and Deaconess Home in Brooklyn made her an honorary life member of the association and sent her a greeting she must have received just a few days before her death:

> In loving remembrance of your splendid and faithful work for the Norwegian Hospital and Deaconesses Home, Brooklyn, board of managers and sisters send their heartiest congratulation and best wishes on your seventieth birthday. As long as the hospital exists your service will not be forgotten.[453]

A friend, Sigmund Feyling, wrote a tribute to her reporting on the recognition in the local paper when she received the award from Brooklyn. In it he gave a thorough biography, including many facts about Elisabeth from his own knowledge. One of them was a wry comment on her life as a farm wife.

> She was not exactly like other farm wives. What she was and had done could not be easily hidden. She always had the kind of authority that people understood. Sister Elisabeth as many still called her continued to care for the ill who came to the farm. And she has continued her work with the county doctor and with the school board.[454]

The house where Elisabeth grew up and which she bought after returning to Norway

He continued by saying that she was very quick to set herself in the background and not take credit, even if it were due. These tributes sound as though people knew she was near death. At the memorial service in her honor in May of that year, the speaker said as much, noting that this honor seemed to be, in hindsight, something like a bouquet on her coffin since she had probably received the honor just before she died.

Death and Burial

Sister Elisabeth died on February 25, 1921. The church book says she was buried on March 4, 1921, in the Egersund cemetery. The announcement had come to the Brooklyn hospital from Ole, her husband. *Nordisk Tidende* announced it on its front page of its March 3, 1921, issue. It was not surprising to hear that she had died, according to the paper, as those nearest to her expected that her illness would lead to her death. All who knew her could say that Fedde still shone like a radiant beam for those who had the honor to know and admire her.

> There was no woman and very few men who had such a powerful influence on the Norwegian community in Brooklyn as Sister Elisabeth. She was gifted with a keen understanding, firm will, clear administrative talents, a rare person with a

self-sacrificing sense and strength to give her community her brand.[455]

Immediately on hearing of her death, the hospital sent a telegram to Sigmund Feyling in Egersund asking him to represent the hospital at the funeral and place a wreath on her casket with the following words on one side of the card: "The Norwegian Hospital, Brooklyn." On the other side: "An expression of our deepfelt gratitude." He wrote later in an article on both Ole and Elisabeth after they were gone, that their final days had been wearing (*"slitsomme"*). A poem in her honor, by O. A. Kjellberg, appeared in *Dalernes Tidende* and then in several other papers, among them *Nordisk Tidende*. It refers to Fedde's days of suffering as she was dying :

> The days of suffering and pain
> of many years have now passed by
> you bore the pain without complaints because
> your hope was in the Lord
> who helped you day and night.[456]

Once again, although no one says from what she was suffering, both Feyling and Kjellberg describe an ending with much pain, something like rheumatoid arthritis.

Obituaries and Memorial Services

Her obituary appeared in the *Nordisk Tidende*:

> Sister Elisabeth Fedde is dead. So a life rich in devotion and love for the neighbor is now ended. She served with joy her God and her neighbors with all that she had of compassion and love. For that reason there are many who say with the apostle, 'I thank my God upon every remembrance of you.' With her death, the Deaconess home has lost a trail blazer in her work here among the Norwegians in this country. She was the first and the one who remains for us today, the ideal deaconess. At the last meeting of the Deaconess Home and Hospital Board of Managers it was decided to have a memorial service on May 8, 1921 at the Seamen's Mission Church. Here we will meet as many as want to come together to remember her life and work and thank Him who gave her to us.[457]

Folkebladet, the Norwegian language church paper of the Lutheran Free Church, on March 10, 1921, also published an obituary, as might be expected, given her relationship with the Minneapolis Deaconess Institute. Sverdrup, Oftedal, and Gjertsen had all died, and their memory was fading. Almost all of the details in the piece were wrong, even the day of her death. The account is obviously written by someone who knew little of the story, but knew her legend. It did get her birthday and birthplace right. It assumed she had entered the deaconess house in Stavanger, where there was none, missing that she had gone to the Deaconess House *from* Stavanger. The article said that Sverdrup, with others, had started the Deaconess Motherhouse and Hospital in 1888, and seems not to have known that it was Gjertsen and Oftedal, more than Sverdrup, who had begun the effort. It did know that she had returned to Norway in 1896 to marry Ole Slettebø, concluding that she was a very gifted woman with a strong character by which she had left a deep imprint on the places where she had worked.

The memorial service for her on Sunday afternoon, May 8, 1921, at the Seamen's Mission Church in Brooklyn was led by Lauritz Larsen (1882-1923), president of the National Lutheran Council and of the Deaconess Hospital board, former pastor of Zion Lutheran Church on 4th Avenue in Brooklyn. Larsen preached on Romans 6:8. "If we have died with Christ, we believe we will also live with him."[458]

He noted that there were few women who were as forward looking (pioneering) as Sister Elisabeth.

> Her strong personality and the example she set, will live among us forever. We are gathered here today in recognition of her great trailblazing work. There are few who have exercised a greater influence in this organization. Along with her obedience to God's will, Sister Elisabeth was equipped with keen understanding, strong will and administrative gifts. It was these qualities together that made her a strong pioneer.[459]

The paper reported that his sermon, filled with warmth, concluded with the blessing, "God bless her memory and may it be a blessing." Pastor Christian Bruun, of the Seamen's Church, remembered especially Sister Elisabeth's strong support for and relationship with the Seamen's Church. He praised her for her good work, saying, "Christianity does not consist so much of sitting and hearing God's Word, as working and serving others" as she had. Vice-counsel Haug from Norway gave a greeting from the Norwegian government, praising her work for others, not for herself. The rector of the hospital, Carl Oscar Pedersen (1887-1972), described her as the ideal deaconess. The service concluded with the singing of "O Happy Day When We Shall Stand," (*O Tænk Naar engang Samles skal*) the traditional closing hymn of the Norwegian church after mission festivals or funerals.[460]

Saint?

Today both the Lutherans and the Episcopalians list Sister Elisabeth in their Calendar of Saints; her date is February 25. She would probably find this funny, as might those who knew her well. She was not particularly saintly, but then few saints are. Saints are difficult people, driven human beings who have had a vision of what God wants them to do and what they can do. They brook no opposition and go forward, eager to do the Lord's will, regardless of cost to themselves. That perhaps describes Fedde's life best.

While they loved her, her family tells stories even today of her forceful opinions and personality. One of her grandnieces, Alva, daughter of Gabriel Martin Nathanael, Gabriel's third son, remembers, "She was the one who insisted on my Dad being named 'Nathanael' even though his parents had already decided upon 'Gabriel Martin', so he received the three names. I don't think of her as saintly, but as gifted and devoted to her ideals, and at the same time opinionated and a little 'bossy'—a wonderful and interesting human being."[451]

In 1931, Fedde was featured in the magazine for nurses, *The Trained Nurse and Hospital Review*. Her portrait, the frontispiece of the issue, would later be featured on a calendar of famous nurses. A brief biography of her noted that

> She, with a great faith and a willingness to give her savings and herself, accepted the challenge. Battling and ever battling for the needy, want, misunderstanding and persecution were just the situations that made failure impossible. An unusually sunny disposition, a capacity for making and keeping friends, a willingness to do the most menial service and an absolutely

unshakeable faith in her calling, made her persist in building up step by step the hospital which stands as her most conspicuous memorial.[452]

What are we to make of this very powerful, complicated, and deeply spiritual woman? Like many others who have written about Sister Elisabeth, I wondered why and how she could leave her active, public and exhausting, but satisfying, life to return to her childhood sweetheart and live peacefully and apparently well for the rest of her life. It was only at the very end of this writing that I discovered that she did not feel able to continue her work in Brooklyn for reasons of health. She wanted to be home in Norway with someone who could take care of her as she faced the ravages of her disease, which she well understood as a nurse. She would never recover. From her interview with the paper, we know she wanted to find a place without having to worry about being left alone and indigent.

The quiet routine of the farm with a close friend as husband to take care of her must have given this strong woman a sense of peace. In her embroidered scene from the farm that is the last work we have from her hand, we see her good humored depiction of little children playing around the women, men and older boys working hard with their rakes. Her observant eye, something she has always has shown to be keen, was as quick as ever. We can also see in her acceptance of her retirement, caused in part by her physical condition the strength of her character

Fedde's embroidery on life on the farm in the Fedde exhibit at Lutheran Medical Center, Brooklyn

and deep faith. She had always prayed to do the will of the Lord and now she could rest. She had done what she could. Her only work after her retirement was to record the events of her life. Her trailblazing work as a deaconess needed to be told.

Fedde's original calling was to serve the poor and sick in Brooklyn. In doing so she kept seeing more and more things she should and could do. Her sense of her own calling to help, and her ability to imagine more and more places for her work to be done, outdid itself. That she got the Children's Home in Beloit, Iowa, up and running is a small emblem of her at her best: getting to know the leaders of the Norwegian Danish Augustana Synod, realizing there would be empty buildings in Beloit, seeing they could be used as an orphanage, persuading the leadership to support her plans, and then getting the board to oversee the institution, raise money for it, and send two sisters there. She did this in very short order, like many of the rest of her projects. Why should we wonder that she found it annoying to have to submit to boards who were trying to make policy and get the organizations running smoothly, but did not have her vision? She had little time for these things and often showed her irritation with policies that seemed only to take more time and prevent her from getting the actual work done, as we have seen in her troubles with both boards. These issues are not old, nor will they go away. There is almost an inherent clash between visionaries and managers. It is often difficult

The Deaconess Hospital and Motherhouse in Brooklyn in 1905 The 1889 hospital is to the far left, the Deaconess Motherhouse inbetween and the hospital to the right.

for them to work together, and in this case it is remarkable what they did accomplish together, despite the tensions and conflicts.

It must also be acknowledged that she was an independent single woman in an office and a time when few understood or valued such women or the vocation. Moving into the public vocation of deaconess, working with men in a collegial manner was a new thing for everyone. We have seen that neither she nor the men quite knew how to work this out. Irrespective of patriarchal attitudes and customs, and they were there to be sure, neither the men nor Fedde had any experience with this new relationship, and she made as many mistakes as they did in trying to move from the private sphere where women "belonged"to working with men together in the public sphere. Added to this, however, was the theology and practice of the whole deaconess movement. It was based on an understanding of the place of men and women that simply could not continue. Kristin Norseth and others have looked closely at these power relationships and noted that the Deaconess Houses were expected to adopt the rules of the home in their work, so these rather formidable single women had to submit to the pastors on the boards as a wife or

The Deaconess Hospital in Minneapolis, 1910

daughter would have to submit to a husband or father in the home at the time. As time went on, more women were leaving home to work, and their self-understandings were changing.

This story is, in some ways, a morality tale of two complicated people: Fedde and Everson played out their drama as characters against a background of liberal and conservative politics and pietist and orthodox theologies. Everson's constant needling of her and lack of respect, even his failure to give her any credit in his accounts of the work, show how difficult these relationships could be regardless of political and theological disagreements. They brought Fedde much spiritual agony as she tried to figure out what to do with him and the board in its most trying times. As a pietist, she was quite ready and willing to imagine in her own heart that she could be at fault in things spiritual, but on the other hand she did not doubt that she was right about her vision for the spiritual and medical side of things.

We cannot see very clearly whether her own private agonies, spiritual and physical, registered on others in her professional relationships with them. Only in her letters to Sverdrup do we see her revealing herself to another. It is significant that she confided briefly in Sverdrup that she had considered becoming a doctor in order to go deeper into the medical side of her vocation. While she did have good relations with many of the doctors, according to her own testimony, things broke down completely with Dr. Laws in Minneapolis. He felt that she did not respect him nor had confidence in him, and he tried to resign many times. It is not difficult to imagine that she could communicate quite clearly her lack of confidence in him without saying much, even if he continued to be a respected doctor for years after she left. The board wisely did not accept his resignation probably because Sverdrup had assured them that she would resign before too long. She did treat Sverdrup as something of a confessor in her frank and often distraught correspondence. She felt free to speak truthfully to him about her hurt when his wife gossiped about her. Sverdrup's actions also show him to be a shrewd reader of her character. He knew she needed more autonomy and power in the organization. In fact, the documents of the deaconess organization suggested she be on the board. Putting her on the board when he reorganized the Minneapolis Motherhouse and Hospital showed he had taken her measure. He did not have the formal objections to Fedde's being on the board that Everson in Brooklyn did. When she returned to Brooklyn, she was appointed Sister Superior and essentially ran the entire operation until she left, something all agree she did well. The fact that the only sisters consecrated under her leadership—Sister Mathilde and Sister Elise—were consecrated after her return to Brooklyn suggests that she had not learned how to mentor her students until after Minneapolis. Her difficulties with the first sisters who came to work with her reveal that. She may have expected far more than they could deliver and demanded too much. Her experience with both Sister Othilie and Sister Bertha show that her first attempts in this work were not successful, although some of the sisters in Minneapolis remained very loyal to her.

The vocation and calling Sister Elisabeth had entered was probably well suited to her at first, but as she grew in her powers and her sense of how much needed to be done and how much she could do, it expanded beyond what her physical abilities could endure. In the Kaiserswerth documents, and also in Mother Guldberg's understanding, the word "self-denial" was basic. Wanting to fulfill one's own desires was proscribed by the rules. Sisters who wanted to have more autonomy over their lives and demanded, for example, they be able to buy a coat, as Sister Mathilde did once, to the dismay of the Board of Managers in Brooklyn, began to chafe under the restrictions of having to get permission for the smallest purchases from the Sister Superior and board. One cannot read the records of the Evangelical Lutheran Deaconess Motherhouses in the United States, all run by men with only men speaking on how the deaconesses should be obedient and deny themselves as Jesus did, without seeing the problem.

The conflict for these powerful women seemed to have been built into their vows and theology. Several incidents among deaconesses in America illustrated this problem. On May 10, 1893, *Nordisk Tidende* reported that two sisters, Martha Bergh and Amalie Kittelson, (Marie Langaunet had since died) had fled the Chicago Deaconess Home because of the onerous demands placed on them by the hospital there. The three had gone to Chicago to work with Pastor Nils C. Brun after their resignation from the Minneapolis Motherhouse, which as we have seen outraged the Minneapolis board. Now they were suing the deaconess board in Chicago for $15,000 because they averred it had broken their contract with them in addition to $10,000 for the damage to their health the work at the hospital had caused them. Part of the problem had been the unclear nature of the several competing organizations which could not agree whether to have a Deaconess Motherhouse associated with the hospital or not. More galling to them, it appears, was that the hospital had hired a "trained" nurse to be over them. As we have noted, deaconess training as nurses was reputed to be somewhat slender, something nursing schools would later address. It became a more and more urgent critique of the deaconesses as the century came to a close. They did not have enough medical expertise. When ordered, the Chicago sisters refused to visit a patient in his home; this refusal caused the board to ask if there was anything they would do if ordered. The relations between them and the board had so deteriorated they said no. The Chicago board released them and told them they should regard themselves as finished at the hospital, but they could not leave until they found another place that would take them in. They left after being received by the hospital in Rochester, Pennsylvania, near Pittsburgh, in what was left of the Motherhouse institution there, where Passavant had built a hospital for those with epilepsy. How the case was solved I have not been able to discover, but the fact that it happened and the fact that it was reported in *Nordisk Tidende,* indicates a problem that many could see coming. Passavant reported in his autobiography that both women left for Norway two years later, about 1895.

It is not surprising, then, to see the letter to the editor that Fedde wrote in 1896 asking for her Norwegian-America sisters to contribute to the statue of Camilla Collett, praising her for her work to win the rights of women in Norway and around the world. While she may have done this in loyalty to Mrs. Børs, a cousin of Collett, the letter has the sound of her convictions in it. She had observed from the inside what it was like to work without a sense of her rights and had to taste the bread of "self-denial," which by her vows she had chosen to eat. By the time she was ready to leave, she had achieved all she needed to and had succeeded in keeping things running as a good administrator. That gave her much satisfaction. The testimony of the board, the doctors, and others are fairly unanimous in their assessment of her as a successful and effective administrator.

The satisfying and apparently serene last years in Brooklyn happened, I would argue, because of her troubled time in Minneapolis. What she suffered there was a mid-life crisis. The cry of dereliction we hear in her letter to Georg Sverdrup after she returned for good to Brooklyn and its sense of utter depletion is evidence of such a moment. Something broke in her, and something broke through to her. While it is easier to say this because we do not have a daily record of her feelings or accomplishments such as a diary after her return to Brooklyn, she seemed to have accepted that her vocation in Brooklyn, to which she returned gladly, was to run the hospital, not build new institutions wherever she saw the need. If she did have ideas for improving their service to the community, such as the ambulance, she got that done. Much has been said and should be said about her sense for God's call. Most mid-life crises, if they are properly settled, involve a rededication or reorientation to what one has been doing in the past and decided to do in the future. In a way it is a revision of one's call that if successfully navigated results in a more focused and fruitful ending to one's working life. One hears that several times in the minutes or in other contemporary records of her life. "This has been one of my best years ever," she commented to the Board at the end of 1892 and would say again a couple more times before she left. She had settled in to the work, and they had figured out how to work with her more successfully. Her *Memoirs* also give us a sense for her mellowing and growth. Events that she once would have thought catastrophic she later narrated with good humor and pleasure. That was a sign of maturity and ripeness. The accolades for her on her retirement and the honorary life-time membership she received from the Brooklyn board just before she died were rich with appreciation of her strong character and good leadership abilities. They also give us a good sense for how she appeared to her public, which we cannot see as well from her own testimony of failures and feelings of despair that she did not apparently share with those around her. Today we can count as her legacy the Lutheran Medical Center in Brooklyn, the Fairview Hospitals in Minneapolis, as well as Lutheran General in Chicago which absorbed Chicago Deaconess, now part of the Advocate chain of hospitals in the Chicago area. Standing in any of those huge establishments bustling with thousands of employees and patients, thinking back to Sister Elisabeth who started out with only herself and few resources along with her faith and her determination, is to understand how great trees do grow from small seeds. We cannot celebrate that enough.

In 2003 the Fedde family in America designed and cast a bronze monument for the Feda churchyard, where Sister Elisabeth was baptized. It now stands there as a tribute to this remarkable woman who should be better known and celebrated. As far as we know, she lived peacefully and serenely in her new calling to do the Lord's will on the farm with Ole. She kept the sardonic glint in her eye as she watched the human comedy around her. She did this, as far as we know, without expressing any bitterness of which we are aware about this turn of events. That in itself, absent public heroics, shows her character as much as anything. She submitted to the limitations caused by her declining health and prayed to live well still doing God's will. Her legacy extends around the world even today, not only in the institutions she and her students founded and served, but in her example which teaches us to forsake sin, death, and the power of the devil, and, with God's help, send people on their way washed up and clean, in good health, with a basket of food and clothes, salve for their wounds or a good word for them as they cross over into the light.

COURTESY KAREN FEDDE MAY

This monument to Sister Elisabeth stands in the Feda churchyard.

THE DIACONATE QUESTION

The messiness of the diaconate goes back to Stephen in Acts 7 who was chosen by the apostles to serve the poor and needy, so the apostles could be doing the work of preaching and evangelism. The irony is that he died preaching the longest sermon in the New Testament. From the beginning of the deaconess movement in the nineteenth century, one of the main courses of study for each sister was the office of the diaconate, never very clear in the Bible or church history. As we can see in Appendix 1, the deaconesses traced their calling back to Phoebe described by Paul in Romans 16:1 as a deaconess; they thought of themselves as "reviving" her ancient office. Cynthia Jurisson, in her entry on the deaconess movement in the *Encyclopedia of Women and Religion in North America,* cautions against thinking of their work as a "revival" of the ancient office and more as an "appropriation" of the term deaconess.[461]

Deaconesses tried to find their place in their particular church hierarchies. The Roman Catholic Church does have a three-fold ministry into which a male diaconate fits, and these offices are usually stepladders into clerical offices: from deacon to priest to bishop. It might be possible in these communions to draw a bright line between the three offices and think theologically about them, mainly in terms of what the people in the offices could do or more correctly what they could NOT do. Deacons cannot do the sacrament; priests can do the sacrament, but cannot ordain other priests; bishops can do all of the previous plus ordain priests and pass on the his-

AT HIS FEET.

The logo for the Minneapolis Deaconess Institute

toric episcopate by the laying on of hands. The Roman Catholic Church has recently made an order of deacon that is permanent. Men in it can be married, but cannot view their office as a step up the ladder to the priesthood unless their wife dies and they want to become priests. For Protestants, making the deaconess' vocation into a minor clerical order had its reasons, but it has been fraught with complications. Did it let women think they were almost clergy before they could be? The order was almost gone by the time women could be ordained. Did consecrating them make them feel better about their nursing duties, as basic as they were? Informed Lutheran laity with a strong sense of their own vocations might wonder about this. When the ELCA began rethinking ministry, there was still a vibrant deaconess community in the Lutheran Church–Missouri Synod tradition, begun in 1919, some of which came into the ELCA conversation through the forming of the Seminex breakaway. Now called the Lutheran Deaconess Association, it considers itself to be inter-Lutheran. Some thought it looked like a natural way for Lutherans to adopt a three-fold ministry of the kind the historical catholic churches have. It was the question facing the Task Force on Ministry that the ELCA commissioned before its merger and which went on for five years. At the end, in 1993, the Churchwide Assembly voted to retain its one office of ministry, the pastor. Still the question is being asked with a new proposal for the diaconate before the ELCA again.

Mary and/or Martha?

The Minneapolis Deaconess Institute had as its emblem a figure of Mary of Bethany sitting at the feet of the master. The contradiction in the emblem is clear to anyone who has thought deeply about the Mary and Martha story. As my mother used to say when forbidding my preacher father ever to preach on the Mary and Martha text, "You laud Mary for sitting there, but you want your pie and coffee as well."

While any Martha can meditate like Mary, and the deaconess rules made it likely they would contemplate more than most others, perhaps, the last thing a deaconess might want to do is sit and contemplate while the needy around them cried out for help. It was this contradiction, finally, that probably brought the deaconess movement as we knew it to an end. Women began to prefer nursing as a vocation. It is no wonder that the movement gradually lost members as the numbers of nurses continued to rise. Nurses without deaconess training could, of course, give spiritual care, and many did. Their education had made them more skilled as nurses, something the administrators of deaconess institutions must have realized as the nineteenth century came to a close. As early as the conference in Christiania in 1894, one could hear the anxiety about the future of the movement—as it was becoming clear women preferred training as nurses rather than deaconesses. One solution was educating Christian nurses for the profession without the deaconess vocation. More women were being attracted to the profession of nursing and finally that of a physician for obvious reasons.

In 1909, the Brooklyn Deaconess Hospital began granting nursing degrees to women who chose not to be deaconesses. In 1916, Deaconess Institute in Minneapolis started a nursing school to

> give young women in congregations who might not feel called to enter the diaconate a chance to receive their nurses' training in a Christian institution. The arguments in favor of a Christian School of Nursing are the same as those in favor of the Christian College in the field of education,

wrote Dr. Thorvald Olson Burntvedt, president of the Lutheran Free Church for the golden anniversary of the hospital.[462] Taking vows of self-denial and obedience were not necessary for those who wanted to be nurses. So one could regard the great progress made by the deaconesses as a beginning, a stepping stone to an entirely different sense for the nursing profession. Without the deaconess movement, things might have developed rather differently.

Florence Nightingale had marked these problems clearly and led the way to a different model. By the end of her life she had rejected the deaconess model with some vehemence because she had seen the problem built into the deaconess vocation. While she had learned much at Kaiserswerth about her role and vocation, she thought its day was over. For her it became important that the "entire control of a nursing staff as to discipline and teaching, must be taken out of the hands of men, and lodged in those of a woman, who must herself be a trained and competent nurse," who could function as an administrator as much as a nurse,[463] as Anna Sticker, historian of these issues, writes. Although Nightingale had begun at Kaiserswerth and picked up many of its practices, she had gone far beyond the patriarchal ways of Kaiserswerth when she established her own school of nursing. In 1897 she rejected rather sharply the notion that she had been formed by the venerable Deaconess House. Now, as Sticker wrote, Nightingale

> stood at the head of what she herself had achieved while German Deaconess Nursing was failing to meet the obvious demands made by an age of further progress, of which Florence Nightingale had been one of the pioneers. Hence the English woman could not endure to be called a pupil of Kaiserswerth.[464]

The contradictions built into the office from Kaiserswerth made the Motherhouses impossible to maintain. Florence Nightingale saw that when she argued that women should be in charge of the nurses. The issue that she did not quite see at the time is that these jobs did not need to be determined on the basis of the gender of the applicant. That would come a century later.

There was also, in America, a strange thing happening to women as they began entering the professions. Anne Douglas in her important book, *The Feminization of American Culture* (1977) argues that while the women on the farms in the early part of the nineteenth century were part of the production of wealth for the family, after the Civil War, women became sentimentalized, objects of beauty and sentiment, not to be taken seriously in the public sphere exactly when they were becoming active in the public sphere. While this was not true of all women in nineteenth century America—there was still a large majority of women on the farm and in the parsonage contributing much to the financial status of the family—it was the regnant view of society as women turned from being producers to being consumers. This was the notion that men worked outside of the home while women were the keepers of the hearth, in other words, public and private. While this caused many difficulties for women trying to find their voices and their place in the society, it was not the problem of the nurse.

Nurses cannot be sentimental or judgmental. They have seen life at its most basic and physical. I can think of no place in the life of Fedde where she was sentimental or judgmental with a patient. She dealt with the situations of each of her patients as they came to her, no matter how much they could have avoided their illness by behaving differently; she viewed life with a steady and level gaze that saw pretty much everything one needed to diagnose the situation and deal with it. Pastor Everson used his theology not to diagnose the situations, but to give the formulaic answers he thought were required by his theological commitments. Although he upset Fedde greatly, he seemed not to have given her the vapors or held her back (although he may have caused her stress enough to make her ill). Actually he may have been the weakling, she the strong one who had to take care not to offend his sensibilities. He was the one who got the vapors. He was blowing up, firing off angry letters to the paper attacking colleagues and friends for some theological error. Today they look unseemly. His hysterics about the bazaar laws and the misuse of the bazaar seem histrionic and inappropriate from this distance.

Everson's personal and theological issues with Fedde and the diaconate show that it was the pietists who were the liberals on these issues and the orthodox the conservatives. For a while the orthodox ended up opposing women's suffrage and the diaconate for theological reasons, as well as their political convictions—although one must be clear that in American politics it was the Republicans who favored women's vote long before the Democrats did, seating two women delegates at its 1892 convention in Minneapolis. The pro-suffrage men, however, who were liberals, and with whom Fedde worked did not appear to be all that easy for her to work with either.

The sentimental language of Henry Ward Beecher and others about woman having a higher moral character than men at the same time demanding that women in the public sphere be more masculine was probably an operating assumption of the men who ran the deaconess boards around the world. It worked at the beginning, but could not be sustained. It is difficult to think Fedde would have ever used her feminine wiles, if she even had them to use, on Everson or anyone else to get her way. Her sense that she was homely made her think probably that she was free of having to flirt! She demanded and got her way.

Pastor Emil Petersen in his 1894 article on the consecration of deaconesses in Brooklyn stated two objections to the office that many Lutherans have had, even as they approved and supported the work and place of the deaconesses. Consecrating women into a "half-clerical" office involved several theological contradictions for some Lutherans who since the Reformation had tended to be opposed to any other clerical office than the pastor. The idea that these women were taking vows to serve the church as something like "brides" of the church—language taken directly from medieval talk about nuns—struck many Lutheran clergy and theologians as contrary to the Lutheran notion of vocation—a calling which Lutherans believed all Christians had as they served their Lord and their neighbor, in any honorable profession. Vigilant lay men and women have been quick to see that this elevated the work of the deaconesses into a level different from the laity. Does the elevation mean better? Peterson, reporting on the service, knew well this was not consistent with the Lutheran doctrine of vocation, one of the most deeply held doctrines of the Lutheran tradition. Second, that the service invited the sisters to the Lord's Table without the rest of the congregation also seemed to raise the deaconesses into kind of status over the laity, something like reserving the wine for the clergy. This also offended Petersen. That the hymns written especially for the service also used the imagery of the bride of Christ only exacerbated the discomfort the pastor felt in observing the service, as it would have many other Lutherans. Did sanctifying this particular work make it easier or more effective to do?[465] Why not have a ceremony for everyone entering any other profession or vocation, something some have argued the traditional commencement ceremony at graduation from the university was designed to do.

Once again, the sacralizing of work was something Luther did theologically in his theology of vocation but not ritually. In fact, one could argue as many have that Luther wanted to desacralize the minister's office by changing the ordination service to something more like an installation service. One hears in the rules for the diaconate (Appendix 1) a defensive tone on these issues very clearly insisting they are not doing what the pastor accused them of doing. These debates go round and round, it seems, century after century. Now there are diaconal ministers in churches who once again are trying to revive the ancient order, looking to the deaconesses like Elisabeth Fedde for help in understanding their office or vocation, although not always with nursing as a major part of the calling. (Candidates were encouraged to enter other professions such as teaching or social work besides nursing in the 1930s.) When the ELCA was formed, deaconesses were still active from the Motherhouse in Valparaiso and the Gladwyne House in Pennsylvania. Since 1993 and the conclusion of the ELCA Task Force on the Study of Ministry, and its provision for diaconal ministers and associates in ministry, an active deaconess program continues in the ELCA, with many of the same commitments of the old deaconess program of service, although different from that of Fedde and her generation. While service and community are important to both groups, self-denial and obedience have not been brought forward in the same way, although they would argue that the office of deaconess makes them accountable to their community. A frequent phrase diaconal ministrers use now is that they are ministers of Word and Service, not Word and Sacrament, something the first principles of the deaconess movement in America proscribed. (See appendix I, 1, 3.) Today there is a flourishing international deaconess community, DIAKONIA: World Federation of Diaconal Associations and Deaconal Communities, which meets in conference every four years around the world. All of the deaconess programs had to radically redefine their understanding of the office during the middle of the last century, which many did with resounding success. (See the website, DIAKONIA-world.org.) Efforts continue as Christians seek to help people in ways that will be effective and evangelical. Today Neuendettelsau has a vibrant diaconal ministry with both men and women serving thousands of people in Germany as does Kaiserswerth, now a major medical center in northern Germany with diaconal ministries flourishing and even a few sisters continuing as a deaconess community on the original model. The Lovisenberg Diakonissehuset and the Lovisenberg Diakonale Sykehus in Oslo, where Fedde received her training, continues as one of the major hospitals in Norway with a strong emphasis in diaconal service even today. Its archives are a rich trove of the history for the deaconess movement, remembered especially in the life and work of Mother Guldberg with a statue of her on the grounds and a restored building showing what some of the rooms looked like in her day. One can see churches at the moment searching for a way to find people willing to serve without being trained as pastors. This unstable, but creative office, has always been there for new kinds of ministry. I would argue that the more clearly the lines are drawn between the office of pastor and the diaconate, the less creative both offices will be. Its very messiness makes it adaptable to new realities and circumstances. More students at seminaries are working for M.A.s in some part of biblical or theological studies so they can avoid the strictures of being rostered. They are at the creative edge of ministry today.

It must be said clearly, however, that when Fliedner and Loehe began the Motherhouses in Kaiserswerth and Neuendettelsau, the idea of women being able to take up this new role was exciting and challenging for women who were looking to serve their Lord outside of the home. They transformed the vocation of nursing and in doing so participated in the changing roles of women as well. Their work, selfless and exhausting, made a huge difference. The movement was extremely important to the Lutheran churches and women. It helped North American Lutherans and other Protestant bodies face the social dislocations caused by immigration, rapid urbanization, and poverty rampant in the nineteenth century. Something had to be done, and these Christians tried to do something. As Isabelle Horton (1853-1933), a Protestant deaconess in Chicago, said, "The world wants mothering. . . . The deaconess movement puts the mother into the church."[466]

This understanding of woman's nature and gifts went largely unchallenged in the work of the deaconesses of Fedde's time. Loehe and Fliedner were not at all radical in their understandings of women's natures: Both believed the commonplace, "the state for man, the family for the woman."[467] Jurisson argues that the dislocations of the day began to change the way people thought about "gender roles and duties." The deaconess movement made it possible for women to enter into a public and professional occupation, even with its careful circumscribed sphere.[468] It would be wrong not to understand that. Despite all that, it was an important marker for women in the Lutheran church as well as the secular world. In creating this office Protestants found a way to meet the needs of the day creatively with a movement that probably could not continue in the form it took during the years 1836 to 1910. Not even Wilhelm Loehe thought the movement would last longer than ten years.[469] While he was wrong, he was not wrong by much. The high point of the movement was probably about 1910.

Those of us who still remember deaconesses did not think they were powerless. They were formidable women, to be reckoned with. When devout women preferred becoming nurses to being deaconesses, things were beginning to change. As women could become doctors, and now as men can become nurses, things have even more radically changed. Regardless of where we are now, attention must be paid to the women who saw their opportunities in the office of deaconess and took it on with courage and devotion. We are the richer for them today.

CERTIFICATE OF INCORPORATION.

We, the undersigned, Carl Ullenæs, Gabriel Fedde, Theodor Siqveland, Emil Eriksen, Rudolph Bang, Martin H. Hegge, A. Sommerfelt, A. Gundersen, Kr. K. Saarheim, M. Rosenquist, Samuel Harris, C. S. Eversen, all of full age, being desirous of forming a body politic and corporate, for the purpose of establishing, maintaining and operating a hospital and home for the reception and maintainance of persons physically afflicted under and in pursuance to the provision of the act entitled " An act to authorize the formation of corporations for the establishment and maintainance of hospitals, infirmaries, dispensaries, and homes for invalids or aged and indigent persons," passed March 29th, 1889, have associated and do hereby associate ourselves together for the purpose of becoming with our associates and successors, a Society and body corporate; and pursuant to said act and for the purpose aforesaid, we do hereby certify and declare

First. That the name and title of said corporation shall be " THE NORWEGIAN LUTHERAN DEACONESSES' HOME AND HOSPITAL.'

Second. That the object for which said corporation is formed is to own and maintain a Home and Hospital and to administer to the wants of the sick and needy.

Third. The names of the persons who shall form the Board of Managers of said corporation for the first year are as follows: Carl Ullenæs, Gabriel Fede, Theo. Siqveland, Martin H. Hegge, Anders Gundersen, Samuel Harris, Emil Ericksen, T. A. Lohne, M. Rosenquist.

Fourth. The term of duration of said corporation shall be one hundred years.

Fifth. That the said Home and Hospital shall be located in the City of Brooklyn, County of Kings and State of New York.

C. Ullenæs,	Rudolph Bang,	Kr. K. Saarheim,
G. Fedde,	Martin A. Hegge,	M. Rosenquist,
Theo. Siqveland,	A. Sommerfelt,	Samuel Harris,
Emil Ericksen,	A. Gundersen,	C. S. Eversen.

STATE OF NEW YORK, COUNTY OF KINGS, CITY OF BROOKLYN. } S.S.

On this, the 14th day of November, before me personally came C. Ullenæs, Gabriel Fedde, Theo. Siqveland, Emil Ericksen, Rudolph Bang, Martin H. Hegge, A. Sommerfelt, A. Gundersen, Kr. K. Saarheim, M. Rosenquist, Samuel Harris, C. S. Eversen, to me known, and known to me to be the individuals described in and who executed the foregoing certificate and they severally acknowledged to me that they executed the same.

{L.S.}

FRED. PITCHER,

NOTARY PUBLIC.

STATE OF NEW YORK COUNTY OF KINGS } S.S.

I, John Cottier, Clerk of the County of Kings, and Clerk of the Supreme Court of the State of New York, in and for said County (said Court being a Court of Record), *Do Hereby Certify*, that I have compared the annexed with the original Certificate of Incorporation of The Norwegian Lutheran Deaconesses' Home and Hospital filed and recorded in my office November 15, 1892, and that the same is a true transcript thereof, and of the whole of such original

In Testimony Whereof I have hereunto set my hand and affixed the seal of said County and Court this 4th day of February 1893,

{L.S.}

JOHN COTTIER,

CLERK.

APPENDIX ONE

THE PRINCIPLES OF THE FEMALE DIACONATE[472]

I

As evangelical Christians we look to the Word of God for a sound basis of the Female Diaconate. We believe that this ministry of the Church of Christ rests on a sure and indisputable Scripture foundation. But at the same time we freely admit that present form of this ministry cannot be traced in all its details to certain clearly defined rules or precepts of the New Testament.

In its present organization the Female Diaconate is the result of a growth and development, in which we recognize the sound Lutheran principle, that nothing can be tolerated in the Church of Christ that would in any wise be in conflict with the Word of God, but that there may be a great deal in the details of the present characters, and *modus operandi* of the Female Diaconate, which cannot be found directly in certain Scripture passages.

II

The Scripture passages which speak directly of women as recognized office-bearers of the Church—as female (διαχονία)—are very few indeed. With Rom. 16:1-2, and I Tim. 3:11 their whole number is completed.

III

The office or ministry (διαχονία) for the building up and governing of the Church of Christ is originally one, and one only—the Ministry of the Word, committed to the Apostles, bishops, presbyters or pastors.

IV

At a very early time in the history of the Apostolic Church this ministry of the Word called in for its assistance certain helpers, with other gifts, functions, and ministrations. They were appointed for the support of the ministry of the Word as circumstances might require for the "daily ministration" (διαχονία χαθημερνή)

V

To this ministry of love, during the Apostolic times already, women also were called, who, like Phoebe of Cenchrea, served the congregation as female δίαχονοι thus becoming a succourer of many and even of the Apostle himself.

VI

The Female diaconate is not a ministry of the Word. We do not recognize or train deaconesses as preachers or evangelists. The New Testament nowhere makes provision for the ordinary preaching of the Word by women, but rather forbids it in direct words, I Cor. 14:34, 35. I Tim. 2: 11,12.

This we maintain, notwithstanding the exceptional cases mentioned in the Old and New Testament of prophetesses who by a direct and special divine call and inspiration were privileged to speak the Word. Nor is the position in conflict with the fact that we train and employ teaching sisters for the instruction and education of our female youth.

VII

The Deaconess, then, is one who accepts and performs the ministry of charity as the calling of her life, discharging her duties in the name and to the honor of the Lord, as a member and helper of the Church of Christ.

VIII

While in the ancient Church the sphere of the Deaconess work was confined to the congregation, the present organization of the Female Diaconate has most successfully adopted the idea of the Motherhouse as a training school of the Deaconess, both for the religious and the technical side of her calling; as an association of those that are united in the same faith and for the same life-work; and as a guarantee for the protection and support of the Deaconess in time of infirmity and old age.

IX

Whilst this idea of the association in a sisterhood of a Motherhouse has been adopted after the model of certain organizations established by Vincent de Paula in the Roman Church of the seventeenth century, the Female Diaconate of our Lutheran Church preserves its truly evangelical character over against Rome in the following points. There is

1. No special vow in distinction from the baptismal vow.

2. No binding obligation to a life of celibacy.

3. No "religious life" as distinguished from the life and calling of any other Christian.

4. No special "order" in the sense of the mediæval Church.

5. No merit or expectation of special reward for a work of supererogation.

X

As the indispensable condition of true unity and a sound development we demand for a Deaconess Motherhouse, the unity in the faith, which finds its expression in a clear confession, and gives to the institution an unmistakably churchly character. In every aspect the life of the Motherhouse must reflect the life of the Church whose faith it professes. And as a small community, based upon the voluntary union of its members, it is able to unfold the life of the Church in even greater purity, richness and consistency than larger congregations. To insure this churchly character of the Motherhouse, the Ministry of the Word, as represented by one or more pastors, must have a permanent and leading position in its organization.

FUNDAMENTAL PRINCIPLES OF THE DEACONESS MOTHERHOUSES CONNECTED WITH THE KAISERSWERTH GENERAL CONFERENCE[473]

I. The Motherhouse in its External Relations.

1. The Motherhouse should endeavor to possess itself of the rights enjoyed by corporations and benevolent institutions.

2. A most vital, yet unfettered union between the Motherhouse and the Church is desirable. (Parochial rights.)

3. The Pastor of the Motherhouse remains the pastor in fact of Sisters on out-stations, especially in all matters pertaining to themselves and the Sisterhood. Nevertheless, for the sake of their joint work, confidential relations should exist between the Sisters and the pastors in whose parishes they labor.

II. The Board of Trustees and the Direction

1. Women as well as men may serve on the Boards of Motherhouses. The Rector and the Sister Superior should belong to the Board, and wherever possible, should be accorded the right to vote.

2. The Rector, by virtue of his office as a Minister of the Word, is also the head of the Sister Superior. The latter, as the housemother, is the immediate head of the Sisters.

3. For all their doings the Rector and the Sister Superior are responsible to the Board. Into their hands, under specific instructions, is commit-

ted the internal management of the Motherhouse, and with this the Board does not directly interfere.

III. The Sisterhood

1. The Deaconesses are set apart for their work by an act of consecration, preceeded by a season of special preparation. A probationary period precedes the training and examination. In deciding upon the consecration of Probationers the Sisterhood should be permitted to have a voice. A woman with a tarnished reputation cannot become a Deaconess.

2. Each Motherhouse furnishes its Sisters a garb of fixed and uniform design, which they are obliged to wear. From Sisters who relinquish the work the surrender of this garb is to be demanded, and every effort must be made to prevent such from wearing the distinctive dress of the Motherhouse after they have severed their connection with the Sisterhood.

3. As members of the Motherhouse the sisters receive no compensation, but all their needs in health, in sickness, on duty during vacations, are supplied by the Motherhouse. Pocket money is furnished for ordinary expenditures.

4. a) The Sisters should steadily grow in the conviction that their vocation as Deaconess is their life-work.

   b) Every Deaconess who is no longer capable of performing active service is cared for by the Motherhouse.

   c) Should a Deaconess receive a proposal of marriage, the authorities of the Motherhouse to which she belongs, expect, like parents, to be informed of the fact, and to be asked for their advice before a decision is reached. Otherwise she is under no constraint; and if she decides upon marriage the Motherhouse dismisses her with its blessing. Should a Sister, however, act deceitfully in matters of this kind, she is dishonorably discharged.

   d) If parents or guardians, in spite of their consent once given, insist on having a daughter or ward permanently returned for the purpose of serving them, the Motherhouse interposes no obstacle, even though it should itself be the sufferer. Should in isolated cases the command: "Thou shalt honor thy father and thy mother" be used as a cloak to forsake the deaconess calling with apparently good motives, the guilty one herself will suffer the consequences of her wrong-doing.

e) If other relatives ask a Deaconess to relinquish her calling, she may refuse to do so, inasmuch as she has the same freedom of independent action in choosing a calling and remaining in it as have those who ask her. In such a case the Motherhouse has a right to refuse permission to withdraw. If, however, in cases of severe illness and upon earnest solicitation, the Motherhouse can serve the relatives of a Deaconess by furnishing a nurse, it will respect their wishes by sending either the related Deaconess or another Sister, Nevertheless relatives cannot demand such service as a right; nor can the Sister ask it on their behalf.

f) If the Motherhouse is conscientiously convinced that the withdrawal of a Sister is willful and unjustifiable, and in conflict with the rules of the Motherhouse, it becomes the duty of the latter to tell her so, and to show her why her course is wrong. In such a case the Motherhouse must also announce the withdrawal to the rest of the Sisterhood, ask their prayers in behalf of the erring one, and cease to have communication with her.

5. Morphia and similar narcotics are not to be used by the Sisters themselves, nor administered by them to the sick unless specially ordered to do so by the physician. If in consequence of the latter a Sister feels burdened in her conscience, she submits the case in all its details to her Motherhouse, which, after careful consideration of the facts, will give her the necessary advice.

6. a) Sisters are sent to outside stations only after a contract has been made with the authorities. The stationing of but one Sister at a place is avoided as much as possible. In their supervision of the work of Sisters on out-stations the authorities of the same must not go beyond the instructions given the Sisters by the Motherhouse. The Sister-in-charge has full authority to act in the name of the Motherhouse. She directs the Sisters individually, and is primarily responsible for good order among them.

b) In nursing male patients, the Deaconesses and Probationers are permitted to perform only such duties as, in the judgment of the Motherhouse, do not offend female modesty. They undertake nursing in the male wards of hospitals only with the assistance of male nurses.

e) Sisters are not required to assist at autopsies.

d) All contracts with out-stations stipulate that for themselves and their Protestant patients the Sisters must be accorded the right to hold daily devotions in conformity with the instructions furnished them by their Motherhouse.

APPENDIX THREE

APPLICATION FORM FOR THOSE WHO WISH TO BE ACCEPTED AS NURSES IN THE DEACONESS HOUSE IN CHRISTIANIA

1. Those who wish to be accepted to the Motherhouse should send in a written application to the institution's board. The application should contain a note on what has caused the applicant to apply and should also include

    a. The parents, guardians or others permission to apply if the applicant is not herself of an age and free

    b. Letter of recommendation from a pastor

    c. Letter from a doctor

    d. A short biography written by the applicant about her life thus far

    e. A note from a known or responsible man or women promising to receive the applicant if for some reason she is not accepted as a deaconess

2. The applicants age should not be under 18 or over 40 years.

3. She should be in possession of a least as much book learning as an ordinary clever confirmand, that is she should be able to write and do arithmetic

4. She will be received first as a student or teaching daughter for a time of at least six months and will receive during this time no pay. After that time and she shows herself to be able to make it through the teaching and practice she will be accepted as a probationary sister. As such she will remain at least one year in that position, but the time can be as long as three years. During this time and in this position, she will receive a salary of 15 specie dollars yearly, together with her work clothes. As a student and as a probationary sister she can leave when she wants to, or the head sister may dismiss her, if she is not

found capable or serviceable. What her travel to and from the deaconess house costs is irrelevant.

5. When she had completed the two levels and has shown herself to have the knowledge and modesty necessary to show the truth of her calling to service she will be accepted as a deaconess. As such she is bound to serve for at least five years in conditions that will bring her nearer to a permanent appointment.

6. The students as well as the probationary sisters will be educated in the institution with changing courses and practical education. Therefor they should have the willingness to forego all bad habits no matter how minor they can be, they shall be judged by their order, teachability, and punctual obedience; all willful self-reliance is proscribed.

Second version of the application form

1. Application must be hand written in the applicant's own hand. It should be addressed to the Sister superior and must contain

   a. The parent's or guardian's permission for the applicant to apply, unless the applicant is of age

   b. A sealed letter from the pastor who is best acquainted with her entire background

   c. A sealed letter from a doctor—after the form of the Deaconess house

   d. Agreement from a responsible man or women that they will take care of her if she fails to be taken in as a deaconess

   e. A short autobiography written by the applicant herself telling her life story: Tell a little bit about your parents, your childhood home, your schooling, your time as a confirmand, and your situation since confirmation—where you have been, what you have done, etc., on why you decided to make the application, why you believe God has called you to this vocation, what you honestly think of the calling, and what you expect for your own part.

2. The applicant must belong to the Norwegian Lutheran Church

3. Her age cannot be under twenty years or over thirty-six years.

4. She must have as much education as a clever confirmand, reading, writing and arithmetic.

If she is accepted she must have the following clothes: 8 linen shirts, 8 pair underpants, 6 nightshirts, 12 pocket handkerchiefs, 4 colored undershirts, 6-8 pair stockings, 2 large work aprons, 3 to 4 pair slippers or shoes, 3 to 4 dresses, 1 scarf, 2 meter long wooden chest, 1 laundry bag, 1 umbrella, 1 set of toiletries, with comb and tooth brush, 1 clothes brush. A Bible and Landstad's Hymnal.

RITE OF CONSECRATION

Vows: The sister kneels at the altar, and each one is asked after her name is named

NN Is it of your own free will that you are choosing to become a deaconess? Yes.

Will you, so long as God grants you to remain in this calling, in loving and willing obedience seek to fulfill it to the honor and glory of God's name and of your neighbor's good? Yes

Will you in prayer and self-denial seek to win and preserve the right Deaconess sense? Yes

Give me your hand! The pastor lays his hand on the Deaconess and says, I consecrate you to be the Lord's Deaconess in the name of the Father, Son and Holy Spirit.

Your verse to remember——-to each sister an appropriate one.

NUMBER OF LUTHERAN DEACONESSES IN THE U.S.

1897—163
1916—362
1922—361
1926—396

ENDNOTES

1   *Nordisk Tidende*, February 28, 1933.

2   *Brev fra Mrs. G.F. (Marie) Heiberg til Bestyrelsen for Diakonissehus i Kristiania April 30, 1886.* Lovisenberg archives.

3   The General Council included several American Lutheran groups, most of which came to form what became the Lutheran Church in America begun in 1962.

4   Among those who heard the speech was Erik Alfred Fogelström, (1850-1909), the Swedish Augustana pastor who would establish a Motherhouse in Omaha for Swedish young women in 1890. Whether he attended the meeting in Gjertsen's home we do not know, but he had spoken at the General Council meeting and had already begun a ministry with four deaconesses in Omaha the year before in 1887. He knew some of the issues the Minneapolis Norwegians would have to face.

5   Carl Gustav O. Hansen. My *Minneapolis: A Chronicle of What Has Been Learned and Observed About the Norwegians in Minneapolis Through One Hundred Years* (Minneapolis: Standard Press, 1956). Hansen treats the lives of many including Gjertsen in his book.

6   "Søster Elisabeths Optegnelser," *Nordisk Tidende* (4 April 1933).

7   Georg Sverdrup, "Diakonissehjemmet i Minneapolis," *Fra Kirkens Arbeidsmark: Samlede Skrifter i Udvalg* IV (Minneapolis: Frikirkens Boghandel, 1911), 1.

8   Ibid.

9   While she says 1873 in her memoirs, the record is clear. Her application materials are dated 1874, a date probably to be more trusted than later documents such as the novel, *The Borrowed Sister*, and the diary republished in the *Nordisk Tidende* in 1933 on the fiftieth anniversary of the Motherhouse. These both say 1873. Her application and her patron's recommendation, however, have the same date of June 26, 1874. The records in the archive for the deaconesses in Oslo state she was enrolled at the home on December 4, 1874.

10   Sister Elisabeth says in an English account of her call to be a deaconess that her father had been at sea, but when his wife, Elisabeth's mother, became ill he returned home to farm in order to be with her and help her in her decline.

11   Elisabeth's siblings were Anne Marie Elene Andreassen (1845-1914); Villum Andreassen (1846—died at birth); Anne Sophie Andreassen (1848-1909); Andreas Andreassen (1853-1875); Villum Andreassen (1856-1888); Olene Margrethe Andreassen (1858-); Ole Andreas Andreassen Fedde (1862-1951). Elisabeth remained close to many of her nieces and nephews, both those who came to America and those who remained in Norway.

12 Erich Pontoppidan, *Truth Unto Godliness.*

13 "Read for the minister" is a literal translation of the Norwegian *"lese for presten."* It may well be associated with the requirement that all confirmands in Norway be able to read in order to be confirmed, so that pastor became a teacher of reading.

14 This is from her application letter, June 26, 1874, from the Lovisenberg Archives. Elisabeth says it is this Bang, but trying to put him in the West Agder where she is at this time, 1863-1866, is difficult to do.

15 Among his followers were Henriette Gislesen (1809-1859) and Berte Kanutte Aarflot (1795-1864), the hymnwriter who influenced many with their hymns and letters of spiritual advice.

16 Dag Kullerud, *Hans Nielsen Hauge: Mannen som vekket Norge* (Oslo: Forum Aschehoug, 1996).

17 *Fra min Diakonissetid*, 3. These page numbers are from Kristin Adriansen's transcription of the handwritten version of the original document. I have chosen to use those numbers since most scholars will use her transcription to access the original which is very difficult to read.

18 Ibid.

19 *Fra min Diakonissetid*, 4.

20 Ibid.

21 Ibid.

22 *Fra min Diakonissetid*, 4.

23 Note from Iver Siqveland, June 26, 1874.

24 These dates/days are not correct. The First Sunday of Advent in 1874 was December 6. Saturday was December 5, not December 4.

25 Lytton Strachey, *Eminent Victorians.* Loc 1490.

26 "Jeanne Madeline Weimann, "Refined Avenues of Effort," in *The Fair Women: The Story of the Woman's Building, World's Columbian Exposition, Chicago, 1893* (Chicago: Academy Chicago, 1981), 548.

27 Sister Julie Mergner, *The Deaconess and Her Work*, freely translated from the German by Harriet Spaeth (Philadelphia: General Council Publication House, 1915), 47.

28 Florence Nightingale, *The Institution of Kaiserswerth on the Rhine, for the Practical Training of Deaconesses*, 12.

29 Ibid.

30 Ibid., 1. Florence Nightingale, *Notes on Nursing: What It Is and What It Is Not* (London: Harrison, 59, Pall Mall, 1859), 6.

31 Judith Lissauer Crommwell, *Florence Nightingale: Feminist* (Jefferson, North Carolina and London: McFarland & Company, Inc., 2013), 137.

32 Florence Nightingale, *Notes on Nursing: What It Is and What It Is Not*, 6.

33 Ibid.

34   Ibid., 14-15.

35   Crommwell, 232.

36   Crommwell, 244.

37   Adolf Spaeth, "Loehe's Influence upon the Deaconess Work," in *Proceedings and Paper of The Seventh Conference of Evangelical Lutheran Deaconess Motherhouses in the United States* (Philadelphia, 1908), 17-18.

38   Georg Sverdrup, "Minder fra Norge: Den Johnsonske Vækkelse: Bibelskse og Kirkehistoriske Skrifter," *Samlede skrifter i udvalg* I (Minneapolis: Frikirkens Boghandel, 1911), 194.

39   Rikke Nissen, *Diakonissehuset i Kristiania: En Oversigt over dets Historie, Indberetning og Virksomhed, med Forord af Julius Bruun, Stiftsprost* (Kristiania: P. T. Mallings Boghandel, 1883), 13.

40   Kristin Kavli Adriansen, *Elisabeth Fedde: En studie av kallet i lys av søster Elisabeth Feddes diakonissegjerning 1873-1896* (Bergen: Masteroppgave Institutt for samfunnsmedisinske fag, 2007), 55.

41   Adriansen, 56.

42   Nissen, 13.

43   Nissen, 14.

44   Nissen, 16.

45   Nissen, 21.

46   Lars Dahle, the head of the Norwegian Missionary Society, visited Neuendettelsau as did August Weenaas, future president of Augsburg Seminary, and both made similar remarks on the physical beauty of Loehe. Reynolds Spaeth in her book *The Deaconess and Her Work* repeats the story of Loehe's effect on Schleiermacher when he was teaching a class: "The piercing look of his bright eyes almost hopelessly confused the celebrated Professor Schleiermacher, who was lecturing," 53.

47   Nils Bloch-Hoell, *Diakonissehusets første hundre år 1868-1968: at vi skulle vandre i dem*. (Diakonissehuset i Oslo, A S. Furuset Boktrykkeri, 1968), 16.

48   Hoell-Bloch, 18.

49   *Memoirs*, Folkedahl, 5.

50   Martinsen, 1984, in Adriansen's thesis, 69.

51   *Fra min Diakonissetid*, 6.

52   *Memoirs*, Folkedahl, 5.

53   *Fra min Diakonissetid*, 8.

54   Ibid.

55   Adolph Spaeth, "Thesis on the Training of Deaconesses," *Proceedings and Papers of The Second Conference of Evangelical Lutheran Deaconess Motherhouses in the United States* (Philadelphia: Press of Edward Stern and Co., Inc., 1897), 4-6.

56   Katherine Stokker, *Remedies and Rituals: Folk Medicine in Norway and the New Land* (St. Paul: Minnesota Historical Society, 2007). This book gives a

well-documented picture of how Norwegians dealt with many diseases and health issues before the establishment of hospitals and clinics.

57   *Fra min Diakonisstid*, 7.

58   *Memoirs*, Folkedahl, 6.

59   *Fra min Diakonissetid*, 7.

60   Ibid.

61   *Fra min Diakonissetid*, 23-24.

62   *Memoirs*, Folkedahl, 6.

63   Ivar Welle, *Norges Kirkehistorie: Kirkens Historie III* (Oslo: Lutherstiftelsens Forlag, 1948), 216.

64   *Memoirs*, Folkedahl, 6.

65   Kristin Adriansen in an email to me suggested that the Siqvelands continued to support Fedde.

66   *Fra min Diakonissetid*, 9. Essendrop (1818-1893) was a student of Johnson and shared his piety.

67   *Memoirs*, Folkedahl, 7.

68   Erling Nicolai Rolfsrud, *The Borrowed Sister: The Story of Elisabeth Fedde* (Minneapolis: Augsburg Publishing House, 1953), 35.

69   *Fra min Diakonissetid*, 12.

70   Ibid.

71   A. S. Dancke, *Erindringer*.

72   *Fra min Diakonissetid*, 14.

73   Ibid, 12.

74   Heuch, a conservative both politically and theologically, would later become the Bishop of Kristiansand. In the cultural debates of the day he was considered a high orthodox Lutheran, much like Gisle Johnson, but as bishop became quite friendly to the lay movement still very strong in Norway and tended to be associated with the Liberal parties. He opposed Bjørnstjerne Bjørnson with whom he had many debates. He became a bitter opponent of the women's movement as represented by Bjørnson as it developed through the end of the century.

75   This must be the Norwegian composer and musician who may have been teaching literature at the time, but it seems rather unlikely.

76   *Fra min Diakonissetid*, 13.

77   *Memoirs*, Folkedahl, 7.

78   Email from Beret Hovland to Gracia Grindal, April 30, 2014.

79   Adriansen, 67.

80   *Memoirs*, Folkedahl, 7.

81   *Fra min Diakonissetid*, 17.

82   Ibid.

83   "Midt i Livet ere vi/Dødsens Vaade…" *Landstad* No. 323, *Lutheran Book of Worship* hymn 350.

84   *Fra min Diakonissetid*, 19.

85   Ibid., 20.

86   "Sister Elisabeth Fedde: A Norwegian Pioneer in America," *The Trained Nurse and Hospital Review* (January 1931), frontispiece.

87   About this Sister Elisabeth was right. The few pastors who made it to America quickly realized they would get little help from the home church and soon built their own seminaries and church to serve the Norwegian immigrants in America.

88   *Fra min Diakonissetid*, 20

89   Gabriel Fedde was from the same area in Norway as Elisabeth and her sister, whom he married. He had taken the same name from the place as was common for many immigrants.

90   David Mauk, *The Colony that Rose from the Sea: Norwegian Maritime Migration and Community in Brooklyn, 1850-1910* (Northfield, Minnesota: Norwegian American Historical Association, 1997), 3-16.

91   Herman Amberg Preus, *Vivacious Daughter: Seven Lectures on the Religious Situation among Norwegian in America*, tr. Todd W. Nichol, (Northfield, Minnesota: Norwegian American Historical Association, 1990), 101-111.

92   Ole Juul, *Erindringer* (Decorah, Iowa: Lutheran Publishing House, 1902), 101.

93   Andreas Mortensen, *Over Havet: Fortætellinger fra Sjømandsmissionen* (Kristiania: Steen'ske Bogtrykkeri og forlag, 1900).

94   Mauk, 104.

95   Gabriel Aanensen Fedde, *Pennestrøg-Oplevelser* [unpublished mss., 1912], 16.

96   Ibid., 57

97   Mauk, 267.

98   *Memoirs*, Folkedahl, 9.

99   The minutes of the board, according to Kristin Adriansen, said Sister Elisabeth was on a sick leave to recover her health.

100 Ibid.

101 Sister Elisabeth's diary says she arrived in New York on April 8, but the ship's list information says the *Geiser* landed on April 10 in Hoboken. One explanation is that the very first entry is not contemporary. She began writing it three weeks after she had arrived.

102 *Fra min Diakonissetid*, 43-44.

103 "Søster Elisabeths Optegnelser," *Nordisk Tidende* (February 28, 1933), 4.

104 Everson served Our Savior's in Brooklyn at the same time he was serving the Perth Amboy congregation in New Jersey. There was an Our Savior's Danish Lutheran congregation in Perth Amboy, which he served from 1873-1889. Everson also served Trinity (*Treenighets, Trefoldighet*—or *Den Skandinavisk evangelisk lutherske Treeingheds menighet*) in Hoboken with Sårheim from 1890 to 1892 and Woodbridge congregation from 1874 to 1889.

105 *Diary of Sister Elisabeth*, May 18, 1883.

106 Minutes, April 17, 1883.

107 "Søster Elisabeths Optegnelser," *Nordisk Tidende* (February 28, 1933), 4. The undersigned to this agreement were Carl S. Everson, pastor, 56 Monroe Street, New York; Cornelius Dankel, 337 East 25th Street, New York, T. K. Skov, emigrant missionary, 56 Monroe Street, New York; Andreas Mortensen, pastor, 117 William Street; Carsten Hansteen, pastor 122 Second Place, Brooklyn; E. J. Hanstad, tailor, 234½ Clinton Street, Brooklyn; O. H. Jensen, master carpenter, 31 Garnet Street, Brooklyn; Gabriel Fedde, ship chandler, 169 9th Street, Brooklyn.

108 *Diary of Sister Elisabeth*, April 1883.

109 *Diary of Sister Elisabeth*, May 13, 1883.

110 *New York Sun*, May 11, 1883. *The Report of the House of Representatives of the Commonwealth of Massachusetts, during the Session of the General Court, 1883* (Boston: Wright and Potter Printing, 1883). The article describes this mistreatment in horrifying detail.

111 The American Siqueland probably spelled it in an American way.

112 *Diary of Sister Elisabeth*, June 13?, 1883. The date has disappeared from the document.

113 *Diary of Sister Elisabeth*, June 17, 1883.

114 Mauk, 109.

115 *Nordisk Tidende*, February 27, 1891.

116 *Diary of Sister Elisabeth*, November 2. 1883.

117 *Diary of Sister Elisabeth*, July 3, 1883.

118 *Diary of Sister Elisabeth*, July 4, 1883.

119 *Diary of Sister Elisabeth*, July 26, 1883.

120 *Diary of Sister Elisabeth Fedde*, August 3, 1883, tr. P. J. Hertsgaard, 10.

121 *Diary of Sister Elisabeth Fedde*, August 10, 1883.

122 *Diary of Sister Elisabeth Fedde*, August 10, 1883, 8.

123 Johannes Gossner, convert to the Lutheran faith while a Catholic priest, founded a highly regarded mission, which still continues its work, to India and other parts of Asia.

124 *Diary of Sister Elisabeth*, August 10, 1883

125 Ibid.

126 "Søster Elisabeths Optegnelser," *Nordisk Tidende* (March 7, 1933), 5.

127 *Diary of Sister Elisabeth*, November 3, 1883.

128 Schiotz, 1980, 65, as found in Adriansen, 76.

129 Ibid.

130 *Diary of Sister Elisabeth*, September 10, 1883.

131 *Diary of Sister Elisabeth*, September 14, 1883.

132 Ibid.

133 Andreas Mortensen, "Trampen" *I Sing-Sing Fængsel og Andre Fortællinger* (Kristiania: Steen'ske Bogtrykkeri og Forlag, 1902), 55.

134 "Søster Elisabeths Optegnelser," *Nordisk Tidende* (March 14, 1933).

135 Bjørnstjerne Bjørnson, *Land of the Free: Bjørnstjerne Bjørnson's America Letters, 1880-1881* (Northfield, Minnesota: Norwegian American Historical Association, 1978), 68-69.

136 Ibid.

137 "Discord Among the Women," *The Brooklyn Eagle* (January 22, 1885).

138 Herman Preus, *Kirketidende*, xv (May 1, 1870), 139.

139 *The Brooklyn Daily Eagle* (December 9, 1886).

140 *Diary of Sister Elisabeth*, December 31, 1883.

141 *The Brooklyn Eagle* (January 2, 1884).

142 *"I Jesu Navn skal al vor gjerning ske,"* from Kingo's 1699 hymnal.

143 *Diary of Sister Elisabeth*, January 1, 1884. *Gjerning* which I have translated "work" is a bit bigger than that. I would say it has more of calling or vocation in it than work, but work is the easiest way to translate it.

144 *Diary of Sister Elisabeth*, January 9, 1884.

145 *Diary of Sister Elisabeth*, January 9, 1884.

146 *Diary of Sister Elisabeth*, January 14, 1884.

147 *Fra min Diakonissetid*, 37.

148 Ibid.

149 Ibid.

150 *Diary of Sister Elisabeth*, January 15, 1884.

151 *Diary of Sister Elisabeth*, February 22, 1884.

152 *Diary of Sister Elisabeth*, March 22, 1884.

153 *Diary of Sister Elisabeth*, May 24, 1884.

154 *Diary of Sister Elisabeth*, May 31, 1884.

155 *Diary of Sister Elisabeth*, June, 1884.

156 *Diary of Sister Elisabeth*, June, 1884.

157 Adriansen, 78.

158 *Memoirs*, Folkedahl, 18.

159 There were two deaconesses consecrated under Fedde's leadership according to Fredrick S. Weiser, *Pioneers of God's Future: A Directory of Deaconesses of the Evangelical Lutheran Church in American who have served in the United States and Canada 1848-1991* (Gladwyne, Pennsylvania: Lutheran Deaconess Community, 1991). The probationary sister upon her admittance was given the garb and called sister, making it somewhat difficult to see who were consecrated and when.

160 *Diary of Sister Elisabeth*, December 1884.

161 *Diary of Sister Elisabeth*, January 15?, 1885.

162 *Diary of Sister Elisabeth*, January 15?, 1885

163 The Norwegian Relief Society Minutes of board meeting, January 20, 1885.

164 Ibid.

165 Ibid.

166 *Diary of Sister Elisabet*h, February 20, 1885.

167 Ibid.

168 *Diary of Sister Elisabeth*, January 20, 1885.

169 *Diary of Sister Elisabeth*, January 21, 1885.

170 *Diary of Sister Elisabeth*, February 9, 1885.

171 *Diary of Sister Elisabeth*, February 22, 1885. *"en frigtilig ??and spetake*l"

172 *Memoirs*, Folkedahl, 16.

173 "Søster Elisabeths Optegnelser," *Nordisk Tidende* (March 14, 1933).

174 *Diary of Sister Elisabeth*, January 28, 1885.

175 *Fra Min Diakonissetid*, 66.

176 *Diary of Sister Elisabeth*, February 2, 1885.

177 *Fra Min Diakonissetid*, 34.

178 *Diary of Sister Elisabeth*, February 8, 1885.

179 "Søster Elisabeths Optegnelser," *Nordisk Tidende* (March 14, 1933).

180 Mortensen, "Tale ved Optagelsen af den første Prøvesøster i det nye Diakonisse-hus i Brooklyn," *Fra Diakonissethuset* (December 2, 1885), 176-180.

181 "Søster Elisabeths Optegnelser," *Nordisk Tidende* (March 21, 1933).

182 Rolfsrud names the Captain Hofstead, but Sister Elisabeth only says, Captain H.

183 *Fra min Diakonissetid*, 36.

184 *Diary of Sister Elisabeth*, March 16, 1885.

185 *Diary of Sister Elisabeth*, March 13, 1885.

186 *Diary of Sister Elisabeth*, March 15, 1885.

187 *Fra min Diakonissetid*, 32

188 Carsten Hansteen, *Søndagsskolen: Haandbok for Lærere ved Søndagsskolen* (Bergen: Lunde & Co.s Forlag, 1922).

189 Ibid.

190 *Diary of Sister Elisabeth*, March 31, 1885.

191 *Diary of Sister Elisabeth*, April 5, 1885.

192 It is of some interest that they did not name a particular synod as their denomination.

193 *Minutes*, April 7, 1885.

194 See footnote 473.

195 Kristin Norseth, *La oss bryte med vor stumhet! Kvinners vei til myndighet i de kristelige organisationene i 1842-1912.* (De teologiske Menighetsfakulet, 2007), 232.

196 Ibid. 253.

197 *Minutes*, April 7, 1885.

198 *Diary of Sister Elisabeth*, April 7, 1885.

199 *Diary of Sister Elisabeth*, April 15, 1885.

200 *Diary of Sister Elisabeth*, April 16, 1885.

201 *Diary of Sister Elisabeth*, April 25, 1885.

202 *Diary of Sister Elisabeth*, April 30, 1885.

203 *Diary of Sister Elisabeth*, May 1, 1885.

204 *Diary of Sister Elisabeth*, May 13, 1885.

205 Here is one of the difficulties of trusting Fedde's memory for dates. The only ship of the Thingvalla line that landed in New York the day after Ascension Day, May 15, was the *Island*. Her date is wrong as well. It is not May 16, but May 15.

206 *Diary of Sister Elisabeth*, May 15, 1885.

207 *Diary of Sister Elisabeth*, May 16, 1885.

208 *Diary of Sister Elisabeth*, June 2, 1885.

209 *Diary of Sister Elisabeth*, June 2, 1885.

210 *Diary of Sister Elisabeth*, June 5, 1885.

211 *Diary of Sister Elisabeth*, June 5, 1885.

212 *The Brooklyn Eagle* (June 15, 1885).

213 Mortensen, "Tale ved Optagelsen af den første Prøvesøster i det nye Diakonisse-hus i Brooklyn," *Fra Diakonissethuset* (December 2, 1885), 176-180.

214 *Fra Min Diakonissetid*, 38-39.

215 *Diary of Sister Elisabeth*, July 8, 1885.

216 *Fra min Diakonissetid*, 39.

217 Ibid.

218 His book on traveling among the Mormons gives a fascinating history and de-scription of the Utah settlement which was a threat to Scandinavian Lutheran churches since a significant number of Scandinavians were attracted to the reli-gion and the place.

219 Andreas Mortensen to Georg Sverdrup, March 3, 1886. Augsburg Archives.

220 See letter from Marie Heiberg to the Deaconess Home in Norway, above. Augs-burg Archives.

221 *Diary of Sister Elisabeth*, September 24, 1885.

222 *Diary of Sister Elisabeth*, September 30, October 1, 1885.

223 *Diary of Sister Elisabeth*, November 12, 1885. The diary is difficult to read at this point, but it is at least in the character of her prayers at the time.

224 *Diary of Sister Elisabeth*, November 15, 1885.

225 *Diary of Sister Elisabeth*, November 15, 1885.

226 *Diary of Sister Elisabeth*, November 17, 1885.

227 *The Brooklyn Eagle* (January 2, 1886).

228 *Diary of Sister Elisabeth*, January 1, 1886.

229 *The Brooklyn Eagle* (January 2, 1886).

230 *Diary of Sister Elisabeth*, January 4, 1886.

231 *Diary of Sister Elisabeth*, January 14, 1886.

232 *Minutes*, November 3, 1885.

233 *Diary of Sister Elisabeth*, January 19, 1886.

234 *Diary of Sister Elisabeth*, January 21-22, 1886.

235 *Diary of Sister Elisabeth*, January 27, 1886.

236 *Diary of Sister Elisabeth*, February 4, 1886.

237 *Diary of Sister Elisabeth*, February 7, 1886.

238 *Diary of Sister Elisabeth*, March 5, 1886.

239 *Minutes*, March 9, 1886.

240 *Diary of Sister Elisabeth*, March 9, 1886.

241 *Diary of Sister Elisabeth*, March 31, 1886.

242 *Diary of Sister Elisabeth*, April 11, 1886.

243 *Diary of Sister Elisabeth*, April 11, 1886.

244 *Minutes*, April 13, 1886.

245 Wettergreen was an important person in the spiritual life of many at this time. He had gone to work with Schreuder in the Zulu mission for ten years and then returned to Norway where he became the pastor of the first Lutheran Free Church congregation in Arendal. He had a tumultuous career after returning from Africa, something that may have affected Fedde's view of him later.

246 The spelling of this captain's name is never very clear in Sister Elisabeth's hand.

247 *Diary of Sister Elisabeth*, April 23, 1886.

248 In one version of her *Memoirs*, Sister Elisabeth says Sister Othilie left to marry; in her *Optegneleser* published in the *Nordisk Tidende* in 1933, she says the engagement was broken off.

249 *Fra min Diakonissetid*, 40.

250 *Fra min Diakonissetid*, 45.

251 *Minutes*, April 27, 1886.

252 Copy of the Certificate of Incorporation, May 26, 1886.

253 *Minutes*, May 25, 1886.

254 *Diary of Sister Elisabeth*, October 10, 1886.

255 *Diary of Sister Elisabeth*, October 10, 1886.

256 *Diary of Sister Elisabeth*, October 5, 1886.

257 *Diary of Sister Elisabeth*, October 20, 1886.

258 *Minutes*, November 11, 1886.

259 *Diary of Sister Elisabeth*, November 18, 1886.

260 *Diary of Sister Elisabeth*, November 18, 1886.

261 *Diary of Sister Elisabeth*, December 31, 1886.

262 *Diary of Sister Elisabeth*, December 31, 1886.

263 "Søster Elisabeths Optegnelser," *Nordisk Tidende* (March 28, 1933).

264 *Fra min Diakonissetid*, 43.

265 *Fra min Diakonissetid*, 43

266 Ibid.

267 *Diary of Sister Elisabeth*, 1887.

268 Before leaving for Norway he visited Norwegian American churches and gave a speech on November 1 in Chicago recommending they start a Deaconess Motherhouse there, which resulted in the establishment of a Tabitha Circle beginning to work on the idea with Brun. Because of internal conflict on what the goal should be—a hospital or a Deaconess Motherhouse—it took the group some time to found the Motherhouse in Chicago.

269 The anonymous friend was later revealed to be Alfred Corning Clark, (1844-1896), heir to the Singer Sewing Machine Company and a good friend of Severini-Skougaard.

270 *Memoirs*, Folkedahl, 25.

271 *Minutes*, February 8, 1887.

272 *Minutes*, February 8, 1887.

273 *Diary of Sister Elisabeth*, February 8, 1887.

274 *Minutes*, February 15, 1887.

275 *Minutes*, February 15, 1887.

276 *Diary of Sister Elisabeth*, February 16, 1887.

277 *Diary of Sister Elisabeth*, February 11, 1887.

278 *Minutes*, March 8, 1887.

279 Ibid.

280 *Minutes*, March 8, 1887.

281 *Diary of Sister Elisabeth*, March 7, 1887.

282 *Minutes*, April 12, 1887.

283 *Diary of Sister Elisabeth*, April 16, 1887.

284 *Minutes*, May 10, 1887

285 Everson is the subject of a long letter to Georg Sverdrup from Pastor Hegge who was at this time serving the Trinity congregation.

286 Carl Severin Everson, "Sjømandsmissionen i New York," in *Festskrift til Norske Synodes Jubilæum, 1853-1903* (Decorah, Iowa: Norske Synodens Forlag, 1903), 308-313. See also letter to H. A. Preus, September 1887, Preus Library archives.

287 "The union committees of the Synod and the United Church, unanimously and without reservation, accept that doctrine of election which is set forth in Article XI of the Formula of Concord . . . and in Pontoppidan's *Sandhed til gudfrygtighed*, Question 548. Madison Agreement, Article I, 1912."

288 Mauk, 125.

289 Pastor Everson, "Beviser for Kirkefolket i Brooklyn at der findes mange og store Mistag," *Nordisk Tidende* (January 22, 1897; January 29, 1897; February 5, 1897).

290 *Fra min Diakonissetid*, 45.

291 *Diary of Sister Elisabeth*, May 1888.

292 "Søster Elisabeths Optegnelse," *Nordisk Tidende* (April 4, 1933).

293 Ibid.

294 "Fra diakonissehuset," *Folkebladet* (October 13, 1888), 4.

295 Sister Elisabeth remembers this as being October 11. Ibid.

296 Carl Christlock argues in his history of Augsburg College, *From Fjord to Free-way*, that the Augsburg faculty minoritized itself by supporting the Prohibition party for too long. At this time the party was at its height in this election.

297 Carl Christlock, *From Fjord to Freeway*, 38.

298 M. Falk Gjertsen, "Diakonissegjerningen," *Folkebladet* (February 6, 1889).

299 This was the precedent for people of the Association of Evangelical Lutheran Churches who had left the Lutheran Curch—Missouri Synod in the early 1970s to call for a merger of the three Lutheran bodies which became the Evangelical Lutheran Church in America.

300 As Sven Oftedal pointed out at the first meeting of the United Church, this fund was vastly over-exaggerated, containing as it did worthless notes and other pledges they had no hope of receiving. See Fevold and Nelson, II, 22.

301 Andreas Helland, *Augsburg Gjennom Femti Aar*, (Minneapolis: Folkebladet Publishing Company, 1920), 214.

302 "Direktiansmøde for Diakonisse Hjemmet afholdte i Dr. Laws Kantor," Mandag 26 November, 1.

303 Ibid., 5.

304 Ibid.

305 *The Press*, April 23, 1889.

306 Ibid.

307 "Søster Elisabeths Optegnelser," *Nordisk Tidende* (April 4, 1933).

308 "Direktiansmøde for Diakonisse Hjemmet afholdte i Konferencens Kirke," March 17, 1889.

309 Ibid. Dr. Laws Kontor, March 25, 1889.

310 Ibid. April 25, 1889.

311 Ibid. April 25-26, 1889.

312 Letter from Sister Elisabeth to Georg Sverdrup, Brooklyn, May 4, 1889. Augsburg Archives.

313 Ibid.

314 Letter from Sister Elisabeth to Georg Sverdrup, Brooklyn, May 11, 1889. Augsburg Archives.

315 Letter from Sister Elisabeth to Georg Sverdrup. Augsburg Archives.

316 See letter to Georg Sverdrup, November 27, 1901 from Hansteen and Laur Larsen in the Georg Sverdrup papers in untitled bound volume of documents concerning M. Falk Gjertsen in Augsburg Archives.

317 Many of the pastors and professors of the church had cabins or places near Saga Hill on Lake Minnetonka. The Deaconess Institute bought a large home there called Solbakken where the sisters could enjoy some free time and rest.

318 Letter from Georg Sverdrup to Sven Oftedal, July 2, 1889. Augsburg Archives.

319 Sverdrup, "Diakonissehjemmet i Minneapolis," 2.

320 Andreas Helland, *Georg Sverdrup: The Man and his Message* (Minneapolis: The Messenger Press, 1947), 241.

321 "Søster Elisabeths Optegnelser," *Nordisk Tidende* (April 11, 1933).

322 Letter from Gabriel Fedde to Georg Sverdrup, September 5, 1889. Augsburg Archives.

323 Dr. G. A. Hansen, *Virchons Archives*, 1888. See Charles N. Hewitt. "Leprosy and its Management in Minnesota," 1889.

324 "Søster Elisabeths Optegnelser," *Nordisk Tidende* (April 11, 1933).

325 *Minutes of the Norwegian Lutheran Deaconess Institute*, November 5, 1889 (St. Paul: Minnesota Historical Society), 28.

326 "Søster Elisabeths Optegnelser," *Nordisk Tidende* (April 11, 1933).

327 This phrase is so common it is almost a mantra in the stories of Norwegian American gatherings from the dedication of the first main building at Luther College in 1865 to the 1925 celebration of the 100th anniversary of Norwegian emigration when King Haakon appeared at the Hippodrome at the State Fairgrounds in St. Paul. Until then the number was always put at about 6,000. That it recurs so often raises my suspicion—how could they know without counting? On the other hand, maybe there were about 6,000 Norwegian Americans who came to these events!

328 Nils C. Brun, *Fra Undomsaar: Den forenede Kirkes historie i femogtyve aar* (Minneapolis: Augsburg Publishing House, 1915), 44.

329 Ibid.

330 "Søster Elisabeths Optegnelser," *Nordisk Tidende* (April 11, 1933).

331 Georg Sverdrup, "Diakonissesagen," *Beretning om Det 1ste Aarsmøde for Den forende norsk-lutherske Kirke I Amerika, afhold i den svenske Augustana Menigheds Kirke* (June 1890), 145-150

332 Ibid.

333 More on this topic will be included in a chapter on Red Wing Ladies Seminary in my forthcoming book, *The Norwegian Synod Educates Its Daughters*.

334 *Minutes*, November 3, 1890.

335 "Den norsk luthersk diakonisse institution ser sig ikke istand til af hensyn til arbeidet ved dens egen anstalt, at efter komme anmodningen," *Minutes*, October 4, 1890.

336 *Minutes*, December 12, 1890.

337 Letter from Fedde to Georg Sverdrup, Mary 11, 1891. Augsburg Archives.

338 "Søster Elisabeths Optegnelser," *Nordisk Tidende* (April 11, 1933).

339 Deaconess Ingeborg Sponland, *My Reasonable Service* (Minneapolis: Augsburg Publishing House, 1938), 34.

340 *Minutes*, May 3, 1891.

341 *Minutes*, January 6, 1891.

342 This is very confusing. The Tabitha organization in Chicago started a Tabitha Deaconess hospital, but its history is absorbed by other institutions. At issue according to Odd Lovoll was whether or not to have a hospital that was connected with a Deaconess Motherhouse.

343 See Andreas Helland, *Augsburg Gjennom Femti Aar 1869-1919*, 24.

344 Georg Sverdrup, *Folkebladet*, January 14, 1891.

345 Nils Nilsen Rønning and W. H. Lien, *They Followed Him: The Lutheran Deaconess Home and Hospital: Fiftieth Anniversary, 1889-1959* (Minneapolis: The Lutheran Deaconess Home and Hospital, 1939), 48. This is taken from comments by Lina Nelson, according to the book, but not very well documented.

346 Letter to Georg Sverdrup from Julius Disselhoff, Kaiserswerth, January 14, 1891. Augsburg Archives.

347 *Minutes*, February 10, 1891.

348 This is something like a Freudian slip—there should be an "enough" at the end of the sentence.

349 *The North* (February 11, 1891), 4.

350 *Folkebladet* (February 11, 1891).

351 This is proof that things were afoot with Brun and Fedde. The deaconesses had gone to Chicago, and the Tabitha Society and Brun were set on a Deaconess House there, but the histories simply say that because they were divided on whether to build a hospital only or include a Deaconess Motherhouse they could not start until 1896.

352 *Folkebladet* (March 11, 1891).

353 *Minutes*, March 4, 1891.

354 Andreas Helland, *Georg Sverdrup: The Man and his Message* (Minneapolis: The Messenger Press, 1947), 235.

355 Letter from Sabine Leschly-Hansen to Georg Sverdrup, April 23, 1891: *"Maa jeg bøie mig for min broders vilje, og han tillade mig ikke paa nogen maade reise saa langt uden paa forhaand vore sikkret optagelse i hjemmet."* Augsburg Archives.

356 Leschly-Hansen to Sverdrup, April 23, 1891. Augsburg Archives.

357 Ludvig M. Biørn, the vice president of the United Church, took his place.

358 Grand Forks hospital was established directly from the Minneapolis Motherhouse in 1892 just after Fedde was there, but Sverdrup was the chief connection. Many letters from the doctor there to Sverdrup recount their difficult financial needs and struggles.

359 "Søster Elisabeths Optegnelser," *Nordisk Tidende* (April 11, 1933).

360 *Minutes*, August 27, 1892, Folkedahl, 29.

361 Pastor Martin Hegge to Georg Sverdrup, March 18, 1891. Augsburg Archives.

362 "Among the Norwegians," *Brooklyn Daily Eagle* (April 5, 1891).

363 "Søster Elisabeths Optegnelse," *Nordisk Tidende* (April 18, 1933).

364 Ibid.

365 Ibid.

366 *Fra min Diakonissetid*, 58.

367 Ibid.

368 *Minutes*, October 12, 1891.

369 *Minutes*, October 12, 1891, translation Folkedahl, 50.

370 *Minutes*, 1894.

371 *Minutes*, January 11, 1892.

372 *Nordisk Tidende*, March 25, 1892.

373 Ibid. Until the discovery of penicillin, in 1943, there was no cure for gonorrhea or syphilis.

374 "Søster Elisabeths Optegnelser," *Nordisk Tidende* (April 25, 1933).

375 We have to take Sister Elisabeth's word on this. I could not find the article.

376 "*Søster Elisabeths Optegnelser*," *Nordisk Tidende* (April 25, 1933).

377 *Inherrads Posten* (April 28, 1898).

378 The history of the deaconess movement says this was a consecration. Another such event would happen in 1894, attended by Pastor Petersen who critiqued it. Oftentimes the ceremony of receiving novices is confused with consecreation.

379 Folkedahl, 2.

380 "Søster Elisabeths Optegnelser," *Nordisk Tidende* (April 25, 1933).

381 The Brooklyn Eagle (January 1, 1893).

382 "Søster Elisabeths Optegnelser," *Nordisk Tidende* (April 25, 1933).

383 "Søster Elisabeths Optegnelser," *Nordisk Tidende* (April 25, 1933).

384 *Nordisk Tidende* (September 27, 1892).

385 O. H. Henrikson to editor, *Sjöfartstidende* (August 17, 1892).

386 The incorporators were C. Ullenæs, Gabriel Fedde, Theodore Siqueland, Emil Ericksen, Rudolph Bang, Martin H. Hegge, A. Sommerfelt, A. Gundersen, Kr. K. Saarheim, M. Rosenquist, Samuel Harris and Carl Severin Everson.

387 *The Norwegian Lutheran Deaconesses' Home and Hospital: A Brief History. Published on the occasion of the fortieth anniversary of the Norwegian Lutheran Deaconesses' Home and Hospital*, April 19, 1923, 12.

388 Folkedahl, 33.

389 *The Brooklyn Eagle* (January 1, 1893).

390 Ibid.

391 Ibid.

392 *Nordisk Tidende* (January 24, 1893).

393 *Fra min diakonissetid*, 64.

394 Jeanne Madeline Weimann, "Refined Avenues of Effort," in *The Fair Women: The Story of the Woman's Building, World's Columbian Exposition, Chicago,*

1893 (Chicago: Academy Chicago, 1981): 454.

395 Weimann, 450

396 Ibid.

397 See the *Fair Women* for an exhaustive and well-written account of all the difficulties of this event.

398 *Nordisk Tidende* (May 21, 1893).

399 "Søster Elisabeths Optegnelser," *Nordisk Tidende* (May 2, 1933).

400 "Søster Elisabeths Optegnelser," *Nordisk Tidende* (May 2, 1933). Sister Elisabeth is tentative about the source for this report. I have tried to find it in *New York Herald* microfilm from this year, but have not been able to find it partly because the microfilm was bad.

401 "Søster Elisabeths Optegnelser," *Nordisk Tidende* (February 1895).

402 *Nordisk Tidende* (November 1896).

403 H. G. Stub, "St. Paul Hospital," *Festskrift til Norske Synodes Jubilæum. 1853-1903* (Decorah Iowa: Norske Synodens Forlag, 1903).

404 *Nordisk Tidende* (April 24, 1894).

405 "Søster Elisabeths Optegnelser," *Nordisk Tidende* (May 9, 1933).

406 Ibid.

407 "Søster Elisabeths Optegnelser," *Nordisk Tidende* (April 18, 1933). Almost all of this is a direct translation of Sister Elisabeth's account. She gets wiser and funnier in these memoirs, much more so than when she was in the midst of the work.

408 "Søster Elisabeths Optegnelser," *Nordisk Tidende* (April 18, 1933).

409 Emil Johan Petersen, "En merkelig og ny Slags Indvielse," XXI *Evangelisk Luthersk Kirketidende* (May 26, 1894), 331-332. Who these women were is not clear.

410 "Søster Elisabeths Optegnelser," *Nordisk Tidende* (April 18, 1933).

411 *Aftenposten* (June 4, 1894).

412 Augustus B. Jahnsen, *Kvindelig Diakoni: i Norges Kirke Gjennem Femti Aar: et mindeskrift ved Diakonissehusets femtiaarsjubilæum* (Christiania: Johannes Bjørnstads Bogtrykkeri, 1919)

413 Bloch-Hoell, 63.

414 Heinrich Arnold Thaulow, *Prospekt övfer Sandefjords Svafel och Havsbad i Norge* (Stockholm, 1885).

415 *Nordisk Tidende* (November 16, 1894).

416 "Søster Elisabeths Optegnelser," *Nordisk Tidende* (May 9, 1933).

417 *Nordisk Tidende* (October 19, 1894).

418 *Nordisk Tidende* (October 19, 1894).

419 Ullenæs, *The Brooklyn Eagle* (October 22, 1894), 4.

420 *Nordisk Tidende* (December 14, 1894).

421 *Nordisk Tidende* (January 4, 1895).

422 *Evangelisk Luthersk Kirketidende* (August 18, 1894), 521

423 *Evangelisk Luthersk Kirketidende* (October 20, 1894), 657.

424 *Lutheraneren* (September 1895), 1.

425 *Lutheraneren* (October 31, 1895), 137.

426 *Lutheraneren* (December 12, 1895), 225

427 *Lutheraneren* (May 21, 1896), 321.

428 *Lutheraneren* (August 11, 1897), 528.

429 *Lutheraneren* (July 7, 1897), 425.

430 *Evangelisk Luthersk Kirketidende* (February 13, 1897), 116

431 "Søster Elisabeths Optegnelser," *Nordisk Tidende* (May 2, 1933).

432 "Søster Elisabeths Optegnelser," *Nordisk Tidende* (May 2, 1933).

433 *Nordisk Tidende* (1894).

434 *Nordisk Tidende* (September 6, 1895).

435 "Søster Elisabeths Optegnelser," *Nordisk Tidende* (May 16, 1933).

436 "Søster Elisabeths Optegnelser," *Nordisk Tidende* (May 16, 1933). In her will, Mrs Børs left the Brooklyn deaconess hospital 50,000 kroner, *Stavanger Aftenblad* (September 23, 1915).

437 *Fra min Diakonissetid*, 76.

438 *Fra min Diakonissetid*, 77.

439 *Nordisk Tidende* (February 28, 1896).

440 Although the drive began in 1896, the progress of the statue took more time. Gustav Vigeland won the commission after submitting about a hundred drawings. It was placed in the Palace Park in Oslo and dedicated by a group of feminists struggling to win the vote for women, Gina Krog, the Susan B. Anthony of Norway, among them, in 1911, two years before they finally won the vote in 1913.

441 *Fra min diakonissetid*, 78.

442 Elisabeth Feddes "Brev til Anders Severin Slettebø," January 12, 1896.

443 Where the letters of what must have been a continuing and rich correspondence are is a mystery to family and friends, to say nothing of scholars!

444 *Stavanger Aftenblad* (November 28, 1906).

445 Aamund Salveson, *Jubilæum og Bygdebok for Eigersund Herad* (Stavanger: Eirik Gjostens Boktrykkeri, 1937).

446 *Nordisk Tidende* (April 28, 1904), 4

447 At Everson's death, some weeks before Sister Elisabeth died, Our Savior's, where he had served for forty-one years, expressed its grief in his death and praised him for remaining "faithful to his ideals of duty and Christian principles," *Nordisk Tidende* (January 1921).

448 Folkedahl, 42. Where he has written this is not clearly noted in Folkedahl, but her sense of the sources has proven to be trustworthy as I have noted in my work with her materials.

449 Folkdahl, 53.

450 Ibid.

451 *Stavanger Aftenblad* (December 23, 1948).

452 Email from Karen Fedde May, April 4, 2014.

453 *The Trained Nurse and Hospital Review* (January 1931).

454 *Nordisk Tidende* (March 3, 1921).

455 Sigmund Feyling, *Dalerne Tidende*, in *Nordisk Tidende* (March 5, 1921).

456 Ibid.

457 O. A. Kjellberg, "Fru Elisabeth Slettebø," *Dalerne Tidende*, in *Nordisk Tidende* (March 5, 1921).

458 *Erindringer*, 12.

459 The *Nordisk Tidende* report on this service incorrectly identified the selection in Romans as 6.v. It is 6.8.

460 *Nordisk Tidende* (May 12, 1921).

461 *Nordisk Tidende* (May 12, 1921).

462 Cynthia Jurisson, "The Deaconess Movement," *Encyclopedia of Women and Religion in North America*, ed. Rosemary Skinner Keller, Rosemary Radford Ruether, Marie Cantlon (Bloomington: Indiana University Press, 2006), 821.

463 T. O. Burntvedt, *Golden Anniversary of the Lutheran Deaconess Home and Hospital Minneapolis, Minn.,* 1939.

464 Anna Sticker, *Florence Nightingale, Curriculum Vitae with information about Florence Nightingale and Kaiserswerth* (Dusseldorf-Kaiserswerth: Diakoniewerk, 1965), 18-19.

465 Ibid., 19

466 When I was serving on the ELCA's Task Force on the Study of Ministry 1987-1993 I was surprised to hear from a Catholic man serving in the office of permanent deacon that because of his ordination into the diaconate and his being ontologically changed by the service that what he did when he served his neighbor was completely different from what it would have been before his ordination. Lutherans could not go there, but it is the theology of the historic churches who believe ordination gives one the *character indelibiles*, or the indelible character. Protestants do not understand this theology.

467 Ibid.

468 Roland Liebenberg, Klaus Raschzok, Gury Schneider-Lurdorff, and Matthias Honold, *Diakonissen für Amerika: Socialer Protestantismus in internationaler Perspektive im 19. Jahrhundert* (Leipzig: Evangelische Verlaganstalt, 2013), xlii.

469 Ibid., 828

470 Erika Geiger, *The Life, Work, and Influence of Wilhelm Loehe 1808-1872*, tr. Wolf Dietrich Knappe (St. Louis: Concordia Publishing House, 2010), ebook, 4034.

471 Alfred Spaeth, "The Principles of the Female Diaconate," *Proceedings and Papers of The First Conference of Evangelical Lutheran Deaconess Motherhouses in the United States* (Philadelphia: Edward Stern & Co. Inc., September 16-18,

1896), 5-7. These were theses presented by Spaeth to the conference and were not adopted officially, but the conference "disclosed a remarkable unanimity of sentiment, and it became evident thus early in the sessions that, as regarded principles, the different Houses were practically of one mind and one accord", 7.

472 *Proceedings and Papers of Fourth Conference of Evangelical Lutheran Deaconess Motherhouses in the United States* (Baltimore, Maryland: Edward Stern, Inc., 1903), 24.

473 "Fundamental Principles of the Deaconess Motherhouses Connected with the Kaiserswerth General Conference," *Proceedings and Papers of The Fifth Conference of Evangelical Lutheran Deaconess Motherhouses in the United States* (Philadelphia, April 26-28, 1904): 9-11. English translation presented of the Fundamental Principles of the Kaiserswerth Conference. They were adopted at the 1904 conference of the Evangelical Lutheran Deaconess Motherhouses in the United States. Note that this document approves women serving on the Motherhouse board "and the Sister Superior, wherever possible, should be accorded the right to vote."

INDEX